# Asian Storm

# Asian Storm

## THE ECONOMIC CRISIS EXAMINED

Philippe Riès

Translated by Peter Starr

Tuttle Publishing   BOSTON • RUTLAND, VERMONT • TOKYO

Library of Congress Cataloging-in-Publication Data
Riès, Philippe.
    [Cette crise qui vient d'Asie. English]
    Asian storm/Philippe Riès ; translated by Peter Starr.
        p. cm.
    ISBN 0-8048-3235-8
    1. Financial crises--Asia. 2. Asia--Economic conditions--1945- 3. Asia--Foriegn
economic relations. 4. International finance. I. Title
HC412 .R4913 2000
222'.095 21--dc21                                        99-042135

Distributed by

USA
Tuttle Publishing
Distribution Center
Airport Industrial Park
364 Innovation Drive
North Clarendon, VT 05759-9436
Tel: (802) 773-8930
Tel: (800) 526-2778

Japan
Tuttle Shuppan
RK Building, 2nd Floor
2-13-10 Shimo-Meguro, Meguro-Ku
Tokyo 153 0064
Tel: (03) 5437-0171
Fax: (03) 5437-0755

Canada
Raincoast Books
8680 Cambie Street
Vancouver, British Columbia
V6P 6M9
Tel: (604) 323-7100
Fax: (604) 323-2600

Southeast Asia
Berkeley Books Pte Ltd
5 Little Road #08-01
Singapore 536983
Tel: (65) 280-1330
Fax: (65) 280-6290

First edition
06 05 04 03 02 01 00    10 9 8 7 6 5 4 3 2 1

Design by Dutton & Sherman
Printed in Singapore

To my father, Georges

For Adelia and Carlota
And for Martine.

# A C K N O W L E D G M E N T S

Chance or intuition led me to live in Hong Kong between January 1997 and June 1998. My initial posting by the French news agency Agence France-Presse (AFP) was to cover the return of the last important outpost of the British empire to China on July 1, 1997. But beginning in February 1997, a personal interest in economics and finance allowed me to observe developments in the wider region, without realizing that the obvious difficulties in Thailand would lead to the major event of the end of the century—the collapse of the "Asian miracle."

Throughout this period, Hong Kong functioned as a nerve center, a regional hub and a resonance chamber. A large part of the primary material for this book was collected firsthand from dozens of interviews, news conferences, seminars, and other gatherings of analysts or investors.

I would like to thank once again my colleagues in AFP bureaus across the Asia-Pacific region, those from our affiliate AFX-Asia, and other journalists working in this part of the world.

I would also like to thank the long list of actors in the drama who helped me understand developments and contributed to the writing of this book, either voluntarily or involuntarily. I would particularly like to thank Michel Camdessus, Kenneth Courtis, Philippe Delhaise, Marc Faber, Toyoo Gyoten, John Mulcahy, and Russel Napier.

The observations and criticisms of friends who re-read the manuscript at different stages were invaluable and encouraging. Many thanks to Daniel Bouton, Jean-Pierre Landau, Brian McManus, Laurent Maduit, and José Vitoria Fernandes. Any mistakes are entirely my fault.

Finally, thanks to Adelia and Carlota who for eight months put up with a husband and father completely absorbed by this project.

*Hong Kong, Paris, and Aldeia do Meco*

# CONTENTS

# I N T R O D U C T I O N

The Asian "miracle" crashed on the slippery road to globalization. The victims of the accident were hundreds of millions of human beings plus a profusion of institutions, companies, ideas and concepts, moral and social values, and dreams and illusions.

In a region celebrating its graduation from underdevelopment to prosperity in barely a generation, the "boat people" returned. But unlike the mid-1970s, these new boat people were not fleeing the communist victory in Vietnam but the inflation, food shortages, and massive unemployment of Indonesia—the fourth most populous nation on earth.

The end of colonialism in Asia was marked by Hong Kong's return to China on July 1, 1997. But at the same time, 1997 was also haunted by the returning specter of foreign domination, with financial-market participants playing a role similar to nineteenth-century gunboats.

The financial storm had its origins in the Gulf of Thailand in early July. Gaining intensity over the following weeks, it eventually displayed the destructive force of the typhoons that regularly swept through the South China Sea around the same time every year. Buildings that seemed to be solid were knocked down and roofs were torn off as the hard work and savings of an entire generation were carried off by the unleashed elements.

Like the typhoons, the Asian financial turmoil had its origins in the violent meeting of opposing masses—rigid monetary arrangements versus the chronic instability of the yen against the dollar; the power of international capital flows versus fragile local banking systems; and the complexities of the market economy versus the weakness of institutional mechanisms.

There was no Richter scale to measure the intensity of financial and economic crises—only historical comparisons. And on the Asian scale, the crisis was unprecedented. It may be true that the region was adversely affected by the first oil shock of 1974 and suffered from an economic downturn in the mid-1980s, but these setbacks were more limited and spread out.

With the exception of the Chinese yuan, protected by its nonconvertible status, not a single Asian currency managed to avoid the speculative pressures. And only one currency managed to avoid depreciation—the Hong Kong dollar—albeit during a brief but bloody clash with speculative forces. The Indonesian rupiah, worth twenty-five hundred to the dollar at the beginning of 1997, had fallen to as low as seventeen thousand a year later while the Thai baht lost half its value. Even the Singapore dollar and the Taiwan dollar lost ground.

Seismic tremors across the region even rattled distant ground in Brazil, Russia, and Ukraine; the Asian crisis more or less becoming a crisis for all emerging markets—and for the United States in 1998 when the hedge fund Long-Term Capital Management failed.

The Russian debacle came at the tail end of the Asian storm. As severe recessions spread across the economies of East Asia, which accounted for twenty-three percent of world Gross Domestic Product (GDP) and twenty-five percent of global trade in 1996, demand dried up for energy and other commodities—the only products Russia was capable of selling on the international market. Toward the end of 1998, the commodity index calculated by the *Economist* fell to its lowest level in a quarter of a century.

South Africa, Australia, Brazil, and Canada were among the other major resource-based economies adversely affected. Russia got full marks for the sorts of deficiencies that explained the depth of the crisis in East Asia—the mushrooming of sixteen hundred banks over the space of several years, financial markets resembling a casino, irresponsible politicians, and the birth of an oligarchy controlling the wealth of the nation. But that didn't bother foreign investors who were dazzled by Russia's charms and promises (unkept) that left everyone hoping for a long and happy relationship.

To pretend that the advanced countries of North America and Europe would avoid the negative fallout because they accounted for almost half the global economy was either wishful thinking or pure folly. In terms of GNP, Asia represented twice its own weight in the creation of global wealth. The recession signaled the disappearance of twenty percent of the combined growth of Asia and the Group of Seven (G7) industrialized countries: United States, Japan, Germany, France, Britain, Italy, and Canada.

## TWO TRILLION DOLLARS TAKES FLIGHT

Toward the end of October 1997, when the "war of the peg" was raging in Hong Kong (see chapter 3), the financial world from Wall Street to Kabutocho lived in dread of the anniversaries of the stock market crashes of 1927 and 1987. In East Asia, the destruction of financial assets was massive—about seven hundred billion dollars, was the estimate of Alan Greenspan, chairman of the U.S. Federal Reserve, toward the end of 1997. By June 1998, British bank Standard Chartered estimated that stock market capitalization in East Asia had been slashed by two trillion dollars over the previous year (with Japan alone accounting for 1.2 trillion dollars). The figure was equivalent to a twenty percent slump on Wall Street at the time. The destruction of wealth was even more alarming if the meltdown in property and debts markets was included. Those who still hadn't understood that the value and circulation of capital determined all exchanges in a capitalist economy could reassure themselves by saying that the wealth only existed on paper. With Japan's bubble economy bursting at the beginning of the decade, that gave time for the Japanese to consider the impact on the "real" economy.

## HEADING FOR A DEPRESSION

The mechanics behind the Asian financial crisis are now well known. The International Monetary Fund (IMF) christened it a "convergence play" in its analysis of the tremors that rocked the European Monetary System in September 1992 and July-August 1993. The same phenomenon was seen in Mexico in December 1994. The belief that currencies would remain stable against the dollar, or the mark in the case of European currencies, encouraged influxes of foreign capital hoping to enjoy a "holiday" with high returns because interest rates are always higher than the "anchor" currency. When an external shock came along, foreign investors packed their bags and liquidity dried up. But the ability of different economies to survive in the new climate was not the same.

In East Asia, the financial tempest signaled disaster for banks. In four of the five countries in the front line—South Korea, Indonesia, Malaysia, and Thailand—the damage was huge (the Philippines was the exception). Dozens of financial institutions had to close their doors or merge. Others owed their temporary survival to nationalization. All this was further aggravated by the slow pace of financial reform in Japan, whose bubble had burst almost seven years earlier.

The third stage in the spiral was economic recession, with its retinue of bankruptcies and layoffs.

But the economic downturns were even more painful because they followed periods of exceptionally high growth. Thailand, for example, plunged from 6.4 percent growth in 1996 to zero in 1997, with the economy shrinking by 8.0 percent in 1998. The Indonesian economy, still expanding by 8.0 percent in the third quarter of 1997, declined 15.0 percent in 1998. South Korea's economy shrank at a similar rate after growing by almost 6.0 percent the previous year.

At first, the macroeconomic impact of the financial squall was underestimated. But quarter by quarter, growth forecasts were downgraded. No one, including those who saw the early danger signs in Thailand, anticipated the power of contagion. What initially seemed to be a simple hiccup for the Asian miracle soon gave way to warnings about the risks of a wave of deflation descending upon the region and spreading to the rest of the world. And finally, in remarks that triggered something of a shock after so much bad news, Jean-Michel Séverino, the World Bank vice president for Asia, raised the specter of a "depression"—the word used to denote the darkest hours of modern capitalism. "So where are we today?" he asked his audience at a seminar in Melbourne in June 1998. "My very straightforward answer would be to say that we are probably at the end of a first cycle of crisis and we are entering into a deep recession, or you could even use the term 'depression.' This depression may be very long lasting if one does not manage it very, very carefully."

## GOLD TURNS TO LEAD

For the countries most seriously affected, the pendulum swung from economic performance to scenes typical of the dramatic social consequences already suffered during the Mexican crisis of 1994 and 1995 as well as the Latin American debt crisis that dogged the region throughout the 1980s.

In Indonesia, the unemployment rate jumped from five to fifteen percent. The number of jobless in Thailand, which had an unemployment rate of 1.1 percent in August 1996, was estimated at two million at the end of 1998. The country's young middle class, lured into speculating on stocks to finance its appetite for Western luxury goods, was also wiped out. In South Korea, where recession deepened with lightning speed from the beginning of 1998, the number of people with jobs plunged by 686,000 in January alone, down 3.4 percent from a year earlier. In only a few months, South Korea went from a country recently suffering from labor shortages to a nation that in 1998 had 1.24 million jobless, amounting to 4.7 percent of the working population and rapidly approaching European levels of unemployment.

"Adverse developments of this magnitude constitute, in themselves, a substantial shock to any social system," the International Labor Organization (ILO) reported in April 1998 in a study of the "social impact" of the crisis. But these effects were amplified by two additional features. "The first is the absence of a meaningful social-safety net," it said, noting that Indonesia and Thailand were particularly vulnerable in the area of unemployment insurance while the recently introduced system in South Korea was still limited. "The vast majority of displaced workers will thus have to fend for themselves during the crisis," the ILO study noted. The second feature "lies in the fact that social expectations in these countries have been shaped by a long period of increasing employment opportunities and this makes the current shock in the labor market all the ruder."

The crisis shattered lives. A Korean father, who couldn't admit to his family that he'd lost his job, spent the day in a park before going home in the evening as if nothing has happened. A young Indonesian girl stopped going to school because her family didn't have enough money to buy her a uniform. A stockbroker in Thailand was forced to make ends meet by selling sandwiches. East Asia once dazzled the outside world with its fortunes made in one generation, racing to build the tallest office towers and the most lavish shopping malls selling expensive designer-label goods from Europe. But the good living and society pages of newspapers soon changed as the gold turned to lead.

## INTELLECTUAL STORM

The storm also ravaged people's minds.

Out and out optimism and self-satisfaction bordering on arrogance gave way to disbelief and disarray among victims of the disaster. Some people were understandably tempted to seek scapegoats and started blaming "speculators," the usual suspects. Working day and night as they shifted through the ashes, the firemen from the IMF were overwhelmed with advice.

By being openly discussed "live" on the Internet, the East Asian crisis marked a first in the history of applied economics. Before long, Professor Nouriel Roubini of New York University had created a web page compiling the vast array of writing on the subject by all sorts of experts (starting with himself). Paul Krugman, the highly controversial professor from the Massachusetts Institute of Technology (MIT) famous for denouncing the "myth of the Asia miracle" since 1994, posted well-defined arguments on his own website. The IMF meanwhile posted its own analyses as well as the responses of leaders to damning evidence, and in the case of Indonesia, the third draft of its agreement with the government in Jakarta. Other frequently visited sites include those operated by the World Bank, the Asian Development Bank (ADB), the Bank for International Settlements (BIS), the Institute for International Finance and the U.S. Treasury.

The crisis prompted a wave of editorials and other opinion pieces in the *Wall Street Journal*, especially its Asian edition, as well as the *Financial Times* and the *International Herald Tribune*. Hundreds of analyses were published for and against the IMF and financial policy issues from the "currency board" system of setting exchange rates to Chilean-style capital controls. Newspapers in the Asia-Pacific region weighed in, ranging from the *South China Morning Post* of Hong Kong, which posted a daily chronicle of the crisis on its Internet site, to the *Bangkok Post* and the *Chosun Ilbo* of South Korea.

The nature and cause of the crisis triggered a particularly animated debate with extremists on both sides.

For some, such as Jeffrey Sachs of Harvard University, the Asian crisis was purely and simply a financial panic. Nothing in East Asia could objectively justify such fears among foreign investors. The IMF therefore made an error in its diagnosis by prescribing severe structural adjustments, throwing oil on the fire. A less scientific version of this theory was seen in the bitter diatribes of Malaysian Prime Minister Mahathir Mohamad. For Mahathir, the financial debacle of mid-1997 was a conspiracy to deny Asians the right to prosperity.

At the other extreme were Paul Krugman and other eleventh-hour converts who blamed "crony capitalism" for the crisis. The economic miracle was nothing but an "Asian mirage" and the crisis merely reflected a return to harsh realities for a model of development that wasted capital.

## ADOLESCENCE CRISIS

"One of the greatest prices of economic wisdom is to know what you do not know," wrote American economist John Kenneth Galbraith. The crisis became less and less "Asian" and was far from over as the twentieth century drew to a close. The East Asian drama had not given away all its secrets. Nevertheless, this writer drew some beliefs from events witnessed during the extraordinary eighteen-month period between January 1997 and June 1998:

The East Asian crisis was the result of a double shock whose origins were outside the countries most severely affected. The first was the end of the Cold War, which subjected two billion people to the forces of global competition, including 1.2 billion Chinese. The second was changes in exchange rates of the world's two biggest economies, the United States and Japan. "We cannot deny that Japan always considered the level of exchange rates between the yen and the dollar as primarily a problem for Japan," said Toyoo Gyohten, a former Japanese vice minister of finance for international affairs. "However, the explosion of the East Asian crisis proved this wrong."

The concept of "Asia" should be approached cautiously given the diversity of races, religions, and cultures in the region and the different political systems and approaches to economic management. But there was nevertheless a "red line" that could be drawn across the region, from east to west and from Tokyo to Jakarta—demarcating a region whose lack of attention to capital returns bordered on distrust. The carefree attitude was encouraged by years of record growth and credit cycles allowing for exceptional levels of liquidity. In such particularly favorable conditions, speculative bubbles flourished like Japanese cherry blossoms in April. "Capitalism without bankruptcy is like Christianity without hell," wrote David Roche, strategist for *Independent Strategy*. In 1997, Asian capitalism discovered that hell existed after all, and capital sought its revenge. East Asia therefore went through a crisis of adolescence. It was painful, especially when it was thought that the "adults"—the advanced Western countries—could be taught a lesson. But adolescence was also the obligatory stage toward maturity.

Wild speculation, endemic corruption, and "crony capitalism" were not the exclusive rights of a geographic region, a period in history, or a race of people. Nor was the concentration of wealth into a handful of groups of families, be they Chinese tycoons, South Korea's *chaebol*, or the *keiretsu* system of interlocking shareholdings in Japan. In the nineteenth century, "robber barons" were a fact of life in the United States, arguably the first emerging market of the modern era. Financial panics and scandals, along with speculative manias, were also common. And at the end of the twentieth century, they were also common in post-Soviet Russia, with the Mafia playing an additional role.

To the disappointment of those still nostalgic for government planning and controls, the East Asian crisis was not caused by excessive liberalism. In fact, greater freedom would have allowed countries of the region to become real market economies. With the notable exception of Hong Kong, this had not been the case. In a way less institutionalized and less transparent than continental Europe, the countries of Southeast Asia were subjected to the heavy hand of intervention by their governments and politicians, all too often for personal interests. Such intervention seriously distorted markets. Japan and South Korea meanwhile pursued a hybrid growth model incorporating both socialist planning and feudal practices.

Liberalization was frequently the target of a mundane misunderstanding, namely, that the process involved the market economy assimilating the law of the jungle. The truth was exactly the opposite—the balanced workings of a modern economy went hand in hand with the rule of law. Liberalization required that the rules of the game were fair and well defined. They had to be applied with transparency, with an independent and respected judiciary, with honest and efficient authorities, and with an unbiased government. Such a requirement was both an ideal and a goal that no country could pretend to have completely achieved. But the East Asian crisis highlighted weaknesses in the political, social, and legal systems in this part of the world.

The crisis also highlighted the backwardness of regional methods of financing. East Asia was like a Europe whose banking system was still dominated by the merchants of Venice and the bankers of Lombardy. The ownership of major banks in Thailand, Indonesia, and the Philippines was dominated by families from the Chinese diaspora (the situation was less pronounced in Malaysia due to policies favoring ethnic Malays). The dominance of Chinese family networks was even more pronounced in Hong Kong, Taiwan, and Singapore. Such traditions could not necessarily be easily adapted to the winds of global change. Banking systems, financial markets, and business relations needed to be closely re-examined as money, know-how, and technology were required, especially from outside. Did this signal a "recolonization" of Asia?

The regional financial crisis resulted in "Asian values" losing much of their appeal. Even Singapore's former prime minister Lee Kuan Yew, the high priest of Confucian authoritarianism, allowed his doubts to emerge. And numerous voices in Asia itself, notably South Korean President Kim Dae Jung, indicated that such "values" actually helped to precipitate the crisis. To achieve a sustainable recovery, East Asia had to create a "second miracle"—a democratic adjustment: political democracy, social democracy, and economic democracy.

The "nonsystem" that characterized the international monetary scene from the early 1970s resulted in chaos. Capital flows gathered strength and freedom to move at a fearsome pace. The logic was inescapable—the rich, old countries had to send part of their savings to the poor, new countries—helping them to reduce their poverty. Experience showed that it was not a zero-sum game, even if the results in terms of efficiency and distribution could have been better. Navigating in such stormy waters required rigor and skill from national political authorities. Each false move was punished more quickly and with greater severity. One could always dream of a return to the calm seas, the "good old days" when the gold standard and fixed exchange rates held sway. But failing the removal of borders, rigid currency regimes had to be accompanied by economic and social flexibility as people adapted to a constantly changing world. Hong Kong paid the price of defending its fixed exchange rate with a severe recession and asset price deflation. And the European Union required considerable effort to achieve economic and monetary union.

In economics, extrapolation was dangerous and also mundane. The past was no guarantee of the future, as the crash of the Asian miracle clearly showed. Michel Camdessus, the managing director of the IMF, described the Mexican peso crisis as "the first financial crisis of the twenty-first century." Without even waiting for the third millenium, the Asian storm erupted as a "force ten" gale. Could something similar happen at the heart of the system—in New York, London, or Frankfurt? What about "The End of History," a change in cycle, a "new paradigm," or a "new economy"? The crisis of 1997 devalued many of these new versions of tomorrow. If economic cycles still existed, especially credit cycles that played such a key role in Asia, they would return to haunt the advanced countries.

## AMERICA WILL PAY?

In the West, the Asian crisis was initially seen as good news. Let's ignore those who were quietly happy to see Asians finally being put in their place. More simply, it was the idea that lower prices in East Asia would perpetuate disinflation in a booming American economy and in economies in Europe that had recently resumed expanding. But was there a risk that disinflation would led to deflation and finally depression? Which "D" would define the end of the twentieth century?

The impact of the Asian crisis on the rest of the world was not difficult to identify. Asian countries and other emerging countries would buy less from industrialized countries and do everything they could to boost exports. The swing from current account deficits to surpluses for East Asia would be in the order of hundreds of billions of dollars by the start of the twenty-first century.

Among the G7 countries, Japan was in the front line. Its economy was already sick and the rest of Asia had been absorbing forty percent of its exports before the crisis. And some Japanese industries, notably steel, electronics, and cars, were suffering from increased competition from South Korea. Toward the middle of 1998, South Korean exports were growing by volume, but the value was stagnating. Prices were falling and declining prices affected everyone.

"America will pay" became the refrain for optimists. Maybe, but how much and for how long? In the second quarter of 1998, American exports dropped eight percent by volume—the sharpest fall since 1982 when Latin America's debt crisis was just starting, leading to the "lost decade" for an entire continent. America's trade deficit was hitting new records and corporate earnings were starting to suffer after an unprecedented boom lasting twenty years. The bears were out on Wall Street, consumers were spending like there was no tomorrow, and America was relying more than ever on its financial market holding up. It looked like it was time to rush for cover.

The savior would be a seventy-two-year-old man, somewhat hunched, who wore tortoise-shell glasses. He spent much of his time going over figures and was a master in the art of speaking for long periods and saying as little as possible, a sure sign of a great central banker. Alan Greenspan was the man who could cut interest rates in the United States. But monetary tools weren't neutral, even in the hands of the chairman of the Federal Reserve Board. How could lower interest rates be reconciled with the maintenance of a strong dollar, or at least a stable dollar, which had contributed so much to monetary stability in the United States while helping to push growth along in Europe?

Just like before the 1929 crash, Europe believed the illusion that it was immune from a deflationary spiral. The Euro was the reassuring shelter, even for those who were still skeptical about European monetary union six months earlier. But things weren't that simple.

Excluding trade between other members of the European Union (EU), the share of exports going to Asia was about one third—the same as to the United States. And EU exports to Asia had grown by an average of sixteen percent a year for a decade. Japanese and South Korean investment had breathed new life into some of Europe's dying industrial areas. And the EU was also exposed to the Russian crisis, both directly and indirectly through its eastern European neighbors.

Furthermore, European banks were heavily exposed to Asia—less than their Japanese rivals but much more than American banks. When the Asia crisis erupted in the middle of 1997, they had committed the equivalent of half their capital to East Asia and eighty percent to all emerging markets including Russia, eastern Europe, Turkey, and Latin America. Japanese banks had 109 percent of their capital in Asia and 118 percent in all emerging markets. But for American banks, the figures were only twelve percent and thirty-four percent.

Europe wasn't immune to bubbles bursting. And there was also asset price inflation in Europe, encouraged by the convergence of interest rates ahead of the launch of the single currency in 1999 and the "flight to quality" as capital fled the collapsing emerging markets.

And Europe lived under another illusion—that the recent resumption of economic growth would compensate for the failure to resolve its serious structural problems. The private sector may have made progress, but public spending was still profligate, corporatism was rampant, pension systems were stifling, and the labor market remained inflexible, which could be seen in massive unemployment across Europe.

## DISASTER SCENARIO

The possibility of the Asian crisis turning into a disaster couldn't be ruled out, and the progress of events in Japan, Indonesia, and even Hong Kong showed what might lie in store.

Across Asia, the incompetence of politicians from Japan to Malaysia couldn't be underestimated. Politicians had already managed to combine a cyclical downturn with a banking crisis to produce the most serious economic debacle since the Great Depression of the 1930s. And the politicians could always strike again. In Japan, the success of market forces winning out over the old Japanese model seemed like a reasonable bet, but after how many costly battles with its trading partners, both near and far?

Asia didn't have a monopoly on political irresponsibility. Thanks to the U.S. Congress, the IMF was in danger of running out of cash. And the IMF was the only international fireman. It was also the only doctor in town, even if its methods of treating patients weren't always pleasant. But neither were the "alternative" cures that would only make the patient worse—isolation, quarantine, protectionism, and renewed controls on the movement of capital, goods, and people. The worst-case scenario was never certain. But it wasn't impossible either.

CHAPTER     ONE

# High Tide, Low Tide

"Wait for the tide to go down to see who's not wearing their
swimming trunks."

*—Chinese President Jiang Zemin,*
*quoting a "proverb" to foreign bankers*

Did the world wake up after a long dream to discover one fine day in 1997 that the "Asian economic miracle" was only a mirage? Grim prophecies suddenly replaced all the hoopla surrounding the imminent coming of the "Pacific Century" that was supposed to see the center of world economic gravity shifting from the West to the East. But to have dismissed Asia would have been equally pompous. Those who previously exaggerated the economic progress of the region frequently mistook their desire for reality. Such desire was replaced by fear.

Asia's economic performance had long been unrivalled, even if the anticipated scale of the recession triggered in 1997 was taken into account.

From 1955 to 1999, the average rate of GNP growth in South Korea was nine percent a year and almost as high for Singapore between 1961 and 1999. Thailand's growth averaged 7.5 percent a year between 1955 and the end of the century while Malaysia grew at an average annual rate of seven percent between 1966 and 1999. Indonesia's average rate of expansion was 6.5 percent a year between 1961 and 1999.

China, which took off much later, grew twice as fast from the late 1970s when economic reforms were first introduced.

Even the Philippines, long considered the "sick man of Asia," grew at an annual rate of almost four percent between 1955 and the end of the century.

East Asia went through an exceptional period of economic growth even when compared with other outstanding periods in recent history such as the nineteenth-century industrial revolution in Britain, the emergence of the United States at the beginning of the twentieth century, and the rebuilding of Japan after World War II.

The economic growth led to sharp increases in living standards across Asia. Toyoo Gyohten recalled the grinding poverty that typified much of Southeast Asia when, as a junior Japanese finance ministry official, he was sent to the Manila-based Asian Development Bank. "It is fair to say that because of the very rapid growth, Asia eliminated very fundamental problems of poverty," the future vice minister said. In 1975, according to the World Bank, six out of ten inhabitants of East Asia survived on less than a dollar a month, considered the threshold of "absolute poverty." By 1992, the ratio had dropped to about two. In Indonesia alone, the ratio of those living below the absolute poverty line plunged from sixty percent to eleven percent in twenty-five years.

In the more advanced "tiger" economies of South Korea, Taiwan, Hong Kong, and Singapore, GNP per capita rose progressively, sometimes reaching the same level as the old industrialized countries.

## MIRACLE OR MIRAGE?

The scale of catching up achieved by East Asian economies was partly explained by the level of development in the advanced industrialized countries. Asian economies grew stronger at a faster pace because the summit they had to climb to reach the industrialized countries had shifted to an even higher elevation. "The growth phenomenon has put East Asia on a course many parameters of which were followed earlier in the old industrial economies. It is faster than anything known elsewhere, but that is at least partly because an economy can move more quickly when it is bridging a large gap between its own productivity levels and the world's frontiers," said Ross Garnaut, economics professor at the Australian National University.

Another way of looking at Asia's economic growth was expressed by those who questioned the "miracle" notion. For them, the region's performance was just as rosy as in other parts of the developed or developing world that were going through painstaking periods of adjustment.

Then there were the total skeptics like Paul Krugman, the American academic who denounced "The Myth of East Asia's Miracle" in an article published in Foreign Affairs in 1994. Drawing a parallel with the Soviet Union, which seemed to be catching up with the West in the 1950s and 1960s, Krugman asserted that rapid growth in the newly industrializing economies of Asia largely reflected "an astonishing mobilization of resources" such as labor and capital rather than gains in efficiency. "Singapore grew through a mobilization of resources that would have done Stalin proud," Krugman wrote. "The miracle turns out to have been based on perspiration rather than inspiration."

"Sustained growth in a nation's per capita income can only occur if there is a rise in output per unit of input," Krugman said, noting that "throwing money nonstop into things like machinery without increasing efficiency would lead to diminishing returns....Because input-driven growth is an inherently limited process, Soviet growth was virtually certain to slow down." Japan suffered a similar fate in the early 1990s, burying once and for all predictions that Japan would overtake the United States in the first decade of the twenty-first century.

In the same way, economic growth in the rest of East Asia faced diminishing returns. And even if these economies manage to keep narrowing the gap with the advanced economies, their growth would be slower. "From the perspective of the year 2010, current projections of Asian supremacy extrapolated from recent trends may well look almost as silly as 1960s-vintage forecasts of Soviet industrial supremacy did from the perspective of the Brezhnev years," Krugman wrote.

So if there was nothing miraculous about Asia's growth after all, the causes and effects of the miracle—be they the superiority of authoritarian political regimes or the inevitable decline of the West—should be approached with caution.

## THE INFAMOUS STUDY

As impressive as they may have been, rates of growth in absolute terms hardly meant much at all. The choice of periods was also a determining factor. An infamous study published by the World Bank in September 1993 covered the period from 1960 to 1985. The study, *The East Asian Miracle*, ranked economies according to GNP per capita and found that eight "high-performing Asian economies" were all among the top twenty...behind Botswana! Six Asian economies were ranked from second to seventh place while Malaysia was ranked seventeenth and Thailand ranked twentieth.

Despite ranking nineteenth, China was excluded from the study. So too was the Philippines, ranked thirty-fourth and considered at the time as the dunce of the regional class.

Should the same arbitrary approach to statistics used to define the Asian miracle in 1993 be used again to illustrate the meltdown?

"The Holy Roman Empire is neither holy, nor Roman, nor an Empire." For Andrew Freris, head of Asian research at Bank of America in Hong Kong, this quote from Voltaire summed it all up. "There is no such thing as Asia, but there are Asian economies," he wrote in early 1988. "The 'Asian banking and financial crisis' was neither pan-Asian, nor wholly banking, nor a crisis in some cases."

The tendency to put all East Asian economies into one basket was misleading. "One need do no more than list the East Asian economies that have sustained rapid growth over the past decade to draw attention to the heterogeneity of their economic and political systems and of their economic experience," Ross Garnaut told an international monetary conference in Sydney in June 1996.

"What is now clear is that there is nothing miraculous about sustained rapid growth in East Asia. It occurs in a wide range of institutional settings once a number of conditions have been met."

In its 1993 study, the World Bank evaluated such conditions, contradicting the title of the work and showing that there was nothing "miraculous" taking place in the "high-performing" Asian economies. "It is largely due to superior accumulation of physical and human capital," it reported. These economies succeeded because they got their policy fundamentals right—high savings and investment rates in the private sector along with rapid population growth, helped by improvements in education and public administration, as well as improved controls over demographics. The macroeconomic policies that followed were usually sound and provided stability while being friendly to the private sector.

But in most of the Asian economies, governments systematically intervened through various means to boost development of the economy in general and certain sectors in particular. They were open to foreign technology, even if the countries of Northeast Asia imposed restrictions on direct investment from abroad. And they also used sectoral policies to promote exports.

## THE MISSING INGREDIENT

Ross Garnaut refined the analysis.

"The most basic condition is that there must be an effective state, capable of delivering stable economic policies and a range of public services necessary for development against the pressures of international and domestic pressure groups," he told his audience in Sydney. "The state's services must be able to enforce the security of property and contracts that underpins markets. While this seems obvious, 'the absence of this condition in most developing countries explains main instances of development failure'."

Rapid growth must also be accepted as a priority by the community. "Rapid economic growth sustained over long periods is disruptive and destructive of established elites, interests, institutions, and ways," he said. Widely distributing the benefits of growth—in areas such as education, health, housing, and land reform—also helped, as did high population densities that enabled countries to develop labor-intensive industries in the early stages of development.

Another requirement was economic stability—low inflation, convertible currencies, and modest levels of domestic and foreign borrowing by governments.

Other conditions for catching up included being open to foreign trade and capital flows as well as foreign technology, management, and ideas. This required high rates of savings and investment, especially in education.

Finally, sustained rapid growth bridging the gap with advanced economies required "acceptance of continuing large and rapid changes in industrial structure," Garnaut said. "This, in turn, requires acceptance of a large role for markets in resource allocation, and the integration of domestic into international markets for goods and services."

How and for what reasons did Asian economies stop adhering to the disciplines behind their success? What was the missing ingredient—democracy, the rule of law? And did the Garnaut model not underestimate conditions now essential for the stability of the advanced economies such as solid financial systems, efficient and independent monitoring mechanism, and controls over corruption and nepotism?

## NEW RULES OF THE GAME

According to William Overholt, head of Asian research with Bankers Trust in Hong Kong, "The good guys won and then they tended to relax." The assertion, advanced half seriously in October 1997, referred to the end of the Cold War in the late 1980s coinciding with the emergence of speculative "bubbles" across Asia, starting with Japan and South Korea. These bubbles signaled the end of sound economic policies that allowed rapid growth to develop. "What was miraculous was that the politicians implemented the right policies because they were scared," Overholt said. "The normal politician's behavior is patronage not rational economics." Behind this strangely virtuous behavior lurked fear, especially fear of neighbors. The greatest example was the dictatorial South Korean President Park Chung-hee, for whom industrial expansion was a strategic policy of national security against the persistent threat from his communist cousins in the North.

Directly linking the disappearance of the communist threat to becoming less disciplined may be somewhat exaggerated.

But the end of the Cold War did prompt leading industrialized nations to reorient their approach to economic development in emerging Asia.

It was no longer a case of the West, meaning the United States, trying to achieve strategic military objectives such as "containing" communism in Asia, while largely subordinating economic activity in the region to the raising of bilateral and multilateral aid.

Once private capital, open markets, and direct investment started to flourish, what counted was capital returns and not anticommunist credentials.

"In the 1950s and 1960s, government loans provided more than half of all capital flows to developing countries," wrote Professor Jeffrey Winters. "Since 1984, private flows to these states have increased at a rate five times faster than official flows. In 1995, private capital accounted for three-fourths of all investment resources delivered to the developing world. Portfolio capital rose to fifty percent of total net capital flows to developing countries by 1996 from just two percent in 1987. And three-quarters of this staggering sum is in the hands of fewer than one hundred emerging-market fund managers."

At the beginning of the 1990s, fund managers from rich countries were allured toward previously exotic investment destinations. An added incentive was the low returns on financial assets in the industrialized countries, the result of mediocre economic performances and low interest rates.

In 1990, net inflows of foreign portfolio investment in emerging equity markets totaled 3.2 billion dollars. By 1995, it had shot up to 45.8 billion dollars, according to the World Bank's Global Development Finance report issued in 1998. Net purchases of bonds issued by developing economies rocketed from one hundred million dollars in 1991 to 53.8 billion dollars in 1997. Commercial banks, burned heavily by their misadventures in Latin America in the 1980s, were initially cautious. But they eventually succumbed, with net lending jumping from 8.9 billion dollars in 1994 to 41.1 billion dollars in 1997. Foreign direct investment—largely directed toward subsidiaries and joint ventures, and therefore more long-term and stable— leapt from 23.7 billion dollars in 1991 to 120.4 billion dollars in 1997.

"It is one thing to call attention to the long-term potential of many of these countries," American economist Henry Kaufman said. "But it was quite another matter to interpret large-scale flows of funds into the emerging debt and equity markets as proof that these countries were immunized from economic and financial problems. There was inadequate attention to the fact that when access to credit becomes too easy, excesses normally follow."

Nothing gave a better idea of the prevailing euphoria than the plunge in risk premiums on bonds issued by emerging economies. The premium over U.S. Treasury bonds with equivalent maturities narrowed from sixteen hundred basis points (sixteen percentage points) in early 1995 (just after the Mexican shock) to just 350 basis points (three-and-a-half percentage points) in September 1997. In the case of Thailand and Indonesia, secondary market yields were only one hundred basis points (one percentage point) above the equivalent Treasury yield—indicating that the credit quality of a borrower in Bangkok or Jakarta was almost as good as the government of the United States.

East Asia entered the new era of "globalization" at the right time, taking advantage of an exceptionally favorable international environment. Competitors from other regions were either weakened—as in the case of Latin America after the "lost decade" triggered by the debt crisis in the early 1980s—or simply too delicate as in Eastern Europe and Russia where political adjustment only occurred after the fall of the Berlin Wall in 1989. After a promising start, China put itself out of the game that same year when the country's aging leadership ordered a violent crackdown on students in Beijing's Tiananmen Square. The time for relaunching reforms wasn't considered ripe until 1992, when Chinese leader Deng Xiaoping visited the booming provinces of the south.

The "Asian miracle" was undoubtedly partly artificial, but the idea was nevertheless important as it reinforced the perceptions of the major economic participants, either domestic or foreign. In this sense, there was an "Asian miracle" as people had faith. And an "Asian crisis" when they lost it.

## AN ESSENTIAL KEY

To explain the fall of the Asian dominos one after the other, factors before the event should be distinguished from justifications after. With reverse engineering, a finished product is dismantled to discover the secrets of how it was built—as Toyota Motor Corporation did by pulling apart a Mercedes "S" model before conceiving the Lexus, its top luxury model. In the process, Toyota discovered it could achieve a similar result at sharply reduced costs.

By submitting the "Asian miracle" to the same treatment, we can find the flaws that justified—after the event—the massive outflow of capital from the region, estimated at one hundred billion dollars or about ten percent of GDP. The weaknesses ranged from "crony capitalism" and excessive debt burdens in the private sector to fragile banking systems and corruption in general. Such weaknesses of the "Asian model" were more or less known, but either voluntarily underestimated or ignored. Moreover, they reinforced the contagion but were not the cause.

Three factors played a key role in spreading the crisis.

The first, and most important without a doubt, was the realignment of exchange rates between the world's two biggest economies.

Analyzing the crisis of 1997 without going into the history of economic and monetary relations between the United States and Japan is impossible. Japan accounted for two-thirds of the GNP of Asia including China, and the United States was not only the military power that guaranteed peace and stability in the Asia-Pacific region, it remained a major destination for Asian exports, the main center of production, and an attraction for capital flows.

Two dates in contemporary monetary history provided an essential key for understanding recent developments. The first is September 20, 1985, when the world's five leading industrialized countries reached the "Plaza Accord" in New York, agreeing to bring about a sustained decline in the dollar's value in foreign exchange markets. The agreement was named after the Plaza Hotel where the meeting took place between finance ministers and central bank governors from what was then the Group of Five (G5). The second event was much more discreet and took place in the spring of 1995. Although an exact date was not easy to pin down, the United States and Japan effectively concluded a "Reverse Plaza Accord"—the term coined by Kenneth Courtis, chief economist for Deutsche Bank in Asia.

In February 1985, the greenback was worth 260 yen. Ten years later, the dollar fetched only 80 yen. But from April 1995, the dollar began to soar against the Japanese currency, gaining thirty percent in eighteen months. For the Asian countries with currencies fixed to the dollar, that represented a swing of sixty percent. "No wonder we have crises that overwhelm small countries," said Paul Volcker, former chairman of the U.S. Federal Reserve Board.

East Asian economies from Indonesia to South Korea, having linked their monetary destiny to the dollar, were initially buoyed by the rising tide of the yen, and were happy to be carried by the "divine wind," the *kamikaze*, blowing from Japan. But when the pendulum swung in the other direction, the wind turned nasty.

The second factor behind the contagion was that the surge of Japanese investment in Southeast Asia redrew the regional trade map. Intraregional trade grew more rapidly than world trade. Japan exported components, machinery, and entire factories to the rest of Asia, and a growing share of manufactured goods were re-imported into Japan. Trade between other East Asian economies followed a similar pattern. So between 1987 and 1997, such intraregional trade grew from about one-fifth of all trade in the region to one-third.

Americans and Europeans soon got involved and the first-generation "tigers"—South Korea, Taiwan, Hong Kong, and Singapore—also started venturing forth outside their domestic economies. But greater interdependence also increases vulnerability in times of difficulty—hence the competitive depreciations of other Asian currencies following the Thai baht's float on July 2, 1997, when the baht collapsed and other regional currencies soon followed suit.

Finally, the fruits of financial growth were attacked by worms in 1994-95. Current account deficits started ballooning to frightening levels—ten percent of GDP in Malaysia in 1995 and eight percent in Thailand the following year. As their dollar-linked currencies surged, Asian economies that relied heavily on exports saw their international competitiveness sharply eroded. At the same time, China largely avoided the adverse impact of the "Reverse Plaza Accord" and its economy remained strong. Circumstances deteriorated when global demand in key Asian export sectors fell in 1995-96. South Korea, for example, was devastated by shrinking demand for semiconductors.

At the same time, private capital inflows were ballooning to alarming levels. As a proportion of GDP between 1994 and 1996, such inflows soared from 0.3 percent to 6.1 percent in Indonesia, from 1.2 percent to 4.9 percent in South Korea, from 1.2 percent to 8.4 percent in Malaysia, and from 7.9 percent to 12.7 percent in the Philippines. In Thailand, inflows of private capital jumped from 14.3 percent in 1994 to 17.3 percent in 1995 before easing to 14.5 percent in 1996.

Such inflows of foreign capital largely reflected short-term debt denominated in strong currencies, mainly the dollar—a perverse fallout for those countries with more or less fixed exchange rates against the greenback. Monetary stability had existed for such a long time—1983 in the case of Thailand—that nobody seriously thought it could be threatened. And so the borrowers failed to hedge their loans against the risks of currency depreciation.

It was as if huge volumes of water were endlessly gushing and accumulating on the other side of a badly built dam, which was straining under the pressure. When the barrier finally gave way at the beginning of July in Bangkok, the disaster shocked the vast majority of the population that was still asleep, deluded by dreams of prosperity and grandeur.

One of those dreamers was called Philip Leigh Tose.

C  H  A  P  T  E  R      T  W  O

# The Fall of the Falcon

---

**"We are the company people love to hate."**
*—Philip Tose, founder of Peregrine and one*
*of the first big victims of the crisis*

The Hong Kong press pack was difficult to keep in check even at the best of times. It was the product of intense competition between more than a dozen daily newspapers and standard Cantonese behavior. Basic courtesy was so lacking among the Cantonese that the government of the special administrative region ended up financing a public campaign to promote it.

On January 13, 1998, the pack of journalists rushed through the slightly tattered corridors of the Ritz Carlton Hotel to witness a deathblow.

In an overheated atmosphere, two photographers were fighting. Television cameramen screamed for more space around the tiny table covered with microphones. The setting would have been perfect for local movie stars Jackie Chan or Michelle Yeoh. But the stars of this show were two investment bankers by the names of Philip Tose and Francis Leung.

The two bankers always appeared together when dealing with the media. Tose would make the presentation and respond to questions in English while Leung would address the local Chinese reporters in Cantonese before interpreting his remarks into the language of the former colonial authorities.

In 1988, these two men walked out of Citicorp Scrimegeour Vickers together to start their own securities company. In the tradition of Scottish hunting, Tose came up with the name and logo of this latest arrival on the Hong Kong financial scene—Peregrine—named after the swift bird of prey.

Within the space of a few years, although Peregrine had come to instill fear among many of the big names in international finance, it commanded no respect. Peregrine was heartily despised for its legendary aggression, the arrogance attributable to its founder, and the ruthlessness with which the company ruled over its terrain, the "miracle" economies of East Asia. "We are the company people love to hate," Tose used to say.

Peregrine was the only local investment bank with a network throughout Asia, from Tokyo to Bombay. By the beginning of 1997, it employed two thousand people and was also present in London and New York. Initially incorporated with only twenty-five million dollars in start-up capital, in 1997 Peregrine reported 5.3 billion dollars in assets and shareholder funds of more than nine hundred million dollars.

And despite the early warning signs in Thailand and South Korea, the company had reported glowing profits for 1996.

Less than a year later, Philip Tose and Francis Leung found themselves in the basement of the Ritz Carlton in the presence of another man—David Hague, from international accounting firm Price Waterhouse. Earlier that morning, a court had ordered Hague on a tough mission—to liquidate Peregrine and carve up the assets of the company that had become the pride of Hong Kong and one of the chief symbols of the territory's entrepreneurial spirit.

## A TASTE FOR RISK

It was a novel idea—appearing in public to tell the tale of one's failure. In similar circumstances, most people would flee from the cameras. But Philip Tose was never afraid of looking death in the face. He entered the world of finance after a brief career as a racing car driver in the 1960s. And his inordinate taste for risk was behind the exceptional performance of Peregrine before it fell.

The physical features of the founder possibly contributed to the company's reputation for being arrogant. His lips were so thin that they almost disappeared into that ironic smile. The voice was firm with a peremptory tone. Any journalists who thought they had come to hear a confession would be sadly mistaken.

"I am not here to answer very detailed questions, I'm warning you," Tose said. "What is important is that the facts are put straight and that we get away from a lot of sensationalism reported in the press."

What the press reported less than two weeks earlier on January 2 was indeed sensational—Peregrine's fixed-income department had committed a third of its capital in a 260-million dollar bridging loan to a company called Steady Safe, a modest Indonesian outfit running a fleet of taxis in Jakarta. The idea was that Peregrine would get to lead manage the company's up and coming bond issue in the United States. But the company was neither steady nor safe, and there were two tragic consequences for Peregrine as the Indonesian rupiah went into free fall in the first few days of the New Year. The first was that the bond issue would never take place. The second was that the bridging loan would never be repaid. The Indonesian taxi company was insolvent.

"I am not going into specifics," Tose said. "Some say credit control was too lax. It is very easy to say with hindsight. But you are missing the point. What happened was a complete meltdown in a country. Indonesia clearly disappointed everyone."

For Philip Tose, the admission had a personal flavor. Here was a man who had not only built his professional success and personal fortune on the rapid economic growth in countries like Indonesia. He was also an apologist for figures like President Suharto and he gladly offered his opinions to Western democracies. And that's how Philip Tose was dragged into the Indonesian debacle.

## JUNK BONDS FOR ASIA

"What's going on at Peregrine?" asked the financial director of a large Hong Kong company in September 1997. Like other corporate treasurers, he had been approached by Peregrine officials to see if he was interested in acquiring the company's entire portfolio of Indonesian bonds. At around the same time, Philip Tose started to court fund managers, some of whom were a bit taken aback by such unusual soliciting.

The development of Asia's corporate bond market, along with the emergence of China as a major economic power, was supposed to be the springboard propelling Peregrine to the heights of international finance.

Asian companies had traditionally borrowed funds from banks. This usually let the owners, often Chinese families, maintain control and avoid any dilution of their shareholdings. Banks often developed close relationships with their clients and tended to lend funds to the shareholders without poking their noses too much into company accounts. A risky business, as the Asian crisis would show.

Raising funds from equity markets was an alternative to borrowing directly from banks. But stock markets in many Asian economies were limited with various restrictions on foreign ownership. There was also the danger of losing control. Not to mention the annoying problem of dealing with minority shareholders.

Debt markets were the ideal solution, allowing companies to raise funds by issuing bonds at a fixed rate of interest over several years before repayment came due. There was no danger of the owner's shareholdings being diluted. And under certain conditions, there was access to the international capital markets.

But for financial intermediaries involved in the fixed-income markets, the work involved in arranging and underwriting bond issues as well as distributing the paper required a solid financial base and a vast sale network reaching institutional investors across the globe. Peregrine's main competitors would be big, well-established names including Merrill Lynch, Goldman Sachs, and Morgan Stanley from the United States, and European rivals such as Deutsche Morgan Grenfell, SBC-Warburg, and ING-Barings.

Peregrine didn't stand a chance. Taking advantage of its regional roots, its connections, and its willingness to take risks, the company instead set about developing a new market all for itself. The new market was modeled on the market for "junk bonds" that appeared in the United States in the 1980s, allowing second and third-rate borrowers to issue high-yielding pieces of debt.

The high returns for junk bonds denote high risk, in this case the risk of default, and the term "junk" was used by credit rating agencies to warn investors that the borrowers were less creditworthy than the traditional issuers of bonds.

Michael Milken, considered the founder of the junk bond market in the United States, was something of a genius—he created a marriage of convenience between ambitious companies desperately needing money and investors who were audacious enough to place bets with the hope of winning higher returns. Milken's tale was well known—it ended with a huge financial scandal, legal proceedings, a prison sentence, and the bankruptcy of Drexel Burnham Lambert, the investment bank that came to dominate the junk bond market. Despite the demise of their creator, however, junk bonds continued to exist and were at least partly responsible for the entrepreneurial dynamism that paved the way for the renaissance of American business toward the end of the twentieth century.

### RED FERRARI IN SEOUL

Philip Tose had found his Michael Milken in André Lee.

Lee, a young American of Korean and French-Canadian extraction, was barely thirty when he was poached from Lehman Brothers where he had been selling commercial paper denominated in various Asian currencies. Poaching entire teams was already the norm for the investment banking industry in New York and London, making the financial market environment unstable by definition. The lure of quick gains, overblown ambitions, and sharp swings in results frequently led such bands of mercenaries to offer themselves to the highest bidders.

And so in 1994, André Lee and a dozen of his colleagues at Lehman Brothers in Hong Kong packed their bags and headed for Peregrine.

Their success was rapid and spectacular. Within two years, the fixed-income department was generating more than half the company's profits and by the end of 1996, it was employing more than two hundred people. Peregrine had become the biggest arranger of junk bond issues in Asia, helping companies in the region raise some thirty-five billion dollars from the international capital market.

When Philip Tose, again flanked by Francis Leung, announced the company's earnings in April 1997, he showed that he was particularly happy with the fixed-income department in a financial climate that had already become more difficult. The market in Thailand was almost dead, he said, and Peregrine was now focussing on issues for Indonesian borrowers, selling the bonds to South Korean investors.

Using his Korean roots, Lee had found the perfect market. South Korea's banks, especially the investment banks, were as hungry for exotic high-yielding bonds as they were negligent with their own accounts. In 1996, the ability to offload paper to the South Koreans was a gold mine. André Lee earned five million dollars that year and could be seen driving around the hugely congested streets of Seoul in his red Ferrari. Hardly an oddity in Hong Kong, Ferraris were almost a mundane fixture to the territory's roads. But a real curiosity in South Korea, where trade barriers and prevailing xenophobia had confined all foreign vehicles to a tiny share of the local market.

Unlike stockbroking, the real profession of Philip Tose, substantial capital was needed for fixed-income operations. To win a mandate from the borrower, the lead manager must not only offer the best price—the lowest interest rate, expressed in terms of the spread over U.S. Treasury bonds of similar maturities, the main benchmark for the market. And not only did the company arranging the issue have to be capable of distributing the paper to international investors. When a bond issue was launched, the lead manager was also required to advance some or even all of the proceeds to the issuing company. So when investors didn't like an issue, the arranger risked getting stuck with paper that nobody wanted to buy.

All of this required money—a lot of money for a company with Peregrine's ambitions.

When the company was born back in 1988, the capital provided by Tose, Leung, and their Chinese tycoon sponsors was thirty-eight million dollars. By mid-1997, shareholder funds had ballooned to 865 million dollars. But even that wasn't enough for Peregrine's fixed-income activities. So the company had to rely on lines of credit from its banks, which were used to finance an alarming expansion in the size of its balance sheet. By June 1997, the company's assets had grown to 5.3 billion dollars, six times the size of its capital.

"By the summer, Peregrine had become a massive warehouse for Asian junk bonds," a member of the company's executive board said later. Thailand's decision to float the baht on July 2 was the signal for international investors to rush for the exits. Unpegged from its long-standing fixed-rate against the dollar, the Thai currency began its perilous descent. By the end of the month, the Indonesian rupiah, the Philippine peso, and the Malaysian ringgit had been sucked into a downward spiral of depreciation. The Asian financial crisis was entering its active phase. The tropical depression became a squall and eventually a typhoon. Peregrine was sitting on a mountain of paper with 3.5 billion dollars worth of bonds on its books. As for the South Korean banks, they were more preoccupied with their own growing problems back home, illustrated by the collapse of the Hanbo conglomerate at the end of 1996. The Koreans weren't interested in André Lee. The market had just fallen from under his feet.

## THE FRANKENSTEIN OF FINANCE

A little earlier, the young head of the fixed-income department sent an internal memo to reassure the troops. "We have prepared for Indonesian rupiah devaluation, we have prepared for Malaysian ringgit devaluation, we have even taken steps to position ourselves in case of Hong Kong dollar devaluation," he said.

"I love chaos. I love things undefined, a picture that can be painted from scratch," André Lee said. "Except that in the last six months, I've been disheartened sometimes when I look over my shoulder and think of the monster that I've created."

Peregrine would try to put this Frankenstein of finance back into its cage before it was too late. The company's bond portfolio was radically slimmed down and Peregrine's assets were halved between June and November, falling to 2.4 billion dollars, less than the level in late 1996. Peregrine sold everything that was reasonably liquid. Even the fatal loan to the Indonesian taxi outfit was sold off to the Koreans at the right moment. But it would eventually come back and haunt the company when the Koreans exercised a repurchase clause.

Around the same time, a Peregrine source said, André Lee was going around as if nothing was happening in the rest of Asia. The investment bank Credit Suisse First Boston (CSFB) approached Peregrine to negotiate the purchase of its fixed-income portfolio. Lee indicated that he was ready to sell, not at a discount but at par or even a small premium! "If that's your starting position, the discussions end here," one of the CSFB negotiators reportedly replied.

On October 27, the company took out a newspaper advertisement: "Peregrine's fixed-income group, including foreign exchange, has seen market conditions deteriorate since June 30, 1997, although revenues have held up better than expected. Peregrine's bond inventory is not significantly different from the amounts reported in the 1996 annual report. Substantially all of the inventory is denominated in U.S. dollars and—to the extent that positions are held in local currency—they have been hedged into U.S. dollars prior to the recent currency devaluation."

At the same time, Peregrine said it had engaged the services of American private-detective firm Kroll Associates to find the source of recurring rumors about the difficulties of the fixed-income department. Tom Grimmer, the man who had the formidable job of Peregrine's public relations manager right up until the company was liquidated, later said that British investment bank Robert Fleming had offered its apologies for spreading the rumor.

## FAVORITE SON

André Lee had his own ideas about the rumors. He was convinced they were coming from inside the company. In April 1998, Lee ended his long silence to give his account of the story in an extensive interview with *Euromoney* magazine. The most interesting aspect of this exercise in self-justification was the public revelation of deep tensions between two sides of the company, the Hong Kong brokerage and the regional investment bank—and a permanent conflict with the overpaid stars of the fixed-income department, especially for those on the more traditional equity side of the business.

"I wasn't sure whether hiring private detectives was actually going to solve the problem," Lee said. "From the third and fourth week of August and first week of September, the content of the rumors suggested to me that they were coming from those of an equity background not a fixed-income background." While Lee acknowledged that the rumors were an opportunity for competitors, he said he also believed that "the source of many of these rumors was from within."

When Lee and his boys arrived at Peregrine, the equity side of the business was depressed. Asian stock markets, including Hong Kong, were not doing too well and the situation would persist until 1996. Tose decided to liven things up a bit by importing the entire fixed-income team from Lehman Brothers. Asked if he encountered any resentment from other people at Peregrine, Lee said: "From day one, definitely. That was always there."

The resentment grew with the expanding role of the fixed-income department. "In an indirect way, we did subsidize parts of the firm," Lee said. "There is scope for a discussion as to whether or not Peregrine would have been around in 1995 and 1996 if fixed income hadn't been there."

The fixed-income boys had the highest salaries—around five hundred thousand dollars a year for the more experienced. Then there were the annual bonuses—five million dollars for André Lee alone in 1995 and again in 1996.

Philip Tose was meanwhile using the fixed-income department to groom future managers. In 1995, he changed the management system whereby country managers throughout Asia lost much of their power, becoming more like administrative heads. Actual decisions were made on a "product-line" basis in Hong Kong by the heads of the equity and corporate finance departments as well as the head of the fixed-income department that was Lee himself. At the same time, people from Lee's department started to get sent out as country managers. These were the same people that used to travel across Asia, negotiating deals in hotel rooms without telling the local country managers they were in town. Fixed-income people were appointed country managers in Thailand and South Korea, "generating not only resentment but outright hostility" from local staff. "When it came to changing the country head of Indonesia and Philip wanted to nominate one of the fixed-income guys to do that, I really wasn't up for it any more," Lee said.

Asked if there was a sense that he was being groomed to take over from Tose one day, Lee replied: "I believed that might have been the sense."

The fact was, according to a company source, that Peregrine remained a "very paternalistic organization" despite efforts to change the management structure. "Philip was the father and you don't argue with your dad," the source said. "André came along and was the favorite son."

## THE FATHER OF RED CHIPS

The crash of the Hong Kong stock market sped things up considerably. Peregrine didn't only lose money. The sky also darkened for what was a source of pride and power for the company—its privileged role as a go-between between China and the international capital markets.

If André Lee founded the Asian junk bond market, Francis Leung was considered the father of "red chips"—companies that were incorporated and listed in Hong Kong but were owned by mainland Chinese interests such as the central, provincial, or local governments and state-owned enterprises. Thanks to its privileged access to the Chinese leadership, Peregrine captured a fat slice of the business of arranging stock market listings for these companies.

The Peregrine boardroom on the twenty-sixth floor of the New World Tower in central Hong Kong left no doubts about the price the company attached to its relations with Beijing. The pictures hanging from the walls showed Philip Tose and Francis Leung surrounding Chinese President Jiang Zemin, Philip Tose being welcomed by Jiang, and Francis Leung shaking hands with Vice President Rong Yiren.

The last picture was the most revealing. Red chips were born in 1990 when Peregrine helped CITIC Hong Kong (Holdings) Ltd. acquire a shell company enabling it to be listed on the local stock exchange. The parent company, China International Trust and Investment Corp. (CITIC), was directly owned by Beijing. As the foreign investment arm of the Chinese government, it was also the most important holding company in China. The newly listed Hong Kong subsidiary, renamed CITIC Pacific, became its bridgehead in Hong Kong and soon outgrew its status as a red-chip stock, joining the blue-chip issues of the Hang Seng index. All this took place under the leadership of Larry Yung, who was none other than the very son of Vice President Rong.

Hong Kong was hit with a heavy bout of "red chip fever" in 1997 as the British colony prepared for its "handover" to China on July 1. Red chip prices soared, taking the price-earnings ratios of these companies to multiples that defied the laws of gravity (forty times earnings in 1998). The vast program of restructurings and privatizations anticipated for state-owned enterprises in China could only mean one thing—a new El Dorado as hundreds, maybe thousands, of mainland companies came to list their shares in Hong Kong over the next few years. And Peregrine had the goose that laid the golden eggs.

The "Black Thursday" of October 23 put an end to the euphoria. The Hong Kong stock market went into a downward spiral and entered a period of high interest rates and massive volatility. Access to the international capital markets for Chinese companies had closed for the time being. It would be months, maybe even years, before it would open again in healthier conditions.

Peregrine, the killer falcon, now had both of its wings clipped.

## HOPE FROM ZURICH

The Swiss arrived.

Not so long ago, the job of Swiss bankers entailed sitting in opulent offices in Bahnhofstrasse in Zurich, quietly waiting for foreign customers to bustle their way in through the doors of the institutions housing the biggest bank vaults in the world. Rival banks were envious to the point of sarcasm. "When the Swiss start arriving, it's time to get out," the saying went. "And when the Japanese arrive, it's already too late."

But times had changed and the financial institutions of the confederation had left their picturesque mountains to discover the world at large.

So there was a real sense of relief in Hong Kong, especially among Peregrine's creditor banks, when it was announced on November 16 that Zurich Group was going to inject some capital into the company.

The Swiss insurance company, through its New York subsidiary Zurich Center Investments (ZCI), indicated that it would subscribe to a special issue of convertible preference shares for two hundred million dollars. ZCI would end up with 24.1 percent of Peregrine after the transaction was completed, emerging as the biggest shareholder. Peregrine International Holdings, the company established by Philip Tose, Francis Leung, and their powerful Chinese friends, would be the second-biggest shareholder with 20.3 percent.

The Swiss weren't there by accident but through the intermediary of Alex Adamowicz, the head of Peregrine Direct Investments Ltd. and one of the most discreet persons in the complex company web.

At a time when Tose was desperately in need of cash, Adamowicz was in the process of negotiating plans to establish an investment fund oriented toward Asia. Negotiations were already at an advanced stage when Tose sat down at the table. Tose said the talks initially focussed on the investment fund before the Swiss gradually got around to talking about Peregrine itself. Another half-truth.

The Swiss weren't stupid. They may have had international ambitions with the purchase of Chicago-based financial services group Kemper Funds in 1996. But they also knew how to count.

First, they were getting a good price, at least in terms of appearances. The deal valued Peregrine at eight hundred million dollars, a substantial discount. Still, the company's share price had lost forty percent of its value since August.

Second, the potential buyers were going to examine the deal from every angle with a "due diligence" exercise that, according to Tose, would last from four to six weeks.

But for ZCI, director Steven Gluckstern was already saying the deal was a foregone conclusion. The transaction would only fail "if an earthquake hit Hong Kong and Hong Kong fell into the sea," he said.

For a while, the promise of an agreement with the Swiss boosted the company's share price. Believing Philip Tose, the banks reopened the taps and the credit started flowing once again.

When he met with reporters on December 12, Tose had just fired 275 employees in Hong Kong and elsewhere in the region.

The announcement was hardly surprising. Across Asia, the stars of the financial industry knew the party was over. From Japan, where bankruptcies were multiplying, to Thailand, where fifty-six finance companies had just been shut down, the white collar massacre had just begun.

"This industry is going to shed tens of thousands of people throughout Asia during the course of the next year. We have to be realistic. If market capitalization has gone from two hundred billion to thirty, you cannot have the same staff," Tose said, adding that Microsoft Chairman Bill Gates "could buy any one these countries."

"One thousand dollars invested in Thailand in 1993 is now worth 150 dollars. Nobody likes to shed people. But we admit what we do. Others don't."

## SOLITARY FLIGHT

But there was also good news—Peregrine was in touch with four new investors who were going to inject an additional one hundred million dollars in fresh capital. The financial conditions were the same as the Zurich Group deal and one of the new investors was Peregrine's main bank, First National Bank of Chicago.

The arrival of the Swiss would have no impact in the day-to-day running of the company. "The only change is that they will have three people on the board. There will be a management committee but the business will be run by Francis and I," Tose said.

But the history of stock market crashes showed that independent securities companies disappeared under the pressure of deregulation and globalization, getting swallowed up by huge commercial banks. Who remembered Alexander Laing and Cruikshank, which became Credit Lyonnais Securities Asia? James Capel was devoured by HSBC, Morgan Grenfell was slowly digested by Deutsche Bank, and Crosby was gobbled up by Société Générale.

But the falcon thought it could defy history, becoming the only bird left in the sky. "Independence can be maintained, providing you have the proper capital basis. And that is what we're doing with this operation," Tose said.

Tose was so certain that Peregrine was immortal that he left town at the end of the year for the Moghul palaces of the Indian state of Rajastan. He was accompanied by his beautiful Chinese-Indonesian wife Jennifer, the pillar of Hong Kong charity balls, and the darling of *Hong Kong Tatler*, the glossy high-society magazine in the former British colony.

## ABANDONED BY THE BANKS

When he returned, Hong Kong had not fallen into the sea; Indonesia had exploded, and for Peregrine the impact was equally catastrophic.

The Indonesian rupiah, worth twenty-five hundred to the dollar only six months earlier, plunged through the barrier of ten thousand to the dollar in the first week of January. The financial system could no longer function. And on January 6, it was learned that the bond issue by Steady Safe would not take place as the Indonesian authorities had not given the green light. The Jakarta taxi company had been planning to use the proceeds of the bond issue to repay the 260 million-dollar loan received from Peregrine in June the previous year. But Steady Safe was now heavily indebted in dollars worth four times their value six months earlier and the company was now virtually bankrupt following the rupiah's collapse. The scenario was the same for thousands of other companies across Asia.

Back in Zurich, it was as if all of Switzerland's cuckoo clocks were striking at the same time. The Swiss immediately headed for a Hong Kong in full disarray. In the race against time, Philip Tose himself gave an account of the latest developments.

"Our discussions with Zurich started on Tuesday last week in order to renegotiate the pricing levels. A verbal agreement was reached that evening. But faced with more volatility, it took us a further two days to find a preliminary agreement," Tose said.

"We went to see the regulators on Thursday," he continued. "Part of the transaction reclaimed a funding line on Friday of sixty million dollars from one bank for four days . Around five p.m. Thursday, it became apparent that this funding line promised to us was no longer there. The next day, we went to the banks and authorities to see what could be done. We went into default on Friday night. Proposals to the banks made on Sunday were not judged satisfactory and you know the rest."

A source familiar with the situation qualified this account. Credit line or not, the truth was that the Swiss were no longer interested. Peregrine managers put on a "pathetic" performance during their last-chance meeting with creditors on that Sunday. "They hadn't prepared anything," the source said. "They just expected people to trust the Peregrine name."

## DREXEL-STYLE COLLAPSE

On Monday afternoon, at 4.46 p.m. on January 12 to be precise, a brief statement was sent to business editors. "The board of Peregrine Investments

Holdings Ltd. regrets to announce that the company has taken preliminary legal steps in the preparation of an application for liquidation. A decision will be made on staffing levels by the liquidator when appointed, probably tomorrow (13 January). END."

There were some surprising coincidences. The sixty million dollars that Philip Tose said Peregrine needed to prevent bankruptcy was exactly the same amount that Mellon Bank of Pittsburg refused to lend Drexel Burnham Lambert ten years earlier, prompting the collapse of the American junk bond house. In Peregrine's case it was another U.S. bank, First National Bank of Chicago, which decided to turn off the life-support system.

That was not the only parallel. As an investment bank, Drexel didn't have a network across the United States, limiting the impact of its closure to Manhattan and the suburbs of New York. The U.S. Treasury let Drexel go to the chopping block. Peregrine was in a similar position, as it didn't take deposits or extend loans either. Its bankruptcy was not going trigger failures at other banks in Hong Kong.

The idea of financial institutions being "too big to fail" was for commercial banks whose bankruptcy would create systemic risks. That's what Hong Kong Chief Executive Tung Chee-Hwa and Finance Secretary Sir Donald Tsang told Philip Tose when he appealed for their help on that fateful Sunday.

"There are very strict regulations as to the use of public funds in bailing out institutions. One of the things was whether it would create systemic risk for Hong Kong," the Peregrine chief said. "Obviously, we made the case that it would. But I think the financial secretary felt that was not really the case. Which is extremely disappointing to us. But frankly, it probably was the right decision."

Although Peregrine's collapse triggered a fresh slide on the Hong Kong market and a few waves on foreign markets, the effect was short-lived.

## FRONT AND BACK

From Peregrine to troubled French bank Credit Lyonnais to Barings, the oldest British investment bank destroyed by the speculative activities of a rogue trader in Singapore in 1995, all failures of financial institutions showed an ignorance of basic principles. "In banking, there are rules based on common sense," said an executive from one of Peregrine's European rivals. "When a bank fails, it's because the rules were not followed. You don't lend a quarter of your capital to a single company. We're ten times bigger and would have never gone into that deal."

It was discovered later that Steady Safe was only the biggest in a very large barrel of rotten apples—Indonesian bonds held by Peregrine accounted for 750 million dollars at the end of October 1997. The total bond portfolio was worth 1.19 billion dollars, exceeding the company's entire capital. In their final offer, Zurich Group offered fourteen cents for each dollar, a discount of eighty-six percent for a mountain of paper that had become almost worthless.

But why Steady Safe? Apart from its fleet of taxis and a rare talent for smooth talking by its chief executive Jopie Widjaja, the company had the indispensable requirement for success in Indonesia at the time. This was its link to the "first family" of President Suharto—who would be ousted in May 1998 after more than three decades in power—through his eldest daughter Siti Hardiyanti Rukmana, also known as Tutut. Jopie Widjaja had spent 145 million dollars to acquire fourteen percent of a highway toll company belonging to Tutut, the de facto first lady since the death of Suharto's wife. Tutut had amassed a fortune estimated at two billion dollars. She was also vice president of Golkar, the ruling party that would later be defeated in mid-1999 in Indonesia's first free elections in four decades.

"Everyone knew we got the shares at a very good price, and her being the president's daughter will help us have a better chance to get better contracts. I don't deny that," Jopie Widjaja admitted in a candid interview after Peregrine's collapse.

Other investment banks including Nomura Securities of Japan and Credit Lyonnais Securities of France tried to win the mandate to arrange the bond issue. But André Lee's boys were faster, loyal to the philosophy of Peregrine's founder, stockbroker, and former racing car driver Philip Tose who loved nothing more than cutting the grass from under his competitors' feet.

"One of our strengths is we don't have to hang around waiting for committees or whatever to commit deals," he reportedly said in 1994. "I can make up my mind instantaneously, whether we'll bid for a deal or underwrite a deal...I've done many deals, very, very big deals, on the telephone instantaneously."

At Peregrine, the person in charge of controlling risks was the financial director Peter Wong, who joined Philip Tose and Francis Leung when they left Citicorp, Scrimegeour, and Vickers to form Peregrine in 1988. Thanks to Peter Wong, the Citicorp affiliate emerged virtually unscathed from the crash of October 20, 1987, when the Hong Kong stock market suspended trading for a week. At the beginning of that fateful month, he prevented Philip Tose from losing his shirt by closing numerous margin-trading accounts opened by clients.

"A real bean counter," a former colleague said. Such comments are typical for the "back office" staff of any company. But in financial institutions, the level of distrust between the accounting department and the stars "upfront" who made the deals could be particularly acute. Peter Wong's reputation was so fierce that André Lee wanted to escape his oversight as soon as he joined the company. Responsibility for controlling risks was transferred to corporate treasurer John Lee, who like André Lee, was also a former Lehman Brothers man. Insiders say they recalled John Lee denying—somewhat unconvincingly—that he was on André Lee's payroll.

During the news conference on January 13, Tose systematically refused to say whether he authorized the fateful deal with Steady Safe. It was obviously one of those "details" he didn't want to talk about. And he hasn't since.

## NO REPLY FROM SUPERMAN

So where was Superman when all this was happening? Li Ka-shing, one of the richest men in Hong Kong, used to make plastic flowers. In a lightning stock market raid, his company, Cheung Kong, exacted the revenge of generations of Chinese "coolies" by taking control of the Hutchison Whampoa conglomerate, a pillar of the colonial establishment. He was known as "KS" among the British, as well as those Chinese who maintained their colonial vocabulary. But for most Cantonese, he was the living incarnation of dreams of wealth. A real Superman.

Of the two men in Philip Tose's life, one was his father, who sent him to Hong Kong in 1972 after a serious car-racing accident. The other was Li Ka-shing, whose company Tose analyzed in the first-ever report on Cheung Kong.

Li and other Chinese tycoons such as Hopewell Holdings chief Gordon Wu and Larry Yung of CITIC contributed a substantial part of the start-up capital for Peregrine when it was founded by Philip Tose and Francis Leung back in 1988. All were joint shareholders in Peregrine International Holdings and the Chinese tycoons provided the irreplaceable introductions to Beijing that Tose, and especially Francis Leung, would exploit to maximum benefit.

Ten years later, when the future of Peregrine was hanging by a thread—a small loan of sixty million dollars—Li Ka-shing was nowhere to be found, even though he was still a big shareholder and a major client of the company. Also absent were the "big brothers" in Beijing, whose photos on the walls of the deserted offices in the New World Tower would soon be coming down.

## CHINESE AND GWAILOS

Tose put it all down to fear.

"On Friday, who did know what was going to happen in Indonesia," he said. "Having said that, a lot of our Chinese friends did help us significantly...I can understand some of the thought process that must have been going on. They were scary times. But you look three days later and it is all peace and quiet."

The truth was that Li Ka-shing and his tycoon friends didn't need a Peregrine transformed with the unfortunate complicity of André Lee. "The Peregrine affair became too complicated for them," the company's legal adviser, Alan Mercer, said.

Relations between Li and Tose cooled. "Philip neglected his relationship with the investors," a former Vickers and Peregrine executive said a few days

*Asian Storm*

after the company was liquidated. "Also, he's a brilliant stockbroker but not a strategist. For him, strategic thinking lasts sixty seconds. When it came to strategic advice, Peregrine didn't provide anything to Cheung Kong, CITIC, or New World. On the other hand, Li Ka-shing supported Francis Leung—namely, helping to finance companies in Hong Kong and China."

The liquidation of Peregrine highlighted two groups with divergent interests within the company. Francis Leung and those involved in the financial activities for "Greater China"—Hong Kong, China and Taiwan—would seek a separate agreement with France's Banque Nationale de Paris (BNP) and its affiliate Prime East. At the same time, they were opposed to Andrew Jamieson, the head of Peregrine Securities International who wanted to find a buyer for the entire company.

One of the first difficulties for Jamieson was that the "Chinese" working on the "Greater China" team accounted for 150 of the 600 employees of the securities arm but eighty percent of revenues. They didn't particularly want to keep working for Jamieson and the other *gwailos* (literally "ghost guys") of the international network. Eighteen months earlier, Andrew Jamieson was chosen to run Peregrine Securities International instead of Peter Fu, the head of stockbroking in Hong Kong. Fu threatened to walk out with his entire team and cross over to rival securities company Deutsche Morgan Grenfell. Francis Leung persuaded him to stay, putting him in charge of corporate finance for Greater China. But the episode left scars.

Francis Leung, his right-hand man Alex Ko, Peter Fu, and other Chinese said they wouldn't stay if Peregrine Securities International was taken over by Banco Santander, a big Spanish bank with a strong presence in Latin America but a newcomer to Asia.

BNP on the other hand brought with it almost one hundred years experience in Asia, a strong presence in China, and close ties with the Chinese tycoons of Hong Kong. On the sidelines of the annual meeting of the IMF and the World Bank in Hong Kong in September 1997, local Chinese bigwigs attended a luncheon hosted by Michel Pébereau, the chairman of the French bank. BNP eventually acquired the jewel in Peregrine's crown for forty million dollars.

## SIR WILLIAM'S LESSON

"What did André Lee change his name to after Peregrine's collapse? André Leeson." This was the joke doing the rounds of the yuppie bars of Lan Kwai Fong when the falcon fell. Nick Leeson was the "rogue trader" who ruined Barings, the oldest securities firm in the City of London. Leeson, released from a Singapore prison in 1999, had been speculating on Japanese stock-index futures in Singapore. Both men made huge amounts of money for their companies before bringing about massive losses. And both did it behind the backs of the bean counters.

But the comparison ended there. Leeson was trading out of an office far removed from the Barings headquarters while Lee was at the heart of Peregrine. Under the protection of Philip Tose, he became the de facto number two of the company, effectively eclipsing the other cofounder Francis Leung. André Lee appeared not to have broken the law while Nick Leeson was still languishing in a Singapore prison before his release in mid-1999 for falsifying documents. Faced with disaster, Nick Leeson fled and was being sought worldwide when Bank of England Governor Eddy George convened an emergency weekend meeting in London to sort out the mess.

André Lee's crime was to make the dreams of Philip Tose come true. Insiders recall hearing during company meetings that Peregrine would not only become a new Morgan Stanley but also the next Jardine Matheson, the diversified British trading company that dominated life in the colony for decades. Asia's rapid expansion would continue for another fifty years and the killer falcon would fly higher and higher, just like in the company's advertisements.

Peregrine also fell victim to wanting to monopolize the market it had created, like Drexel Burnham Lambert a decade earlier. Such a strategy can be extremely dangerous in the world of finance where competition can be intense but where everyone has to work with everyone else. "As a result of wanting to be first and distrusting others, the process of elimination gets you in the end," said a former executive with Drexel and French investment bank Paribas. "When you don't share your business with your competitors, it blows up in your face as soon as you hit a snag. You can't go around telling everyone your rivals are idiots and then expect them to help you out in a crisis."

The moral of the Peregrine story came from Sir William Purves, former head of HSBC Holdings that owned Hongkong and Shanghai Banking Corp. Under his direction, the pillar of the colonial financial establishment became one of the world's most powerful financial groups. "To put it very bluntly, it is a question of having one foot on the ground and not two feet off the ground," he said on February 28, 1998, as he announced the group's annual results for the last time. His advice came too late for Philip Tose...and a lot of other people across Asia

# Joseph Yam in the Storm

**"It is obvious that compared to the others, we deserve an A-plus."**
*Sir Donald Tsang, Financial Secretary of Hong Kong*

On October 23, 1997, the world came to realize that globalization was a two-way street. Almost ten years to the day after the "Black Friday" on Wall Street on October 19, 1987, it was Hong Kong's turn to shake the world. The Hang Seng index plunged ten percent in a single session, setting off alarms around the globe—not only in neighboring Asian markets. The storm that had been sweeping across Asia for almost four months suddenly took on an added importance. European and American savings were threatened. The first soothing words on the developed world's immunity to the Asian contagion came from government officials.

In late 1994 and early 1995, the Mexican peso crisis triggered a global epidemic that became known as the "tequila effect." The Hong Kong market's plunge signaled that authorities had failed to contain the turmoil that had so far been largely limited to Thailand, Indonesia, Malaysia, and the Philippines, the four main economies in the Association of Southeast Asian Nations (ASEAN).

But Hong Kong was not Mexico, and not even a country. The tiny territory was basically a port and a few rocks. But it was also a nerve center, being the second largest financial center in Asia after Tokyo. And unlike the Japanese capital, which still resisted foreign ideas and money, Hong Kong was anything but insular. The hive of foreign banking activity in the newly born Special Administrative Region (SAR) of China was just as great as under

British colonial rule that ended almost four months earlier at midnight on June 30. Foreign capital flows moved in and out at such speed that current account statistics weren't even maintained.

Hong Kong had become the gateway to China after two decades of economic reform. The territory's manufacturing base had been sharply reduced as companies moved their operations across the border where cheap labor was abundant. Hong Kong investors were among the most adventurous in China, along with their cousins in the neighboring southern province of Guangdong and the coastal metropolis of Shanghai, the biggest city in China and also the birthplace of many Hong Kong tycoons.

Hong Kong was one of the economies most highly rated by liberal economists. Under British colonialism, the territory of 6.5 million people had developed with the rule of law, a small and efficient government, and some of the world's most robust financial institutions as well as a financial infrastructure and regulatory system to match.

By reaching Hong Kong, the financial fury that started in Southeast Asia was moving onto a new path taking in the southern coast of China and moving northwards into Northeast Asia—Taiwan, South Korea, and Japan.

Over the previous months, speculative pressures on the four ASEAN countries involved currencies pegged to the dollar under semi-rigid arrangements. The Thai baht, the Indonesian rupiah, the Malaysian ringgit, and the Philippine peso all sank when their pegs to the dollar were removed. The Hong Kong dollar was a different animal—a rare and curious beast by which the value was set by a system known as a "currency board," a nineteenth-century British invention.

## THE WAR OF THE PEG

"On October 21st, we noticed quite substantial orders to sell Hong Kong dollars for U.S. dollars," said Joseph Yam in his account of the currency crisis.

It was November and the chief executive of the Hong Kong Monetary Authority (HKMA) was speaking to a group of correspondents from the foreign media. Yam wanted to explain what happened during the "war of the peg"—the arrangement whereby the value of the Hong Kong dollar had been rigidly fixed to the U.S. dollar since 1983.

At the beginning of that terrible week in October, it was obvious that the Hong Kong dollar was next in line for speculators after the four ASEAN currencies.

"It continued and intensified on Wednesday the 22nd," Yam said, referring to the classic pattern of "short selling" something in the hope of making a profit by buying it back at a cheaper price in the future.

"The interesting date was on the twenty-third, settlement date for the twenty-first trades, that is, four billion Hong Kong dollars in settlements for U.S. dollars. But the net amount of outstanding Hong Kong dollars was quite low—less than one billion, maybe no more than five hundred million. So the banks had to go to the interbank market during the day," he said, referring to the market where banks lend each other money on a short-term basis—from overnight to several months. As in any market, prices rise when there are more buyers than sellers—signaling upward pressure on interest rates if there are more borrowers than lenders.

"At one time, the overnight rate went to three hundred percent," Yam said, noting that this was only natural. "When Bank A lends to Bank B, the total sum of money in the interbank market will not increase unless the HKMA steps in."

As a quasi central bank, the HKMA's role was to regulate the market by injecting or withdrawing liquidity to keep interest rates within the desired range. In normal times, the monetary authority would turn on the liquidity taps if there were more borrowers than lenders, a sign that funds had run dry. But would it suck liquidity out of the system if there was too much money slushing around when there were more lenders than borrowers.

But October 23 wasn't any normal day. Joseph Yam was at war with speculators. "We waited for the money that didn't exist to come to us," he said.

Yam was referring to the system whereby the "currency board" required reserves to be held in the reference currency, in this case the U.S. dollar. Put simply, if a bank wanted to acquire Hong Kong dollars, it had to give the equivalent in U.S. dollars to the "exchange fund" overseen by the HKMA at a fixed rate of 7.8 to the U.S. dollar. While the reality was a little bit more complex, the main thrust of the system was that the HKMA only created Hong Kong dollars when it received U.S. dollars in return.

"When people criticize us for squeezing the banks, in a way it is not true," Yam said, noting that the system itself was designed to prevent speculative attacks as soon as they occurred by automatically reducing the monetary base.

The Hong Kong system was not a pure "currency board" in the strictest sense due to reforms introduced in 1988. Under the reforms, the HKMA introduced a "liquidity adjustment facility" (LAF) whereby banks could borrow funds at a rate fixed by the monetary authority. On October 23, when speculative selling of the Hong Kong dollar was at its height, the HKMA effectively turned off the liquidity tap. The prevailing rate of 6.25 percent would no longer apply and banks repeatedly seeking to borrow funds from the facility were warned that they would be punished with a penalty rate, imposed on a case by case basis.

"Banks have the responsibility of organizing their funding in a prudent manner," Yam said, referring to his warning to the banks on October 23. For the banks that weren't prudent—those suspected of selling Hong Kong dollars they didn't have—it was turmoil. By the end of morning, the Hong Kong Interbank Offer Rate (HIBOR) had jumped from 10.6 percent to 37.3 percent for three-month borrowings while the one-month rate soared from 10.7 percent to 47.5 percent.

"They couldn't get the money and started to resell their U.S. dollars to the exchange fund," Yam said.

But there was a problem—October 23 was a Thursday and any sales of U.S. dollars would not be settled until the following Monday. The banks had to clear their "short" positions the same day. "We made an exception and accepted to settle on the same day," Yam said. "We relieved them for the weekend by creating Hong Kong dollars in order for them to pay us on Monday."

During that Thursday afternoon, the HKMA injected seven hundred million Hong Kong dollars into the system, helping to relieve the pressures that had sent interest rates skyrocketing in the morning. "By providing liquidity in the afternoon through lending into the market, we made sure that lending would be made in anticipation of U.S. dollar settlement with us on Monday."

Although a pure currency board system didn't even have a central bank, the HKMA played the role of lender of last resort, guaranteeing the stability of the banking system. "You need to provide liquidity and look at the way you provide liquidity. If I had done nothing and waited until the LAF opened in the afternoon, overnight rates could have shot up to one thousand percent. I exercised discretion only to that extent. We were actually relieving pain in the market rather than increasing pain."

"Because the short positions in Hong Kong dollars were quickly unloaded, on Friday interest rates went down and that was the end of the story," Yam said. "Banks have learned their lesson on how rates behave under such a system and they have been rather more cautious."

Modesty was not one of the strong points for Joseph Yam, crowned "central banker of the year" by a specialist magazine in 1997. He and Finance Secretary Sir Donald Tsang, knighted by Britain's Queen Elizabeth II just before Hong Kong's return to China, had staked their reputations on defending the peg. What they underestimated was the price they would have to pay. Presenting the Hong Kong government's annual budget in February 1998, Sir Donald asserted: "It's obvious that compared to the others, we deserve an A-plus." Within months, however, Hong Kong fell into recession and the government—long accustomed to posting budget surpluses—suffered its first budget deficit in fifteen years. The unemployment rate doubled to the highest level since 1983. Surrounded by "D-minuses," the grades of the most outstanding student in the regional class started suffering too.

## AN IMPREGNABLE CITADEL BUT...

If it existed to defend the level of exchange rates, the currency board system displayed its efficiency throughout the crisis. The currency stayed on the strong side of the peg, hovering around the level of 7.75 units to the U.S. dollar and never even touching the nominal rate of 7.80. "I wanted very much to leave the market alone," Yam said. "If there is no speculation, 7.75 or 7.85 doesn't matter. But if the activity in the market suggests that there is a wave of speculation, we have to deal with it at whatever rate." On another occasion, Yam said: "There is a degree of what I would call 'constructive ambiguity' that does not involve any meaningful departure from the discipline of the currency board system. And I see no reason why I should show all my cards to the speculators."

Hong Kong's enormous foreign exchange reserves, among the highest in the world, were hardly mobilized at all during the October battle. By the end of 1997, they stood at 92.8 billion U.S. dollars, about ten billion dollars more than when the regional crisis began six months earlier. "Perhaps there has been a flight to quality, with Hong Kong being very much regarded as the typhoon shelter of the region," Yam said.

For currency board systems to work, the narrow definition of money supply—notes and coin in circulation, known as M-1 by economists—must be covered one hundred percent by the reserve currency. In the case of Hong Kong, the coverage rate was eight hundred percent. Also included in the calculation of money supply were bank deposits with the HKMA to settle transactions in the interbank market, as well as the deposits of the banks and the HKMA themselves. Include China's foreign exchange reserves, amounting to 140 billion dollars at the beginning of 1998, and Yam had a veritable war chest to play with against speculators.

At the same time, the HKMA had another weapon in its arsenal—its real-time gross settlement system that helped to identify immediately any potentially speculative positions. Meanwhile, surpluses in Hong Kong's current account indicated that the local currency was less likely to fall into foreign hands.

Determined speculators could always acquire the cash physically. But that was easier said than done. "To borrow money, you've got to find lenders," noted Patrick Gillot, head of Asian foreign exchange, treasury, and capital markets operations at French bank Credit Lyonnais. In Hong Kong, eighty-five percent of cash deposits were held by three banking groups—Hong Kong and Shanghai Banking Corp. and its subsidiary Hang Seng Bank, both part of London-based HSBC Holdings; the Hong Kong branch of Bank of China and a dozen mainland Chinese affiliates; and British bank Standard Chartered.

Under an arrangement with the HKMA, the three groups also printed the territory's bank notes (that looked similar but bore the name of each bank). To speculate against their own currency would be pointless, especially considering that Hong Kong Bank, Bank of China, and Standard Chartered all held vast foreign exchange positions at the rate of 7.8 units to the U.S. dollar.

The currency board system operating in Hong Kong was therefore like a citadel virtually immune from speculative attacks—unless there was a panic among those who held the cash, namely the population at large. But in Hong Kong, where financial transactions were completely free, anybody could open an account in a foreign currency—ranging from dollars and yen to ecus and New Zealand dollars. Hong Kong dollar deposits nevertheless accounted for 45.5 percent of all deposits in the June quarter of 1997, up from 33.4 percent in 1991. Taking into account the HKMA reserves, the ratio would have theoretically had to have fallen to twenty-six percent for the peg to collapse.

The financial turmoil in Hong Kong did in fact see billions of dollars flow out of Hong Kong dollar deposits into U.S. dollar deposits in October and November. But the flows were reversed in December and January as calm returned. The currency board worked with higher interest rates luring funds back into Hong Kong dollars. Joseph Yam had won the battle—but not the war—by teaching speculators a lesson. But not all speculators.

The "Achilles heel" of the Hong Kong system was the stock market. If speculative selling of the local currency triggered a rise in interest rates, the price of financial assets such as stocks had to fall. What Patrick Gillot described as "intelligent speculators" did exactly that—while short selling shares at the same time in the hope of making huge profits as the stock market declined. Such two-pronged strategies appealed to some of the larger market participants such as hedge funds—frequently blamed for much of the Asian crisis. During the October crisis, Joseph Yam said such activities had been detected but that was about it. In August the following year, however, the HKMA took the unprecedented decision to intervene in the stock market in a bid to arrest market turmoil that followed the financial meltdown in Russia. The government intervention in both the cash and futures markets went against Hong Kong tradition and created a frightening chain of events—equity prices resumed sliding every time the government stopped pouring reserves into the stock market. The costly event raised questions about how long the population, especially the business community, could afford to support the peg.

## CHINA SUPPORTS THE PEG

Faced with an unprecedented crisis in its new territory, China behaved with tact. Chinese officials declared unambiguously that they wanted Hong Kong's monetary stability to remain stable but never gave the impression of wanting to intervene directly. The "one country, two systems" formula for Hong Kong's return to the motherland had clear financial echoes—two currencies and what Yam called two "mutually independent" central banks.

China's support of the peg was never really in doubt. Breaking the fixed exchange rate less than four months after the handover would have been deeply humiliating for Chinese officials. Moreover, maintaining confidence in Hong Kong was crucial given its important role in modernizing the mainland.

One false step by Beijing would have had disastrous consequences—in the same way as the creation of the peg in 1983 was a response to growing jitters during Sino-British talks on the future of the colony. The "joint declaration" by London and Beijing was eventually signed in 1984. But in mid-1983, the talks were at an impasse. The financial stability of Hong Kong had been rocked a year earlier by the Carrian affair, the biggest bankruptcy in the colony's history. Amid fears of a banking crisis, the Hong Kong dollar plunged from 7.67 to the U.S. dollar to 9.50 during the course of the summer, despite increases in interest rates.

The solution came from a thirty-six-year-old economist called John Greenwood who envisaged a return to the gold standard abandoned in the early 1970s—but with the U.S. dollar taking the place of the yellow metal. The two banks issuing currency in the colony at the time—Hongkong Bank and Standard Chartered—would be required to deposit U.S. dollars each time they issued a banknote.

Greenwood, chief economist at GT Management, also proposed setting up a central bank with control over interest rates as part of a paper entitled "How to Rescue the Hong Kong Dollar—Three Practical Proposals." At the time, the colony had what was known as a "monetary affairs branch" dominated by officials seconded from the Bank of England. Greenwood's ideas were influenced by economists such as Milton Friedman, the high priest of the "monetarist" school in Chicago at the time, and Allan Walter, the anti-European free-market guru of British Prime Minister Margaret Thatcher.

The colonial government, unsure of which path to follow, summoned Greenwood for an emergency meeting on September 25. The representatives of the British Treasury and the Bank of England were apparently persuaded to adopt Greenwood's idea.

Under the new system going into effect on October 14, 1983, the rate of 7.80 to the U.S. dollar was chosen arbitrarily by the then Financial Secretary John Brembridge, who nevertheless declared publicly shortly beforehand that he was against the idea of a peg. The most important thing was to have a credible exchange rate as close as possible to the earlier level. "This is not a precise science," Greenwood said fifteen years later in 1998. "It is a matter of credibility and more importance will be attached to the true autonomy of the currency board than to the exchange rate itself."

## THE ECONOMY ADAPTS

It paid off. The system would successfully pass its first test in mid-1984 when Sino-British talks on the future of Hong Kong almost broke down But interest rates jumped to as high as forty percent for several weeks. The peg also survived the stock market crash of 1987 as well as the crisis of confidence triggered by the Chinese military's massacre in Tiananmen Square in 1989. The Hong Kong dollar meanwhile followed the sharp swings of its U.S. counterpart against other foreign currencies throughout the 1980s and 1990s.

"When Hong Kong went to a currency board in 1984, we had some ideal conditions—a highly flexible economy, and a political system precommitted to allow the currency board to remain autonomous," Greenwood said.

Such a system involved the complete "depolitization" of monetary policy, frequently subject to executive and legislative interference in many countries. It achieved on a day to day basis—with no compromise—what the Maastricht Treaty stipulated, with much hostility from politicians, for European economic and monetary union.

For Hong Kong, the last major colony from an empire of a bygone era, this was not really a problem. Any links with the British pound had long since been forgotten and the United States was by the far the biggest trading partner of the colony by the time the 1980s rolled round. Moreover, the colonial administration had long been practicing Thatcherism to the letter, described as "positive nonintervention" by one financial secretary, Sir John Cowperthwaite. Sir Donald Tsang, the first finance secretary under Chinese rule, noted many years later that there had long been a tacit understanding between government and business in Hong Kong that it was better to let entrepreneurs and investors make their own decisions.

The peg therefore allowed Hong Kong to avoid setting up a central bank, leaving the conduct of monetary policy to the Federal Reserve Board in Washington. As Joseph Yam said: "We actually do not have an interest rate policy. Our interest rates should be at the U.S. level in normal conditions."

For a long period, Hong Kong's interest rates followed those in the United States. Prime rates charged by banks in Hong Kong were more or less based on the federal funds rate—the rate U.S. banks borrow funds from the Federal Reserve—with adjustments for the differences in the rate of inflation in the two economies. Although inflation was structurally high in Hong Kong, the reality was that inflows of fund—notably from China—allowed Hong Kong interest rates to closely follow U.S. interest rates for most of the 1990s.

From the end of 1990 to the beginning of 1995 when the Americans followed a tight monetary policy triggering a mini bond market crash at one stage, Hong Kong was actually benefiting from negative real interest rates.

As seen with what happened under speculative pressures, the Hong Kong system basically operated on automatic pilot—leaving nothing to human intervention. According to John Greenwood, "The government obligation is to defend the monetary base and let the consequences feed through the system."

## RED CHIP FEVER

When the storm broke out in Thailand on July 2, 1997, Hong Kong was going through an euphoric stage. Two days earlier, under torrential rain that mixed with the tears of the last departing governor Chris Patten, the British had handed over the keys of the territory along with a giant bank vault—Hong Kong's foreign currency reserves. Prince Charles, representing his mother, shook hands with Chinese President Jiang Zemin and left town with the Union Jack under his arms, joining Patten for the final voyage of the royal yacht *Brittania*. The deluge would continue for the rest of July, becoming the wettest on record. But over at the Stock Exchange of Hong Kong, the sun was still shining.

During 1996 and the first half of 1997, the Hong Kong market benefited from the best of both worlds. Like the rest of "emerging" Asia, it was being inundated by inflows of foreign capital, leading to zero or negative real interest rates. As a result, the property market was going through an unprecedented boom.

The other big factor was the "China play"—a combination of blind patriotic fervor ahead of the "handover" on June 30 and the ability to make quick profits through trading "red chips"—shares of the growing number of subsidiaries of mainland Chinese companies being listed in Hong Kong.

Real-estate fever and red chip fever—a fateful combination. But just another one of those speculative manias that litter the history of world finance.

Huge crowds gathered for lotteries held by property developers, the prize being the right to acquire—for the same price as a penthouse in Manhattan—a tiny apartment in the suburban New Territories bordering China. Others rushed for a chance to buy shares in the newly listed Beijing Enterprises, a hodgepodge of diverse assets bundled together by the municipal government of the Chinese capital. The issue was oversubscribed 1,250 times.

"With red chips, people were investing in a concept without even knowing what the companies did. It's typical for emerging markets," said John Mulcahy, managing director of Indosuez W. I. Carr. "After becoming a mature market, Hong Kong is now becoming an emerging market or rather a reemerging market with the volatility, the influx of new capital, and the number of newcomers."

Analysts at Paribas Asia Equity put out a "red alert" warning clients of the predictable consequences of the party that, it turned out, would last until the middle of that summer with the Hang Seng Index hitting successive record highs.

The days of the Hong Kong market plunging on the slightest whiff of a rumor about the health of paramount leader Deng Xiaoping had long gone. Deng died in February and the market surged with relief, helped by massive buying by mainland interests as well as the pro-Beijing lobby in Hong Kong.

"From now on, investors are buying Hong Kong because of China not despite of China," Mulcahy said in July.

Such "irrational exuberance"—to use the expression of U.S. Federal Reserve Board Chairman Alan Greenspan—had started to worry the Chinese authorities. In a bid to cool the red chip fever, they indicated that the injection of mainland assets into the newly listed Hong Kong companies would be more strictly controlled. Beijing had good reasons, as many of the assets were being transferred under dubious conditions.

Real-estate fever was meanwhile proving to be a major preoccupation for the new government of the Special Administrative Region of China, led by Chief Executive Tung Chee-hwa. In his first policy speech, the most salient point was a promise to provide more low-cost public housing while bringing about a "soft landing" in the overheated property market. The government had already implemented anti-speculative measures at the beginning of 1997, recalling policies introduced in early 1994 that depressed prices by twenty-six percent over the ensuing eighteen months. But in 1997, the pressure was too strong—prices had already surged forty percent from the previous low by the middle of the year, especially at the top end of the market. The surge in luxury housing prices also started spilling over into the rest of the market, raising prices in the huge housing complexes with thousands of apartments where the vast majority of middle-class people lived.

At the same time, many of the professional people who left Hong Kong and emigrated to countries like Canada, Australia, and the United States in the wake of the Tiananmen massacre in 1989 had started returning to Hong Kong as fears about the Chinese takeover receded.

The colonial government, which owned much of the land in Hong Kong, was meanwhile being accused by pro-Beijing interests of inflating prices by deliberately auctioning off limited parcels of "crown land" to maximize returns.

Reality was, of course, more complex. Hong Kong, which had some of the most densely populated areas on earth, did have a serious problem with lack of space. Urban development required long and complex authorization procedures for the massive apartment blocks being built, whether on reclaimed land or the sides of mountains. The government was simply overwhelmed by the demand for housing in the last few years of colonial rule.

A plunge in the number of building permits in 1994 and 1995 led to a decline in the number of new apartments coming to the market in 1996 and 1997, by which time the waiting period for public housing had grown to seven years with some 170,000 families on the list. Between 1992 and 1996, prices rose forty-six percent despite the downturn in 1994.

The government nevertheless had an interest in maintaining booming real-estate prices because thirty percent of its revenues came from property taxes. "It is for this reason that the maximum personal income tax rate is so low at fifteen percent and corporate tax is only 16.5 percent," said Michael Green, real estate analyst at Salomon Brothers in Hong Kong. "Property in

Hong Kong is a form of taxation whether one buys or rents. But it is an ideal form in many respects because it is the renters' or buyers' (that is, taxpayers') choice how much rental or pre-paid tax one wishes to pay."

## THE PASSION FOR CONCRETE

Property accounted for a disproportionate share of the Hong Kong economy. Companies from colonial establishments like Jardine Fleming to conglomerates owned by Chinese tycoons such as Cheung Kong and New World invested in concrete, as did the "red billionaires" from the communist mainland. Property accounted for a major share of bank lending and half the market capitalization on the Hong Kong stock exchange.

Property crashes were a common feature of Hong Kong's economic development, but banking regulations on exposure to the sector were strict. David Carse, the number-two man at the Hong Kong Monetary Authority, said at the beginning of 1997 that property prices would have to fall by forty percent before banks started to suffer.

But the heavy dependence on property investment had negative consequences. Hong Kong was one of the best places in the world to do business, but also one of the most expensive. In mid-1998, a survey by The Economist Intelligence Unit found that Hong Kong was the third most expensive city in the world for expatriates after Tokyo and Osaka.

For couples where both people were working and living in their own apartment, the entire salary of one would go toward paying off the mortgage. The labor market was destabilized as people shifted from job to job, seeking the slightest increase in salary to help make ends meet.

Property speculation also affected income distribution. In 1996, the top ten percent of households accounted for forty-two percent of income while the bottom fifty percent accounted for only nineteen percent. "It appears obvious that a major cause of the disparity is due to the rich participating in the property market and the poor being unable to do so," said Michael Green of Salomon Brothers.

In his first policy speech in 1997, the new Chief Executive Tung Chee-hwa promised to accelerate the release of government land for housing purposes while putting eighty-five thousand new apartments on the market each year. The target was for seventy percent of the population to own their own homes by 2005.

But the arrival of the Asian financial assault in Hong Kong would compromise the scenario for a soft landing in the property sector.

## SUFFERING FOR THE PEG

Apart from reversing the surge in equity prices, the October 23 stock market crash took the heat out of the property market and led to the first prolonged period of high, real interest rates since the peg was introduced in 1983.

From its peak of 16,673 points on August 7, the Hang Seng Index dived to a low of 9,059 points on October 28, reducing market capitalization by almost half. The plunge in real-estate prices would exceed thirty percent over the next six months. Shares and real estate became the sacrificial lambs to defend the peg.

With the option of a competitive devaluation of its currency effectively out of the running, the challenge was twofold. Would the adjustment through lower prices for financial assets, goods, and labor be sufficient for Hong Kong to maintain its international competitiveness? And second, would the legendary flexibility of its economic and social structures be up to the job?

Two days before the crash, Hong Kong Chamber of Commerce Chairman James Tien publicly declared that it might be time for a "revision" of the peg following the recent moves by monetary authorities in Taiwan and Singapore to let their currencies slide. Hong Kong was much more sensitive to developments in Taiwan and Singapore than it was to events unfolding in Thailand, Indonesia, Malaysia, or the Philippines.

James Tien was the spokesman for the thousands of companies and merchants who made up the Hong Kong economy. These ranged from the dozens of real-estate companies that would shut down with the loss of thousands of jobs over the next few months to the shops that extended their sales to well after the Chinese New Year in a desperate bid to move stock. Others included the hundreds of restaurant owners who would be forced to cease business and the hotels whose occupancy rates would plunge despite big discounts.

It soon became clear that this was the price Hong Kong would have to pay to maintain the peg. China encouraged the view, as did the IMF.

During a visit to Hong Kong between October 27 and November 5, an IMF mission led by David Goldbrough applauded the policies adopted by the government in dealing with the crisis, notably the move to keep monetary conditions tight. "We are confident that the authorities will be cautious and avoid a premature loosening of monetary conditions, despite the short-term pain that high interest rates bring. Indeed, a period of tighter monetary conditions may help facilitate a desirable unwinding of the asset price inflation, rapid credit growth, and labor market tightness that emerged during the past year," the head of the IMF mission said.

## JAPANESE CAKE PANIC

The comforting assurance was that the banking system was not threatened—unlike Thailand, Indonesia, South Korea, Malaysia, and the Philippines. Peregrine Investment Holdings Ltd. would fail in early 1998 but it was an investment bank and not a commercial bank, posing little risk to the system at large.

There was a brief panic over a small bank called International Bank of Asia (IBA) in early November. Rumors of difficulties, falling share prices, and lines of depositors lining up under the watchful eye of police and television cameras—all the ingredients of a classic bank run were in place. But it tuned out to be a false alarm. IBA had solid shareholders—Arab Banking Corp. with fifty-five percent and the Chinese government-owned Everbright group with twenty percent. IBA received an injection of funds, allowing all twenty-five branches to stay open and satisfy those who wanted to withdraw their funds. The HKMA declared it was monitoring the situation and that it considered the rumors baseless. The whole affair was over in forty-eight hours.

"You don't need to do much here before you start seeing lines forming outside banks," one analyst commented.

All things considered, the IBA affair was nothing compared to the Japanese cake panic that would erupt a few days later.

Another rumor, this one after the stock market had closed, said the Saint-Honoré chain of cake shops wouldn't open the next day as the parent company, Yaohan International Caterers Ltd., was in difficulties. It was a credible rumor considering that the holding company had closed its doors the week before. Lured by the promises of the Chinese market, the chairman of the Japanese department store operator moved much of the company's international operations to Hong Kong shortly after the Tiananmen massacre in 1989, taking advantage of low prices at the time. The Japanese founder of the Yaohan International Holdings Ltd. led a flashy life in Hong Kong but eventually overextended himself and watched his dreams of conquering the Chinese retail market go up in smoke. The problem was that Yaohan International didn't control Yaohan Caterers anymore, and the Japanese company had recently sold off its remaining share of seven percent. But Hong Kong's cake lovers weren't concerned with small details like that. Before long, they had invaded the forty-seven Saint-Honoré outlets across the territory. Huge lines of people, mostly women, formed on the sidewalks. Hong Kong suddenly looked like Moscow under Brezhnev. Even more so as the people in the lines were holding coupons—a common feature of the retail industry in Hong Kong where customers were rewarded with coupons as a prize. In 1996 alone, Yaohan Caterers had distributed fifty million Hong Kong dollar's worth of coupons. That's a lot of chocolate eclairs and egg tarts. The foray would last for several days as cake factories worked around the clock to meet demand from the thousands of panic-stricken coupon holders. The Japanese cake panic eventually ended when people's refrigerators and stomachs were full.

Such was life in Hong Kong as 1997 drew to a close—active, frantic, noisy, whimsical, and harsh. "Vibrant" was how the last governor Chris Patten used to describe it before he sailed out of town after midnight on June 30 when the British flag came down for the last time. Patten wasn't known as "Fat Pang" in Cantonese for nothing. He had a particularly strong weakness for egg tarts.

## BEARING THE PAIN

Patten never ran out of praise for Hong Kong's people's endurance, energy, and willingness to adapt. Societies got the currencies they deserved, if that's what they wanted and were able to maintain. For Bank of France governor Jean-Claude Trichet, the strong mark or the weak franc wasn't simply rates on a grid. They reflected the performance and behavior of the respective economies.

Several months later, Yam conceded during a speech in London that high interest rates were the pain Hong Kong had to bear. "There were suggestions for the HKMA to sell insurance products, guarantees, structured notes, options, and other derivatives, so to speak, to put our money where our mouth is in holding the exchange rate fixed," he said. "Such a demonstration of confidence, it was argued, would bring down Hong Kong dollar interest rates to levels close to those for the U.S. dollar."

But Yam said he doubted that such moves would be seen as a demonstration of confidence. "It could be seen as a lack of resolve to defend the currency and bear the necessary interest-rate pain," he said. "Keeping interest rates artificially down when there is capital outflow amounts to providing cheap funding to those who are shorting the currency. These derivative products, however they are structured, in effect amount to discretionary intervention in the forward foreign exchange market, involving possibly an uncontrollable commitment of foreign reserves that even those with very large reserves would find the situation difficult to hold. This was the mistake of one or two Asian economies now in financial difficulty," he said. It was certainly the case for Thailand, which lost its foreign exchange reserves in the forward currency market.

David Liu, of Schroders Investment Management, said it was a fact of life that interest rates in Hong Kong and the United States sometimes diverged. "People only want to have the good side and get away from the bad side. That is not realistic," he said. Lower housing prices were "all for the benefit of Hong Kong in the long term. People will have to spend less on property and can diversify their spending."

## CHINA'S MANHATTAN

Compared with the hysterical clamor among French exporters for a competitive devaluation in 1992 when Britain and Italy devalued their currencies, Hong Kong businessmen were remarkably quiet. But the reason was simple—Hong Kong didn't compete with Southeast Asia.

"Hong Kong is the leading example of the virtual economy with 84 percent of GDP derived from services compared with 72 percent in the United States and 70.8 percent in Britain," Joseph Yam said.

As a nerve center, Hong Kong was servicing the Chinese economic machine where twenty years of reforms had put the mainland on the path toward modernization and opening up to the outside world.

As an island, the northern coast of Hong Kong bore a remarkable resemblance to Manhattan whereas the south was more like the French Riviera. But as an economy, Hong Kong was the Manhattan of China. The image was from Irishman Russel Napier, the ace stock market strategist at Credit Lyonnais Securities Asia. "Prices in Manhattan are significantly higher than Kentucky. Both share the same currency. But despite its much higher costs, Manhattan is highly profitable and successful. Much to the chagrin of middle-America, the folks of Manhattan achieve above-normal wages by acting as the service center of America's business hinterland. Similarly, the six million people of Hong Kong represent the service economy of the 1.2 billion people of China. The hinterland is still the home of the world's cheapest labor."

Hong Kong would face difficulties if China failed to overcome the huge challenges to its modernization and development. And its role as a financial center was threatened in the long term by China's biggest city, Shanghai, notably the Pudong central business district on the other side of the river from the Bund.

That was the prediction by Marc Faber, the legendary "Doctor Doom" of Hong Kong who saw the place becoming just like any other Chinese city. In 1997, the Swiss economist, previously with Drexel Burnham Lambert, loved nothing more than to shock his audiences with gloomy forecasts for the territory. With the financial community packing their bags and moving to Shanghai, he forecast weeds growing on the streets of central Hong Kong in the early twenty-first century. But most financial professionals thought Shanghai would need a generation to develop to the same level as Hong Kong. As Tokyo and Paris showed, dreaming about becoming an international financial center was not enough. As the twentieth century drew to a close, China showed no intention or interest in endangering Hong Kong's status for the time being—as seen by the way Beijing acted during the crisis.

The Asian storm validated Hong Kong's recipe—the rule of law, sophisticated capital markets, solid banks that were well capitalized and properly regulated, an adaptable economy, a modest government that was usually competent, and a constant effort to stamp out corruption.

There was no doubt that the fixed exchange rate played a positive role in structural development. Hong Kong's system would always be one of the options available for East Asian countries considering what sort of long-term exchange rate arrangements they wanted to implement after the crisis.

CHAPTER    FOUR

# Amnuay's Anger

"In 1897, there was King Chulalongkorn, and in 1997, there
was the IMF."

*—Ammar Siamwalla, economist at the Thailand*
*Development Research Institute*

Amnuay Viravan was angry. Very angry. The question had obviously touched a
raw nerve. And the reply was that of an exasperated man.

"Why do I have to learn from the Mexican crisis? It's an entirely different story in this part of the world," he snapped.

It was an afternoon in February 1997. We were in the Peninsula Hotel, a
palatial colonial-era establishment on the Kowloon side of Hong Kong, and
afternoon tea was being served. And the man who suddenly flew off the han-
dle was the deputy prime minister and finance minister of Thailand. I had
committed a grave sacrilege by daring to suggest that there might be a parallel between Asia—the land of "miracle" economies, the paradise of Asian
"tigers" and "dragons" with their unprecedented growth and record savings
rates—and Latin America, that backwater of siestas, hyperinflation, and currency devaluation that IMF missions were constantly trying to revive. How
ridiculous!

The reaction of Amnuay, the former head of Bangkok Bank Ltd. who had
gone into politics with prime ministerial ambitions, was what IMF managing director Michel Camdessus would later call the "denial syndrome"—the
belief that Asia was somehow different from the rest of the world, that "it
can't happen to us."

Across Asia, the refrain was common and most political leaders refused for months to look reality in the face, even after the tempest hit in some cases.

But Amnuay Viravan and other politicians were not the only ones to reject comparisons between Asia and Mexico— comparisons that exploded under the weight of a massive current account deficit and huge short-term borrowings in foreign currencies at the end of 1994.

Peter Churchhouse, managing director of Morgan Stanley Asia Ltd., responded to the same question, "We absolutely don't see in Thailand the same conditions that triggered the Mexican crisis." If Churchhouse had the dubious distinction of being distinguished in the small crowd that didn't see anything coming, it was in his deranged forecasts. At the beginning of 1997, six months before Hong Kong's return to the motherland, he predicted that the local market's Hang Seng Index—which was then around 13,000 points—would skyrocket to between 26,000 and 28,000 points by the end of 1999. A year later, after the October 1997 crash slashed the index to the 9,000-point level, he managed to provoke much mirth by predicting a recovery to 16,000 points by the end of 1998.

## THE DENIAL SYNDROME

Thailand said it wouldn't become a new Mexico. And after Thailand fell, South Korea said it wouldn't become a new Thailand. By November 1997, four months after the Thai baht collapsed following the decision to float the currency on July 2, the assault that had been sweeping around most of Southeast Asia finally hit South Korea. In an attempt to prevent the world's eleventh biggest economy from being relegated to the ranks of other victims of the epidemic, South Korea's finance and economy ministry led a desperate battle with foreign investors and even started writing letters to the editors in major international publications. Betty Strakey, sovereign risk analyst at international credit-rating agency Thomson Bankwatch, chose Hong Kong to announce the latest downgrading of South Korean debt. And mingling with the reporters attending the news conference at the Foreign Correspondents Club of Hong Kong that day were officials from the consulate general of South Korea who had come to preach the gospel from Seoul, handing out a statement from the finance and economy ministry back home.

The statement, dated November 10, argued that considering the country's basic fundamentals such as economic growth, inflation, and the trade balance in addition to political reform, there was "almost no chance" of South Korea suffering the same fate as Thailand.

The statement listed errors committed by the government in Thailand, highlighting the contrast with South Korea. As for the truth of the claims, the comment by newly elected President Kim Dae Jung on December 24 set the record straight. "I'm shocked. I had no idea things were this bad," Kim declared after the outgoing government showed him the books.

But the tendency to downplay the bad side of things was not the only factor behind the denial syndrome. Many Asian politicians simply failed to understand the financial crisis, and after so many decades of success had difficulty in identifying and accepting the implications. What happened in 1997 was a "shock" for politicians in all regional capitals and leaders had "still not recovered" from the shock, Singapore bureaucrat Kishore Mahbubani told a round-table discussion at the East Asia Summit organized by the World Economic Forum in Hong Kong in October.

## FUNDAMENTALS

When the sky fell on Thailand's head, the Land of Smiles had just enjoyed thirty exceptional years.

From 1966 to 1996, growth averaged 7.4 percent a year. The last recession was in 1958. And although things got a little rough for the rest of East Asia in the mid-1980s, it was clear sailing for a Thailand that was starting to enjoy the fruits of a Japanese investment boom. Over the following years, Japanese companies would flock to Thailand to reduce their production costs as the yen rose higher and higher in the wake of the Plaza Accord of late 1985.

Thailand's spectacular growth was accompanied by remarkable monetary stability. The baht was effectively fixed to a basket of currencies dominated by the dollar that was followed by the yen. The exchange rate of twenty-five baht to the dollar had barely changed in almost fifteen years.

"We believe that the fundamentals of our economy are strong," Amnuay Viravan declared in February in comments that would be echoed across the region by political leaders and economists when the fury eventually hit. Malaysian economist Jomo Sundram, a professor at Universiti Malaya, later remarked that the whole notion of "economic fundamentals" would have to be redefined as markets and economists no longer provided them the same significance.

From 1988 to 1997, Thailand's annual rate of inflation hardly ever rose above five percent. Its public finances were exemplary—the government's budget was in surplus throughout the entire period, rising above four percent of GNP between 1989 and 1991.

Strong growth, low inflation, monetary stability, tight fiscal policy—Thailand should have been the model student of the IMF.

There was the problem of the current account deficit, but that was a common trait of all developing economies. Besides, foreign exchange reserves were strong—almost forty billion dollars in 1996—and more than five times monthly imports throughout the 1990s, well above the three-month level recommended by the IMF. In this area, Thailand was a lot better than South Korea, not to mention Indonesia, Malaysia, and the Philippines. It was also better than Hong Kong and almost as good as Singapore.

In hindsight, two events can explain the problems Asian politicians had with recognizing the danger signs—a strong rebound in exports after 1991 and the resistance of Asian currencies to the Mexican crisis in late 1994 and early 1995.

Export growth for the four main ASEAN economies—Thailand, Indonesia, Malaysia, and the Philippines—dropped from almost fifteen percent in 1988-89 to less than four percent in 1990-91 when the United States and Europe were in recession and when Japan was entering a long period of stagnation. But annual export growth recovered sharply to almost twelve percent between 1993 and 1995, boosted by the weak dollar—to which their own currencies were pegged—and recovery in the United States.

## RESISTING THE TEQUILA EFFECT

The other factor explaining the psychology in Asia at the time was the region's immunity to the "tequila effect"—the huge outflows of capital from emerging economies following the Mexican peso's collapse at the end of 1994. At the end of the day, only Argentina would be seriously affected. But it quickly recovered, thanks to the efficient functioning of its "currency board" system of exchange rates similar to that prevailing in Hong Kong. And the Mexican crisis itself was quickly overcome by the joint intervention of the IMF and the United States.

"In retrospect, what happened was that the tequila effect wasn't taken seriously," said Russel Napier of Credit Lyonnais Securities Asia. He and Jim Walker, a Scottish economist at the same company, were among the first to be alarmed. "Once the Southeast Asian currencies survived the tequila crisis, then everybody thought they'd be pegged forever," he said. "Capital inflows accelerated and bankers thought then we can really lend money to these guys here because if they can survive the tequila crisis, their currencies are never going to break. People were never so bullish than right before it burst."

The figures told the story—net inflows of private capital into Thailand came to a record 12.7 percent of GNP in 1995. The breakdown was even more interesting. Foreign direct investment—mainly companies setting up subsidiaries or injecting more equity into existing ventures—fell to a record low of 0.7 percent. Portfolio investment in stocks and bonds was only 1.9 percent. The rest, amounting to a record ten percent of Thailand's gross national product, was "other net investment" and the highest figure in dollar terms since 1991. Similar imbalances were seen in 1994 and in 1996.

## OPEN INVITATION

Where did this money come from? Mainly European banks and their Japanese rivals. Beginning in 1993, they engaged in an orgy of lending to Thailand. Short-term lending. Encouraged by the government in Bangkok.

For both lenders and borrowers, it was like waving a red flag under the nose of a snorting bull. The red flag in question was the Bangkok International

Banking Facility (BIBF), an offshore banking center that could easily merit a place as the biggest monster ever created in financial history.

The establishment of the BIBF was considered a move toward opening up the financial sector to foreign participants. For decades, the Thai banking sector was dominated by some fifteen banks, almost all of which were owned by local Chinese families. Authorities protected the cartel by refusing to grant new licenses. The BIBF, which was also open to local banks, would allow foreign banks to lend to Thai borrowers. But as the foreign banks were not allowed to accept deposits, the funds lent would have to be raised abroad. At the same time, authorities encouraged reckless lending by foreign banks by making the granting of future banking licenses conditional upon the volume of BIBF loans.

Thai banks also benefited as they could suddenly borrow foreign currencies, mainly dollars, at much lower interest rates. The local banks then used the proceeds to make loans to Thai companies at higher rates, earning fat margins on the side. Foreign exchange risks were considered nonexistent as the baht was pegged to the dollar. Even worse, the Bank of Thailand dealt with the influx of money by applying orthodox policies to what was an extremely unorthodox situation—it tightened credit to mop up the excess liquidity, driving domestic interest rates higher and encouraging even more Thai borrowing in dollars.

By 1995, Thailand's external borrowings, including BIBF loans, accounted for twenty-three percent of GNP and forty-nine percent of exports, up from only eight percent of GNP and fifteen percent of exports two years earlier.

## INVESTMENT FRENZY

In Bangkok, it was Christmas all year round for investors and consumers.

Private capital investment accounted for thirty-seven percent of GNP in 1995. Although the country's savings rate was high, like other countries in East Asia, it was not enough to finance the frenzy of investment. Between 1988 and 1995, lending to the private sector swelled from sixty percent of GNP to 130 percent.

Where did the money go? For anyone who visited Bangkok in the 1990s it wasn't difficult to see—luxury hotels, sumptuous office towers, and opulent residential complexes manufactured by the Asian miracle for the new rich and the urban middle-classes.

Foreign investment was also directed toward developing an industrial base, especially in the automobile sector where Japanese carmakers predominated. The Americans and Europeans were also present, but well behind the Japanese. Visitors to Bangkok at the time couldn't fail to notice that Thailand made cars. The traffic jams defied imagination. Driving at a few kilometers an hour was considered normal in off-peak periods. The traffic was so bad that the riverside Oriental Hotel, considered the best in the world, even provided water shuttles from the airport. People travelling by car eventually adapted—installing phones and fax machines in their vehicles. Bottles for urinating were another popular item. Children going to school would finish the night's sleep on the backseat of the car.

An empirical observer at this stage might have asked whether such a development model still made sense. But such questions were immediately suspect if raised by Western visitors who were nostalgic for the old days when Asian capitals still had their colonial charm. The Royal Selangor Golf Club and the surrounding tree-lined avenues of Kuala Lumpur, for example. And if the frantic pace of development led to urban misery for much of the population, on what basis could outsiders criticize the aspirations of the developing world to create its own urban model. Experience, perhaps?

From Singapore to Shanghai, most Asian cities realized too late that construction and aesthetics didn't necessarily contradict each other. After knocking almost everything down, Singapore started restoring what remained of its heritage, including the magnificent Raffles Hotel, and opening museums to get tourists to stay a little bit longer than the average visit of one-and-a-half days which was enough time for shopping and little else. "What we learn from history is that we don't learn anything from history," said Tess Johnston, the American diplomat who spent the first few years of her retirement recording the architectural heritage of Shanghai.

## THE DEBT GETS BIGGER AND BIGGER

The *Global Development Finance* report published by the World Bank in 1998 included an interesting new element on the cause and effects of the Asian crisis—a net decline in the quality of investment just before the meltdown. "An increase in incremental capital-output ratios in East Asia may reflect the poor quality of a large portion of new investment during the 1990s," it reported. "For example, the efficiency of Korean investment declined in the years preceding the crisis, with the share of investment in GDP rising from thirty percent in 1983-89 to thirty-eight percent in 1996-98 while GDP growth fell from ten percent to eight percent.

"Although East Asia has high savings rates—averaging more than thirty percent of GDP in Indonesia, Korea, Malaysia ,and Thailand during 1993-96—foreign capital was required to finance its even higher investment rates that rose to about forty percent of GDP in Korea, Malaysia, and Thailand and thirty-four percent in Indonesia during 1993-96. Still, financial crises result more from a loss of confidence in borrowers' ability to repay than simply from the existence of large current account deficits," it said, noting that there only appeared to be a "weak" link between such deficits and the onset of the crisis.

"The sustainability of large current account deficits partly depends on how the funds are used. If East Asian borrowers had invested the funds in diversified, high-productivity investments, the deficits would have been sustainable. But instead, much of the capital inflow (and the coincident surge of domestic investment) appears to have been directed into risky, low-productivity investments," it reported.

The report noted that real-estate loans amounted to twenty-five percent of all lending in Malaysia and the Philippines and about twenty percent in Thailand. But the surge in real estate rapidly outpaced demand and vacancy rates jumped to fifteen percent in Bangkok and Jakarta in 1996. In Thailand, the stock market index for building and furnishing companies collapsed from a peak of almost 8,200 points in late 1994 to eleven hundred points in late 1997.

A study of the Bangkok property market by Hong Kong real-estate company First Pacific Davies found that 600,000 square meters of office space came onto the market in 1996. Only 450,000 square meters were rented out. And while 25,000 new residential units came on to the market between 1996 and 1998, the vacancy rate was thirty percent in the March quarter of 1997.

All this was financed by an orgy of lending to the property sector—eight hundred billion baht in Thailand alone. The impact was dramatic, with Thailand's debt amounting to one hundred percent of GNP at the end of 1996, up from 64.5 percent six years earlier. In 1993, the ratio was as high as 175.8 percent. Worse still, external debt almost doubled from 45.8 billion dollars in 1993 to 88.6 billion dollars in 1996. More than half was in the form of short-term debt, and the private sector alone accounted for sixty-seven billion dollars. Thanks largely to the Bangkok International Banking Facility.

## HOSTAGE TO DEBT

The problems were economic but the solutions were political. This rule would be seen in the coming months—that once the crisis hit, the quality of the response became the determining factor. In Thailand, the response was a disaster.

In some ways, Thailand never stood a chance. In 1996 and 1997, the country suffered from having the most incompetent government in Thai history, the Singapore-based Political and Economic Risk Consultancy (PERC) wrote in early 1998. In the fourteen-month period before the baht was floated at the beginning of July, Thailand had no fewer than four finance ministers. The team of Prime Minister Chavalit Yongchaiyudh, the former general who would relinquish power in humiliating circumstances toward the end of 1997, was supported by a parliamentary coalition that was divided and volatile, and remarkably corrupt, even by Thai standards. It was a recipe for disaster.

When IMF officials pressed Thailand to allow greater exchange-rate flexibility in 1994, the idea was to allow the baht to rise with interest rates to help cool down the overheated economy. The IMF made a similar recommendation in 1996. But as time passed, such a move became increasingly difficult.

Toward the end of 1996, the first speculative attacks started to test the strength of the Thai currency. From this point on, greater flexibility in exchange rates meant allowing the baht to fall.

Exchange-rate policy was soon hostage to the private sector's mountain of external debt, which was mostly unhedged against adverse currency movements. Any depreciation of the baht would inflate the value of the debt in foreign currencies. And if the depreciation was major, the creditors led by Thai banks might be unable to meet their external obligations.

"Very clearly, the ability of a country to deflate its way back to competitiveness is limited by the extent of its indebtedness," said Michael Taylor, chief economist at Indosuez W. I. Carr in Hong Kong. "Deflation means that real interest rates rise and real debt levels rise. Japan discovered this, and so now has Thailand."

Southeast Asia was on the threshold of a debt crisis such as that of Latin America in the 1980s—except that most of the debt was held by the private sector. "When looking at the pressures likely to emerge on the rest of Southeast Asia, we must look not only—or perhaps not even primarily—at issues of export competitiveness but also at debt levels," Taylor wrote a day after Thailand floated its currency.

## BANKERS AND POLITICIANS

The situation Thailand faced in 1996 would have been a frightening challenge for any strong and resolute institution. The Bank of Thailand was neither.

PERC recalled that Thailand's central bank was widely respected for its prudence and skillful management of national finances before being "politicized" in the early 1990s.

"The new men appointed to head the bank turned out to be political animals with a work philosophy much different from their predecessors. A precept for them was that no Thai bank or finance house could even be allowed to fail," the consultancy wrote.

Rudiger Dornbusch, an outspoken economist from MIT, explained. "In Thailand, every politician owns a bank and every bank owns two politicians," he said.

Appointing politically linked figures to the Bank of Thailand from the governor's position down to ordinary clerk weakened the central bank's ability to deal with the diverse pressures resulting from the euphoria of the 1990s. Many central bank officials left for the private sector, lured by fat salary packages. Among those who stayed were those who started to play the stock market.

Symptoms of the malaise manifested themselves in a banking scandal that exploded in 1996.

The saga of Bangkok Bank of Commerce (BBC) was a textbook example of what not to do—take a sleepy commercial bank and transform it into an aggressive investment bank overnight, financing the takeover of potentially profitable companies, and lending generously to politicians—seven billion baht, according to the final inquiry by the central bank. The scandal itself was a fairly mundane affair—in response to rumors and a panic among depositors, the central bank decided to inject sixteen billion baht into BBC in May 1996, acquiring thirty-two percent of its capital. The central bank discovered the following month that BBC was weighed down by nonperforming loans amounting to seventy-seven billion baht, leading to a further capital injection of forty-eight billion baht by the government-owned Industrial Finance Corp. of Thailand (IFCT). When IFCT finally took control of the bank in April the following year, it was discovered that half the bank's loans were nonperforming, amounting to 5.6 billion dollars (before the baht's depreciation). BBC had been headed by a former central bank official, Kirkkiat Jalichendra. The scandal claimed the job of Bank of Thailand Governor Vijit Supinit who resigned in July 1996 at the height of the affair. Subsequent events would show that the episode was no accident but was setting the stage for things to come.

## ASTOUNDING FIGURES

The events leading up to the floating of the baht of July 2 were about as clear as the haze from the Indonesian forest fires that enveloped much of Southeast Asia later that year. The air was cleared the following March by the new government headed by Prime Minister Chuan Leekpai, known as the "Mr. Clean" of Thai politics.

In his testimony before the cabinet, Bank of Thailand Governor Chaiyawat Wibulswasdi revealed that the central bank had spent an astounding 1.1 trillion baht (more than twenty-five billion dollars) in keeping the financial system afloat since 1996. The figure exceeded the government's entire budget in 1997.

Among the beneficiaries of this largesse that wiped out a decade of fiscal surpluses was BBC that absorbed forty-eight billion baht alone. The central bank also advanced a further 717 billion baht to financial institutions facing a liquidity crisis of which 430 billion baht went to fifty-six of the country's fifty-eight finance companies, ordered shut down in August 1997 in exchange for the IMF's financial assistance. Finance One, the insurance company founded by the flamboyant Pin Chakkaphak, alone received almost forty billion baht from the Financial Institutions Development Fund (FIDF). The central bank also spent 53.7 billion baht on buying shares in troubled institutions and 62.4 billion baht on compensating the holders of paper issued by the finance companies. Another 196 billion baht was allocated to paper maturing in five years.

These figures didn't included money owed to foreign creditors or the elevated carrying costs of the FIDF, a sort of bank guarantee fund established in the late 1980s.

The Bank of Thailand also borrowed 23.4 billion dollars in its increasingly desperate attempt to defend the baht against the speculative attacks that started in late 1996.

Thailand had left almost its entire reserves in the hands of Paibon Kittisrikangwan, the head of the central bank's foreign exchange operations who was later described as young and inexperienced. Thanong Bidaya, who succeeded our angry friend Amnuay Viravan as finance minister on June 25, discovered that Thailand's reserves had fallen to the equivalent of *two days* worth of imports when he visited the central bank. The baht's fate was sealed.

"Information that was hidden for a long time has now been made public and it's understandable that people are shocked," government spokesman Akapol Sorasuchart said after the cabinet meeting on March 3, 1998.

Perhaps even more shocking was the fact that the future and savings of more than sixty million people had been gambled away by a handful of individuals that included Amnuay himself.

Following the revelation by the new government of Chuan Leekpai, former central bank governor Rerngchai Marakanond—the main culprit—had his version of events. In an interview with *Manager Daily*, he said that a triumvirate of Amnuay, Chaiyaway, and himself headed a secret group of central bank and finance ministry officials in charge of operations.

The group had its moment of glory in May 1997 when it successfully repelled a speculative attack on the baht—with the assistance of monetary authorities from Hong Kong, Singapore, and Malaysia. The defensive strategy also involved raising interest rates and ordering commercial banks not to advance funds to speculators.

Amnuay and his friends from the Bank of Thailand celebrated their victory by cracking open a bottle of champagne in public, asserting to reporters that the central bank had thirty billion dollars in its coffers. The truth was that most of the reserves were committed in forward currency contracts. In the case of a depreciation, Thailand would lose its shirt.

## FAVORITISM

Thailand was trapped. With the external enemy now prowling around its very doorstep, the financial system started to crumble under the weight of its own debt.

On February 5, real-estate company Somprasing Land became the first company to default on a Eurobond issue. At the end of February, the government tried to arrange a merger between the leading finance company, Finance One, and Thai Danu Bank. Horrified by what it found in Finance One's books, Thai Danu declined. In March, just after his angry outburst in Hong Kong, Amnuay Viravan came up with the idea of using four billion dollars in public funds to acquire the nonperforming loans of the credit union. The public started to lose confidence and pulled money out of credit unions believed to be suspect. The Bank of Thailand ordered the immediate recapitalization of ten credit unions. Such policies of reflating the financial system to protect particular institutions, notably the fifty-eight finance companies, would continue unabated until the IMF put an end to the party several months later.

Central bank officials used the classic argument of protecting the public in defending their actions. "We had to protect the financial system or the public will take the fall," assistant governor Tanya Sirivedhin said the following year. "The situation then required us to move quickly to restore confidence in the financial system. If we didn't do anything, depositors would end up losing their money when financial institutions collapse."

Chaiyawat said the central bank lent money to the finance companies to maintain the liquidity of the financial system. Japan and Sweden had used public funds in such a way, so why not Thailand?

Maybe. But in March 1998, two weeks after his first cabinet testimony, the central bank governor was ordered back to explain a troubling detail. Why did the Bank of Thailand fail to order the recapitalization of the biggest four finance companies a year earlier when it was demanding the same treatment for smaller companies with smaller exposures? The four—Finance One, CMIC Finance and Securities, General Finance and Securities, and Thana One Finance—had collectively borrowed only 2.4 billion baht from the central bank. By the time Chaiyawat was testifying before the new government of Chuan Leekpai a year later, the figure would exceed one hundred billion baht.

"The discrepancy implies there was favoritism to these four companies," said Akapol, the government spokesman. Why? It would all eventually be revealed in a commission of inquiry headed by Nakul Prachuabmoa, another former central bank governor. Unlike some of his successors, however, he was one of the men who ran the Bank of Thailand in the old days when it was still revered after the monarchy as one of the country's most respected institutions.

Nakul Prachuabmoa was also part of the government of technocrats led by Anand Panyarachun in 1990, undoubtedly the most competent and most honest government Thailand had ever had. After clearing up some of the mess left by the latest military coup, Anand and his team were sent packing by the old guard of corrupt politicians who had dominated Thailand for decades.

## IMF APPEAL

When he was forced to resign as finance minister amid coalition infighting on June 19, 1997, Amnuay Viravan was still refusing to look reality in the face. The baht, he said, would never be devalued.

And it would take another two weeks for his successor, Thanong Bidaya, to find out. He was head of Thai Military Bank and joined the government reluctantly under the orders of Prime Minister Chavalit, the former general.

Chavalit was the incarnation of a whole class of Thai politicians who were corrupt, incompetent, and co-opted by money in elections where vote buying was considered normal and where village chiefs considered themselves the overlords of the voters under their jurisdiction. Such practices were conveniently overlooked during the days of rapid economic growth. Rampant corruption had become the stuff of legend, as had the frequent military coups of which Thailand had witnessed seventeen in half a century.

"Before the financial meltdown in July, most Thais thought politics were a separate entity from economics," wrote Kavi Chongkittavorn, editor of The Nation. "They cited the numerous coups in the past that did not seem to have any economic consequence. So long as the economy continued to grow, they were complacent and willing to ignore official corruption that put the interests of politicians before interests of the country."

"It was not until the baht devaluation that they realized the high cost that backstage politicking and infighting among coalition partners was having on the country's once dynamic economy."

When the reserves ran out and Chavalit decided to stop defending the currency on July 2, the baht was floated—and immediately sank. The level of debt denominated in foreign currencies ballooned. The financial system was asphyxiated as borrowers rushed to buy dollars to meet their repayments, exerting more downward pressure on the baht. Several economists had warned of such a scenario if the currency was allowed to depreciate.

Within weeks, the Thai economy was threatened with paralysis. The country was about to default. The IMF, whose advice had been systematically ignored since mid-1996, was called in. On August 14, the Chavalit government agreed to adopt a severe restructuring program in return for 17.2 billion dollars in multilateral assistance. The package was the biggest since the rescue of Mexico in 1995.

## WHITE-COLLAR REVOLT

But the denial syndrome was still there. The Chavalit government, an unstable coalition of six parties, was reluctant to adopt the measures dictated by the IMF amid jostling by various interest groups—notably the shareholders of the banks and finance companies—who wanted to avoid the punishment of the market.

Within a few months, the financial and monetary turmoil degenerated into a full-blown political and institutional crisis. The discredited team led by Chavalit owed its survival to the opposition, dominated by the Democratic Party. To avoid dissolution of parliament before a new constitution was passed, the government would have to agree to a series of safeguards against the shameless use of money in the electoral process. Without the economic pressures, PERC wrote in September, the reforms would never have survived due to the opposition of Chavalit and leaders of the other coalition parties.

As was often the case in the Kingdom of Thailand, the military played a key role—but not by mounting another coup. The bloody events of the latest major unrest in 1992 showed that the vast middle class produced by decades of rapid growth could not be ruled by the barrel of a gun. The head of the armed forces, General Chettha Thanajaro, undoubtedly encouraged by King Bhumidol Adulyadej, put pressure on Chavalit to pass the political reform legislation.

Things came to a head on October 19 when Thanong Bidaya, the new finance minister, announced his resignation after Chavalit reversed moves to increase taxes on petrol and diesel. The unpopular measure was aimed at raising twenty-four billion baht and was a key element of the IMF program.

The press denounced the latest government dithering and by October 20, thousands of white-collar workers from the financial sector gathered in Silom Road in the heart of Bangkok's central business district. By the following day, they had moved to Government House. Faced with the pressures coming from the streets, Chavalit was let down for a second time by the military, which quashed his plans to declare a state of emergency.

On November 3, Chavalit finally announced he was stepping down. The stock market welcomed the announcement with a 7.2 percent surge in prices. The baht also strengthened.

The new government led by the Democratic Party had more to offer in terms of economic management. Prime Minister Chuan Leekpai was joined by Supachai Panitchpadki as his deputy and Tarrin Nimmanhaeminda as finance minister. Both had been in the Chuan government that ruled Thailand between 1993 and 1995. Moreover, they were clean—Chuan had the reputation of being the poorest prime minister in modern Thai history.

"One of the lessons the crisis has taught us is that a lot of our structures and institutions were not ready for this new era. We should adapt to achieve international norms. The whole society hopes for a better and more transparent government," Chuan said.

There was a precedent one hundred years earlier. "In 1897, there was King Chulalongkorn, and in 1997, there was the IMF," quipped Ammar Siamwall, economist at the Thailand Development Research Institute. Known as Rama V, the monarch reigned for forty-two years, bringing his country from nineteenth-century feudalism to a modern nation of the twentieth century. After returning from a visit to Europe in 1897, the king put an end to slavery and nationalized the tax system while creating an education system and a central administrative structure. Railways, steamships, and the telegraph came to Thailand and even monetary reforms were introduced, with the silver standard used to determine the currency's value changed to a gold standard.

The crisis of 1997 dragged Thailand and the rest of Asia out of the twentieth century. But the road to the third millennium would be long and full of dangerous traps.

# CHAPTER FIVE

# Mahathir versus Soros

---

"Markets have restricted the ability of politicians to promise
paradise to their constituents and led them to hell."

*—The Economist*

The annual meetings of the International Monetary Fund and the World Bank
were not usually known for their passion. The autumn meeting of the two
"sister" organizations founded in Bretton Woods in 1944 was usually dominated by the arcane details of esoteric discussions on IMF quotas or the latest calling of the World Bank, an organization that spent much time trying to
define its purpose in life. As this was going on, thousands of commercial
bankers from all corners of the globe descended upon the meeting seeking
ways to lend the money of their depositors to "emerging" economies (the
term "developing" was unfashionable in the late twentieth century, having
gone the same way as "Third World" countries). Emerging economies were
more than happy to borrow the funds, especially when they could invest
them in questionable projects and avoid repayment. The hotels of Washington
liked this time of the year—the movers and shakers of international finance
came back year after year and their expense accounts were generous.

Every three years, the international financial jamboree left the banks of
the Potomac for exotic places. The local reception could always introduce a
bit of fantasy into these largely ceremonial occasions—like in Berlin in 1988
when huge protests against the "money assembly" by German leftists briefly
recalled the finest moments of the 1960s. But the state of siege in Berlin was
an exception to the rule.

That's why excitement swept through the immense corridors of the newly built Hong Kong Convention and Exhibition Center on September 20, 1997. A rare performance was about to take place. It would be a sellout.

By deciding to hold its annual meeting in Hong Kong several years earlier, the IMF and the World Bank knew that the territory would have been under Chinese rule for barely three months. But they couldn't have known that the Asian miracle would have just collapsed, giving the annual jamboree an unusual resonance. Mahathir Mohamad had been invited to speak at a seminar on the sidelines of the main meetings. And George Soros would address another seminar the following day in the same amphitheater. Mahathir versus Soros, the dream fight, the financial equivalent of Muhammad Ali fighting George Foreman to be heavyweight champion of the world.

## JEWISH CONSPIRACY

For several weeks, everyone knew the Malaysian prime minister would heat things up. As soon as the Asian financial crisis erupted in July, the hotheaded Mahathir climbed up onto his favorite horse—to blame the West. And during the annual meeting of the Asean in Kuala Lumpur the same month, he identified the scapegoat—George Soros, the American billionaire of Hungarian origin, the pioneer of highly speculative financial instruments known as hedge funds, and the man behind the British pound's collapse in 1992.

Dr. Mahathir's theory was simple, if not simplistic—the financial storm was a plot hatched by rich Western countries to reverse twenty years of economic growth in Asia. Appealing to his country's Muslim majority, he then started blaming the Jews.

"We are Muslims and the Jews are not happy to see Muslims progress," he declared in October. "We may suspect that they have an agenda but we do not want to accuse them…We cannot make wild accusations…They will twist our arms."

This reluctance to make accusations didn't stop Mahathir from labeling international fund managers as "racist" for selling their shares in Malaysian companies. Soros was meanwhile branded as a "criminal" and a "moron."

Between July and September, Mahathir not only insulted foreigners. He threatened them too. Market analysts who were found to be spreading rumors would be punished. He also took initiatives, like banning the short selling of stocks on the Kuala Lumpur Stock Exchange. And in early September, a sixty billion ringgit (twenty billion dollar) fund was established to buy back shares at prices higher than those prevailing on the market. The scheme, partly financed by the public pension fund system, was limited to Malaysian investors.

"What Malaysia is saying to foreign investors is that we don't want you," said the chief economist of a foreign investment bank in Singapore. Each new inflammatory remark or initiative from Mahathir was greeted by a bloodbath on the stock exchange. In Kuala Lumpur, the job of stockbroker or foreign exchange dealer became simple—just listen to the latest outburst by Mahathir...and the following day's clarifications by Deputy Prime Minister Anwar Ibrahim who went around cleaning up the mess. Mahathir's anti-Jewish remarks eventually triggered a backlash among congressmen in the United States. At one stage, Anwar even asked journalists for suggestions on how to reverse the damage created by the outburst against Jews. The seeds were being sown for an extraordinary clash between Mahathir and Anwar, who had long been groomed as the prime minister's successor.

## BAN CURRENCY TRADING

In power since 1981, Mahathir was in his early seventies but didn't look his age. He still had a good head of hair and it was still black, although hardly uncommon in Asia where cosmetics manufacturers had an important male clientele. He was slim and his voice was firm. And even if he was incoherent, his speeches were required listening. At the time, the idea that the crisis was part of a Western "agenda" struck a vibrant chord in Asian public opinion. The conspiracy theory was appealing—that Asia's emerging economies were being forced to return to the miseries of the past for daring to challenge American and European supremacy.

"When I was invited to speak at this World Bank and IMF gathering more than three months ago, things were going very smoothly indeed for Asia," Mahathir said in his opening remarks to his hushed audience. "There was much talk then of Asian dragons and tigers, and of course, the East Asian miracles. We were flattered. We thought they were admiring our strengths and skills...We did not realize how close we were to a manipulated crisis."

"But now we know better. We know why it was suggested that Malaysia would go the way of Mexico. We know that even as Mexico's economic crash was manipulated and made to crash, the economies of other developing countries too can be suddenly manipulated and forced to bow to the great fund managers who have now come to be the people to decide who should prosper and who shouldn't," he said.

"All along we had tried to comply with the wishes of the rich and mighty. We have opened up our markets, including our share and capital markets...We were told that we must allow our money to be traded outside our country...We must allow for speculation. We did all that we were told to do. But we were told that we have not done enough. We were told to slow down our growth. We were told that it could not be sustained."

"You don't like us to have big ideas. It is not proper. It is impudent for us to try, or to even say we are going to do it. If we say that when we have the money we will carry on with our big projects, you will make sure we don't have the money by forcing the devaluation of our currency," he said, prompting some audible rumblings in the hall.

"But Malaysia and its Southeast Asian neighbors continued to grow, to prosper. Disobedient, recalcitrant, and at times impudent, these upstarts—Malaysia in particular—had the temerity to aim higher than developed countries, the powerful, the movers and shakers of the world."

"Despite our bitterness over the attempts to push us back by a decade through forced devaluation of our currency, through the rape of our share market, we in Southeast Asia and Asia are still keen to receive investments from Europe and America," he said. "But we will have to be more circumspect. We still believe there are sincere investors out there. But there are also quite a few rogues who can cause an avalanche forcing others to run for cover."

But Mahathir hadn't come to Hong Kong with empty hands.

"I know I am taking a big risk to suggest it but I am saying that currency trading is unnecessary, unproductive, and immoral. It should be stopped. It should be made illegal. We don't need currency trading. We need to buy money only when we want to finance real trade. Otherwise, we should not buy and sell currencies as we sell commodities."

"No one, I think, would want to return to fixed exchange rates. But if anarchy is abhorred by good citizens everywhere, there is no reason why we should not abhor anarchy in the world financial system."

If Mahathir had hoped to have an impact on the international bankers attending the conference, he would not be disappointed.

It was inevitable that the Asian financial crisis, an earthquake of similar magnitude to the collapse of the Bretton Woods system in the early 1970s, would raise the tide against "speculation." Here was another attempt to clamp down on speculators.

Stanley Fischer, first assistant managing director of the IMF, had already anticipated the nature of the latest outburst from the Malaysian prime minister. "Every currency crisis produces demands to do something about hedge funds and speculators," he said the day before Mahathir spoke. "Usually the anger at the speculators would be better aimed closer to home, and in practice nothing much has yet to be done to tame them."

In the case of Mexico, cited by Mahathir as a precedent, studies reported that Mexicans themselves took the initiative to start speculative selling of the peso. Subsequent events in Malaysia would show that Malaysian banks were big sellers of the ringgit as well.

But Malaysians weren't the last ones to speculate against their own currency. The assault on the ringgit largely came from dealing rooms in Singapore and Hong Kong. As the Malaysian crisis got worse with Mahathir's shouting match with foreign investors, Malaysian depositors rushed to open accounts with foreign banks. As in any financial crisis, the fallout was automatic—as capital fled the country, the "flight to quality" accelerated.

If calls to restrain "speculators" fell on deaf ears, it was because they tended to be regressive—a return to the era of controls, regulations, distortions, bureaucracy, and arbitrariness.

Mahathir's policies were bound to isolate his country from the rest of the world.

A year after his outburst in Hong Kong, Mahathir's clashes over economic and monetary policy with Anwar would degenerate with the resignation of the central bank governor and his deputy in late August. On September 1, the government announced a return to capital controls and fixed exchange rates with plans to phase out external convertibility of the currency by the end of the month. Mahathir dismissed Anwar the following day and had him arrested as a threat to national security two and half weeks later, triggering Malaysia's biggest street protests in decades. In what was largely seen as a political show trial, Anwar would eventually be sentenced in 1999 to six years in jail on four corruption charges. Anwar, who was too close to the IMF and the World Bank for Mahathir's comfort, repeatedly insisted that the charges of corruption and sodomy were trumped up and that he was the victim of a political conspiracy hatched by the prime minister and his various cronies.

## WHAT KEYNES THOUGHT ABOUT SPECULATION

Questions over the pros and cons of "speculation" were discussed in the early part of the twentieth century by John Maynard Keynes. Speculation, he wrote in *The General Theory of Employment, Interest and Money* first published in 1936, was "forecasting the psychology of the market" while enterprise was "forecasting the prospective yield of assets over their whole life." A day after Mahathir's blistering attack, World Bank President James Wolfensohn invited a couple of speakers representing these two sides of modern capitalism in the late twentieth century—speculator and financier George Soros and businessman Jerôme Monod, chairman of French group Suez-Lyonnaise. Monod had spent thirty years extracting profits from the company's assets in the sewage and water treatment industry. Soros would spend thirty days, sometimes thirty seconds, on devaluing currencies.

"Speculators may do no harm as bubbles on a steady stream of enterprise," Keynes wrote. "But the position is serious when the enterprise becomes a bubble on a whirlwind of speculation. When the capital development of a country becomes the by-product of the activities of a casino, the job is likely to be ill-done."

Given the excess liquidity on Wall Street at the time, Keynes suggested that "the introduction of a substantial government transfer tax on all transactions might prove the most serviceable reform available with a view to mitigating the predominance of speculation over enterprise in the United States."

"The spectacle of modern investment markets" prompted him to wonder if making investments "permanent and dissoluble like marriage…might be a useful remedy for our contemporary evils."

"For this would force the investor to direct his mind to the long-term prospects and to those only," the British economist wrote.

But "this expedient brings us up against a dilemma, and shows how the liquidity of investment markets often facilitates, though it sometimes impedes the course of new investment," he said. "The fact that each individual investor flatters himself that his commitment is 'liquid' (though this cannot be true for all investors collectively) calms his nerves and makes him much more willing to run a risk."

The advantages of free trade and transfers of technology along with movements of people and capital were difficult to question, especially when they contributed so much to Asia's rapid growth.

The second half of the twentieth century saw continuous efforts to dismantle borders, barriers, obstacles, and protectionist measures erected during the first half. The growth of world trade was one of the major factors behind economic expansion and even the most distant observer could see that the second fifty years were better than the first fifty years.

In his response to Mahathir on September 21, George Soros noted that economic benefits were not the be all and end all.

"Equally important are the noneconomic benefits, the freedom of choice associated with the international movement of goods, capital, and people, and the freedom of thought associated with the international movement of goods, capital, and people, and the freedom of thought associated with the international movement of ideas," Soros said.

"To appreciate the noneconomic benefits, we only need to remember what it was like to live in the Soviet Union or China when it was cut off from the rest of the world or what it is like in Burma or North Korea today. Global capitalism does not bring political freedom and prosperity to all parts of the world but it certainly helps."

## RICH COUNTRIES TOO

Was the system without risks? No, risks were part of the system. And they materialized during crises. But they could be limited by the quality of institutions and macroeconomic policies.

"International capital flows tend to be highly sensitive to the conduct of macroeconomic policies, the perceived soundness of the domestic banking system, and unforeseen economic and political developments," the IMF's Stanley Fisher said. "Accordingly, market forces should be expected to exert a disciplining influence on countries' macroeconomic policies."

"Of course, policy makers do not always welcome discipline of which they are the object, even if it is appropriate. Nor are they likely to admit when trouble comes that the capital markets were the only messengers, delivering a verdict on their performance. Rather, they may be tempted to shoot the messenger."

Mahathir's frustrations in late 1997 echoed those of British Prime Minister Harold Wilson who denounced the "gnomes of Zurich" when his country became the last industrialized economy to seek the assistance of the IMF back in the 1960s.

Roger Altman, a former assistant secretary in the U.S. Treasury, recalled that President Jimmy Carter unveiled a long-awaited budget in 1979. The foreign exchange market didn't like it and the dollar collapsed. Within two weeks, Carter had withdrawn from the battle and drawn up a tighter budget to submit to Congress.

When the socialists came to power in France in 1981, capital fled the country. Finance Minister Jacques Delors, a devout Christian, managed to avoid going cap in hand to the IMF by getting down on his knees—to the Saudi Arabian Monetary Authority (SAMA). Michel Camdessus, the head of the French Treasury who would later become IMF chief, was quickly dispatched to Riyadh to arrange a four billion dollar line of credit. Camdessus was accompanied by his assistant Philippe Jaffré, who would later become chairman of French oil giant Elf-Aquitaine. In Riyadh, they met with SAMA officials and their advisor—David Mulford, the future number two man in the U.S. Treasury. Negotiations were about to break down when the Saudis (on an American suggestion, perhaps?) proposed that the socialist government put up a guarantee in the form of gold to be held by the Bank of France. An about-face avoided the French being humiliated.

And in Britain in September 1992, it was the conservative Prime Minister John Major who delivered his sermon against speculators from the doorsteps of 10 Downing Street. Speculative attempts to push the pound out of the European monetary system's exchange rate mechanism (ERM), he said, would never succeed. A few days later, Major made a humiliating retraction and the accompanying "Black Wednesday" for the British pound signaled the beginning of the end for the long Tory rule.

In all of these episodes, and innumerable others, markets reacted to economic imbalances. Britain under the Labor government of Harold Wilson was living beyond its means and was accumulating current account deficits. And under Socialist President François Mitterrand, France implemented expansionary policies at a time when the rest of the industrialized world was either in recession or slowing down—a fatal step for the country's external accounts resulting in three devaluations of the franc in less than two years.

In the case of Britain in 1992, John Major was confronted with a difficult heritage—the policies toward Europe left by Margaret Thatcher's rule. The pound rejoined the ERM too late to be solidly anchored to the system when tensions arose over German reunification, and its exchange rate against the mark was too high. Foreign exchange markets also had reason to doubt the government's willingness to impose the necessary sacrifices to keep the pound in the system.

Whatever the country and whatever the circumstances, currency devaluations were always difficult for the politicians who had to assume responsibility. Since time immemorial, money had been associated with power and sovereignty. A government that devalued its own currency was therefore devaluing itself.

In the European monetary system, currency adjustments were never cut-and-dried—even if frequent changes of parities between ERM currencies managed to take some of the drama out of the Sunday meetings of the European monetary committee in Brussels during the early years of the system. But if there was a battle, and if large amounts of reserves were mobilized and lost, and if the public became aware of those losses, government failures to beat speculators became a humiliation.

Devaluation of a national currency always made a country poorer, and popular wisdom rarely accepted justifications after the event. And in a world where trade competition was intense, devaluations should be followed by austerity measures to contain the fallout, notably inflation. France's excessive dependence on currency depreciations between the end of World War II and the mid-1980s didn't just have an impact on French economic behavior. It started to affect fundamental rights, such as the freedom to spend money and circulate freely. Capital controls even imposed strict limits on the amount of currency carried by tourists heading for Costa Brava. When northern Europeans started discovering the joys of summer holidays abroad in the 1960s, currency restrictions were still in force. And these restrictions still were in Malaysia at the end of the century, thanks to the controls reimposed by Mahathir toward the end of 1998. "If devaluations can make a country richer, Argentina should be the richest country in the world," Nobel Prize-winning economist Merton Miller once said.

## THE HUNTER GETS CAPTURED BY THE GAME

Politicians of all stripes didn't like markets, and Mahathir's outbursts were hardly unique. French politicians, for example, had a long tradition of denouncing the "dictatorship" of markets and their "blind power" going back to the jaw rattling against the "pit" by President Charles de Gaulle. Many years later, Prime Minister Edith Cresson declared: "I don't give a damn about the stock market."

Statements by politicians contained, however, an embarrassing contradiction—they were the ones responsible for the power of markets. In all industrialized countries, the need to finance public spending from funds other than tax revenues gave birth to markets for government bonds. Confronted with the choice of reducing spending or lifting taxes, governments often chose public debt as an alternative. And improving the management of that debt became one of the driving forces behind deregulation—to reduce the cost of borrowing with more sophisticated financial instruments and to broaden the investor base with bond issues carrying longer maturities of up to thirty years while being opened up to nonresidents and denominated in foreign currencies.

The power of bond markets was such that "you can intimidate anybody," said James Carville, the guru behind President Bill Clinton's first election campaign.

In most Asian countries besides Japan, real bond markets had not developed along the same lines because most governments traditionally ran balanced budgets, usually with surpluses, which obviated the need for additional funding.

## ETHNIC INTERVENTION

Politicians found it difficult to accept the power of markets. "What the prime minister has been saying is not entirely wrong but he speaks like a politician not an economic expert," said Malaysia's then Foreign Minister Abdullah Ahmad Badawi during a visit to Paris in late 1997. "He's expressing the feelings of a man who certainly feels very angry, very furious, and very sad as well."

For Mahathir, who would later reward Abdullah by appointing him deputy to succeed the jailed Anwar, the financial crisis came at a particularly bad time—it complicated his plans to retire in full glory from the domestic and international scene after two decades in power.

Mahathir's trade policy was based on nationalism—ethnic nationalism for the Malays who along with other indigenous people accounted for sixty percent of the population. Ethnic Chinese accounted for about thirty percent while Indians and others made up the remaining ten percent. Generations of Chinese immigrants came to work in the tin mines in what was then the British colony of Malaya. Indians tended to work in rubber plantations. And when the whites left in 1957, the remnants of the British "divided and rule" policy gave birth to a nation that was largely divided along ethnic lines with the Chinese dominating commerce amid growing resentment from the Malays, culminating in anti-Chinese riots in 1969.

The riots gave birth to an "affirmative action" program in favor of the bumiputra residents, the "princes of the soil" who were neither Chinese nor Indian. But unlike such programs for blacks and other minorities in the United States, the so-called "New Economic Policy" was directed at the majority. Such ethnic nationalism among the leaders of the dominant ruling party, the United Malays National Organization (UMNO), was one of the main reasons why Singapore left the enlarged federation of Malaysia in 1965.

When Mahathir came to power in 1981, he continued the same policies of redistributing wealth to the ethnic Malays which were introduced by his predecessors. At the same time, however, he managed to skillfully use the influx of Japanese and other foreign capital from the mid-1980s to start forging a nationalist spirit transcending racial lines.

"Since the late 1980s, Mahathir has worked toward the development of a more encompassing nationalist spirit that transcends ethnic divisions," the

Singapore-based PERC said. "While not abandoning the socioeconomic restructuring goals of earlier years, slogans such as 'Look East,' 'Malaysia Incorporated,' and 'Vision 2020' have sought to emphasize the development of the nation as a whole rather than the interest of a particular ethnic group."

Ordering people to "Look East," of course, had a strong anti-Western flavor—look east, look toward Japan, an Asian country of nonwhite people who hauled themselves up from the war to the same level as the industrialized countries of the West. Ironically, the concept of "Malaysia Inc." was blindly based on the term "Japan Inc."—created by Western critics of the Japanese model of development. In any case, "Vision 2020" became the new slogan for Malaysia to become an industrialized nation by the early twenty-first century. Another irony—this was the same date for the free-trade target for the Asia-Pacific Economic Cooperation (APEC) forum, whose Western members Mahathir repeatedly criticized in the early 1990s for stifling his own plans for an East Asian Economic Caucus (EAEC—jokingly referred to as East Asia Excluding Caucasians among Mahathir's critics).

The different phases of Mahathir's economic strategy had a common element: state intervention, the weight of government policies. The acceptance of market rules that Mahathir boasted about in Hong Kong was not being questioned. Malaysia was open to foreign investment in export-oriented industries. It was undeniable. But inflows of foreign capital paved the way for Malaysia to pursue a voluntarist government-directed strategy of development that recalled those of Latin American military regimes and African despots, including the white elephants that came with them. And two very large white elephants could be seen clearly from the air as one approached Kuala Lumpur—the Petronas Twin Towers. At 451.9 meters, the towers allowed Malaysia to swell with pride as the country had for a while the world's tallest buildings. The towers of glass and steel glittered in the clouds. They were magnificent, and expensive at 460 million dollars. Designed by an American architect, they were built by Japanese and South Korean construction companies. Malaysia provided the money and the manpower. Started in 1992, they were barely finished in 1998 when the Asia crisis had rendered hundreds of thousands of meters of office space redundant in a highly saturated market.

According to PERC, Malaysia's rapid rate of economic growth took place despite the government rather than because of it. While encouraging foreign investment, especially in the manufacturing sector, the government tried to manipulate the international tin and palm oil markets on several occasions (Malaysia was a major producer of both commodities). Government-led campaigns boycotted countries such as Britain and Australia, deemed to have offended Malaysian sensitivities. And to shield the domestic economy from competition, Mahathir also imposed protectionist measures in the petrochemical, steel, and automobile sectors.

## SOROS AGAIN!

It was well known—old whores ended up running charities. While Mahathir didn't have harsh enough words for speculators in 1997, his own central bank, Bank Negara Malaysia, had plunged into the dangerous game of currency speculation several years earlier. After some initial successes, the Malaysian central bank managed to lose an enormous sum—12.8 billion ringgit (4.7 billion dollars at the time)—in the turbulence that rocked the European Monetary System in 1992. The final outcome resulted in further losses of 5.7 billion ringgit in 1993, according to the bank's annual report. Mahathir and Anwar publicly defended the central bank's management but governor Jaffar Hussein resigned. It was a pity that Bank Negara Malaysia had been betting against and not with the man who broke the Bank of England, the man behind the most famous attack on the British pound, the man who would haunt Mahathir for years to come—George Soros.

"We have privatized more than four hundred government departments, companies, and functions. We have succeeded and we are still going on," Mahathir declared in Hong Kong.

But the process of privatization in Malaysia was everything but a conversion to market economics. Public assets were simply transferred to private companies. The individuals who took over the public services were compensated with the ability to make money out of government properties and commercial privileges. Government assets and franchises didn't go to the highest bidders in public tenders—they were transferred by mutual agreement. And the head of the government was the one who made the decisions.

The development of Malaysia Inc. was supported by the building of infrastructure ranging from roads, bridges, and dams, to ports, power plants, and sewage facilities—not to mention residential projects and other Pharaonic monuments. But entrepreneurial drive played a secondary role to the distribution of government favors that aimed to develop a new class of "bumiputra" entrepreneurs.

For such an edifice to keep standing, regardless of the pros and cons, there were two requirements—rapid economic growth and lots of cheap money.

## THE RENONG AFFAIR

Mahathir's speech in Hong Kong contained a curious passage that would turn out to be the glint of something much bigger—the Renong affair. For the international financial community, this episode would be just as devastating as Mahathir's inflammatory remarks.

"A few decades back, some enterprising people hit on the idea of acquiring controlling interest in companies and then stripping their assets. The shell left by them was incapable of giving any return to the small shareholders. Thousands of people lost money," Mahathir said.

"Again the government stepped in and required anyone acquiring more than a certain percentage of shares to make an offer for the rest. That way the small shareholders were able to dispose of their shares at the offered price."

Now let's observe how this worked in practice, comparing Mahathir the speaker who defended the rights of small shareholders to Mahathir the prime minister.

In November 1997, United Engineers (Malaysia) Bhd. (UEM) announced plans to acquire 32.6 percent of Renong Bhd. for 2.34 billion ringgit (550 million dollars at the time). UEM was in fact a subsidiary of Renong that held thirty-seven percent of the company. The announcement triggered a plunge in Malaysian share prices. Why? Because authorities decided to exempt UEM from making a general offer to buy the shares held by the minority share-holders. In the following weeks, UEM would suffer massive paper losses as a result of the stock market's collapse, the emergence of problems with risky investments, notably in the Philippines, and a climate that had turned gener-ally hostile toward heavily indebted conglomerates. The losses would be equivalent to four-fifths of the value put on the stake in Renong.

Renong wasn't just any company, it was closely linked to the main ruling party, UMNO, which had ruled the country without interruption for forty years. In the late 1980s, UMNO assets were transferred to Renong, a property company owned by Halim Saad, a protege of party treasurer Daim Zainuddin. Hailing from the same village as Mahathir in the northern state of Kedah, Daim was named finance minister at around the same time and became the spiritual father of "Malaysian-style" privatizations.

Thanks to its unrivalled patronage, Renong acquired a considerable portfo-lio of assets in various privatizations. The company became the ultimate blue chip of Malaysia Inc. with assets ranging from telecommunications concessions and a light-rail network to the newly built North-South highway that ran the entire length of the peninsula linking Singapore to Thailand. One contract was typical of Mahathir's style of privatizing public assets with Renong receiving government land to develop in central Kuala Lumpur in exchange for building a sports complex for the Commonwealth Games hosted by Malaysia in 1998.

Given the violent negative reaction from the international financial com-munity, Anwar—still deputy prime minister and finance minister at the time—told parliament that the exemption for UEM would be withheld and that the whole deal would be subject to an inquiry. But in January 1998, the inquiry was declared closed and the exemption confirmed once again, trig-gering a new plunge of the Kuala Lumpur Stock Exchange. In a bid to put an end to the scandal, Halim offered to buy Renong shares at the initial transac-tion price—but not until the year 2000.

Shortly after Anwar's dismissal and arrest in September the same year, Daim, who returned to the cabinet as Mahathir's right-hand man in the mid-dle of 1998, announced a bailout for Renong—2.7 billion dollars.

## A MENACE TO HIS OWN COUNTRY

George Soros exercised his right of reply to Mahathir a day after the prime minister spoke. It was the same hall in Hong Kong where Mahathir had spoken.

"Dr. Mahathir's suggestion yesterday to ban currency trading is so inappropriate that it does not deserve serious consideration," Soros said. "Interfering with the convertibility of capital at a moment like this is a recipe for disaster. Mahathir is a menace to his own country."

Until now, the Hungarian-born American financier had patiently ignored the torrent of abuse from Mahathir. He had denied that Qantum Fund, his star-performing hedge fund, had ever been involved in speculative attacks against the ringgit. And he had even proposed—unsuccessfully—to meet personally with Mahathir to smooth over any misunderstandings. But it was now time to settle scores.

"I have been subjected to all kinds of false and vile accusations by Dr. Mahathir," Soros said. "He is using me as a scapegoat to cover up his own failure. He is playing to a domestic audience and he couldn't get away with it if he and his ideas were subject to the discipline of independent media inside Malaysia."

The paradox was that deep down, the reactions of Mahathir and Soros to the crisis were not so far apart.

"The private sector is ill-suited to allocate international credit," the American financier would write several months later in *The Financial Times*. "It does not have the information with which to form a balanced judgement. Moreover, it is not concerned with maintaining macroeconomic balance in the borrowing countries. Its goals are to maximize profit and minimize risk. This makes it move in a herd-like fashion in both directions."

"To argue that financial markets in general, and international lending in particular, need to be regulated is likely to outrage the financial community. Yet the evidence for just that is overwhelming."

Soros proposed setting up an "international credit guarantee corporation" as a sister organization to the IMF. In exchange for getting comprehensive data on the debts of borrowing countries, the new body would guarantee loans up to certain amounts. "Beyond these, the creditors would have to beware," Soros wrote, adding that such an organization would "render any excessive credit expansion unlikely." For international bankers, this was about as exciting as a dog leaping into a game of croquet. But the details of the idea were less important than the way Soros himself was now trying to defy markets. Mahathir should have found a better scapegoat.

By December, after almost six months of waging a sterile verbal guerilla war against "speculators," Mahathir appeared to be toning down his rhetoric but was still bitter and combative. "We in Southeast Asia should accept that we are poor now and the road to recovery is going to be long and hazardous," he told a business conference ahead of a summit of East Asian leaders in Kuala Lumpur. "It will be many years before the economies of Southeast Asia regain some semblance of their past performance."

"It would be wrong to say that their governments and their people, in particular their businessmen, are completely blameless. There have been many abuses and malpractices including, of course, large foreign borrowings and deficits in the balance of payments. These abuses on their own would have resulted in slowing down growth or even reversing it."

Mahathir later told a news conference that "governments and the private sector abused the system." But "those abuses by themselves would not have caused this financial turmoil," he said, blaming "predators" in financial markets who "saw the opportunity for the kill."

With a hint of sarcasm toward his international audience, Mahathir said Southeast Asians had "not understood what is going on in the big world outside. For thirty years, we developed the old-fashioned way. But during the thirty years, concepts and ways of doing business changed. With liberalization, globalization, and market forces came herd instincts. We were caught unaware. And so we have to pay a price, a heavy price. But for the price that we paid, we should at least get a few tips on how to manage, if not a full lesson."

## PROFESSOR CAMDESSUS'S LESSON

Mahathir would eventually prove to be a very bad student. But for those who could bear the pain of listening, the full lesson was available. The theme of the lesson was "corporate governance" and the visiting professor was Michel Camdessus, the managing director of the International Monetary Fund. And as Dr. Mahathir was in a position to know the professor was always willing to give special tutoring to problem students.

Camdessus summarized the theme of the lesson in Hong Kong on September 25 at the traditional news conference that marked the formal end of the annual meeting. After that, reporters assigned to the international monetary beat and a few local colleagues would abandon the sandwiches and instant noodles of the past week for lunch with the heads of the IMF and the World Bank and their top assistants.

"What I would like to say is that when you see speculation somewhere, you must ask yourself why, as speculators never like to lose money. If they speculate, it's because they see somewhere a weakness or a rigidity that would make them very safe conditions for making money. So if speculation is part of market life, what this crisis tells us is that you should not try to outlaw speculators because you will create only parallel channels for speculation. What you must do with a sense of urgency is to compete for excellence in the management for your economy in such a way that you will not attract the attention of the speculators and that they would not dare to speculate against you."

In remarks to the French chapter of Transparency International several months later, Camdessus said there were "varied and complex" reasons for the crisis. But "many of the problems that lie at the heart of Asia's difficulties are bound up with poor governance," he added.

With the encouragement of the IMF, good governance became a major theme for multilateral institutions during the 1990s. The idea was simple—governments should work with markets, and not against them. First, because the essential component of financing growth was private capital, and capital markets didn't come with the diplomatic niceties of donor countries giving bilateral or multilateral aid. If they didn't like something, capital market participants voted with their feet. The second was that markets had become so powerful that clashes weren't worth it—markets didn't care whether governments were big powers or developing countries.

The struggle against corruption was an element of corporate governance but not the only one. There were others such as creating and strengthening the rule of law with rapid and impartial judicial systems, the efficiency and responsibility of the public sector, budget transparency, simple and stable tax systems, and healthy and efficient financial institutions accompanied by independent and reliable supervisory systems.

"Asia is no exception," Camdessus said. "We have seen there that governance problems can also undermine the ability of countries to channel private capital inflows into productive, long-term investment. Moreover, the Asian crisis has demonstrated in a very dramatic way how the lack of transparency about underlying economic and financial conditions can feed market uncertainty and trigger large capital outflows that can in turn threaten macroeconomic stability."

## THE TRANSPARENCY REVOLUTION

One of the cliches most frequently used to describe how markets worked was the "invisible hand"—and one of the most striking things about the evolution of finance in the era of globalization was the magnitude of efforts to increase visibility.

Financial intermediaries and institutional investors spent vast sums on research. Turnover in the world's information sector was estimated at seven billion dollars a year toward the end of the 1990s. A company like Capital in Los Angeles would allocate tens of millions of dollars each year to its research budget. And in the Asia-Pacific region, dozens of investment banks had research networks covering each country. Sectoral analysis was also big business and nearly all financial institutions had research teams in at least two of the main three centers of Hong Kong, Singapore, and Tokyo (although Tokyo was almost exclusively dedicated to research on the Japanese market). All of the big research teams included regional economists who scrutinized macroeconomic developments, putting all sorts of statistics through the grinders.

Much gray matter was used and thousands of graduates were recruited each year to fill high-paying jobs. The research was paid for by the financial industry, in other words investors themselves, and their work was complemented by the research of international organizations such as the IMF and the World Bank in Washington, the Organization for Economic Cooperation and Development (OECD) in Paris, the BIS in Basel, and the Manila-based ADB. Then there were the credit-rating agencies and various research foundations, institutes, and academic bodies.

Globalization made investment decisions more scientific. Rumors in the stock market gave way to the analysis of profit ratios. Risks were not eliminated but assigned values instead.

After the tempest broke, many criticized this army of economists for failing to predict the impending disaster. But this was only partly true. The timing and circumstances weren't foreseen and the depth of contagion was underestimated. But the deteriorating situations in national economies, especially Thailand, were correctly anticipated by many economists ranging from those in institutions such as the IMF to others working in the private sector.

What economists obviously couldn't include in their model was the political response to a crisis. It was clear, for example, that Mahathir's behavior from July 1997 had a negative impact among investors, making Malaysia more vulnerable to regional contagion.

But there was more. The quality of analysis by the private sector and multilateral institutions alike depended on the quality of information coming from governments and individual companies. There's the rub.

Governments that denounced markets for being blind and acting like sheep were often the same governments with the biggest clouds swirling around their own economic management. From Thailand to South Korea to Malaysia and Indonesia, the half-truths and outright lies heavily tarnished the information policies of those in power. As the crisis deepened, increasing intimidation and even direct threats caused analysts to censor themselves or simply shut up. The victims were, of course, the very governments that maintained a tight lid on information, keeping things dark and obscure and encouraging their people to distrust markets. But international investors were like children—they loved to be dazzled but were afraid of the dark.

"The business environment in Asia tends to be influenced more by personal relationships than by hard-and-fast rules and regulations, and there is often a flexibility in the way regulations are applied, statistics are collected, and supervisory duties are performed that can only be described as arbitrary," the Singapore-based PERC said in a late 1997 study of the mediocre performance in Asian economies.

Even Singapore, the best student in the class, barely scored above average and lacked transparency in some critical areas. "For example, try and find out about the real magnitude and trend of Singapore's trade and investment with

Indonesia, the island's largest neighbor and one of its leading trading and investment partners," it said. "This is like trying to analyze the strength of the U.S. trade and investment position without taking U.S. commercial links with Canada into account." Even Hong Kong had problems with transparency. The territory didn't publish current account statistics showing the inflows and outflows of capital. As a result, mainland companies could invest in China from Hong Kong and reap the benefits of being classified as a "foreign" investor. "In other words, Hong Kong's role is to facilitate a game of smoke and mirrors. Its value is its lack of transparency, not its transparency," PERC said.

Legend had it that overseas Chinese companies throughout Southeast Asia kept three sets of accounts—one for the taxman, another for minority shareholders, and the third for the family controlling the company.

The storm left in its trail the sad reality of Asia's unprecedented economic boom—banks crippled by bad debts and companies with excessive borrowings in foreign currencies that hadn't been hedged, along with high-risk investments, questionable business practices, nepotism, and corruption on a grand scale

That's why an important part of the lesson given by Professor Camdessus was devoted to transparency in corporate accounting and the release of government statistics.

"We cannot overemphasize the importance of high-quality statistical data," the IMF chief said. "Such data are an influential factor in improving economic policy and an essential aid to potential investors in evaluating countries' economic policies and performance. They allow the markets to become more informed and selective, and constitute a first-class protection for countries with good policies, which will be less vulnerable to the often capricious fluctuations and herd behavior of the financial markets."

Camdessus admitted he was advocating a veritable "revolution" that would profoundly change the course of events if taken seriously. "Such reforms will require a vast change in domestic business practices, corporate culture, and government behavior. Obviously, this will be a long-term process—a process in which the IMF, the World Bank, and others will assist, but one whose success depends on the efforts of the countries themselves."

# CHAPTER SIX

# Something Brewing on the Eastern Front

"Japan is the third communist country I've lived in but it's the only one that works."
— *Fernando Mezzetti, former correspondent for Italian newspaper*
*La Stampa in Moscow, Beijing, and Tokyo*

"If the current crisis has done nothing more than discredit the Japanese and Korean models and banking practices, then some day we will look back at these days as a blessing," Nobel Prize-winning economist Merton Miller declared in Hong Kong in January 1998.

Amid the smoking ruins of the Asian "miracle" as hundreds of millions of individuals shifted through the ashes of their dreams of prosperity, economists started to settle scores. East versus West, markets versus planning, the American model versus the Japanese model. After years of polemics and entire shelves full of literature on the subject, one thing had finally become clear—it was no longer a fight between equals. Japan had lost.

## THE JAPANESE MODEL

How do you establish a model of the Japanese model? How do you reduce more than half a century of economic and social history, how do you define the tangled web of political commercial and financial relations of a country with more than one thousand years of history into a few simple equations?

John Greenwood tried. The head of LGT Asset Management (Hong Kong) Ltd. was better known for conceiving the "peg," the currency board system of exchange rates established in Hong Kong in 1983. But the economist also had an intimate knowledge of Japan. After graduating from the University of Edinburgh, Greenwood furthered his studies at Tokyo University, the breeding ground for the country's elite and the alma mater of the powerful mandarins of the Japanese finance ministry and central bank. He also did an internship at the Japanese central bank.

Greenwood compared the Japanese model for development with the Anglo-Saxon growth model.

"The current financial crisis in Asia is a revelation of the shortcomings of the 'Japan growth model.' To understand its features, first note the fundamental underpinnings of the Anglo-Saxon model with a balance on all sides of producers, consumers, and politicians," he said, illustrating the model with a triangle showing producers and employers in one corner, consumers and shareholders in the second corner, and politicians radiating power from the third.

"In contrast, the essence of the Japanese model is a centrally-located allocation of resources by government and bureaucrats through a compliant banking system to favored corporations in designated sectors," Greenwood said.

This triangle was dominated by the two corners representing producers-employers on one side and politicians on the other. But they were separated by two new groups—bureaucrats and banks. An intense amount of two-way activity dominated the relationships between all four groups—between politicians and producers, between politicians and bureaucrats, between banks and producers, between banks and bureaucrats, and so on. The consumers and shareholders were isolated out on the third corner of the triangle as powerless spectators.

Greenwood said the model worked well while Japan was in the process of "catching up" with Western-industrialized countries. But the price was widespread corruption.

"The way in which the Japan growth model undermined good corporate governance, transparency, and accountability and promoted corruption is becoming clear with each new bankruptcy," he said.

## LIVING IN AN ANTS' NEST

How did the Japanese economic machine function at full strength?

The basic ingredient was a very high level of savings, a crucial factor in post-war Japan. Salaried workers received biannual bonuses equal to several months' salary. When they reached retirement age, they would leave with an important nest egg. National income taxes were paid through the company and the costs of housing and education were extremely high. This was the type of environment that turned Japan into a mound of activity—and the Japanese into the "ants" that French Prime Minister Edith Cresson once famously described. Her comments triggered diplomatic turmoil between Paris and Tokyo. But at least in terms of statistics, she was not wrong.

Where did all these savings go? Mainly banks, the post office, and life insurance companies. Interest rates were strictly regulated to ensure that the returns on these savings were as low as possible. Competition was minimal and financial markets were underdeveloped. The stock market was dominated by the *keiretsu* system of interlocking shareholdings between corporate groups, representing the reincarnation of the huge pre-war conglomerates known as *zaibatsu* such as the Mitsubishi, Sumitomo or Mitsui groups that dominated the economic life of the nation.

What did the banks do with the money? They lent it to companies, but the lending environment was not free. The banking system was rigidly compartmentalized into the main commercial banks, long-term credit banks, trust banks, regional banks, and specialized institutions such as credit unions. Banks and securities companies operated in two environments strictly separated by insurmountable barriers.

The landscape appeared to be frozen in time. Banks operated under the administrative guidance of the finance ministry that "protected" them from any competition. The market was virtually closed to foreign banks. For many years, a single bank would serve as the main link to the outside world—Bank of Tokyo Ltd., descended from the old Yokohama Specie Bank that used to have the monopoly on foreign exchange transactions.

Each of the main groups in the *keiretsu* system had their own "main bank" that would act as lender and auditor, temporarily assuming management of any companies within the group that fell into financial difficulties.

The rationale behind all this was simple—to guarantee access to capital for the Japanese industrial machine at the cheapest rate possible. The objectives were to invest, to invest more, to expand, to gain market share, to export, to export more, and to keep on exporting forever. The indispensable element for such a system was that shareholders enjoyed the right...to remain silent. Shareholders were only one of the many category of "stakeholders" and came well behind the corporate group, the main bank, and the staff, whose loyalty was ensured by a system of lifetime employment and seniority-based promotion. Other stakeholders included corporate partners and subcontractors (that had to be exploited without being killed).

Japanese companies themselves operated under the vigilant watch of the all-powerful Ministry of International Trade and Industry (MITI). Bureaucrats from MITI determined the priority sectors, fixed the rules of the game, handed out subsidies, and fiercely protected the domestic market from any incursions by foreign companies owned by *gaijin* (literally "outside people").

As Chalmers Johnson noted in his book, *MITI and the Japanese Miracle*, the postwar industrial organization provided for the continuation of the Japanese military structure established during the 1930s. The men in charge were essentially the same before and after the 1945 surrender. Not only did the Americans fail to realize their plans of radically altering the landscape during the Allied occupation, but the Japanese used ideas coming from the United States as a shelter when it was convenient.

An exemplary case was the Glass-Steagall Act, transposed to Japan after the law was passed in the United States to separate banking and stockbroking activities in the wake of the Wall Street crash of 1929.

Like all systems of restraint, the shackles of Japanese bureaucracy occasionally produced dissent and revolt, some crowned with success. Honda Motor Co. Ltd. became Japan's third largest carmaker by defying MITI's order to stay within its assigned territory of making motorcycles. And Sony Corp. shook up the hierarchy of the business establishment thanks to the inventiveness of the company's two founders.

But by and large, the system justified the remark by Fernando Mezzetti that caused so much indignation among Japanese bureaucrats at the time. The Italian newspaper *La Stampa* sent him to Tokyo in the second half of the 1980s after he had served as correspondent in Moscow and Beijing. "Japan is the third communist country I've lived in," he said. "But it's the only one that works."

## MESMERIZED BY SUCCESS

And how could anyone deny that it worked with devastating efficiency for more than three decades? Japan became the world's second-biggest industrial power, the first and for a long time the only Asia member of the Organization for Economic Cooperation and Development (OECD), the Paris-based club of rich countries. Japan's prime ministers were invited to the annual summits of leading industrial countries. Its finance ministers and central bank governors took part in regular meetings of the G5 alongside their counterparts from the United States, Germany, France, and Britain (later joined by Italy and Canada as the G7). Japan excelled in several sectors, notably steel, shipbuilding, cars, electronics, and home appliances. Its people were young, there was no unemployment and the standard of living rose spectacularly. The ruling Liberal Democratic Party (LDP) delivered the goods. Apart from a brief period in the mid-1990s, this conglomeration of conservative factions linked by vested interests and the lucrative benefits of power ruled Japan without interruption since the late 1950s.

But people became blinded by success and so did countries. Everything written about East Asia at the end of the 1990s was equally applicable to Japan only a decade earlier.

"There are several similarities between Japan and East Asia," said Toyoo Gyohten, a former vice minister of finance.

"At the initial stage, a strategy based on export-led growth and close cooperation between government, bureaucracy, and business enjoyed considerable success. But that brought about excessive confidence in that particular strategy. External criticisms were brushed aside. 'After all, we are still growing faster than you are' was the answer made to the Americans and the Europeans."

Gyohten called this a "mesmerizing phenomenon," the idea that strong growth acted like a hallucinogenic drug, taking away all risks and eliminating any pain. "Fast growth can cover many problems successfully," he said.

A good lawyer knew the strengths of his case but also the weaknesses of his client. And Japan couldn't dream of having a better defender than Toyoo Gyohten—which was exactly the role he was conferred with in mid-1998 when Prime Minister Keizo Obuchi appointed him as adviser.

## THE FAILURE OF THE INTERNATIONALISTS

If he hadn't been Japanese, Toyoo Gyohten would have been managing director of the IMF. But tradition dictated that the head of the IMF had to be a European while the president of the World Bank had to be an American.

Even by the high standards of Japanese bureaucrats, his career was outstanding. Promoted to one of the two top posts in the Ministry of Finance (MoF) in 1986, he was the first vice minister for international affairs to have his two-year term extended to three years. When he left the powerful ministry in 1989, he spent the customary two-year "decompression" period in teaching positions—first at Princeton and Harvard in the United States and then at Saint-Gall University in Switzerland. On his return to Japan, he became adviser and then president of Bank of Tokyo, taking an active role in its merger with Mitsubishi Bank to form one of the world's biggest banks in terms of assets. Gyohten also headed the Institute for International Finance, the Washington-based lobby group for global financial institutions. He was also a member of the influential Group of Thirty, an informal group which meets on the sidelines of IMF meetings, and the Bretton Woods Commission.

Gyohten best epitomized the "internationalists," a tiny Japanese elite convinced that Japan had to embrace the times, shed its armored plating, and stop looking at the outside world merely as a market that was otherwise a threat. But this school of thought was always in the minority, treated with suspicion and even outright hostility by the rest of the herd that made up the Japanese bureaucracy. Using the leverage of external pressure or *gaiatsu* to try to force change, the internationalists lost the battle in the 1980s. The status quo won, protected by the sclerosis of the political world, a powerful coalition of vested interests and the complacency that came with success.

"In the early 1980s, we started our efforts by amending the banking law, and modifying the foreign exchange law. We started to change the system," Gyohten said. By 1984, Gyohten was assistant director-general of the ministry's banking bureau and a member of the ad hoc working group of Japanese and American officials who would eventually agree to encourage the yen's sharp appreciation against the dollar from 1985.

"The unfortunate event was that the bubble came and bloated the economy. A superficial sense of achievement superceded. Because of that operation, we stopped our reform efforts. We succumbed to the mirage of success, to the illusion that we could very well succeed without reforming our ways. We wasted almost an entire decade."

As he looked back on this period of Japanese history when he was a key player, Gyohten turned to the events of 1985.

"A fundamental mistake was made after the Plaza Accord. The yen started to rise and Japanese businesses started to ask the government to do something about it. Bureaucrats and politicians rushed to the rescue without thinking too much."

At this point, Japan got caught up in the spiral. With the menace of the rising yen threatening to shoot corporate Japan in the head, it was decided to stimulate the domestic economy. Internal demand would help reduce trade imbalances with the United States and other countries and help Japanese companies adjust to the stronger yen at the same time.

"We had three different tools at our disposal to stimulate demand—fiscal policy, monetary policy, and action at the microeconomic level, that is structural reform. MoF refused to resort to fiscal policy and microeconomic action was voted down by vested interests. But the Bank of Japan (BoJ) agreed to reflate. We eased too much, for too long."

"With hindsight, what we should have done was not to resist the appreciation of the yen and focus all our efforts on structural reforms. Deregulation was the key word. But we could not do it. And the bubble was created."

Gyohten admitted "there are not too many people in Japan who look back to that period in that way."

In the defense of the Japanese, however, they were not the only ones blinded by their success. The Americans thought the Japanese had become invincible giants. Under the weight of a flood of Japanese imports, the "Big Three" carmakers suffered huge losses and automobile workers joined the ranks of the unemployed. The home appliance industry was wiped out. The last bastion, RCA, was taken over by the French state-owned company Thomson that imported its video components from Japan. And Washington negotiated a government-controlled opening of the Japanese semiconductor market as American manufacturers were cutting back in this field and starting to concentrate on other areas of technology.

With pain, corporate America would eventually rebuild itself with Europe becoming a distant second.

In Japan, the bursting of the bubble in the early 1990s led to a massive hangover. "It became very difficult for us to relaunch the reform process," Gyohten said.

## IMPOSSIBLE TO CHANGE

Gyohten himself analyzed how the Japanese system missed an historic opportunity to redefine the rules of the game after 1985 by subjecting the old economic structures to the full pressure of the skyrocketing yen. A symmetrical error occurred in 1991. What changed was the treatment prescribed to the patient—painkillers instead of stimulants. Surgery was postponed once again.

Let's go back to the study by John Greenwood, which compared the structure of the Japanese and Anglo-Saxon models earlier. Now let's see how each model performed in terms of earnings per share.

On the left, the Japanese heavyweight, the Nikkei Stock Average of leading shares on the Tokyo Stock Exchange. On the right, the American champion, the Standard and Poor's 500 index of the New York Stock Exchange.

From the starting line in 1977, the Japanese curve rose from five to twenty in 1985 before reaching its top performance of thirty in 1990 just after the Nikkei peaked at almost forty thousand points. The rise was particularly steep after 1985 when Japanese companies were under the combined influence of monetary and speculative stimulants. From 1988 to 1991, the curve reached a plateau. But it fell away to less than twenty in 1999.

The American curve, by contrast, jumped around a lot more with visible troughs in 1982-83, 1987, and 1992. Since the last trough, it moved violently upwards, reaching forty-five in 1998.

"The contrast between the results of the Anglo-Saxon growth model as practiced in the United States and the results of the Japan model are striking," Greenwood said.

Indeed it was—Japan started flirting with deflation when the bubble burst while the United States entered a rare period of sustained noninflationary growth. In other words, the American model allowed for corporate restructuring and the Japanese model blocked it.

Another graph illustrated the impact of the bubble on Japanese banks. The curve rose sharply between 1983 and 1990 when the global assets of Japanese banks more than doubled from three hundred trillion yen to 750 trillion yen. Then it stopped and remained flat for several years, starting to cave away in 1996 and 1997 when the "credit crunch" hit as Japanese banks took defensive moves in the rest of Asia.

## THE MOTHER OF ALL BANKING CRISES

"During the bubble years, Japanese banks' assets grew vigorously. Since that time, we have been witnessing a zero growth rate," Greenwood noted. And while lending stagnated, the balance sheets of financial institutions were increasingly weighed down by bad debts. Nonperforming loans at the nineteen leading banks were estimated at twenty thousand billion yen in 1993. When the finance ministry finally decided to lift the smokescreen four years later, the figure had ballooned to fifty thousand billion yen at the end of 1997, or fifteen percent of all loans. At the end of March of that year, the "official" figure was "only" 27,900 billion yen.

By the end of the 1990s, the estimates were closer to seventy-five thousand billion yen, more than ten percent of all assets. "Deflation is causing the bad debt problem to worsen and as long as this vicious cycle is not broken, we don't see a recovery in the Japanese economy unless the vicious circle is broken," Greenwood said.

Over at Deutsche Bank, Kenneth Courtis got out his calculator.

In 1989, the hidden reserves of Japanese banks—mainly unrealized gains on shareholdings in various companies—were about four hundred billion dollars. Between 1989 and 1996, banks sacrificed much of their margins and some of their stock market gains to make provisions for bad debts of 250 billion dollars. Deflation, especially the collapse of property prices, remained a problem and Japanese banks depended heavily on the performance of equity markets. Courtis estimated that unrealized gains on shareholdings represented 350 percent of the capital of trust banks and 160 percent for the main commercial banks. Whenever the Nikkei Stock Average fell below sixteen thousand points, these gains became losses.

"That means the banks lost 650 billion dollars since 1989," Courtis said. That was about half of what a country the size of France produced in GNP every year.

On his way to a meeting in Manila in November 1997, Larry Summers stopped over in Tokyo. The number-two man at the U.S. Treasury—who would become secretary in 1999—met his Japanese counterpart Eisuke Sakakibara and Finance Minister Hiroshi Mitsuzuka. Coming out of the meetings, he suggested that Japan should perhaps finally change the way it had been treating its sick financial system for the past seven years. And the example he gave was the costly but eventually successful recipe used to resolve the Savings and Loans crisis in the United States.

America's adventure with deregulation was not all clear sailing. There were the pitfalls, the inevitable excesses and failures, the biggest being those of the savings and loans institutions that began in the mid-1980s. These institutions used their newfound freedoms with catastrophic consequences. Their licentious behavior included high-risk speculative activities and investments in questionable real-estate projects. After the initial spectacular successes, everybody jumped in. Some institutions were plundered by outright criminals. And the wake-up call, partly prompted by a cyclical downturn in the property sector, was devastating, with American taxpayers being asked to foot the bill. The authorities opted for shock treatment with dozens of savings and loans forced into liquidation or mergers. The Resolution Trust Fund Corp., which took over assets before reselling them, funded the operation that came to 150 billion dollars. Not only was the crisis stopped from spreading to the rest of the financial system, but its broader economic impact was limited and the taxpayers at least got some of the money back several years later when the assets were liquidated.

If Summers felt authorized to publicly teach the Japanese a lesson in late 1997, it was because time was of the essence.

Across Asia, banking systems were being sucked into the financial whirlpool. During a conference on Asian debt in Hong Kong that July, Philippe Delhaise, the head of Thomson BankWatch Asia, forecast that the plunge in Asian currency values would be followed by the collapse of banks. The Thai baht had already dropped precipitously, and the Philippine peso and the Malaysian ringgit were coming under downward pressure, with the Indonesian rupiah emerging as the next in line. "If there was a domino effect for currencies, there's a domino effect for banks too," explained Delhaise, whose company, a subsidiary of the Canadian group Thomson, monitored and assigned credit ratings to four hundred banks in Asia. The alarmist prediction would prove to be an underestimate in the months ahead.

Behind the impatience expressed by Summers in Tokyo that November seemed to be two major priorities. The first was to discourage the region from looking to Japan for a solution. As far as banking crises went, Japan did everything it shouldn't have done. The second priority was that if Japan had the ability to let its problems fester, it was at the expense of the rest of the economy. Now was the time for action. Asia's financial storm and Japan's banking crisis would be an explosive combination. In a few days, we would see why.

## TREMOR IN TOKYO

On November 24, the financial world was rocked by a powerful earthquake—Yamaichi Securities had failed.

Speaking before a crowd of stunned reporters, Shohei Nozawa, the president of Japan's oldest stockbroking firm, burst into tears. Nozawa's sobbing gave some indication of the extraordinary tensions in Tokyo over the previous days and nights as authorities did all they could to save the company that was getting ready for its one hundredth anniversary celebrations. The earthquake was, however, preceded by several tremors.

On November 3, when banks were closed, Sanyo Securities announced its financial results. The company was insolvent. Sanyo was one of the leading second-tier brokerages behind the Big Four securities companies that included Yamaichi. During the euphoria of the late 1980s, Sanyo had opened the world's biggest trading room with giant electronic screens in eastern Tokyo. This monument to the Japanese bubble economy could still be seen on the highway to Narita Airport a decade later. The stock market's meltdown throughout most of the 1990s made medium-sized companies like Sanyo especially vulnerable as all securities firms relied heavily on commissions, which fluctuated on a daily basis with the overall market turnover. The failure of Sanyo was the first in the securities sector since World War II and sent an important message to the markets—the finance ministry couldn't find a buyer.

When the banks reopened on November 4, the markets were nervous but there was no panic. International banks had been reducing their exposure to Japanese institutions for months, advances were being cut off to companies that looked the most fragile and the distrust among *gaijin* had hit new highs. Despite the country's status as the world's biggest creditor, the Japan Premium—the higher interest rates charged by international banks on their loans to Japanese banks—widened to more than one hundred basis points, a full percentage point more than what other big banks were paying. And the credit-rating agencies were downgrading Japanese banks even further.

At the same time, anxious depositors were lining up outside the doors of Hokkaido Takushoku Bank, the smallest of the country's ten major commercial banks with most of its network concentrated on the northern island of Hokkaido. Known as Takugin, the bank had seen its share price sink to as low as fifty-nine yen, barely above the fifty yen face value. Takugin, whose share prices had once been worth 1,630 yen, was especially vulnerable after a failed attempt to merge with its local rival Hokkaido Bank.

Taking advantage of the weekend, authorities organized the closure of the bank to avoid the appearance of any "systemic risk"—the worst nightmare for any finance minister or central bank governor. The Bank of Japan would guarantee deposits at Takugin, profitable activities would be transferred to another Hokkaido bank called North Pacific, and the bill would be taken care of by the Deposit Insurance Corp. When it was finally closed, bad debts had mounted to thirteen percent of its loans.

Who was next? That's the question everyone was asking on November 17, given that government promises to warn of any insolvency among the twenty major banks had vanished as quickly as the autumn leaves falling at the time. Drawing up a list was dead easy. You just had to look at the stock market—and start panicking when prices fell below one hundred yen a share.

On November 19, the share price of Yamaichi Securities plummeted forty percent in a single session, closing at fifty-seven yen. Moody's downgraded the company to "junk bond" status two days later, signaling that there was now an elevated risk that Yamaichi wouldn't be able to repay its debts.

The other fatal blow came the same day and was delivered by Yoshiro Yamamoto, president of Fuji Bank. One of Japan's top five banks, Fuji Bank was part of the Fuyo group of companies that also included Yamaichi Securities. When Yamaichi fell into difficulties in 1965, authorities arranged a rescue with Fuji Bank, Mitsubishi Bank, and Industrial Bank of Japan. Yamaichi recovered but was always relegated to last place among the Big Four, behind Nomura Securities, Daiwa Securities, and Nikko Securities. But this time around, Fuji was refusing to help Yamaichi. "My responsibility is to uphold the credibility of Fuji Bank, and the priority is always Fuji," Yamamoto said. "Yamaichi is a valued customer, so as a customer we would help them. But it is a relationship with a customer…at this moment, I can't tell whether they will survive or not."

Three days later, the verdict fell. For the third time in what was to become the "Black November" for Japan, the markets opened on Monday with a major bankruptcy announcement.

The earthquake in Tokyo triggered a *tsunami* worldwide. From the United States to Europe, the crisis that spread from Thailand to other countries several months earlier had been ignored by financial markets. Alarm bells only started ringing in late October when the Hong Kong market collapsed.

But Japan? That was something else. However anemic it was, Japan still accounted for two-thirds of the Asian economy. Japan was like its famous sumo wrestlers. If it fell, watch out. It was big enough to cause a lot of damage—not only to its opponents but to those sitting near the ring as well.

## A VERY CLOSE CALL

The Japanese authorities were aware of this. The announcement of Yamaichi's failure was immediately followed by simultaneous statements appealing for calm by Finance Minister Hiroshi Mitsuzuka and Bank of Japan Governor Yasuo Matsushita.

"We have taken every possible measure to prevent the financial problems of individual financial institutions from spreading and leading to the instability of the entire system," Mitsuzuka said. "We are determined to sustain the stability of the financial system by taking measures such as fully protecting deposits…as well as ensuring the stability of interbank transactions since the deposit-taking institutions such as banks constitute the basis of Japan's financial system. We are also determined to protect the deposited assets of customers at securities firms.

"I have just had consultations with the governor of the Bank of Japan, and I requested that the governor properly address any possible disturbances in the financial markets both at home and abroad. We have affirmed supplying any necessary liquidity to the market. I have conveyed this matter to the monetary authorities abroad, " Mitsuzuka said.

Matsushita, the central bank governor, called for calm. "We strongly request all investors, counterparties, and participants in the financial and capital market to act calmly."

"The environment surrounding Japan's financial system has become increasingly harsh due to recent instability in the stock markets and Asian currency markets, and also due to the recent successive failure of financial institutions. Under these conditions, the Bank of Japan is of the view that we face a very important situation that requires the utmost central bank efforts to ensure the stability of the banking system would not be undermined."

Matsushita added that the Bank of Japan "affirms its readiness to take necessary supportive steps, including the provision of sufficient liquidity into the markets to cope with the risk of an unexpected decline in market liquidity." The actions would be followed by words. During the course of the day, the central bank opened the floodgates, inundating the short-term money market with an unprecedented thirty-seven hundred billion yen in surplus liquidity. The central bank also lent funds directly to the institutions considered most vulnerable. And the finance ministry even entered the interbank market abroad to lend dollars to Japanese banks that had been quarantined by their foreign counterparts.

"MoF and BoJ managed to prevent financial panic from spreading but it was a very close call," Gyohten admitted later.

Fear jolted the politicians and bureaucrats into briefly regaining their faculties. A large-scale scheme to use public funds to clear up the mess in the Japanese financial system was announced—seven years after the crisis began. Although it took years of debate to work out a rescue plan for the troubled *jusen* credit companies that lent heavily to Japan's powerful agricultural cooperatives, the LDP suddenly announced stabilization plans for the Japanese banking system worth thirty thousand billion yen. Japan had come within an inch of a violent financial disaster before the politicians temporarily arose from their slumber.

## FINANCIAL HYPOCRISY

Yamaichi's failure would once again justify the outside world's distrust toward Japan and the loss of credibility toward Japanese authorities.

The statement by the Bank of Japan governor on November 24 contained a surprising passage. "Yamaichi Securities has recently informed the authorities that there is a strong suspicion that the firm has a large amount of off-the-book liabilities," it said. Recently? Strong suspicion?

One of the more exotic manipulations in Japanese financial markets had long been the practice of concealing losses from the accounts of important clients. The losses would be transferred to other accounts, from one financial year to the next, and eventually sometimes to other companies and even other countries. The practice was known as *tobashi*, a Japanese word for removal.

Rumors of *tobashi* activities at Yamaichi were around ever since the early 1990s when the bubble burst. As the losses swelled, the company apparently decided to keep these concealed losses away from prying eyes by transferring them to companies registered in the Cayman Islands.

Yamaichi's *tobashi* losses of 265 billion yen had been a shameful secret. But the secret was shared. After the company's failure, tongues started wagging and it turned out that Yamaichi executives had asked finance ministry bureaucrats what to do five years earlier when *tobashi* activities were outlawed.

The new legislation followed Japanese public outrage over the practice when the first *tobashi* scandal surfaced with Nomura in 1991. At the time, small-time Japanese investors were watching their hard-earned savings go up in smoke as the stock market collapsed. But not the privileged clients of Nomura Securities—the losses on their investments were being "compensated" by *tobashi* accounts. At the time, Nomura was being run by two men who shared the same family name but who were not related: "Big Tabuchi" the chairman and "Small Tabuchi" the chief executive.

Nomura was punished by being suspended by authorities from trading for six weeks, the two Tabuchis resigned to "take responsibility" for the scandal and the affair was quickly forgotten.

But in Japan, scandals rarely proved fatal. Take the case of Prime Minister Kakuei Tanaka, whose wide-ranging influence on Japanese politics survived for fifteen years after he resigned at the height of the Lockheed scandal in the late 1970s.

So in 1997, a new Nomura scandal erupted. The company was accused this time of compensating the losses of a corporate racketeer called Ryuichi Koike. Known as *sokaiya* in Japan, these groups played a special role in a country with limited shareholder rights. Often linked to organized crime, they would gain access to annual meetings of companies by virtue of holding a few shares. They would then disrupt proceedings and ask potentially embarrassing questions of the management. All of this could be avoided, of course, in exchange for a small fee, allowing meetings to proceed in the traditional consensual harmony and brevity for which Japanese annual meetings were renowned.

"The disturbing issue underlying these scandals is the fact that the *sokaiya* trade in information that corporations do not want stockholders, creditors, or the public to know," said Edward Lincoln, a researcher from the Brookings Institution. "What secrets are they hiding? How would revelations alter market evaluation of these companies? Maybe the president is using corporate funds to take his mistress to Las Vegas and gamble (as happened in a scandal involving Japanese telecommunications firm KDD several years ago). Maybe the company is involved in an illegal cartel to fix prices and market shares. Such behavior is endemic in Japanese corporations and should not be surprising given the nature of corporate governance."

Paying off *sokaiya* had been illegal since the early 1980s. But Koike was no fool, as he didn't rely exclusively on blackmail *sokaiya*-style. He edited magazines. And after the second scandal erupted, Nomura cancelled its subscriptions, all seven hundred of them.

The fallout from the second scandal would also prompt Nomura to announce the definitive resignations of the two Tabuchi executives, who resigned six years earlier in the first scandal. Although they had lost their nominal positions back in 1991, they had since been appointed to advisory positions where they still managed to pull the strings at Japan's largest securities firm. In a similar fashion, Ryutaro Hashimoto resigned as finance minister around the same time as the first Nomura scandal in 1991 but had returned to the corridors of power as prime minister at the time of the second scandal.

Investigators probing the second Nomura scandal found similar ties with sokaiya among other Japanese brokers, including Yamaichi.

Yamaichi was severely damaged by tobashi and sokaiya but it wasn't insolvent—its assets more or less covered its losses at the time of liquidation. But it couldn't be saved either—by Fuji Bank, the Ministry of Finance, the Bank of Japan, or even a foreign company. Yamaichi died of shame, its own shame and the shame of others.

## DESCENT FROM HEAVEN

On January 26, 1998, it seemed Japan was entering a new era. Dozens of grim-faced investigators from the Tokyo Public Prosecutors Department marched through the stone archway of a building in central Tokyo to conduct a raid. Similar scenes had been played out across Japan over the preceding years as the bursting of the bubble gave rise to a growing number of corporate and political scandals. But this wasn't just any building. And it wasn't just any raid. It was the hallowed Ministry of Finance, and the dozens of boxes of papers being seized inside were government documents. And the two men arrested, Koichi Miyagawa and Oshimi Taniuchi, were officials from the banking supervision section of the ministry's prestigious banking bureau.

The two men were accused of being wined and dined by the same banks they were supposed to be supervising. In exchange, the banks involved—including top names such as Dai-Ichi Kangyo Bank and Sanwa Bank—were alerted well in advance when ministry inspections were about to take place, giving them the time to remove any embarrassing documents. The ministry officials involved were invited to luxury restaurants and golf outings, with the bill over four years coming to one hundred thousand dollars. The public prosecutors, who used the series of earlier scandals to improve their own public relations, threw a juicy bit of information to the salivating public—the favorite restaurant frequented by Miyagawa and Taniuchi was a very particular type of establishment. The waitresses wore short dresses and no panties, moving about on a mirrored surface as they served shabu-shabu, a Japanese dish consisting of thin slices of raw beef and vegetables cooked in a clear soup. Such no pan (no pantie) establishments were common enough in Japan at the time, but the image of respected bureaucrats and bankers sitting in a no-pan shabu-shabu restaurant conspiring to cook the books was a bit much even by jaded Japanese standards.

Japanese financial scandals were a bit like games of musical chairs, with the music playing for decades. When the music suddenly stopped, the surprised people fell. And everyone waited for the music to start playing again.

"Institutionalized corruption is the best way to describe it," said John Greenwood. But on the scale of international corruption, the "gifts" received by Japanese officials were tiny. The main lever was elsewhere, in the organization of the careers of senior bureaucrats.

When the top students graduated from the faculty of law at Tokyo University and joined the finance ministry, a second process of selection lasting three decades started. Ministry officials retired at the age of fifty-five, which was when their second career began, advising and sometimes heading financial institutions in the private sector.

This second career, marked by material comforts and generous retirement benefits, was known as *amukadari* in Japanese, or descent from heaven. The expression is somewhat paradoxical, as the daily life of a finance ministry official was far from heaven. The workload was never ending, the salaries were modest, and the housing was simple and often involved long commutes to the office. The old Ministry of Finance building in Tokyo was dusty and congested. Up-and-coming officials became "generalists," passing from one section to another and often getting stationed in provincial cities. Postings abroad—to the IMF or World Bank in Washington, to the Asian Development Bank in Manila, or to Japanese embassies that nearly always had their own finance ministry representative—were rare and brief.

But heaven was the seat of power in the administrative mythology inherited from China. The bursting of the bubble nevertheless progressively transformed the ministry into a citadel of incompetence with scandals and attacks on its wide-ranging powers. At the same time, however, it could be comforted by the knowledge that it had friends in high places. In 1998, more than eighty retired ministry officials had seats in the lower and upper houses of Parliament (notably former prime minister Kiichi Miyazawa, who joined the ministry during the war and was serving his second stint as finance minister more than half a century later).

At the same time, another two hundred retired ministry officials were running various financial institutions across Japan.

Japanese bureaucrats were not necessarily better than the public auditors who went on to monopolize top management positions in French banks. But for more than three decades, Japan didn't need bankers in the commercial sense. It needed administrators to oversee a tightly regulated system of allocating capital, and descending from heaven was one of the key elements to make sure the system worked smoothly.

But by the end of the 1990s, it appeared to be the major stumbling block to cleaning up the mess in the financial system. "The incentive to hold back against deregulation is strong as it jeopardizes future directorships," John Greenwood said.

Until the first bank failure in 1995, the finance ministry stuck to the line that it would never allow a single bankruptcy in the Japanese banking system. The policy was to get strong banks to take over weak ones, allowing them to continue business while restructuring their activities. The Japanese banking system would remain frozen in ice for half a century.

## HOOVER RULES IN TOKYO

"I've just come back from Tokyo. I could go on forever. But I'll say one thing only—I'm driven to despair," said David Roche, the iconoclastic economist of Independent Strategy, speaking in the machine-gun oratory he developed as a young communist militant at Trinity College in Dublin.

Despair best expressed the feeling of anyone waiting for the Japanese government to do something. With the Asian crisis, Washington thought it had found a new lever to lift Tokyo out of its political and bureaucratic inertia. Larry Summers, the deputy secretary of the U.S. Treasury, coined a new term—the "virtual" Japanese economy. Even as the rest of Asia came tumbling down around it, the Japanese politicians were unperturbed and still pursuing their policy of patience. Economists and editorialists alike urged them to be decisive like Ronald Reagan. But they preferred to stick to Herbert Hoover.

The comparison between the government of Prime Minister Ryutaro Hashimoto in 1997 and the Hoover administration during the onset of the Great Depression in the early 1930s was made by Kenneth Courtis of Deutsche Bank. "In April 1997, Japanese officials wanted to prove that Herbert Hoover was not wrong by raising taxes during a period of crisis without provoking a recession," he said. The remarks by Courtis would tour the world before coming back to Japan a year later when Sony president Norio Ohga denounced the impotence of the country's politicians. In unusually harsh comments for a Japanese business leader of his stature, Ohga compared Hashimoto with Hoover and warned that the Japanese economy was "on the verge of collapsing."

As part of the finance ministry's plan to "rebuild public finances," the government of Hashimoto agreed to raise the consumption tax from three percent to five percent beginning in April 1997. The tax itself was only introduced in 1989 after a long battle between politicians and the finance ministry, which wanted to broaden the tax base to cope with the dramatic challenge facing Japan—the accelerated aging of its population in the early part of the twenty-first century.

The budget bureau, the most powerful arm of the finance ministry, was never happy with three percent that was a compromise in the negotiations with politicians back in the second half of the 1980s. And the bureau seized the chance when Hashimoto, a former finance minister, was appointed prime minister. The result was a disaster—after an artificial consumption boom before the tax took effect in April, household spending plunged and GDP receded eleven percent in the June quarter. The timing couldn't have been worse—Japan was returning to the earlier stagnation of the 1990s at the same time as the financial fury started hitting other Asian economies.

The saddest thing was that a large part of the deficit in public finances was due to the inappropriate medicine prescribed for the economy when the bubble burst. The loose monetary policy pursued by the Bank of Japan didn't lead to a sustained recovery in the absence of determined action to clean up the banking mess. In an effort to revive the economy, successive governments instead launched massive public works programs, damaging the environment while enriching the coffers of political figures.

But budget subsidies had the same effect on an economy as drugs given to Chinese swimmers at the time—performance dropped when they were taken away. With the exception of 1996, Japan's economy crawled along for most of the 1990s with growth hovering around one percent a year.

## MARKETS AT LAST?

Given such a dismal performance, it was clear that Japan was suffering from something more commonly associated with Latin countries—bad government. Hopes faded of reforming politics to become a focus of competence and authority. The opposition vaporized after a brief spell in power in the mid-1990s, and the old guard, represented by the coalition between politicians and bureaucrats, was unable to find a way out of the labyrinth.

The most lucid Japanese like Toyoo Gyohten realized that the initiative was not going to come from the top. "This time around, changes will not have to come from some self-generated desire to change and not through high hopes of becoming a different country but from the sheer changes that the market will force into the Japanese economy," he said.

Japan had a foretaste in November 1997 when the financial system came close to exploding, the banks of the world's biggest creditor nation being reduced to the status of pariahs of the international financial market. Public opinion came to realize that a statement by a credit-rating agency had more influence on the course of events than all the efforts employed by the bureaucracy. "Nobody could help us. Markets can kill any institution when they become so ferocious. For many Japanese, it was a revelation," Gyohten said.

"Reform will not come from Japan's own initiative but it will be forced upon us by the market—not through gaiatsu. It will be quite real and extend far deeper than those piecemeal changes we had before."

Japan faced a "real collapse of the old system," he said.

CHAPTER SEVEN

# Mr. Yen Makes a Confession

"The U.S.-Japan relationship is the most important bilateral
relationship in the world, bar none."
— *Mike Mansfield, U.S. ambassador to Japan*
*from 1977 to 1988*

By late 1997, the Asian crisis had emphasized the need to rebuild financial systems across the region. The buzzwords were transparency, accurate statistics, allocating resources based on returns, opening to foreign financial institutions, and continuing to allow the free movement of capital. These themes ran through the IMF adjustment programs that some Asian countries were adopting. So it wasn't a bad time to ask that nagging question—why did Japan let seven years elapse from when the bubble burst before announcing plans to throw itself fully into deregulation from April 1998?

"Better late then never" was the reply. The argument was poor but true. But it wasn't Eisuke Sakakibara at his best.

In the comedy of Japanese power, Sakakibara played the role of the "bureaucrat not like the others." His abrupt comments, displays of nationalism, and bursts of laughter made him a favorite with both the local and international media. As vice minister of finance responsible for international affairs in the MoF, he had the nickname of "Mr. Yen."

With a bit of exaggeration, financial market participants followed by reporters gave him the nickname in 1995 and 1996 for his ability to move foreign exchange markets by uttering a few words. Everyone knew that remarks from top officials were an important government weapon to influence market sentiment. But the weapon had to be used with moderation and by early 1998, Sakakibara's words had lost much of their earlier power.

Sakakibara was not the first Japanese bureaucrat to enjoy being "different." One of the pioneers was Makoto Kuroda, an official with the MITI who was promoted to the top position of vice minister in the late 1980s. An imposing figure who spoke perfect English and loved French wines, Kuroda was the man who could tell Americans where to go during the innumerable trade clashes between Tokyo and Washington.

But several years were enough to achieve a complete turnaround. When Kuroda was vice minister in the late 1980s, Japanese success in the global marketplace had prompted what came to be known as "Japan bashing" among resentful Americans. The Japanese model, notably high savings, was held up as an example to address the problems faced by decadent Americans (without even mentioning those poor Europeans). The future of capitalism was in the East, as Ezra Vogel wrote in his book *Japan as Number One*.

But history was cruel. As the author of a book dedicated to the glory of Japanese capitalism, Sakakibara would later have the questionable privilege of having to explain the economic breakdown in Japan, considered the sickest of the leading industrialized countries by the end of the twentieth century.

Confronted by critics, Japan based its defense on a tried and true recipe— the promise of change. With a remarkable lack of imagination, the Land of the Rising Sun would announce a series of economic recovery plans, ritually unveiling them to international audiences attending the annual summits of the G7 industrialized countries.

Each new plan would be greeted by the sententious approval of Japan's G7 partners. There was still hope, after all. Japan also managed to keep its international audience guessing with the countless preliminary reports, intermediate reports, and final reports on various reforms promising better days. One of these was the Maekawa report, the work of a remarkable man called Haruo Maekawa, a former governor of the Bank of Japan. His clear-headed report was full of excellent ideas and was greeted with much fanfare in the late 1980s. He later died with virtually none of the ideas implemented.

## BIG BANG

"I'm doing something MoF officials shouldn't be doing, that is not in the nature of MoF officials," Sakakibara told an Asian conference organized by the World Economic Forum in Hong Kong in October 1997.

Sakakibara was indeed planning a "revolution" in Japan, going a lot further than any of his predecessors.

"There is a misperception about the Japanese bureaucracy, particularly MoF," the vice minister said. "MoF doesn't hold the ultimate power, it is not true. Public opinion has to be nurtured into accepting such a radical revolution."

Sakakibara nevertheless added: "We judged that public opinion was ready, and politicians as well."

So the subversive elements of the finance ministry were themselves taking credit for Japan's proposed "Big Bang," modeled on sweeping changes to the financial sector started in London in 1986.

Under the plan, Japan decided to maintain its gradual approach to reform with a three-year preparatory period stretching to April 2001. The thousands of pages of guidelines would also not break with Japanese tradition. "In Japan everything's forbidden unless it's specifically allowed, while in the West it's the reverse, everything is allowed unless it's forbidden," John Greenwood said.

Japan's Big Bang was nevertheless real, despite its limits. Barriers separating the activities of different types of financial institutions would be lowered or eliminated. Much of the plan was based on Japanese citizens being able to invest their savings freely, both in domestic and overseas markets.

In three words, the Big Bang would make things "free," "equal," and "global," injecting a heavy dose of competition into a system that until then had about as much liberty as a straitjacket.

The idea was to finally transform Tokyo into a real international financial center that matched the size of Japan's economy and its high level of savings. And along the way, it would have no choice but to adapt the "global norms" that it had resisted for so long.

Japan's capacity to resist change for such a long time could be traced back to 1984, when Japan and the United States signed their first agreement on financial liberalization, the so-called "Oba-Sprinkel Accord."

## THE COLLAPSE OF 1971

Of all financial markets, foreign exchange markets are by nature the most unstable. Beginning in the early 1970s, they expanded rapidly thanks to successive technological developments. Operating around the clock and ignoring international borders, daily turnover kept growing and averaged about one thousand billion dollars by the 1990s.

At regular intervals, the currency markets pulled the rug from under the feet of democratically-elected governments, prompting indignation from politicians and commentators that "something has to be done" to control this beast.

But it was governments themselves who created the animal. In August 1971, President Richard Nixon decided to suspend the dollar's convertibility into gold. That meant European central banks could no longer line up at the windows of the U.S. Federal Reserve Board and exchange the dollars accumulating in their official reserves for American gold being held at Fort Knox.

The president knew the United States could no longer finance its war in Vietnam and bankroll the rest of the world at the same time. The Bretton Woods system of exchange rates, built on the smoking ruins of World War II, had survived up until then. It would soon be replaced by a "nonsystem"—the market where rates fluctuated and traders were kings.

Technically, America was bankrupt. The massive pile of dollars circulating around the world represented a financial claim on the United States, a claim the Americans were hardly about to meet. But despite some German grumbling and mutterings from the French, nobody was seriously considering making a fuss—the United States provided the nuclear umbrella against the Soviet Union, and Red Army tanks were only a day's drive from the Rhine.

The collapse of the Bretton Woods system announced by Nixon on August 15 led to a sharp decline in the dollar's value against other currencies. By the end of 1971, the yen and the currencies of other industrialized nations had risen fifteen percent against the dollar.

The United States was the world's biggest economic power by far. Europe was divided and Japan was dependent. Moreover, the U.S. economy was less exposed to the rest of the world with external trade accounting for only ten percent of GNP. Seen from Washington, the dollar's rate of exchange against the mark, the pound, the franc, or the yen was a minor preoccupation. And ensuring the external stability of the dollar was in those days not a major concern for the Federal Reserve, which was more interested in containing inflation and maintaining economic growth. "The dollar is our currency but it's your problem," one American official told whining Europeans at the time. Benign neglect was the privilege of Imperial America.

But times changed and by the early 1980s, America was on the road to becoming an international bum, forced to carry its begging bowl abroad to get enough to survive on every month. The twin deficits—in the budget and the current account—were like millstones hanging around its neck. Banker to the rest of the world at the end of World War II, America had become crippled by ballooning public debt and plunging savings rates while inflation was a serious threat.

The man who put an end to all this was a debonair gentleman called Paul Volcker, who was chairman of the Federal Reserve Board. Volcker was a giant—in terms of height as well as intellect—and raised interest rates sharply in 1981, triggering a deep recession. The secondary effect—worth remembering when examining the causes of Asia's crisis in 1997—was that the higher interest rates triggered the Latin American debt crisis, with Mexico collapsing in 1982.

At the same time, deep structural reforms were being carried out by the administration of Republican President Ronald Reagan—the B-movie actor and former governor of California who had recently been converted to supply-side economics. But the reforms wouldn't really bear fruit until 1998 when Democrat President Bill Clinton was able to draw up a federal budget with a surplus for the first time in a quarter of a century.

But the high interest rates—combined with the sharp rebound in U.S. economic activity from 1983—sent the dollar sailing to record heights against other currencies. A series of all-time highs were set in February 1985 with the dollar soaring above three marks at one stage.

The soaring dollar was meanwhile undoing the previous decade's efforts to correct the cardinal error committed by the Americans—letting Japan benefit for such a long time from the ridiculously low exchange rate set at the end of the war.

The advisors of General Douglas MacArthur set the rate at 360 yen to the dollar during the Allied Occupation, against the advice of some American economists who argued that the rate was too favorable to Japan. But in the smoking ruins of the Pacific War, who could have imagined at that time that Japanese industry would be taking on American companies on their own turf thirty years later. Detroit and Pittsburgh were already dying—and the dollar's surge would be the final nail in the coffin for American industry as foreign competitors moved in, led by Japan.

Washington eventually started listening to the complaints of American industry and unions about the strong dollar, which was threatening to unleash a protectionist backlash.

And with the change in police came a change in the men running the Treasury with James Baker, the pragmatic Texan, succeeding Donald Regan, the Wall Street "gnome" and high disciple of the market.

Big, elegant, sure of himself, and extremely brutal when he wanted to be, James Baker had an innate sense of how to use the media and court public opinion. He showed his skills off to the Israelis in his subsequent position as secretary of state.

## THE PLAZA ACCORD

To proclaim the radical change in White House policy toward the dollar to the whole world, Baker decided to drag the Group of Five out of its complacent obscurity. Although it sounded like something out of children's literature, this was actually the title given to the finance ministers and central bank governors of the world's leading industrialized countries—the United States, Japan, Germany, France, and Britain. The choice was no accident these were the countries whose currencies made up the "basket" that determined special drawing rights (SDR's), the unit of account used by the International Monetary Fund.

On September 22, 1985, members of the G5 walked out of a suite in the Plaza Hotel in New York to read a statement to the waiting media.

What did the statement say? Basically, that the five countries were going to take concerted action in foreign exchange markets and that "some further orderly appreciation of the main nondollar currencies against the dollar is desirable."

For the Republican administration, this was a change in attitude toward the market—government intervention was now okay, as long as it was under certain conditions. If the timing was right and central banks acted together, intervention had the ability to influence this four hundred-kilogram gorilla that the foreign exchange market had become. The principle was the same as *aikido*—using the weaknesses of your opponent to topple him. And the dollar had already started to weaken when the G5 stepped into the ring.

But the Plaza Accord had another dimension, well described by Makoto Utsumi who was counselor for the Japanese finance ministry at the Japanese embassy in Washington at the time.

"The second significance of the Plaza Accord is that major countries started to implement a new strategy. It was to prepare a theater for the audience called 'the markets' and to send effective signals through it.... Up until then, although the G5 had been playing a significant role, its presence was typically never exposed openly to the public. But the G5 that gathered at the Plaza Hotel played a magnificent drama that astounded the markets."

In fact, it was so successful that Italy and Canada insisted on getting up on the stage too by virtue of the fact that their prime ministers took part in the annual summit of seven industrialized countries. Italy and Canada had no technical qualifications—their currencies weren't in the SDR basket—but the summit in Tokyo in 1986 nevertheless decided to expand the group that became the G7. As Utsumi pointed out, "the Plaza Accord is actually the first and last communiqué that came out from the G5 finance ministers and central bank governors of the G5."

By the late 1990s, Utsumi presented himself as a modest professor of international finance at Keio University in Tokyo, advising major stockbroker Nikko Securities in his spare time. But having also served a two-year stint as vice minister for international affairs at the finance ministry, Utsumi was a close advisor to former Prime Minister Ryutaro Hashimoto, himself a former finance minister. And as one of the architects of the Big Bang, he was one of the most influential figures on the Japanese financial scene as the twentieth century drew to a close.

"The third impact of the Plaza G5 is that it clearly stated that macroeconomic policy coordination and concerted actions in foreign exchange markets were as indispensable as the two wheels of a bicycle in order to achieve stability in the foreign exchange markets while reflecting economic fundamentals," Utsumi said.

This was the real change at the time. Suddenly, the major economic powers of the world institutionalized the "right to meddle" in each others' affairs in public. The change recognized the powers of markets and the need to maintain an open dialogue. It also recognized that economic sovereignty didn't stop at borders, and that countries had to be aware of the impact of their behavior on their neighbors and partners.

Looking at each others' economic policies was not new—the practice already existed within the IMF, the OECD, and the G5 itself. But the fact that this was now taking place in public—in full view of the international press and especially the financial markets—would change everything.

The principles of the Plaza Accord were borne out by experience. These were negative in the case of 1987 when the United States and Germany clashed publicly over monetary policy, triggering the crash of Wall Street that year. But they were also positive in the sense that relations among North America, Europe, and Japan progressively stabilized. Talks on the coordination of economic policies focussed attention on structural factors behind growth. The United States was forced to take note—nothing more—of criticisms that its low savings rates were a major factor behind external imbalances. With Britain having distanced itself after the Thatcher revolution, the continental European countries meanwhile accepted questioning over the rigidities of their labor markets as unemployment soared to record highs. And Japan, under constant attack for its huge trade surpluses, produced a series of plans to boost domestic demand while promising to…change.

But Japan either couldn't or wouldn't adapt its behavior to the new international environment for fifteen years. In the United States, Reaganomics deregulated the transport, telecommunications, and finance industries. The information society was born with Microsoft, Intel, and others leading the way, and traditional industries were restructured. For Europe, the results were not less impressive but focussed on modifying institutional arrangements—moving toward the single market and monetary union, absorbing the shock to German reunification, and opening the borders to the East.

And while all this was going on in America and Europe, Japan resisted change.

## A PATHOLOGICAL RELATIONSHIP

"The U.S.-Japanese relationship is the most important one bilateral relationship in the world, bar none," Mike Mansfield liked repeating. Mansfield occupied the American ambassador's residence in the hills of Akasaka in central Tokyo for more than a decade. But the relationship had its roots in the U.S.-led Allied occupation of Japan from 1945 to 1952, and was deeply unbalanced, sometimes neurotic, and always subject to periodic crises of intense passion. The Americans wanted Japan to be like the United States—open, democratic, and transparent. And the Japanese perpetuated the attitude adopted during the occupation—arching its back, accepting the appearance but not the reality of change, and basically following to the letter the prescription of Tancrede in *The Leopard*, the novel by Italian writer Giuseppe Lampedusa: "Everything must change so everything stays the same."

On the economic front, the United States and Japan were the two sides of the same problem that was the huge imbalance between the world's two biggest economies. Japan's surplus in savings was the driving force behind its powerful export machine and the chronic deficit in savings in the United States turned Americans into gluttons for imports.

By contrast, relations between America and Europe were remarkably balanced over the longer term.

With capital flows, the relations between the United States and Japan were identical. Japan's surplus savings financed America's budget deficits. And when it wasn't Japanese investors, notably life insurance companies, buying United States Treasury bonds, the Bank of Japan would step in.

The tragedy of the affair was that Mike Mansfield was right—this pathological relationship between the two big economies dominated international economic relations with deeply destabilizing effects for other countries. A relatively stable area like Europe could protect itself from the fallout of this tormented relationship and was one of the strongest arguments for putting European economic and monetary union in place.

But the fragile emerging economies of Southeast Asia found themselves overwhelmed when they were hit by the fallout one fine day in the middle of 1997.

## ENDAKA

Thirteen years earlier, Tsutomu Oba was a distant predecessor of Sakakibara as vice minister of finance for international affairs. Oba and his American counterpart, Beryl Sprinkel, number two in the Treasury, signed an agreement known as the yen-dollar accord in 1984. Under the deal, also known as the Oba-Sprinkel agreement, Japan agreed to deregulate its financial system, notably by accepting a timetable for liberalizing interest rates. The Americans were trying to strike at the heart of the Japanese system—poor returns of Japanese savings that were being allocated in an authoritarian manner by the ministries of finance and trade to the Japanese export industry.

At the same time, Washington was exerting pressure on Tokyo to dismantle—sector by sector—various tariff and nontariff trade barriers that made the Japanese market an impregnable fortress. The Japanese procrastinated over implementing the yen-dollar accord to defend their protectionist citadel—house by house and street by street.

With the Plaza Accord in 1985, the Americans brought the monetary weapon into play. And they didn't stop using it for another ten years. The yen was worth 360 to the dollar when the Bretton Woods systems collapsed in 1971, the same rate imposed after the war. By February 1985, the currency had strengthened to 260 yen to the dollar. And by 1995, it had risen as high as 80 yen to the dollar.

During this period, the high yen—known as *endaka* in Japanese—profoundly affected monetary policy and industrial strategy in Japan. To reduce the initial shock in the second half of the 1980s, the Bank of Japan adopted an easier monetary stance that was too loose and maintained for far too long.

The era of cheap money unleashed the bubble economy, characterized by galloping "asset price" inflation that sent the price of shares and property skyrocketing.

At the same time, Japanese industry started shifting to cheaper locations to offset the higher costs of production at home. Japanese production facilities were soon sprouting like mushrooms across paddy fields in Southeast Asia. The main beneficiaries—Thailand, Malaysia, Indonesia, and the Philippines a bit later on—would become the focal point of the tempest unleashed in 1997.

In 1989, the Nikkei Stock Average of leading shares on the Tokyo Stock Exchange was still rising and approaching forty thousand points. Calculated in dollars, GNP per capita in Japan had surpassed that of the United States. Calculations showed the value of land occupied by the Imperial Palace in central Tokyo was worth more than all of the land in California. Japanese investors, armed with overvalued assets as collateral, embarked on a buying spree in the United States. Mitsubishi Real Estate, the premier landlord in Tokyo's business district, snapped up the Rockefeller Center in New York. Fifty years after Pearl Harbor, Japanese tourists and investors flocked to Hawaii. European artworks were suddenly popular, especially Impressionist paintings. Usually genuine but sometimes fake, they came out of their private collections and galleries in Europe to find themselves on the walls of Japanese financial institutions. One of Picasso's major works, Les Noces de Pierette, was moved to a prefabricated building at a Japanese car-racing track.

To put an end to this orgy, the Bank of Japan should have started tightening monetary policy from 1987. Unfortunately for Japan, the world stock market crash came along in October that year and the U.S. Federal Reserve led an international effort by central banks to inject massive amounts of liquidity into the system. The expected recession never happened and the world economy slowly got back on its feet. In Japan, the party was still going on.

Moreover, the Japanese party was being encouraged by the United States. Given the failure to achieve an authentic opening of the Japanese market, Washington insisted that stimulating domestic demand would whet Japan's appetite for imports. Excessively loose monetary policy and repeated stimuluses were substitutes for real policies of deregulation. Makoto Utsumi helped to try to get a "structural impediments initiative" between Tokyo and Washington off the ground in the late 1980s and early 1990s. It was a quid pro quo arrangement along the lines of America consuming less in exchange for Japan saving less. After a few difficult rounds of negotiations, the initiative got bogged down by a lack of goodwill on both sides.

## MIENO BURSTS THE BUBBLE

After the party, the hangover. The painful awakening came in 1990 when the governorship of the Bank of Japan passed from Satoshi Sumita, a former finance ministry man, to central bank veteran Yasushi Mieno under an unwritten rule whereby the two institutions took it in turns to be governor.

The reversal of monetary policy was brutal—Mieno raised the official discount rate in five stages from two percent to more than five percent. The bubble burst. The Nikkei Stock Average dived to a series of new lows, and property prices collapsed in the Kanto area around Tokyo and also in the Kansai area around Osaka, Kobe, and Kyoto. Thousands of speculators and tens of thousands of dubious transactions were suddenly exposed.

The balance sheets of Japanese banks were devastated as bad debts mushroomed. But the bad debts wouldn't see the light of day and would remain buried in their accounts. Led by the finance ministry, the banks began a gigantic camouflage operation.

One paradox was that the monetary manipulation organized by the Americans and the Japanese in 1985 hadn't changed much in terms of the imbalances between the two countries. True, the Japanese current account deficit had been halved from four percent of GNP to two percent. But in terms of value, the U.S. deficit with Japan was still massive whereas its deficit with Europe had practically disappeared. China would start replacing Europe as a major source of friction with the United States from 1993, with the Chinese trade surplus with the United States eventually overtaking the Japanese surplus.

In February 1993, President Bill Clinton succeeded George Bush, putting a Democrat in the White House for the first time in twelve years. But the economy was still in a cyclical recession—the recovery would come a few months too late for the unfortunate Bush—and frictions with Japan resumed.

"As soon as the new administration was in place, U.S. officials—through their repeated 'strong yen talk'—triggered an appreciation of the yen," Utsumi said. "This became the major single element that caused the Japanese economy to drop to its lowest level. Setting aside the argument of whether the U.S. administration officials intentionally used the 'strong yen card' to put pressure on Japan in the context of various bilateral issues, it is clear that these statements by U.S. officials had a tremendous influence on the markets. Many economists who saw the dollar suddenly dropping from the 125 yen level to 100 then 90 and then 80 tried to explain and justify this phenomenon *posteriori*. However, nobody was able to explain this sudden surge of the Japanese yen against the dollar by economic fundamentals. This was a period in which the U.S. economy, in contrast to the Japanese, was showing a strong performance. Moreover, the very peculiar incidents we have witnessed—in which each time Japanese political instability was exposed…the yen strengthened—showed to which degree the foreign exchange markets had been influenced by the 'strong yen card' of the U.S. government. And this 'strong yen card' myth lived in the markets for quite some time, continuously influencing them. We had to await the U.S.-Japan concerted intervention of the beginning of July 1995 to see its end."

This joint intervention was what Kenneth Courtis of Deutsche Bank called the Reverse Plaza Accord.

By the middle of 1995, the Japanese banking system was about to implode. The problem of bad debts hadn't receded with the passage of time. It got worse thanks to an internal process put in place with the complicity of the finance ministry. To avoid having to make provisions for losses, the banks artificially supported their bad clients by lending them more money to pay off their debts. The practice exacerbated the problems already caused by legislation that was lax in identifying nonperforming loans.

Bad debts snowballed. The assets used as collateral for loans had seen their value collapse after the bubble burst. Property prices in the Tokyo area plunged seventy percent. Bank vaults were bursting with overvalued European paintings that couldn't be sold on the international art market except at a loss. With the disappearance of Japanese speculators, the art market had come down to earth.

The Nikkei Stock Average sank to new depths and the unrealized gains on securities held by Japanese financial institutions evaporated. Japanese banks, like their foreign competitors, were subject to the "Cooke ratio," named after Bank of England official Peter Cooke who headed the bank supervisory committee within the BIS in Basel in the 1980s. One of the reasons behind the ratio was to force banks, notably poorly capitalized Japanese banks that were rapidly expanding at the time, to limit their lending in relation to the size of their capital.

The ratio required banks with international operations to have capital equivalent to at least eight percent of their risk-weighted assets, meaning that banks that were poorly capitalized had to raise more capital or reduce their lending.

Although many Japanese banks raised fresh capital, the stock market's collapse was a source of new pressure as they were allowed to include unrealized gains on securities holdings as assets when calculating their ratio. Put simply, if the Nikkei fell below certain levels—estimated at anywhere between fifteen thousand points and twelve thousand points—falling stock prices would "break the banks" in the true sense of the expression.

For the Americans, Japan had entered the "danger zone" in the middle of 1995. Pushed any further, Japanese financial institutions might liquidate their most precious assets—U.S. Treasury bonds.

The consequences of Japanese selling were simple to see—a sharp increase in U.S. interest rates that would threaten the economy's continued expansion just when Clinton was trying to get elected for a second term.

On several occasions in the past, the Japanese had become so fed up with American behavior that they indicated they could always use this trump card.

But the threat of Japanese financial institutions liquidating their holdings of American paper was never taken too seriously.

Besides, it was the Japanese government itself and not just private institutions that took part in the Treasury's monthly auctions between 1993 and 1995. In a desperate bid to halt the yen's surge, the Bank of Japan bought dollars by the fistful. Within eighteen months, the country's foreign exchange reserves jumped from sixty billion dollars to two hundred billion dollars. Japan used the dollars to buy American government debt.

## THE BANKS CREAK

Before long, ten years had passed since the Plaza Accord. The Land of the Rising Sun was screaming for mercy and the first cracks started appearing in the financial system. A couple of small institutions, Cosmo Credit and Kizu Credit, went bust in mid-1995. Their demise was followed by the failure of Hyogo Bank, a mid-sized regional bank.

The international financial community had grown wary of Japan. When Japanese banks wanted to borrow funds in the interbank market abroad, they were forced to pay higher rates than their American and European rivals, including such respected institutions as Tokyo-Mitsubishi Bank and Sumitomo Bank. The "Japan Premium" widened to fifty basis points or half a percentage point in October 1995, although it would be much higher by the time the Asian financial storm rolled around two years later.

Back in April, a G7 meeting of finance ministers and central bank governors in Washington indicated that the yen's surge had come to an end and that a stronger dollar was desirable. The message was confirmed in Canada in June when leaders of the seven industrialized nations held their annual summit in Halifax.

The determining factor was the staggering commitment of the joint market intervention by the Federal Reserve Bank of New York and the Bank of Japan.

And at the same time, the Bank of Japan was lowering interest rates to ease pressures on banks.

When November rolled around, it was time for Makoto Utsumi to host the sole celebration of the tenth anniversary of the Plaza Accord. Given the price Japan had to pay at the alter of international financial cooperation, such a celebration seemed a bit odd. But the decision to hold the gathering reflected the influence of this unassuming man. Whenever he had the chance, Utsumi would travel to Kyoto to seek refuge in the serenity of Daisen-in, the jewel of Daitoku-ji, a group of temples in the northeastern part of the former imperial capital. Utsumi was not only a soldier-monk in his retirement, he was also a monk, period.

Three of the five finance ministers who signed the Plaza Accord turned up for the anniversary in Tokyo—James Baker from the United States,

Noboru Takeshita from Japan, and Nigel Lawson from Britain. Utsumi gave a moving speech for the late Pierre Beregovoy, the former French finance minister who committed suicide after becoming prime minister many years after the Plaza Accord. Gerhard Stoltenberg, the German finance minister who put his name to the G5 statement, had left the political scene after a scandal in his electoral region of Schleswig-Helstein. Among others who showed up were the IMF's Michel Camdessus and Satoshi Sumita, the former Japanese central bank governor who had the courage to admit his mistake in keeping interest rates too low for too long after the yen's initial appreciation.

The meeting provided a chance to visit Eisuke Sakakibara, who had moved to the vast office of the director-general of the finance ministry's international finance bureau. The office—with its ancient furniture, the lace on the armchairs and the electronic real-time display showing the yen's latest value against the dollar—was familiar. It was formerly occupied by Utsumi and before that Gyohten back in the 1980s.

The misery was ostentatious in this grim-looking gray building in Kasumigaseki, the area in central Tokyo where most ministries are located. The walls were flaking, the lighting was dreary, and the red carpet on the stairs and corridors leading to the offices of senior officials was threadbare. The offices of various officials still had their cheap little wooden signs with handwritten titles in Japanese—and English for the *gaijin* who ventured to places like the International Finance Bureau. The men who keep the country's accounts believed in open displays of stinginess.

"What we're doing is simple. We'll transfer five thousand billion yen a year to Japanese banks. This will allow them to resolve their bad-debt problems in two or three years," Sakakibara said. Subsequent events would show he was way off the mark.

Within time, Japanese interest rates fell to record lows. The Bank of Japan's official discount was lowered to 0.5 percent, which was unprecedented anywhere. Banks could raise funds more cheaply than ever before lending to clients at higher rates. The banks could also invest in higher yielding foreign bonds, earning additional funds from exchange-rate gains if they were denominated in dollars. This was the five thousand billion yen Sakakibara was talking about.

## WHEN ELEPHANTS DANCE...

All this was well and good. But when they decided to reverse policy, did the two giants on either side of the Pacific think about the consequences for Southeast Asia? Model students of the IMF, these countries had pegged their currencies to the dollar in exchange-rate arrangements that were more or less rigid. The value of the Thai baht was set by a basket of currencies. Its composition was secret but it was dominated by the dollar with the yen playing a minor role. The Indonesian rupiah meanwhile fluctuated within a sliding range.

"Thailand's more or less forced devaluation is not a one-off accident," Michael Taylor said on July 2, 1997, the day the currency was floated. The chief economist at Indosuez W. I. Carr in Hong Kong said Thailand was merely the latest Asian country to submit to harrowing change in response to forces outside its control.

The reversal in yen-dollar exchange rates meanwhile triggered a chain reaction in Northeast Asia. Producer prices in China started falling in mid-1995. In South Korea in 1996, the central bank let the won slide from 770 won to the dollar to 840 won at the end of the year. Currencies in Vietnam and Myanmar also came under pressure in 1997, signaling that the tsunami unleashed from Japan was being felt in distant corners of Southeast Asia. In Taiwan, central bank authorities signaled a more accommodating policy to let the currency ease against the dollar.

"The Thai devaluation, however, trains the spotlight firmly on the rest of ASEAN," Taylor said on July 2. "There is now every sign that the pattern of devaluation and/or deflation that started in the high value-added economies of Japan and carried on through Korea and (recently) Taiwan—and which has also passed on to the lower value-added economies of China and Vietnam—now has sufficient critical mass to make it very unlikely that the rest of ASEAN will remain unscathed."

If it was true that nobody knew about the scale of the assault that was about to break, it must be said that some were more clairvoyant than others.

## IN THE DOCK

The tempest in Asia was a blessing for those who denigrated the Japanese model. Hit by repeated scandals, the jaded and arrogant bureaucrats of the finance ministry became the targets of investigation and sarcasm from the Japanese press. They also became the global punching bag at international financial conferences. Eisuke Sakakibara himself had to endure an ear bashing at the annual World Economic Forum in the Swiss ski resort of Davos in early 1998.

Suddenly, the old members of the "Japan Bashing" clubs were being swamped with new members like Merton Miller, winner of the Nobel Prize for economics.

"In an attempt to restore Japanese bank capital, the lawyers who ran the Japanese Ministry of Finance had a choice of strategies. They could have insisted that the banks write off the bad loans and raise more capital. But both strategies would have damaged the existing stockholders and forced them to share their control with foreigners. Instead, MoF adopted another strategy that, unfortunately, destabilized the rest of Southeast Asia. The Japanese opted for a strategy of driving down short-term interest rates—and drive them down they did, to levels not seen since the Depression years of the United States in the 1930s."

"The only cloud hovering over such a strategy would be an unexpected rise in the yen, but that was unlikely given the depressed condition of the Japanese economy. And under the pressure of that depression, plus the low interest rates, the yen kept falling," the University of Chicago professor said.

"And now we can put our finger on the real culprit for the financial crises in Southeast Asia—the low and falling yen, the deliberate policy of MoF to let the yen go," Miller said. "The real trouble is on the other side of the coin of a falling yen, namely a rising dollar. Thailand and other countries in Southeast Asia had linked their currencies to the dollar. As the yen fell and the dollar rose, currencies linked to the dollar therefore inevitably seemed overvalued and ripe for attack."

A year and a half later, Sakakibara had another confession. In an interview with The Australian Financial Review in June 1999, he admitted that it was "true" that the sudden weakening of the yen in 1995 helped trigger the Asian crisis. "We should have coordinated with the other Asian countries. But that didn't occur to me at the time," Sakakibara said.

## FEAR OF THE FUTURE

The Asian crisis was the price to pay for the difficulties Japan and the United States experienced in trying to integrate their economic systems more closely. Both nations repeatedly showed that the questioning of long-held practices and vested interests would trigger resistance that was sometimes impossible to overcome. Efforts to reform American banking legislation, for example, had been a monster lurking around the corridors of Congress for decades.

In Japan, the bubble was a consequence of rejecting, at least since the early 1980s, the profound mutations that prevented its integration into the world economy. "Why was the bubble created?" asked Keio University economist Sahoko Saji in early 1998. "Because everyone wanted it."

Why was Japan resigned to accepting these mutations at the end of the 1990s when it was certain that rejecting them fifteen years earlier was the right way to go? Because certainty vanished with the bursting of the bubble, prolonged stagnation, and the threat of implosion when the Asian crisis hit in 1997.

Most Japanese were apprehensive about the new environment. Its value wasn't clear. The old structures of mutual dependence that permeated Japanese society were being weakened. Skyrocketing unemployment, a sign of change, saw the jobless rate jump to a forty-five-year high in 1998, the same level when Japan was still picking itself up from World War II.

As for the United States, which was supposed to embody this new model, Toyoo Gyohten noted a "very deep-rooted sense of resistance"—not just among Japanese, but other Asians as well. "No Asian would really believe that, even if we try very hard, we can convert ourselves into pure Americans. This is a new type of Asian dilemma.

"We are desperately looking to Europe to get a clue on how we can maintain our way of life while being competitive. Are the Europeans really succeeding in reforming themselves and maintaining their own values? Many Asians still doubt it," the former vice minister said.

His remarks were echoed by Sahoko Saji. "Even if Tokyo does succeed in becoming a financial center, not everything is going to be rosy," the economist said. "The fact remains that every aspect of Japanese society and economy must change. This is the end of Japan as we know it."

# Enjoy Your Meal,
# Mr. Summers...

---

"We're witnessing an invasion of foreign capital, especially from
America. A sort of colonization of Asia has begun."
—*Hiromu Nonaka, secretary general of Japan's*
*Liberal Democratic Party (LDP)*

Larry Summers had a nimble mind in a cumbersome body. During closed-
door meetings of finance ministers and central bank governors from the G7
industrialized countries, the Deputy Secretary of the U.S. Treasury would pass
his time "stuffing his face with candy and other junk food," one regular par-
ticipant said. The more agitated Summers got, the more he ate. The number-
two man in the Treasury would then drown all of this with copious amounts
of Diet Coke. His silhouette was a fitting tribute to this gluttonous appetite.

But Summers didn't just crave physical nourishment. The former Harvard
professor, who once served as chief economist at the World Bank, also had a
fine mind—and didn't mind showing it off with a certain degree of arrogance. And Summers obviously couldn't help but give lessons to the people
he was talking with. "When you meet Larry, you always get the impression
you're taking an exam," said a senior French official and long-time resident
of Washington. And the economic brain of the Clinton team never stepped
away from a good controversy. His style could be unpleasant—and not just
for foreigners. Numerous veterans of the department were said to have quit
when he joined Treasury.

But in his role as America's front man for international financial affairs,
Summers had to take on the role of "bad guy," leaving the "good guy" role

to his boss, Treasury Secretary Robert Rubin, the affable banker from Wall Street whom Summers would eventually succeed in 1999.

Relations among the United States and its main partners weren't always easy. The Europeans weren't docile students, especially the German Bundesbank and the duo that comprised the French Treasury and the Bank of France. Earlier clashes between the United States and France had died down by the end of the 1990s. Peter Sutherland, the former Irish head of the General Agreement on Tariffs and Trade (GATT) that preceded the World Trade Organization (WTO), once said he was surprised by the constant "anti-American" reactions of senior French officials. But such clashes shouldn't have been a surprise—they went back to Jacques Rueff, the man behind de Gaulle's policy of defending the gold standard.

America's problems weren't just with the Europeans. In the late 1980s, the number-two man in the Treasury was our Texan friend David Mulford, the former Saudi adviser who dealt with the French in Riyadh. He was now working for fellow Texan, U.S. Treasury Secretary James Baker. Mulford became the bête noire of the Japanese finance ministry that couldn't stand his abrasive style.

For Europeans and Japanese, there was something suspicious lurking behind the American pleas to open financial markets and liberalize capital flows—the voracious appetite of Wall Street giants ranging from the commercial banks like Citibank and Chase Manhattan to investment banks such as Merrill Lynch, Goldman Sachs, and Morgan Stanley.

## RETURN OF THE GI'S

Such fears appeared justified. Financial deregulation, launched in Europe with the "Big Bang" in London in 1986, allowed American companies to move onto the continent from the bridgehead established in Britain by Prime Minister Margaret Thatcher. And the presence of European companies on Wall Street was minimal, despite attempts such as the unfortunate experience between Paribas and Becker.

By 1997, Morgan Stanley ranked number one in France in the lucrative field of corporate advisory services and mergers, and acquisitions. The Americans moved into a French marketplace that had seen incoherent policies of nationalizations favoring mutually owned institutions followed by premature deregulation before a proper banking system was in place. The subsequent disaster at Credit Lyonnais, which would have collapsed if it hadn't been state owned, showed that Asia didn't have the monopoly on making mistakes.

Other European countries with banking cartels or more solid systems such as Germany, Switzerland, and Belgium put up a stronger resistance against the American invasion.

The Japanese record was even more worrisome. The time was long gone when Japan was a major presence in California banking and occupied the top ranks of lead managers in the eurobond market, carried by the bubble and the strong yen.

But the problem was simpler for Thailand, Indonesia, and South Korea. After the Asian financial fury passed in 1997, their banking systems no longer existed. The net value of assets was negative and most financial institutions were effectively dead. Rebuilding the banks was a top priority and foreign capital appeared inevitable.

China presented an interesting case. Their banking crisis was not less severe than countries hit directly by the storm like Indonesia. But it was basically a domestic problem—the government owing money to the government. In other words, the state-owned banks were weighed down by bad loans to state-owned enterprises. But in China too, the role of foreign capital in the financial system couldn't be ignored.

From Tokyo to Kuala Lumpur, East Asian economies had to respond quickly—under very difficult conditions—to the challenges of integrating themselves into the global financial system. For some, this was the equivalent of recolonization. Humiliated in Vietnam and unable to break through protectionist barriers, the Americans were seeking revenge. The GI's were replaced by investment banks. And the general was Larry Summers.

## SPIN DOCTORS

Asian public opinion could be at least partly comforted by U.S. propaganda— the returning American imperialists were not wearing battle dress but Brooks Brothers suits.

Since the Watergate scandal, when a couple of reporters from the *Washington Post* managed to bring down President Richard Nixon with their revelations, the American press had enjoyed an exceptional reputation, especially outside the United States. So-called "investigative reporting" was proposed as a model to young journalists. And the independence of the American press from the established power centers was upheld as a universal model.

But there were occasions when owners used their publications for personal interests. Witness Henry Luce, the founder of *Time* magazine, who gave unconditional support to Taiwan and the corrupt Chiang family dynasty.

Administrations in Washington also went out of their way to get the local and international media to serve their interests. The way they used—and manipulated—the media could be seen every year during the annual summits of leading industrialized countries. But when it came to information, quantity and quality weren't necessarily the same thing. The uninterrupted succession of briefings and statements, complemented by the phenomenal number of transcripts of every utterance by the president and his top lieutenants, were the signs of professionalism when it came to public relations. Delegations from other countries could never compete. American officials were often more accessible than their international counterparts. The environment was relaxed with the officials calling reporters by their first names. Did all this help journalists forge an independent and balanced view of the event? My long experience with the American press corps at these annual summits raises major doubts.

Under the headline "Swat Team From Washington," the U.S. magazine *Business Week* published in February 1998 a glowing portrait of Summers and his two right-hand men—David Lipton, the undersecretary for international affairs, and Timothy Geitner, the assistant secretary for international affairs. "How a U.S. Treasury trio helped to contain the Asian crisis," the subheading gushed.

"Even though the United States. is technically just following the IMF's lead, everyone looks to the United States to anchor any scheme to shore up Asia. That means Summers, Lipton, and Geitner have to use pressure, cajolery, and subtle prodding to move everyone into consensus," *Business Week* reported.

The image of the IMF being kicked around by the United States was a recurring theme among American journalists. And to maintain the image, history was often rewritten. But let's not forget that the "U.S.-led" bailout of Mexico in 1994-95 was, in fact, blocked by Congress itself. The United States only managed to save face—and Mexico its economy–thanks to IMF managing director Michel Camdessus. The American contribution was eventually financed from an old fund left over from the Cold War.

The IMF board of governors decided unanimously in 1996 to extend the five-year mandate of Camdessus for a third term. But *Newsweek* wouldn't have voted for him. Camdessus, the former head of the French Treasury and governor of the Bank of France, was a "colorless bean counter," it wrote a few weeks before the *Business Week* article appeared. "He's about as Asian as an escargot," the magazine reported as it questioned his credentials in resolving the regional crisis. The same issue of *Newsweek* carried an article written by Larry Summers himself under the headline "Riding to the Rescue" accompanied by a photograph of the cavalry riding to the rescue on horses. The theme—"Sustained American leadership can help build a new model of the region's economies." This sort of stuff was manna from heaven for Malaysian Prime Minister Mahathir Mohamad, whose rhetoric had increasingly included loud warnings of a "recolonization" of Asia by Westerners (although he never mentioned the horses).

American officials were aware of the dangers. At the same time, however, they had to galvanize public opinion and legislators who were reluctant and even hostile to the idea of the United States helping foreign countries.

"After the Mexican bailout, Congress made it clear it will not tolerate another administrative action like that," said Richard Holbrooke, the number-two man in the State Department during Clinton's first term.

Jeffrey Shafer, a former senior Treasury official who joined investment bank firm Salomon Smith Barney, said debates on relations between the IMF and the United States were directed toward domestic audiences. America's influence of the IMF was "intellectual influence mainly," he said. "We work very closely with the IMF and other governments as well. Our influence is very important when we have good ideas and we argue them well." But other issues are just as easily dismissed, such as America's frequent objections to the high salaries paid to IMF officials, a subject particularly close to its heart.

The United States controlled 18.2 percent of the IMF's capital—equivalent to the combined stake of Germany, France, Britain, and Italy. "We're four and they're all alone," said Jean Lemierre, head of the French Treasury. "The influence of the Americans reflects their weight. It's a strong influence but IMF policy is not only American."

Holbrooke, who joined investment bank Credit Suisse First Boston after leaving the State Department, agreed. "The United States does not control the IMF, contrary to what people believe," he said. Despite leaving the administration, Holbrooke remained an important foreign policy adviser to the Clinton administration, taking part in diplomatic missions to Cyprus and Kosovo. "I can assure you that the IMF speaks for itself," he said. With the IMF headquarters located a stone's throw from the White House, Holbrooke said he had witnessed several foreign leaders seeking U.S. support in their negotiations with Michel Camdessus. But according to him, such pleas were dismissed.

## LATE WAKE-UP CALL

Richard Holbrooke offered a more sober assessment of the U.S. response to the Asian crisis than the American press. "The United States was belated in recognizing the magnitude of the problem," he lamented in January 1998. Although the tempest erupted six months earlier when the Thai baht collapsed in July, Washington didn't wake up until October when Undersecretary of State Stanley Roth toured the region. And the United States didn't contribute a single penny to the multilateral package of 17.2 billion dollars arranged for Thailand. The Thais, close allies of the Americans, were bitter.

"The United States has an obligation to lead," Holbrooke said. That's what sole superpowers were supposed to do. But while "presidential leadership is a key variable in the U.S. system," such leadership did not take place in a void. It involved a process of reaching a consensus in the top levels of the administration on the relative importance of problems and how to solve them. The number one principle was to "resist the temptation to turn our backs on Asia," Holbrooke said. "We went through the Vietnam catastrophe, and within a few years we were back."

The Asian crisis once again highlighted a permanent contradiction in American foreign policy throughout the twentieth century—the opposition between the desire to be led by the world's leading military and economic power and the deeply isolationist sentiments among most citizens and a large number of politicians. The argument was always the same. Why can't the Asians help themselves? Why don't we put our own house in order first?

But according to Holbrooke, the objective reality was obvious. "For the first time, what is happening in this region is affecting the U.S. economy," he said. Even if the United States, like the Euro countries, was almost self sufficient with external trade accounting for only ten percent of its GNP, the microeconomic impact would be great, especially if there was a sudden influx of cheap imports from Asia. Moreover, Asia had become a big market for Americans ranging from the Boeing workers in Seattle to the farmers of the Midwest. And while American banks were less exposed to Asia than their Japanese and European rivals, a default in Asia would trigger just as much damage.

The second principle was that if something was in America's national interests, the president had to act against public opinion. Having negotiated the Dayton accords on Bosnia, Holbrooke spoke from experience—American troops were sent to the former Yugoslavia despite the opposition of seventy percent of Americans toward U.S. involvement in the Balkan quagmire. "Intervention in Bosnia was much too slow. It should have come much earlier but once it happened, it was decisive," Holbrooke said.

The third principle was that whatever happened, administration officials had to accept criticism both from home and abroad. Holbrooke recalled that Democrat President Harry Truman was attacked by the Republicans over the Marshall Plan and only managed to get it through Congress with dissident support from the other side of the House. The comparison was relevant as the banking systems in some Southeast Asian countries required reconstruction in much the same way as Asian countries that needed to be rebuilt after World War II. But the banks needed private capital, unlike the Marshall Plan, where public funds were used. "In order to get Congress on board, especially in the House, you need to make clear the benefits to their constituents," Holbrooke said.

In Asia, "we are blamed both ways," he added. "First we are too slow and we do too little. Then we are too fast and we do too much. That's the price of leadership and if I had to choose, I would prefer to be accused of too much leadership than for too little."

In early 1998, however, voices were rising against the return of American imperialism under the guise of the IMF. And not just in Kuala Lumpur, where this became the official government line of Prime Minister Mahathir Mohamad, and Jakarta, where the family of President Suharto was struggling to stay in power. Similar voices were being heard in Thailand and South Korea, two of America's closest allies in Asia.

Given the explosive social environments caused by soaring unemployment and massive poverty, such rhetoric was an additional headache for American leaders.

"If we had the 'Ugly Americans' like in the past, Congress will react in an emotional way," said Carla Hills, the U.S. Trade Representative in the Bush administration. But she also warned her compatriots against feeling too triumphant. "There is the idea shared by too many Americans that American capitalism is the only way to go and that Americans had it all right, which implies that the rest of the world had it all wrong."

Indeed, Mahathir referred to "ugly capitalism" in a virulent speech to a conference in Tokyo in June 1998. "People will show their resentment against those outsiders who will lord it over them once again," the Malaysian prime minister said. "Sooner rather than later, they will think of retaining control over their economies. They will regard this as a new war of liberation…There will be a kind of guerilla war which will not be good for anyone."

## LEAVE MY BANK ALONE!

The sensitive issue was the ownership of the financial system. Like the defense industry, government authorities tended to think of banking as a strategic sector. The feeling was particularly strong in postwar Europe and also in Asia as their economies emerged.

Direct ownership and control over credit was considered a necessary instrument of national politics. And the entry of foreigners was considered a threat to national independence—as Mahathir asserted in November 1997. "The moment you open up the financial market, these foreign banks come in and buy up the local banks," the Malaysian prime minister said. "Then we do not have local banks any more and we cannot make policy changes."

Mahathir's remarks were echoed in a discussion paper submitted to ASEAN financial officials ahead of a meeting of finance ministers in Kuala Lumpur in early December. "Countries may desire the existence of a strong domestic presence in the banking system as they would be more amenable to national aspirations and would stand by the country through good and bad times," the discussion paper said. "Hence, in understanding financial reform, countries would wish to ensure that their domestic institutions are not marginalized."

Political concerns coincided with the interests of local participants who lacked the capital and human resources as well as the technology to compete with the big international banks. Except for Hong Kong, all economies in East Asia maintained high formal and informal barriers against the entry of foreign financial institutions.

In Thailand, protectionist policies were virtually flagrant, with the central bank systematically refusing to grant full-banking licenses to foreign applicants to protect the fifteen local banks, mostly controlled by overseas Chinese families. In Japan, the dozens of foreign banks present were stuck with less than five percent of all lending as a result of the tangled web of interlocking shareholdings between companies where all corporate groups had their own main bank.

The results of protection in Japan were worse for the financial sector than for the industrial and agricultural sectors. At least in industry, Japan had world-class manufacturers. Japan's financial adventures abroad were a disaster.

In the Japanese banking industry, the absence of competition encouraged indifference to costs, negligence toward risks, moral complacency, and technological obsolescence. And in all East Asian countries, the belief among depositors and borrowers alike was that government guarantees extended to all practices, even the most questionable. It was clear that institutional reforms would not find a solid base without the injection of foreign competition.

"Subsidiaries of strong international institutions bring to the local market not only the financial strength of their parents—which aids in withstanding shocks—but also the established practices regarding accounting, disclosure, and risk assessment, which strengthens their operations," Carla Hills said. "These practices tend to be contagious in the good sense."

## THE WIMBLEDON EFFECT

"If you don't want foreigners, then suffer," declared Merton Miller following objections, even in Western ranks, to the idea that local banking systems should be recapitalized with foreign money, seen as a serious assault on the national sovereignty achieved over the past half century. But if Asian countries didn't accept such an historic upheaval, Miller said, they had to be ready to reduce their economies to a level that corresponded with their domestic capabilities.

No country in the region, starting with Japan, could escape this dilemma as the twentieth century drew to a close.

Sahoko Kaji, the economist at Keio University in Tokyo, called this the "Wimbledon" effect after the sacred shrine of the All England Tennis Club where tradition—including strawberries and whipped cream—survived despite the absence of British players. An alternative was the "J-League" scenario—the Japan League soccer championship that challenged the traditional dominance of Japanese sport by sumo wresting and baseball in the early 1990s by importing foreign mercenary soccer players from all corners of the world. For some Japanese, the question was whether the "Big Bang" deregulation measures would lead to the emergence of a Wimbledon or J-League model in the financial sector.

"If Tokyo becomes a 'Wimbledon'," Kaji wrote, "that means the location is still in Japan but that the players are all foreign. If Tokyo follows the J-League path, the companies will also remain Japanese but many foreigners will be employed by them. Consensus seems to be building that it will be the J-League. There is the language problem, and Tokyo just does not have the infrastructure of London, Singapore, or Hong Kong. If it succeeds in becoming a world financial center, it will resemble New York."

At the end of the day, it would no doubt be a mix of the two. In certain areas of financial activities, foreigners had already achieved—or were said to have achieved—extremely strong or dominant positions. But global activities would always be dominated by international financial institutions while domestic activities seemed destined to dominate local activities. "To have a foreign presence of ten or even twenty percent is quite normal," Toyoo Gyohten said. "The previous situation was not normal."

The stakes were obviously high, and not just for the foreign institutions that hoped to find a new El Dorado in Japan.

Some twelve thousand billion to thirteen thousand billion dollars in Japanese savings were involved. Japanese households saved for their extravagant American compatriots as well. But that was the problem—Japanese saved too much to enable the revival in domestic demand that the rest of Asia desperately needed. And the tendency to save more only increased with the fear of the future—not only the economic crisis itself, but the more long-term problem of the aging population. Forecasts showed that by 2015, Japan would have 61 people over the age of sixty for every one hundred people between the ages of twenty and sixty—double the ratio in the late 1990s. The result was that Japanese were saving more and more while the rest of the world was waiting for them to spend more. How would the Japanese get out of that mess? Simply by increasing the returns on savings—that averaged a miserable 2.5 percent a year from the early 1980s. The only way would be to allow the "wild" competition from foreign institutions.

## FOREIGN INVASION

By the end of 1997, the combination of financial difficulties, repeated scandals, and the rancor of Japanese investors had undermined the position of Japan's leading securities companies. Wall Street firms such as Merrill Lynch, Goldman Sachs, and Morgan Stanley started to move in. The failure of Yamaichi Securities provided an historical opportunity for Merrill Lynch—it picked up thirty branches and almost two thousand staff from one of the Big Four securities companies in Japan. For the first time, a foreign company was acquiring the distribution network that gave it direct access to the housewives who traditionally ran the finances of Japanese households. One of the most important measures in the Big Bang proposals was to deregulate commissions charged by stockbrokers.

By the middle of 1998, Yamaichi had disappeared from the ranks of the Big Four that had long dominated Japanese stockbroking. Nikko had entered into an alliance with Travelers, the American financial giant that owned Salomon Smith Barney. Nomura, the only Japanese securities firm considered capable of challenging foreign competitors in the international market, signed a strategic agreement with Industrial Bank of Japan (IBJ), widely seen as a defensive move. "It is important to defend our domestic market in cooperation with IBJ," Nomura president Junichi Ujiie said.

The foreign invasion even extended to life insurance and asset management in agreements that once would have been unimaginable in Japan's deeply xenophobic financial sector. In February 1998, GE Capital, the financial arm of the American industrial conglomerate, reached an agreement with Toho

Mutual that was struggling to contain a mountain of debt. Under the deal, 2.5 million policyholders of Toho Mutual were taken over by a joint venture that was ninety percent-owned by GE Capital. At the same time, Toho kept the old liabilities. In other words, the "bad" part of the company remained Japanese— and was declared insolvent in June 1999—while the "good" part of the company was taken over by the Americans. And in May of the same year, American Insurance Group, long established in Asia, got the green light to acquire Aoba, a company established to take over the assets of Nissan Mutual, the first Japanese insurance company to fail since World War II.

In the field of asset management, Bankers Trust tied-up with Nippon Credit Bank, and Fidelity Investments with three commercial banks while Marsh and McLennan reached an agreement with Nippon Life. The deals had all the appearances of the "unequal treaties" that dogged much of Asia's earlier contacts with European powers. Imagine seventeenth-century Dutch merchants languishing for decades in the Deshjima enclave off Nagasaki suddenly having the doors open to the Empire of the Rising Sun. In the late 1990s, foreign banks in Tokyo thought they were dreaming when some of the best names in Japanese industry started coming to them to borrow funds refused to them by Japanese banks, which were still cutting back their balance sheets.

"We're witnessing an invasion of foreign capital, especially from America. A sort of colonization of Asia has begun," said Hiromu Nonaka, secretary-general of Japan's ruling LDP. Ten years earlier, the American press was screaming about the Japanese "threat" when such icons as the Rockefeller Center, the Pebble Beach golf course, and Hollywood film studios were being purchased by Japanese companies. By the end of the 1990s, some newspapers in Japan seemed to have acquired the hysterical tone of their American counterparts.

## THE GOOD, THE BAD, AND THE UGLY

Like the earlier fears of a Japanese "invasion" of the United States, the risks of an American "colonization" of Japan were not real. On several occasions, foreigners refused the opportunity to acquire financial troubled Japanese financial institutions regardless of price—Yamaichi Securities, for example, and Long-Term Credit Bank of Japan (LTCB), one of three long-term credit banks that turned to Sumitomo Trust and Banking after failing to find a foreign savior.

But the small banking systems of Southeast Asia were more vulnerable and the risks of colonization real. Before the crisis, the combined capitalization of banks in Indonesia, Malaysia, or the Philippines was equivalent to that of a mid-sized bank in the United States. Philippe Delhaise, head of Thomson BankWatch Asia noted that the assets of all Philippine banks at the end of 1996 were sixty-five billion dollars—about one-tenth the size of the world's biggest bank. And after the financial storm swept though the region, most of the banking systems had a negative value in terms of net assets. "To run an entire banking system today, you need three to four billion dollars in shareholder funds. What does that represent for HSBC or Citibank or Deutsche Bank? These giants could pick up all these banks of a single country in difficulty," the Belgian bank analyst said.

Delhaise, whose company rated four hundred banks in the region, classified Asian banks into three categories—the good, the bad, and the ugly.

"The good ones are suffering. They lost their shirt but that's all. They can become profitable again with a little bit of extra capital brought in by their owners or local investors. In a nutshell, they'll survive," he said.

Bad banks were those whose shareholder funds had been wiped out. They would have the biggest problems in trying to recapitalize themselves with local funds. "They're like an old car that's just been in an accident where the cost of repairs is more expensive than buying a new car," Delhaise said, adding that foreign banks might nevertheless be interested. "They would be acquiring the right to operate in the country and that would be worth more than the bank itself."

Ugly banks were those whose losses were so big that they required another source of funds to put them back on their feet before being offered for sale. In such cases, "the only technical solution is nationalization," Delhaise said. Liquidating these banks was practically impossible as governments in most countries had guaranteed depositors. Such policies weren't questioned by the IMF when it was called to the rescue in Thailand. And so governments began nationalizing financial institutions as a matter of urgency.

Delhaise said the real dilemma was the "bad" banks where the choice was between nationalization and neocolonialism, the worst case scenario being "Nepalization" where foreign banks were allowed to operate through joint ventures. "They are the only banks that function well, they choose their own activities, and they take everything that's profitable. They leave the rest to local banks that lose a little more ground every year," Delhaise said. "It's a colonial scandal and it should be stopped."

Sir William Purves, the former chairman of HSBC Holdings, more or less agreed, but with somewhat less radical language. "Personally, I would not like to see the demise of local banks as a result of what happened," he said. "We are going to see an amalgamation of local banks to make them stronger and better able to compete with foreign banks."

For Western banks, the situation in Asia in the late 1990s gelled exactly with the Chinese ideogram for crisis—formed from the two characters for "danger" and "opportunity." For the risks taken during the Asian miracle days, banks would have to pay a heavy price in making provisions for bad debts over several years. But for those who hadn't lost the appetite, there were rare chances to get a foothold in markets previously closed, to acquire assets that were never before up for sale, and to expand in East Asia as they had in Latin America. But the banks would have to show they had learned lessons from their repeated domestic and global errors of the past.

## THE TEXAN PRECEDENT

When he was chairman of the U.S. Federal Reserve Board, Paul Volcker would lecture his fellow Americans. And he never stopped denouncing the federal budget deficit and America's tendency to live beyond its means, which was largely responsible for the imbalances in the international financial system. He hadn't changed.

"We have to deal with the simple fact that countries with strong banks, honest and democratic governments, relatively transparent accounting systems, and experienced regulators have not been immune to banking crises. This list includes the United States," he said in a speech to the Paul Nitze School of International Relations in mid-1998.

Volcker recalled the banking crisis in Texas, triggered by the oil and real-estate booms of the 1980s. With an economy the size of South Korea, Texas lost its banking "independence" after the crisis, although it had fiercely resisted ownership by out-of-state banks in the early 1980s. When tiny boats are being tossed about in the sea of capital flows, "the natural defense is to seek the shelter of larger, inherently more diversified and stable ships. By the end of the 1980s, every major bank in Texas—with the encouragement and support of the federal government—had become part of a much larger national banking organization," Volcker said. Similarly, Argentina now had only one sizeable private bank without substantial foreign ownership and Mexico had followed the same route, despite its deep nationalist traditions. Foreign ownership of banks was also common in Eastern Europe and it was now Asia's turn. "The economic logic of living in a world of global capital markets is much more integration, with the present crisis force-feeding the existing tendency. The obvious counterpoint is a growing lack of autonomy in economic management, easily perceived as an affront to sovereignty," he said. "The potential for political resistance that flows from this perception will be all the greater if the changes seem to be forced not by economic logic but by external forces with their own agenda. This is why international advice-givers should be prudent in their tone."

On another occasion in Hong Kong, Volcker noted that globalization had to be accompanied by concrete material advantages. "If financial integration does not appear to succeed at the end of the day in terms of sustained rapid growth, then you have a potential for a political backlash," he said. In other words, the capitalism of free markets won the war against the Japanese model and "crony capitalism." But it hadn't yet won the peace.

# CHAPTER NINE

# Rendezvous in Manila

---

"Neither Japan nor China nor ASEAN took the initiative.
East Asia showed it lacked cohesion."
*—Toyoo Gyohten, adviser to Japan's Prime*
*Minister Keizo Obuchi*

"When Asian leaders meet, I'd like them to spend a little less time playing golf and a little more time discussing their common problems." It was September 1997 and Michel Camdessus had just arrived in Hong Kong for the annual meetings of the International Monetary Fund and the World Bank. As he did every year, Camdessus was touring the press center, accompanied by Shailandra Anjaria, the head of external relations at the IMF. He had stopped by for a friendly chat at the working booth of the French news agency, Agence France-Presse (AFP).

Camdessus was from the Basque country in southern France, where holiday-ing British aristocrats started playing the ancient royal game of golf in the nine-teenth century. But he never caught the obsession with golf, which had become the major pastime of Asian leaders by the end of the twentieth century. And he wasn't among the IMF staff who frequented the Bretton Woods Recreation Center, the organization's exclusive golf course on the outskirts of Washington.

With the Asian crisis, Camdessus saw a chance to renew his crusade to convert Asian leaders to "peer pressure"—the idea of holding the frankest possible dialogues between governments and sovereign states. The same process had been progressively adopted by industrialized countries, helping to resolve several international financial crises.

Asia's financial turmoil didn't just sweep aside the embryonic signs of cooperation between regional central banks. It also underscored the absence of regional mechanisms that could promote a coordinated response.

There were regional institutions, notably ASEAN that celebrated its thirtieth anniversary in 1997. But ASEAN, which evolved into a bulwark against communism in the 1960s, 1970s, and much of the 1980s, upheld the principle of noninterference in each other's internal affairs.

ASEAN's policy of noninterference allowed various countries to live side by side—such as a newly democratic nation like the Philippines after the fall of President Ferdinand Marcos in 1986 and a country such as Indonesia that would be ruled for another twelve years by the family of President Suharto. Noninterference was accentuated by ASEAN eventually admitting Vietnam, a communist state. By the time of the thirtieth anniversary in 1997, ASEAN also embraced the neighboring communist state of Laos as well as Burma, renamed Myanmar by the ruling military junta. Cambodia's admission was delayed until 1999 due to heavy fighting between rival factions in the streets of the capital only weeks before it was supposed to join in 1997.

But noninterference had its pitfalls, as illustrated by the disastrous forest fires in Indonesia that enveloped much of the region in a smoky haze toward the end of 1997. While fires were common in the dry season, they were exacerbated by Indonesian companies burning down forests for land, especially in Sumatra and Kalimantan. Droughts caused by El Niño made the phenomenon even worse in 1997. In Kuala Lumpur and Singapore, two of the cities worst hit, residents started wearing masks outside and the incidence of respiratory complaints soared. But the adverse effects also spread to the Philippines and Thailand. Airports closed and lives came to a stop. The economic effects were almost as dramatic as the long-term impact on public health.

In Indonesia itself, those responsible for the burning were beyond reproach. Members of the Suharto clan had forestry interests as did timber baron and presidential golfing partner Mohamad "Bob" Hasan. And neighboring countries found it difficult to question the Suharto regime.

By the middle of 1998, the policy of noninterference was showing signs of falling apart. Embracing an idea floated by Malaysian Finance Minister and Deputy Prime Minister Anwar Ibrahim, Thailand got the support of the Philippines in pushing for the idea of "flexible engagement" between ASEAN members during the group's annual meeting in Manila in 1998. Bangkok didn't see why it should be compelled to ignore what was going on in Myanmar, for example, when it was exporting drugs and prostitutes to Thailand. But resistance to the idea was vocal from Malaysia, whose foreign policy was dominated by Prime Minister Mahathir Mohamad himself, as well as Indonesia and Singapore.

## ASIA DOESN'T EXIST

Like nature, the modern global economy didn't recognize borders. And like nature, the economy could seek its revenge if it was ignored. "Markets are neither right nor wrong. They simply are," said Andrew Freris, head of research at BankAmerica in Hong Kong.

The progressive integration of Asian economies in the world economy gave rise to regional solidarity. Greater interdependence worked well when everything was fine. But it exacerbated the contagion effect when things started falling apart. Markets were obviously unfair in heaping all of Asia's economies into the "one basket" when the storm hit, ignoring differences in the real economies of each country and the individual capacity to resist shocks. But as Freris remarked, "nobody ever said markets were supposed to be fair."

And despite the solidarity of destiny—at least in the eyes of others—East Asia was unable to come up with an institutional response to the storm.

For Freris and many others, it was simple—"Asia" did not exist, for various complex reasons. As Mahathir noted, Asians were too diverse in terms of race, religion, and culture to have a common desire to dominate others in the same way as the rational white Christians of the West did for five centuries.

The pace with which the people of the former Soviet empire reintegrated themselves with Europe highlighted the power of common historical and cultural identities on a continent stretching "from the Atlantic to the Urals." But in Asia, there was no common identity. With the exceptions of Japan and Thailand, the national identities of all countries including China were influenced by long and difficult periods of colonial domination by Europeans (and subsequently Americans in the case of the Philippines). Decolonization was accelerated by World War II but did not give rise to a real regional identity. In failing to succeed with its reckless military adventurism in Asia, Japan lost the moral authority in the region as well as the power to lead, which had been conferred upon the country by its singular ability to acquire and master Western technology. And after a century of decadence, China became communist and largely withdrew from the rest of the world.

The absence of a regional identity was also reflected in the Cold War, which was nevertheless "hot" in this part of the world with the Vietnam War and the American defeat in 1975. Despite efforts in the 1990s to expand the annual ASEAN meetings into a regional dialogue on security issues, Asia had nothing like the Atlantic alliance for mutual defense.

The Pax Americana that guaranteed peace was based on a bunch of bilateral agreements between Washington and various regional capitals. The most important was the security treaty between the United States and Japan, the "unsinkable aircraft carrier" anchored off the coast of the Asian continent.

In the economic, trade, and monetary fields, Asia didn't exist either. Stages of development were too far apart between Japan, which had already surpassed most Western powers, and the rest of the region, most of which was slowly emerging from underdevelopment.

From the 1960s, Japan started to join various multilateral institutions dominated by Western countries such as the IMF, the OECD, the G5 (the forerunner of the G7), and the BIS. Japan was the only Asian member of the OECD until the mid-1990s when South Korea joined the Paris-based club of rich countries. At the same time, much of Japan's official development assistance was directed toward Asia, and Tokyo jointly controlled the Manila-based ADB with Washington. Aid policies complemented America's policy of "containment" with regard to the advances of communism in Asia. But Japan's priorities were elsewhere—catching up with the West and opening the vast American and European markets to Japanese exporters.

Asia passively witnessed the formation of regional trade areas in Europe and North America, with the main concern being that these markets remained open to Asian products.

Trade between countries in the region was anemic for decades, dominated by raw materials including oil and gas that were siphoned off to the Japanese industrial machine. On the monetary front, East Asia was a dollar zone even in Japan where most of its import and exports were denominated in US currency.

But this changed starting in the mid-1980s when Japanese companies started moving production to other parts of Asia to offset pressure at home arising from the strong yen. The newly industrialized economies (NIE's) of South Korea, Taiwan, Hong Kong, and Singapore emerged in the late 1980s. And China joined the process of regional integration with its open-door policies and other reforms.

But the institutional response to the upheavals triggered in 1997 was surprisingly timid.

## APEC BARELY EXISTS

This absence of a major response from ASEAN was not surprising. It had largely evolved into a grouping dominated by foreign policy and didn't include the regional heavyweights, Japan and China.

More troubling was the failure of the APEC forum. Launched by Australia in 1989 in a bid to reduce trade tensions between Washington and countries on the western side of the Pacific, APEC had become an annual summit of Asia-Pacific leaders by 1993 with the notable participation of the American, Japanese, and Chinese leaders. Following the bad example of the annual summits of the G7, the event rapidly became a media circus with substance giving way to appearance. The high point became the "family picture" of leaders decked out in local attire—batik shirts in Indonesia in 1994, leather jackets in Canada in 1997, and batik shirts again in Malaysia in 1998. The largely ceremonial activities didn't conceal the lack of achievement, especially when

APEC was supposed to be working toward free trade in the region by 2010 for industrialized members and 2020 for the rest. When the leaders met in Vancouver in late 1997, the Asian crisis had just entered a particularly critical stage. The most substantial contribution came from Mexican President Ernesto Zedillo. Drawing on the experience of his own country in dealing with the peso crisis several years earlier, Zedillo advised his Asian colleagues not to waste "one minute" in admitting the gravity of the situation before taking action to correct the problems. The only significant concrete outcome of the Vancouver summit was to expand APEC membership to twenty-one with the inclusion of Peru, Russia, and Vietnam.

"Two things happened to APEC that diminished its effectiveness, one of them America's fault, the other Asia's," wrote Greg Sheridan, the foreign editor of *The Australian* in April 1998. "APEC's membership became so grossly distended that it lost its focus," he said, questioning Washington's insistence on membership for Mexico and then Russia. "In no sense is it an integrated part of the Asia-Pacific economy," he said. "As for Asia, its contribution to APEC's enfeeblement was the insistence that APEC's decisions be nonbinding, and that it be a forum not for negotiation but only for consultations in an attempt to recreate the culture of exhaustive ASEAN consensus that has also paralyzed ASEAN in this instance."

## ASIAN MONETARY FUND

When the storm erupted and reminded everybody of their common destiny, Asians looked for an institutional response—creating a regional version of the IMF. The moment chosen to launch the initiative was a bit unusual—a G7 meeting of finance ministers and central bank governors in Hong Kong on September 20, 1997, just before the annual meetings of the IMF and the World Bank. It was like a supermarket using its annual sale to announce the opening of a new store across the road from a competitor.

Asian countries concocted the idea forty-eight hours earlier on the sidelines of a ministerial meeting of Asian and European countries in Bangkok, and Japanese Finance Minister Hiroshi Mitsuzuka was chosen as the messenger. At the G7 meeting, the Japanese delegation suddenly pulled the rabbit out of its hat—an "Asian Monetary Fund." The other G7 officials present barely had enough time to prepare for Saturday's meeting of ministers. And now this.

"The Japanese put the idea on the table," French Finance Minister Dominique Strauss-Kahn said at the time. "The idea was far from being accepted. It was undoubtedly a serious initiative and those who advanced it were obviously determined. But it raised questions from all the other participants." In fact, the other G7 members—who were also the major shareholders in the IMF—suspected that Japan was under pressure from its Asian neighbors to establish a regional structure competing with the IMF, allowing them to avoid the sort of harsh medicine that Thailand had just been forced to swallow. "The existence of a regional structure could signify less discipline for the countries in question," Strauss-Kahn said. "For this reason, the other participants felt it was not a great idea. Our Japanese friends listened and are going to reflect on the matter." Jean Lemierre, director of the French Treasury, was more explicit. "The reaction of the six other countries and Camdessus was very clear—we will never accept this," he said. "It's important to understand why. First, we were facing a global problem. There was no way a body other than the IMF was going to intervene. We said to the Japanese—'You're going to start supporting countries and impose weak conditions. So who's going to pay?' 'You and us,' they said. 'If this is the case,' we said, 'we want to be on board from the start.'" For the same reasons, several Asian countries gave a lukewarm reception to the Japanese proposal. "Hong Kong and Singapore, which have a lot of money, weren't very warm toward the idea. They feared seeing their reserves being siphoned off," a European official said.

The glacial G7 reception to the Japanese proposal prompted Tokyo to adopt a diplomatic fallback position—it wasn't an Asian fund as such, just a facility. Malaysia's Finance Minister Anwar Ibrahim said two days later that it was being called an "Asia Facility" but that things were at a "very, very preliminary stage." Anwar said that the name of the facility, the conditions imposed, the countries involved, and relations with the IMF would still have to be studied. Or perhaps restudied, as the Japanese proposal was not improvised. "There was certainly important preparatory work carried out by the finance ministry and it was certain that the Japanese government wanted it to succeed," a former Japanese finance ministry official said. Stanley Fischer, the number two man in the IMF, saw a document of several pages detailing the proposal, including contributions amounting to some one hundred billion dollars and the establishment of a secretariat.

The strongest argument against a regional mechanism that was independent from the IMF came from Michel Camdessus himself. "If you were to invent a softer conditionality somewhere...the credibility would not be brought or found in the marketplace. So if you want credibility, it's better to have only one source of conditionality, professional enough, based on solid experience. And so far only the IMF has that," he said, adding that whatever scheme was adopted should be based on IMF conditionality and "be subordinated to the IMF to take risks. If the IMF does not put money somewhere, well you should ask yourselves why before embarking on financing."

## JAPAN PUSSYFOOTS

The episode would have repercussions—the idea of an Asian Monetary Fund was not going to die a sudden death. It expressed the growing frustration of emerging economies with a small group of industrialized countries that were dominating the process of international economic and financial coordination. Before the Japanese proposal, Australia had proposed setting up a regional version of the BIS, the central bank for the world's leading central banks based in the Swiss city of Basel. The BIS saw the danger signs and opened its doors wider to Asian central banks while setting up a regional office in Hong Kong in July 1998.

And almost nine months after the proposal was shot down by its G7 partners, Malaysian Prime Minister Mahathir Mohamad publicly regretted Japan's ceding defeat during a visit to Tokyo in May 1998.

Japanese officials at least didn't underestimate the extent of the crisis by suggesting contributions of about one hundred billion dollars for the proposed Asian fund. The figure was a lot higher than that envisaged by participants in the annual meeting of the IMF and the World Bank in Hong Kong. At that stage, the IMF had put together a package of 17.3 billion dollars for Thailand. Apart from Japan, the G7 countries were limiting their contributions to multilateral institutions that combined their resources with funds from regional economies with high levels of reserves. But by the end of 1997, the IMF had to rush to the assistance of Indonesia and South Korea. The total assistance pledged by the IMF, the World Bank, and the Asian Development Bank along with various countries exceeded one hundred billion dollars.

Behind the idea for an Asian Monetary Fund was the temptation among some Japanese to assert a leadership role for their country in the region. But it was largely a temptation. Due to the sheer weight of its economy, Japan could not play the role of first among equals. How would it have looked, an Asian Monetary Fund financed almost entirely by Japan, whose GNP accounted for two-thirds of the entire East Asian economy including China? Moreover, Japanese officials had effectively opposed internationalization of the yen, which would have prevented Southeast Asia from becoming a dollar zone. And making the yen the anchor currency in Asia, like the mark in Europe, would bring responsibilities when Japanese markets were deregulated. The problem was that Japanese officials did not want to accept the responsibilities.

But it would not be long before talk about internationalizing the yen came back into fashion with the imminent birth of the euro from the beginning of 1999 and fears of the Japanese currency being marginalized in a bipolar global system based on the American and European currencies.

"Under such circumstances where the euro becomes one of two credible currencies in the international monetary system, we would naturally be greatly concerned about whether the yen could keep up with the euro and dollar bipolar monetary system," Bank of Japan executive director Akira Nagashima said in Hong Kong in early 1998. "In this context, what is crucial is how the internationalization of the yen will develop in Asia." Nagashima, who was in charge of international affairs at the Japanese central bank, said two things were "essential" to enhance the yen's use in Asia. The first was "to ensure that Japanese financial and capital markets are highly developed so as to be able to provide Asian countries with enough hedging instruments for exchange-rate risk, that is short-term financial assets." The second essential ingredient was "to maintain the capacity of Japanese financial institutions to supply sufficient yen-denominated funds." The speech was notable for its immateriality. At the same time and in the same place as Nagashima was speaking, Japanese banks were preparing for a credit crunch across Asia, especially Hong Kong.

## BURIAL IN MANILA

The Japanese initiative to establish an Asian Monetary Fund was buried in Manila on November 18 and 19, 1997. There were no flowers or wreaths.

The meeting in the Philippine capital was called to clear up an affair that was threatening to poison relations between East and West. The list of the deputy finance ministers and deputy central bank governors invited showed a bit of last-minute improvisation. Initially, the United States, Japan, and Canada were to be the only G7 countries attending. Canada was present because any decision taken had to be ratified a few days later by APEC leaders attending their annual summit in Vancouver. Following a French initiative, the European members of the G7—Germany, France, Britain, and Italy—extracted a last-minute invitation. "We imposed ourselves in Manila as observers," said Jean Lemierre. "The stakes were global. We suffer the consequences—indirectly and sometimes directly, we have to pay,"

Australia was also present in Manila. The Australian government had made financial commitments to the rescue packages for Thailand and Indonesia, pledging one billion dollars on each occasion. Canberra was worried about the lack of concern from the major industrialized countries as the Asian crisis spread. For more than a decade, Australia had been playing its regional integration card after abandoning its "White Australia" immigration policy in the late 1960s. Markets were opened, deregulation took place, and by no longer turning its back on its neighbors, Australia was able to surf on the wave of regional prosperity that swept over Asia. The country had a lot to lose in the collapse of the Asian miracle but its vulnerability was not purely economic. Australia and Indonesia were close neighbors and Australians lived in constant fear of instability in a country of more than two hundred million people. Australia's shareholding in the IMF was 1.5 percent—the same level as Switzerland—and it would not stop urging the bigger European and American shareholders to do more.

Hong Kong also attended the Manila meeting. The newly born Special Administrative Region of China sat on a mountain of foreign exchange reserves that ranked third in the world. It had already committed one billion dollars to the rescue package for Thailand and an undisclosed sum to the package for Indonesia—the same as the commitment from China that was also at the meeting. South Korea was also present, having committed—like Indonesia—five hundred million dollars to the Thai package before withdrawing the pledge. Donors were becoming recipients. Rumor had it that South Korea was about to seek IMF assistance. United States Deputy Treasury Secretary Larry Summers stopped over in Frankfurt and Tokyo on his way to Manila, and the figures being bandied about for South Korea—between forty billion dollars and sixty billion dollars—would get a prominent hearing.

ASEAN was represented by six of its nine members at the time, including Indonesia, Malaysia, the Philippines, and Thailand that were all directly affected by the crisis. Also present were Brunei and Singapore, the two rich ASEAN members that had already committed large sums to both Thailand and Indonesia. The IMF, the World Bank, and the Asian Development Bank completed the rest of the table.

When they arrived in Manila, the Asian delegates—led by Japan—hadn't given up the idea of trying to revive the Japanese proposal for a specifically Asian fund. Philippine Finance Secretary Roberto de Ocampo said there was talk of a "facility" as opposed to a fund. But Michel Camdessus, who represented the IMF himself, once again warned against the idea of a "gentler, kinder, softer" fund that would lack the credibility to restore market confidence. "Whatever financial mechanism can be put in place, it should not compete...or reduce the strength of the IMF qualities or conditionalities," he said. Exactly the opposite point of view was expressed several days earlier by Malaysian Prime Minister Mahathir Mohamad who said he saw practically no use in having a mechanism that was merely an extension of the IMF.

The affair was eventually resolved on a very basic principle—whoever pays...rules. And so the "Framework for Enhanced Asian Regional Cooperation to Promote Financial Stability" was adopted after forty-eight hours of discussions. "This framework, that recognizes the central role of the IMF in the international monetary system, includes the following initiatives: (a) a mechanism for regional monitoring to complement global monitoring by the IMF; (b) enhanced economic and technical cooperation, particularly in strengthening financial systems and regulatory capacities; (c) measures to strengthen the IMF's capacity to respond to financial crises; and (d) a cooperative financing arrangement that would supplement IMF resources."

On the final point, the statement dealt with the sensitive issue of conditions. Participants could provide, "in consultation with the IMF and on a case by case basis, supplemental financial resources for IMF-supported programs." What would from now on be known as the "Manila Framework" used the same framework as the packages provided to Thailand and Indonesia (and within time, South Korea). Additional funds from countries in the region, industrialized countries, or international financial institutions would be mobilized at the request of the IMF for structural adjustment programs that would be worked out by the IMF and approved by its board of directors—on the recommendation of the managing director.

## PEER PRESSURE

At their summit in Vancouver on November 27, APEC leaders called for the Manila Framework to be implemented rapidly. On December 1, ASEAN finance ministers confirmed their support for the plan during a meeting in Kuala Lumpur. An idea for a specific ASEAN fund, proposed by those who couldn't accept the Japanese withdrawal, would be shown the door. A statement issued at the end of the meeting merely said that ASEAN countries in a position to give financial support would pay particular attention to all members seeking assistance. The statement was interesting as it abandoned the traditional ASEAN approach of noninterference and rallied rather explicitly around the idea of "peer pressure" that Camdessus was trying to get Asian leaders to embrace. The ministers said the monitoring between peers would be based on the G7 format but with its own ASEAN characteristics.

In G7 meetings, the leading industrialized countries already had the habit of discussing certain facts that weren't always nice to hear. In this area of "multilateral monitoring," Camdessus would play the role of "rapporteur," giving good marks and bad marks for data collected by IMF economists.

The value of the exercise had been strongly contested, often because expectations were too high. The G7 couldn't and didn't want to be a "global board of directors"—it functioned best when the national interests of its members converged. Its recommendations were often in vain when they clashed with domestic policy constraints. But governments could also use the pressure of their G7 partners to advance their own reform programs, what the Japanese call "gaiatsu" or outside pressure. On the monetary front, the G7 had undeniably relieved some of the problems stemming from the "nonsystem" of floating exchange rates that developed in the early 1970s. And despite the yawns that generally greeted G7 statements in trading rooms, the group ended up being respected—it didn't cause any miracles but it prevented, at least until the late 1990s, any major disasters.

"The G7 has shown that it has fulfilled its role. There are real debates between the rich countries," said Jean Lemierre.

By transferring such peer pressure to Asia, the IMF managing director Michel Camdessus was hoping that alarm bells would start ringing when policies followed by one country in the region represented a threat to its neighbors. When IMF officials were unable to get anyone to listen to them in Bangkok in 1996, they would have liked to have been able to relay their fears to neighboring capitals in the hope of getting a better response.

Stanley Fisher, the number two man in the IMF, underscored the importance of such mutual monitoring in late 1997, describing it as "group therapy" among countries. Recalling the dialogue of the deaf between the IMF and Thailand the previous year, he noted that many of the countries that felt affected by the crisis were reluctant to talk to Thailand.

Transpose to Asia a practice followed by the world's leading industrialized countries, all Western except for Japan?

"Frankly speaking, it's not always easy," the head of the French Treasury said. But "it's desirable that mechanisms for convergence exist in Asia." The opposition of Western countries to the proposed Asian Monetary Fund didn't reflect hostility to the idea that Asians speak to each other more. "We told them: 'If you want to have dialogues, if you want to create mechanisms for bringing yourselves closer together, go ahead. You have a major interest in speaking to one another.' But Lemierre warned against being overly optimistic even though the Manila Framework was in place. It was a "complicated process, constantly evolving," he said.

Indeed, the next meeting of Manila Framework group—the G7 plus ten countries from the region along with the IMF, the World Bank and the ADB—was in Tokyo in mid-1998 and Japan wasn't just providing the hospitality. It was also proving to be a major topic of discussion with the yen having plunged to within a whisker of 150 yen to the dollar, requiring the United States to intervene in the foreign exchange market jointly with Japan for the first time since 1995. The Federal Reserve bought some two billion dollars worth of yen and the Bank of Japan twice the amount, bringing a halt to the Japanese currency's slide just before the meeting. The following weekend wasn't at all peaceful for Eisuke Sakakibara, who found himself being harassed by critics on all sides. And this time, the European members of the G7 had every right to be present. "We don't play a minor role when it comes to our G7 partners," Lemierre said. But the star of the show was the representative from Beijing. China had just managed to pull off a remarkable public relations exercise by indicating that it could devalue the yuan if nothing was done to halt the yen's slide. Teaching a lesson to Japan was one of those small little pleasures that China could never resist.

## DANGEROUS DEPENDENCE

Having failed to put into place a regional financial infrastructure to deal with the winds of globalization during the period of rapid growth, could Asia now come out of the crisis in better shape?

Many countries would be under IMF supervision for many years to come and it was impossible to tell when they would regain their liberty of movement. IMF programs generally lasted three years. But when the Philippines emerged from its program in 1998, it had been a quarter of a century.

"Perhaps the most under-remarked lesson from the Asian economic crisis is the complete failure of the region's institutions, especially the Asia-Pacific Economic Cooperation forum and the Association of Southeast Asian Nations," Greg Sheridan wrote. "The lead institution in the crisis has been the IMF, although the soundness of its response is the subject of vigorous debate. But the IMF is quintessentially a multilateral organization under effective

American dominance. Other institutions that have played a role, such as the World Bank, are also organizations whose inspiration and leadership lie outside the region. That is a significant lapse. It shows that the East Asian region is dangerously dependent on outside leadership in anything that counts, and has failed to construct even a rudimentary regional institutional architecture that can deal with the challenges of regional life. The result is a state of quasi-colonial dependence for the region, which is all the more depressing because it is self-imposed."

Did the 1997 crisis serve as a lesson? External powers and multilateral institutions should help to consolidate the Manila Framework. The Europeans, through the Asia-European Meeting (ASEM) process, could offer their Asian partners some advice on their own experiences with regional integration. "It's not a matter of giving lessons but explaining concretely how we proceeded, including how to avoid making the same errors we made," Jean Lemierre said. But the responses had to come from Asian countries themselves. What would be the role of China, whose influence on the region was undoubtedly strengthened by the financial assault? How would Japan overcome its own economic difficulties and the serious crisis of confidence in its own future and the country's relations with the rest of the world? And would transplanting "peer pressure" from the G7 to Asia succeed when it implied transparency, challenging the very survival of undemocratic political regimes?

CHAPTER TEN

# Suharto Incorporated

---

"Eat rabbit. The taste of rabbit is just as good as chicken."
— *Tutut, the eldest daughter of President Suharto, advising Indonesians who couldn't afford to buy chicken anymore*

It was going to be the mother of all gold mines. From the Klondike to California, from the deserts of Australia to the jungles of the Amazon, gold fever was a disease that struck human beings at regular intervals. Across the ages, it had triggered massive migrations and colonial adventures, destroyed ancient civilizations, and changed the face of continents. Some found their fortune. Many lost their illusions and also their lives. For central banks managing official reserves, the yellow metal had lost much of its luster in the 1990s due to a prolonged price decline. But gold still sparked dreams of many people. And swindlers too.

It all started back in 1993 in Calgary, Canada. David Walsh, a former broker, was running an obscure mining company called Bre-X. The company was established by a curious trio—Walsh, his wife, and John Felderhof, a geologist of Dutch origin whose reputation rested upon the discovery of a gold mine thirty years earlier in Papua New Guinea. Felderhof, who was the company's vice president, hadn't discovered anything since then. But gold fever was not something you cured overnight. After waiting thirty years, Felderhof sought his revenge in the stinking jungles where he'd spent much of his life. The revenge was called Busang.

The name of the locality, lost in the forests of eastern Kalimantan, the Indonesian part of the island of Borneo, would soon become an international household name. Bre-X had its hands on what could be the biggest gold discovery in the world since Witwatersrand in South Africa. The estimates went from forty million ounces to seventy million ounces and then to two hundred million ounces, one hundred billion dollars at market prices at the time.

While the claim seemed fantastic, it was reasonable. Three-quarters of the world's mining deposits were discovered by small companies that would seek assistance from the major international mining companies if the opportunity arose. Bre-X was among about forty such junior partners working across Kalimantan. And Indonesia was already a gold producer—the Grasberg deposit in Irian Jaya, the western part of New Guinea controlled by Indonesia, had proven reserves of more than eighty million ounces.

The story was believable enough to interest big and small investors alike—the price of Bre-X shares, listed on the Toronto Stock Exchange in April 1996, would soar from two Canadian dollars to a peak of 280 dollars with the successive announcements of the deposit's estimated size.

Busang fever soon spread to Jakarta. In what seemed to be naiveté at the time, Walsh and Felderhof announced their discovery before obtaining a contract for the mining rights from the Indonesian government. Canadian mining giant Barrick Gold was quick to exploit the "mistake," eager to become the major partner for Bre-X as the Busang deposit was mined. To get Bre-X to accept its conditions, Barrick enlisted the services of some of its influential friends in the corridors of Indonesian power including Siti Hardijanti Rukmana. Also known as Tutut, she was none other than the eldest daughter of President Suharto.

Did Tutut play a role? It wasn't clear. But on August 15, 1996, Indonesian Mines and Energy Minister I. B. Sudjana made an unprecedented announcement—he withdrew the preliminary exploration license granted to Bre-X that had paved the way for the company's stock market listing.

Barrick didn't stop there. It enlisted further support from eminent people among its "international advisers," notably former American president George Bush and former Canadian prime minister Brian Mulroney.

But Bre-X didn't back down and Walsh, in turn, tried to get his own backing from the "first family" of Indonesia. In October, Bre-X announced a "strategic alliance" with Panunan Duta, a company owned by Tutut's brother, Sigit Harjojudanto. He would take a ten percent stake in the mine and receive forty million dollars in "consultancy" fees.

The Indonesian family feud triggered chaos. The Busang affair had the big international mining companies concerned. They feared the new uncertainty over how Jakarta applied the rules of the game could frighten off their financial backers. Other mining groups, notably another Canadian giant called Placer Dome, wanted an international tender for the role Barrick was seeking for itself. Placer Dome meanwhile decided to protect its rear by negotiating a merger with Bre-X. Thousands of small and large shareholders were soon up in arms, complaining that they'd been stripped of their gold.

In early 1997, President Suharto asked his best friend and golfing partner, the ethnic Chinese billionaire Mohamad "Bob" Hasan, to look into the matter. Suharto's influential wife Siti Hartinah, also known as Tien, had died the previous year. To resolve conflicts between the enterprising offspring of the Javanese patriarch, "Uncle Bob" had been assuming the role of arbitrator previously held by the woman dubbed "Madame Tien Percent."

Bob Hasan quickly set to work. Barrick and Placer Dome were sent packing. The operators of Busang would be the American mining company Freeport-McRoran Copper and Gold, which had a thirty-year presence in Indonesia and was already operating the Grasberg gold and copper mine. Bre-X got to keep forty percent of the mine—a better deal than Barrick was offering. A further thirty percent would go to two Indonesian companies and their local partners, including Sigit Harjojudanto, who hadn't lost everything after all. Freeport would get fifteen percent and the Indonesian government five percent. Hasan had an indirect interest in the agreement through an investment in Busang by a company called Nusantara Ampera Bakti, also known as Nusamba. Hasan was president of the company and the sole shareholder.

Another strategic move by Hasan, better known as Indonesia's plywood king. But this time, the strategy failed.

On May 5, 1997, an official inquiry undertaken by Strathcona Mineral Resources confirmed what everyone had been suspecting for weeks—there was no gold at Busang and there never was—the soil samples given by Bre-X had been salted with alluvial gold.

Strathcona described the affair as a "fraud without precedent in the history of mining" and fingers were soon being pointed at Michael de Guzman, a Filipino working as chief geologist of Bre-X. But Guzman was not there to tell his side of the story—in March, he fell from a helicopter as it was flying to Busang. Once news of his death was out, the shares of Bre-X went into free fall, collapsing eighty-four percent on March 27 when a huge wave of sell orders jammed the computers of the Calgary Stock Exchange. The outcome for Bre-X shareholders on that black day—1.9 billion dollars went up in smoke.

Walsh claimed he was a victim of fraud. Felderhof was lying low in a luxury house in the Caribbean, bought with the capital gains made on Bre-X shares. Furious shareholders, including some who had lost their life savings, began marathon judicial proceedings in Canadian and American courts. And the industry tried to forget the whole episode that had made fools out of several big mining companies.

## GREAT WHALES

Welcome to "Suharto Inc."

Comparing companies to countries was fashionable among journalists. "Japan Inc." paved the way many years earlier and was followed by "Korea Inc." And in Kuala Lumpur, Dr. Mahathir had even made "Malaysia Inc." a slogan and a national objective. The term may have been a cliché, but it accurately described the collusion between governments and industries, between the public and private sectors, in helping to develop countries. The term was not unique to Asia but it was in this part of the world that it was particularly prevalent.

And here was a new variant—everything good for Indonesia was also good for President Suharto's family, and everything good for the family was also good for Indonesia.

But Suharto Inc. wasn't just a matter of government coffers being mixed up with the fortunes of the "First Family"—and that's what distinguished Indonesia from the run-of-the mill banana republics in Africa. Suharto, a military man from a conservative Moslem family in Java, was no Mobuto Sese Seko, the Zairean president who shamelessly plundered his country for three decades. Suharto didn't even establish the system. He just ran it, putting his family and friends in the middle.

"Indonesians are like tiny plankton in a warm sea where the great whales bathe," wrote Sterling Seagrave in his book *Lords of the Rim*. "They find it reassuring that the biggest whales—President Suharto's family and friends—swallow nearly everything, after running it through their krill strainers. To them, that means everything is not swallowed by the Overseas Chinese. The role of the Chinese in the islands is exactly opposite to that in Thailand, but the result is the same. Instead of the Chinese controlling the economy and the army providing protection in return for kickbacks, as they do in Thailand, in Indonesia the army controls all commerce while the Chinese run it for them in return for kickbacks. Here Chinese are not the army's unwilling victims but its eager bedmates; there is no argument over who gets to be on top, which is important for the army's prestige."

After independence, the Indonesian military took control of the country from the Dutch colonial rulers. Widely known by its acronym ABRI, the army not only had a military role but also had social and political functions. ABRI also used its key role in the power structure to build up its own business empire.

When the Dutch left, the Chinese minority of about three to five percent of the population retained its *compradore* function. The only thing that changed were the masters.

The role played by overseas Chinese throughout Southeast Asian had ancient roots. During the Song dynasty in the thirteenth century, Chinese merchants set up shop in the region. Subsequent internal upheavals sent waves of immigrants following in their footsteps. When European power started colonizing the area, the Chinese—whose relations with indigenous people frequently raised problems—suddenly became useful. They were skilled in business and spoke the languages of both the colonizers and those who were colonized. As many were single men who had left their families back in China, large numbers of Chinese immigrants married local women.

In the nineteenth century, the colonial authorities encouraged mass immigration from China to work in mines and plantations feeding the new industrial machine. In Malaya and Indonesia, generations of Chinese "coolies" were exploited in this way, their miserable existence made tolerable by opium (another colonial business).

Local authorities regarded the links between the Chinese immigrants and China with deep suspicion, both before and after independence. But the links varied over the centuries. If anything, immigrants were more attached to clans or villages in the coastal areas of southern China than the central authorities whose soldiers and tax collectors they had fled.

Following the communist victory in China in 1949, these Chinese immigrant communities were in the same ambiguous position. As an independent power with a permanent seat on the United Nations Security Council, it was perceived that China would eventually guarantee the rights of Chinese in Southeast Asia, especially in countries where they felt threatened, such as Indonesia and Malaya, and subsequently Malaysia from 1963. But the ancestral distrust toward the center of power in China extended to Mao Zedong too. The distrust was reciprocal, and Beijing treated its "overseas compatriots" with caution and discretion—even at the height of anti-imperialist movements in Third World countries in the 1950s and 1960s. In Indonesia, however, the Chinese would pay a heavy price for the activities of local communists.

While full details of the bloody events of 1965 and 1966 were still not clear at the end of the twentieth century, they led to the downfall of Sukarno, the country's founding father and first president. The communist party PKI was accused of preparing a coup, prompting a brutal crackdown by the military. General Suharto, who escaped death in an operation to eliminate part of the top military hierarchy at the time, slowly emerged as the most powerful figure among those who isolated Sukarno before pushing him aside. Anti-communist and anti-Chinese pogroms rocked the country for months. The death toll was estimated at half a million. The PKI was wiped out. Beijing protested feebly. All was in place for the "New Order" that would last more than thirty years.

## THE CHINESE FRIEND

Three decades in power allowed Suharto the extravagance of being able to "personalize" relations between the Indonesian military and ethnic Chinese businessmen.

Among the "friends" of Suharto, nobody could compete with Liem Sioe Liong, founder of the Salim group of companies and a figurehead for the local Chinese community.

The background of Liem, known as Salim in the Indonesian language, is a similar story to those of millions of Chinese immigrants over the centuries. Born in Fuqing in the southern Chinese province of Fujian before World War

I, Liem arrived in Kudus in central Java in 1937. In Kudus, he had an uncle and a brother running a peanut-oil business. Like many Chinese immigrants, he had no plans of staying in Indonesia for the rest of his life and hoped to return to China. But Liem was a resourceful young man and was soon running his own business buying cloves from Sulawesi, used in the production of local cigarettes. In 1946, Liem met Suharto, who was then a young commander in the rebel forces fighting the Dutch for independence. Suharto had received his military training after joining an anticolonial militia set up by Japanese troops that occupied Indonesia during World War II. Liem supplied Suharto's troops with all sorts of items including arms, apparently, and the two men became business partners. Suharto was already showing the kind of mercantile zeal that would eventually raise eyebrows in Jakarta.

When Suharto came to power in the mid-1960s, Liem stopped being a regular Chinese merchant. He effectively became one of the main beneficiaries of that moneymaking machine that made the Suharto system work so well—the monopoly. In 1968, the same year as Suharto won the first of his seven consecutive presidential mandates, Liem obtained one of two clove-importing licenses. The other license went to Suharto's half brother, Probosutedjo.

In 1970, Liem established a company called PT Bogasari Flour Mills that obtained an exclusive contract to supply flour to Bulog, the government agency in charge of ensuring supplies of staple foods. This was the starting point for the food production activities of the Salim group, which would eventually become the world's biggest manufacturer of instant noodles. Next came cement. Like flour prices, cement prices were fixed by the government at levels that were well beyond those prevailing in international markets. But government kindness didn't stop there. When Liem's company Indocement fell into difficulties during a recession in the mid-1980s, the government injected 325 million dollars into the company in exchange for a thirty-five percent stake.

Bruce Gale, of the Singapore-based Political and Economic Risk Consultancy, nevertheless noted that the relationship was "not all one way"— as shown by the rescue of Bank Duta, owned by welfare foundations controlled by Suharto. "In 1990, when Bank Duta ran into serious financial trouble as a result of a 420 million dollar loss in foreign exchange speculation, Liem was one of those who stepped in to rescue it," he recalled.

Suharto's own business dealings went back to 1966 when he established his own company, PT Hanurata, which acquired some three thousand square kilometers of forest in Kalimantan. Suharto later focussed on setting up charitable foundations. In principle, he was only the chairman. The foundations were a great invention—any profits were exempt from taxes. And these foundations were also allowed to accept "donations" from various interests—foreign companies, for example, which might be interested in doing business in Indonesia.

## A FAMILY AFFAIR

The first step in building the Suharto family fortune was simple—collecting commissions and bribes. This was how Suharto's wife came to be known as "Madame Tien Percent."

Oil stocks in 1974 and 1980 brought considerable windfalls. Indonesia was a major producer of crude oil and natural gas, and Asia's only member of the Organization of Petroleum Exporting Countries (OPEC). All Indonesians benefited from the surge in all prices, but some more than others.

Suharto awarded oil-related trading concessions to three of his children—his two sons Bambang Trihatmodjo and Hatomo Mandala Putra, known as Tommy, and his eldest daughter Tutut. The concessions involved state-owned oil company Pertamina's business activities with both clients and suppliers. The concessions were worth several hundred million dollars a year.

When the economy started to take off in the late 1980s, Indonesia tried to wean itself off oil by developing manufacturing activities. Foreign companies started moving in. And Suharto's children were placed at the door.

Bruce Gale described the "typical way" in which members of the presidential family did business: "A company is set up with the express purpose of entering an industry that is either closed or partially closed to private business. Usually, it is also an industry with which they have very little business experience. A license is then obtained from the government, thus greatly increasing the market value of the company. Shares are then sold at a huge premium to foreign investors specializing in the field who have no choice but to buy into the company if they want to invest in the country. After making a substantial profit on the sale of the shares, the founders then sit back and collect dividends as minority shareholders. Historically, this tactic has worked well in heavily-regulated sectors such as telecommunications, power generation, and industrial chemicals."

For being simple intermediaries, this tactic paid off handsomely for opening the right doors to foreign investors; and the Suharto children soon became investors in their own right. This was more profitable and had a longer life span than the one-off "consultancy" fees levied on foreigners. The only thing that didn't change was the professional competence of the Suharto offspring in their business careers—nonexistent or at best weak. And totally superfluous.

Within a few years, the six children of the presidential couple found themselves running major conglomerates with diversified interests—cigarettes, highways, banks, stockbroking, electronics, petrochemicals, timber, pulp and newsprint, telecommunications, plantations, real estate, shipping, aviation, automobiles, and taxis.

The outcome was that a visitor to Jakarta in 1997 had virtually no chance of escaping the First Family from the time he or she left the airport. The taxi, the highway, the hotel, the telephone line, and the water from the shower all bore the imprint of "Cendana"—the presidential palace where Suharto ruled Indonesia for thirty-two years.

Bimantara, the group headed by Tommy, had a list of Japanese partners ranging from trading houses Itochu, Nissho Iwai, and Marubeni to shipbuilder and motorcycle manufacturer Kawasaki Heavy Industries. South Korean industrial giant Hyundai was another partner along with American Express, Swiss food group Nestlé, Alcatel of France, Deutsche Telekom, and Dutch airline KLM.

"The direct role of foreign investors in the build-up of the family's wealth is another consideration," wrote Michael Backman, an Australian specialist in business networks in Southeast Asia. Backman identified 1,247 companies in Indonesia with significant shareholdings by Suharto family members. He also drew up a list of their foreign partners, identifying forty-four Western companies and some fifteen groups from Japan and South Korea.

## BILLIONS OF DOLLARS

How much was the First Family worth before the Asian crisis? How many billions or tens of billions of dollars?

Peter Sutton, the Jakarta representative of Credit Lyonnais Securities Asia, said it was impossible to know in May 1998, which was when Suharto finally stepped down at the height of antigovernment riots sweeping the country. "We don't know. It's not a listed company. They don't publish annual reports and those who give figures are only guessing," he said.

The American media frequently cited an estimate, said to have been made by the CIA, of about thirty billion dollars in Jakarta at the end of the 1980s. That would have made the Suharto clan one of the frontrunners among the world's richest families. Adam Schwarz, author of *Nation in Waiting*, updated the estimate to forty-eight billion dollars, citing his own sources close to the palace. That was five billion dollars more than the forty-three billion dollars pledged by the IMF and the international community in emergency aid to Indonesia in late 1997.

The American financial magazine *Forbes* meanwhile placed Suharto third in its "kings and tyrants" category.

Paribas Asia Equity estimated that the visible part of the iceberg represented eight percent of the Jakarta Stock Exchange's market capitalization in mid-1998. These were the companies in which the children, cousins, half-brother, and Uncle Bob had a stake, usually a minority shareholding. The Paribas study also noted a particular feature. "The Suharto clan's companies are either owned directly or owned through foundations or charitable trusts," it said. "A local magazine, *Warta Ekonomi*, revealed that in thirty-two years of government, Suharto had formed and managed as many as forty such foundations, either chaired by Suharto himself, the late Mrs. Tien Suharto, Suharto's children, son-in-laws, in-laws, brothers, relatives, or friends. Of the forty charitable trusts, however, only seven are known money generators."

Such a system would allow Suharto to declare that he didn't own anything apart from the savings accumulated from his presidential salary and his military pension—with the rank of a five-star general, the highest ever awarded in Indonesia.

But this defense wasn't so easy for the children, whose taste for luxury and extravagant lifestyles was well known in Jakarta. Tutut didn't have thousands of pairs of shoes like Imelda Marcos but she did have a soft spot for silk scarves. And Tommy was a playboy running after starlets in nightclubs until his celebrated marriage fit for a prince in early 1997. He drove around town in a Rolls Royce and his passion for sports cars prompted him to acquire a big chunk of the Italian manufacturer Lamborghini. The children pleaded innocent. They were working for the nation. And all of the assets were in Indonesia. Well, most.

"Of course, there are some significant assets overseas, although the bulk of the family's fortune is tied up in industrial assets in Indonesia," Michael Backman wrote.

Some of the foreign assets were identified—Tutut invested in a highway project in the Philippines, and it was known that Bambang had a stake in Singapore Osprey Marine Ltd. that operated a fleet of oil and gas vessels.

But some Indonesians asserted that the family had at least one billion dollars in liquid assets in banks in Switzerland, Saudi Arabia, and Morocco in addition to property in the United States, Britain (where Tutut did her shopping), and New Zealand.

At the same time, people had to be paid off and that would have diminished the size of the fortune. Peter Sutton noted that Tommy's clove monopoly involved a lot of people and that he couldn't have kept all the money himself.

## JAVANESE EMPIRE

Until the storm erupted in 1997, such "crony capitalism"—that Indonesia perfected more than any of its neighbors—was considered the price one paid for the Asian miracle.

Suharto was the "smiling general" and political and social structures were adjusted accordingly. The ruling Golkar party along with other official parties and opposition groups were all passive cogs in the machinery of executive power with ministers simply carrying out their duties. In foreign policy, Suharto—a virulent anticommunist—put an end to Indonesia's contribution to the assertive solidarity of Third World countries that marked the final years of Sukarno's rule. Indonesia halted its policy of "confrontation" with Malaysia and played a major role in forming ASEAN in 1967, becoming a pillar of stability in the region. But the 1975 invasion of East Timor, abandoned by Portugal as it moved from being a colonial dictatorship to a young European democracy, showed how ruthless Suharto could be when he considered Javanese interests at stake. Mervin Nambiar, a Malaysian journalist who worked for the French and Malaysian news agencies for more than thirty years throughout Southeast Asia, noted that Indonesia was first and foremost an empire before being a nation. The country of more than two hundred million people had more than three hundred ethnic groups and a similar number of languages. Java, the most heavily populated island, ruled over thirteen thousand islands situated around the most sensitive shipping lanes in the world linking East and West, and notably Japan with the Gulf where almost all of its oil came from. Separatist movements were strong in Aceh, on the northern tip of Sumatra neighboring India, and Irian Jaya next to Papua, New Guinea. The 350,000-strong army—relatively small considering the country's size and population—was manned by Javanese and run by Javanese.

Close neighbors, especially Australia and Singapore, lived in constant fear of anarchy in Jakarta that would trigger an explosion across the country. Indeed, when events got out of hand in late 1997 and early 1998, Australia urged the IMF to be more generous and accommodating with the powers in Indonesia in a bid to avert a catastrophe in its own backyard. But that didn't prevent rampaging by pro-Jakarta militias when East Timor voted over-whelmingly for independence in August 1999. And by mid-September, Australia was being used as the launching pad for military intervention by multinational forces under a UN resolution to restore order to the territory.

At the height of the Cold War, Suharto skillfully converted his contribution to regional stability into cash. After all, the Americans weren't so particular about human rights and transparency when the top priority was containing communism.

The West turned up its nose at the most obvious signs of corruption but generally turned a blind eye. And for good reason—the Suharto family was getting rich but so too were Indonesians. Efforts to eradicate poverty enjoyed unprecedented success, and economic growth averaged seven percent a year for three decades. Between the mid-1960s and 1990s, GNP per capita jumped from seventy dollars to more than twelve hundred dollars. As the World Bank applauded, tens of millions of Indonesians rose above the poverty line and a middle class emerged in Jakarta and other big cities. The oil money helped to build essential infrastructure and financed a vast education program. The money was also used to fund industrialization programs to reduce the country's reliance on commodity exports. International aid flowed in as the World Bank sang Indonesia's praises and the country also became an important destination for Japanese industries moving production to cheaper locations in Asia. And when the fashion for investing in emerging markets hit, Indonesia became a favorite target of portfolio investors in the 1990s.

## THE PRICE OF CORRUPTION

After succeeding Sukarno, a flamboyant man who was leading his country to ruin, Suharto soon started playing the role of the enlightened dictator. He filled his government with technocrats, many of whom were educated in the United States, and left them to themselves to run fairly orthodox fiscal and monetary policies.

But like elsewhere in Southeast Asia, rapid economic growth masked structural weaknesses that prevented the country from reaching a new stage in its development.

And the Suharto family's greed knew no bounds. Just before the storm broke in 1997, the payoffs to members of the family and other influential Indonesians were as much as 30 percent of a project's costs. Foreign investors, even the most compliant, started grumbling. Income distribution widened at the expense of the poor. Between the 1970s and the 1990s, the poorest 40 percent of the population saw its share of the national pie drop from 21 percent to 19 percent, according to Prijono Tjiptoherijanto, a professor at Universiti Indonesia. The share of the middle 40 percent also declined, falling from 37 percent to 35 percent. But the share of the richest 20 percent grew from 41 percent to 45 percent. By the end of 1997, riots were breaking out and rapidly turning into major demonstrations of anti-Chinese sentiment across Indonesia, with stores and churches the main targets. The army largely looked on. By 1999, a year after Suharto stepped down, the island of Ambon would become a major focal point for clashes between indigenous Moslems and Christian Chinese. But things were never so clear-cut in Indonesia. In western Kalimantan, local Chinese would join with indigenous Dayak and Malay people in riots against immigrant settlers from the island of Madura off Java. The victorious Dayaks, traditionally headhunters, paraded the severed heads of slaughtered Madurese through the streets for several days. The East Timor crisis came next.

"Corruption in Indonesia has been shamelessly excused by some Western observers as culturally acceptable to Indonesians, dismissed by many aid donors as a small price to pay for economic development, and rationalized by many foreign investors as helping to grease the wheels of an otherwise unresponsive bureaucracy," Adam Schwarz wrote in May 1998. "The events of the last six months have exposed these arguments for the nonsense they always were. There is no doubt that the unchecked corruption tolerated and encouraged by Mr. Suharto deeply affronted Indonesians, undermined the competitiveness of the economy, and weakened the effectiveness of the bureaucracy by eroding the legitimacy of the government."

One could go ever further. With the tentacles of the First Family spreading across every facet of life in Indonesia, Suharto Inc. became the main reason for Indonesia's political paralysis and its inability to cope with the Asian storm as well as its neighbors. From late 1997, it appeared that all decisions ranging from the choice of a future vice president to the sudden interest in a "currency board" system to stabilize exchange rates had only one rational explanation—to preserve the Suharto family fortune.

## FAMILY VERSUS TECHNOCRATS

By early 1998, the Indonesian currency had lost more than eighty percent of its value, tumbling from twenty-seven hundred rupiah to the dollar before the crisis to a low of seventeen thousand rupiah to the dollar.

By contrast, the depreciations of the Thai baht, the Malaysian ringgit, and the Philippine peso were no more than fifty percent. When the baht collapsed, analysts were almost unanimous in predicting that Indonesia was the least badly placed among ASEAN countries.

"If we were to place the regional current account deficits into a beauty contest, then Indonesia's current account deficit isn't exactly drop dead gorgeous, but wins by default nonetheless," Paribas Asia Equity said in August 1997.

Moreover, the sequence of events from July indicated that Indonesia was on stronger footing than some of its neighbors.

Under Finance Minister Mar'ie Mohammad and Bank Indonesia Governor Soedradjad Djiwandono, two respected technocrats, the authorities widened the range in which the rupiah was allowed to fluctuate. The existing range of five percent above or below a set rate was already a lot more flexible than Thailand, allowing it to withstand much of the initial shock.

And while Malaysian Prime Minister Mahathir Mohamad was embarking on his long crusade against "speculators," Suharto projected the image of a responsible head of state. He preceded the calls for IMF help by indicating that Indonesia was willing to adjust to the new reality in Asia, freezing a series of major projects including some that had been promised to members of his family.

By late 1997, there was nevertheless a showdown between the technocrats and the family.

Finance Minister Mar'ie Mohammad and his allies won the first round when the Indonesian government reached an agreement with the IMF on an initial structural adjustment program in early November. The IMF program involved sweeping deregulation including the abolition of cartels and monopolies—like those for cloves and plywood that had made fortunes for the Suharto clan. The subsequent move that provoked so much controversy was the decision to close down sixteen small and medium-sized banks among the 240 operating across Indonesia. Monetary authorities said the banks were considered insolvent and a threat to the stability of the entire banking system. IMF critics attacked the decision, seen as triggering defiance among the banks and panic among depositors. The truth was, IMF sources said, that Indonesian negotiators had deliberately asked for the bank closures to be included in the program and had drawn up the blacklist themselves.

But why these banks, and not bigger institutions that were in just as bad shape? Philippe Delhaise of Thomson BankWatch Asia reckoned that five of the country's biggest banks were technically bankrupt. But closing them down would have triggered an earthquake. The more rational explanation was that the technocrats wanted to send a signal to the owners and share-holders of a banking system that was falling apart and to test the Suharto clan's capacity to react.

The clan reacted, dramatically.

Bambang, the second son of the president, announced plans to take the finance minister to court. He held a quarter of the shares in Bank Andromeda, one of the banks blacklisted for closure. "I personally consider this decision to be an attempt to discredit the family so he is not reelected president," he said. Bambang's allusion to the "election" faced by his father the following April was somewhat surreal. Under the New Order established by Suharto, the constitution required the president to be elected from a one thousand-member assembly. Half the assembly was handpicked while most of the rest were from Suharto's party, Golkar. The risk of a real contest did not exist, as subsequent events showed. "The closure of Bank Andromeda is a farce and undermines my reputation as the head of a company with a good track record," Bambang told the official news agency Antara. He admitted that the bank had violated a rule forbidding banks from lending more than a certain amount to shareholders. But, ninety percent of Indonesia's banks did that, Bambang said. That, of course, was quite true—most of the banks that started mushrooming across Indonesia in the 1980s were used by their owners to finance their own activities. Delhaise noted that loans to executives often exceeded shareholder funds—and didn't even appear on the balance sheet.

The other member of the First Family who sprung to his defense was Suharto's half brother Probosutedjo who owned Bank Jakarta, also targeted to be shut down. The closure order had been accompanied by a ban on owners and executives leaving the country, and he protested against this intolerable abuse of his human rights. Other members of the Suharto clan must have protested as well given that the initial blacklist targeted twenty-seven banks. But these banks were saved by white knights, notably Bank Central Asia (BCA), owned by Liem Sioe Liong himself and one of the country's leading financial institutions. BCA injected funds into Bank Surya, controlled by Tutut, and Bank Utama that was controlled by Tommy.

The first round between the technocrats and the Suharto clan would play an important role in the loss of market confidence in Indonesia. By all appearances, Suharto seemed to be supporting the technocrats—Bambang, for example, met with his father and announced he wouldn't be taking Finance Minister Mar'ie Mohammad to court after all. But from the ashes of Bank Andromeda, a new bank was reborn with a different name. With the IMF and technocrats on one side and clan recriminations on the other, Suharto was sidestepping but would allow family interests to prevail.

And the plywood affair would leave no doubts.

Indonesia's plywood association Apkindo was inseparable from the name of Mohamad Hasan—Uncle Bob, the president's friend of forty years. The plywood cartel was put into place in the mid-1980s, fixing quotas and prices for each producer in a market worth some 3.7 billion dollars a year. Hasan had his own people in offices in Singapore, Hong Kong, and Japan. The cartel provided its own shipping, and Uncle Bob's PT Kara Lines was a natural beneficiary. And freight-forwarding activities were undertaken by a company whose shareholders were companies or foundations run by Uncle Bob. The cartel was justified on the basis that it would prevent the excessive exploitation of Indonesia's vast forest reserves.

At the IMF's request, a letter of intent from the Indonesian government stipulated that "all restrictive commercial agreements, both formal and informal, will be dissolved" starting in February 1998. "No company will be required to sell its products through the joint marketing board nor will they be required to pay premiums or commissions."

But in early February, the press revealed that Apkindo was alive and well. Producers were still being taxed albeit at a lower rate of fifty thousand rupiah a cubic meter, about half the previous rate. This was to cover the "cost of collecting statistics." The shipping service changed its name and producers were told to go through the "new" company.

Similar resistance was seen with efforts to dismantle the monopoly on cloves, the essential ingredient in Indonesia's kretek cigarettes. Established in 1991 as a private consortium, the monopoly was run by Tommy. It offered guaranteed prices to clove farmers. But this proved to be the monopoly's downfall—the prices paid were too high, leading to overproduction and a plunge in clove prices. The government came to the rescue with 360 million dollars.

## SINATRA STYLE

The behavior of the Suharto clan should have come as no surprise. The Javanese patriarch had already shown that he could defy the rules of world trade and the international community if that was the price to pay for defending the privileges of his children. Japan, the biggest source of aid and investment for Indonesia, had been complaining about the plywood cartel for years to no avail. When the "Timor" affair came along, the Japanese decided to get a lot tougher. The Timor was an idea that sprung from the decidedly fertile mind of Tommy. The president's youngest son decided Indonesia should also have its "national car"—in the same way as Prime Minister Mahathir Mohamad promoted the Proton car in neighboring Malaysia in the 1980s. While Mahathir had teamed up with Mitsubishi Motor Corp. of Japan, Tommy found a willing partner in South Korean car maker Kia Motors. The idea was to assemble an Indonesian version of Kia's Sephia model and Tommy had no problems in raising several hundred million dollars for the project. The new company, PT Timor Putra National, would enjoy exceptional privileges—the imported South Korean cars would be exempted from a sixty percent tax on luxury products. That meant the Timor could be sold at half the price of competing models. Car makers in Japan, Europe, and the United States objected, and their governments took the case to the WTO in Geneva. The main victim would be Astra, an Indonesian venture with Japan's top car-maker Toyota Motor Corp. Astra was the biggest automobile concern in Indonesia and included Tommy's older brother Bambang among its share-holders. And so the Timor project triggered a clash between members of the Suharto family in much the same way as the Busang gold fever affair. "The absurdity of the situation became even more apparent in the middle of the year when Tommy announced that since Timor Putra's assembly facilities were not yet ready, the first batch of 'national cars' would actually be assem-bled in South Korea," Bruce Gale said. IMF chief Michel Camdessus later con-fided that Tommy's project received funds diverted from IMF aid for fighting forest fires burning out of control in Indonesia in late 1997, sending a thick haze over regional capitals. The project was obviously one of the first the IMF sought to kill off in negotiations with the Indonesian government. The IMF's timing was appropriate—the South Korean car maker was up to its neck in debts and was on the verge of bankruptcy.

As 1998 dawned, markets reacted violently when they realized the Suharto family had lost contact with reality. Measures dictated by the IMF were being systematically ignored or bypassed. The seriousness of the crisis was being denied. The growing feeling was that Suharto wanted the money—the forty-three billion dollars promised by the IMF and other mul-tilateral and bilateral donors in October—but was refusing to accept the poli-cies that went along with it, namely cutting government spending, cleaning up the financial system, and dissolving the cartels and monopolies that were making fortunes for his clan. Bank Indonesia, the central bank, was printing money and the country risked descending into the chaos of hyperinflation. While Bangkok and Seoul seemed determined to tackle their problems fol-lowing recent changes in government, Jakarta was wallowing in self-denial symbolized by an aging president and his corrupt family.

The straw that broke the camel's back was the government budget sub-mitted by Suharto on January 6. Forecasts for economic growth and inflation were immediately considered unrealistic. Estimates of government revenue and spending were deemed extravagant, especially spending that was forecast to grow thirty-two percent. The technocrats were obviously starting to lose the battle, and the bloodbath on the foreign exchange market began. The cur-rency lost almost half its value in forty-eight hours, plummeting to seventeen thousand rupiah to the dollar at one stage—down eighty percent from its pre-crisis level—before stabilizing below the ten thousand rupiah barrier. Panic spilled into the streets with supermarkets looted and shelves emptied of staples such as rice and cooking oil.

Indonesia had become the epicenter of the Asian financial earthquake. The rupiah's free fall spread to other Asian currencies. And fear spread to foreign capitals. On January 9, President Bill Clinton picked up the phone as he was travelling on Air Force One and spoke to Suharto for twenty minutes. Other calls placed to the presidential palace came from Japanese Prime Minister Ryutaro Hashimoto and German Chancellor Helmut Kohl, whose countries were both major economic partners of Indonesia. United States Deputy Treasury Secretary Larry Summers rushed to Jakarta. Following in his footsteps was Goh Chok Tong, the prime minister of Singapore that lived at the foot of the volcano and broke into a cold sweat whenever the ground started shaking in Indonesia. And finally, IMF managing director Michel Camdessus arrived at the palace on January 15 to sign a revised agreement with the Indonesia government.

Camdessus was an artist when it came to financial diplomacy. He was used to forcing governments—even those of major powers like Russia—to swallow the bitter medicine brewed by his team of international monetary experts. He traveled the world with his eternal smile, putting warmth into the pleas to tighten budgets and open markets. But on January 15, the financial diplomat blundered. As Suharto leaned over a desk to initial the agreement under the eyes of television cameras and photographers, Camdessus folded his arms. For public figures, folded arms were a headache. Keeping them to the side looked too military and moving them about was too casual. And holding hands behind one's back looked impatient. So Camdessus folded his arms. The image of the imperious IMF chief scornfully eyeing the head of state of a humiliated country went around the world, tirelessly repeated on television and printed in hundreds of newspapers. For Asia, it would become the strongest symbol of the turn for the worse in 1997.

What the Indonesian president signed on that day was effectively a bill abolishing Suharto Inc. At least in theory. The agreement and its annexes went a lot further in describing structural reforms and with the consent of the Indonesian government the entire document was posted on the IMF's website. Everyone could read it. Unfortunately, subsequent events would show that Suharto himself hadn't read it.

The pressure exerted by the major powers, including the United States, would not prove to be very effective. New riots would force Suharto to step down in May, relinquishing power to his vice president B. J. Habibie. President Habibie would be defeated in the country's first free elections in four decades in June the following year. And Indonesian politics would come full circle with Golkar being displaced by the party headed by Megawati, the daughter of Sukarno, the country's founding father who Suharto pushed aside in the mid-1960s.

But in the first few months of 1998, the aging general was showing no signs of abandoning the "My Way" approach immortalized by Frank Sinatra. At seventy-six, Suharto had ruled an extraordinary complex country for thirty-two years. Sukarno may have been the father of the nation, but Suharto was the "father of development," as his supporters called him. He would never step down, confirming the crude but realistic assessment of one American official. "Marcos was our son of a bitch but Suharto's his own son of a bitch," the official said.

## DR. HANKE'S MAGIC POTION

Steve Hanke was a mild-mannered American academic, the most unlikely person to play a leading role in the Indonesian drama. It was hard to imagine this thin man—married to a Frenchwoman and used to looking at the world through narrow glasses—erupting in violent polemics against the IMF and prompting angry responses from its executives.

As a professor in applied economics at John Hopkins University in Baltimore, Hanke was a specialist in "currency board" systems of exchange rates. In a world of floating exchange rates, this rigid system had become a life buoy for several emerging economies. Hanke himself was involved in setting up currency board systems in Argentina, as well as countries liberated by the collapse of the Soviet empire such as Bulgaria and Lithuania as well as Bosnia.

As Hong Kong showed, currency boards were a radical means of ensuring currency stability.

In all countries hit by the Asian financial tempest, the stability of exchange rates had become a priority, but even more so in Indonesia where the rupiah's collapse had reached dramatic proportions. Taking into account Indonesia's external debt of seventy-two billion dollars, or more than one hundred and twenty billion dollars if derivatives were included, most Indonesian companies were insolvent if the exchange rate fell to ten thousand rupiah or more to the dollar. The loss of confidence in the rupiah was so great that the payments system wasn't working any more. The currency crisis triggered outflows of capital that depressed the rupiah even further. The real economy was starting to seize up. If the country defaulted on its foreign debt, the cost was incalculable—Indonesia would lose years, possible even decades, of development. This was how things were in early 1998.

In early February, Steve Hanke met Suharto and proposed a currency board system with the rupiah pegged at fifty-five hundred to the dollar. When Hanke went to Suharto's office, it was the president's eldest daughter Tutut who opened the door. Well, almost. She organized the meeting behind the backs of those in the government's economic team including Widjojo Nitisastro, the president's economic adviser who was leading negotiations with the IMF. The IMF had known nothing about the initiative until Hanke got off the plane.

The currency board battle would last several weeks, triggering passionate arguments within the Indonesian elite and between economists and other monetary experts across the world. The debate showed that religious wars between distinguished economists could be punctuated by a violence that was rare in the academic world. Steve Hanke found himself denounced as the "Rasputin of the Rupiah" by another American economist, Paul Krugman. In political circles in Jakarta, being for or against the currency board proposal could determine future career prospects and Suharto himself expressed his support for the idea. On February 11, Suharto signed a decree that got rid of central bank governor Soedrajdad Djiwandono. He was replaced by Sjaril Sabirin, a Bank Indonesia official who had once worked at the World Bank headquarters in Washington. Soedrajdad hadn't been very keen on the idea of a currency board system, and neither were most of the technocrats. Sjaril supported the idea.

The argument for a currency board was simple—as illustrated by Peter Gontha, an associate of Bambang. "Nothing the IMF has done has worked, so unless the IMF can come up with a better way to bring the rupiah down below six thousand, the currency board should be given a chance," he said.

In Washington, the thinking was a little different. Michel Camdessus told Suharto that he could follow Hanke's recommendations. But if he did, Indonesia could say goodbye to the money from the IMF.

The argument was no longer technical—like the financial crisis itself, it had become largely political. But for the experts from IMF, there was an ulterior motive behind the Suharto clan's support for the idea. An IMF official explained later that backing the currency board proposal was an "exit strategy"—it would have allowed the members of the clan to exchange their rupiah for dollars at an exchange rate that had been raised to an artificially high level. In other words, put their hands on the country's remaining foreign exchange reserves that by that stage had fallen to less than twenty billion dollars.

The IMF didn't object to currency board systems in principle. Steve Hanke himself noted that the IMF played an active role in implementing the exchange-rate mechanism in Bosnia as part of the Dayton peace accords. To show that such a system didn't conflict with the IMF's demands, Hanke—who was now Suharto's special economic adviser—suggested the "IMF plus" formula to the Indonesian president. In other words, the Hanke plan was in fact nothing more than the IMF plans plus the stabilization of the rupiah through setting up a currency board system.

But another major problem was that such a system required robust payment systems whereas Indonesia's banking system was a total mess. Nonsense, Steve Hanke responded several weeks later in Hong Kong during a debate between Hanke, Paul Krugman, and John Greenwood, the architect of the Hong Kong system established in 1983. Nonsense because setting up a currency board system was the best way to purge the banking system. "Bank Indonesia is funding the banks because there is no constraint on the huge overdrafts of the banks," Hanke said. The currency board would put an end to practices that were leading to hyperinflation as it would immediately

*Asian Storm*

halt the printing of money. Of the two hundred banks across Indonesia, only about a dozen would survive.

Lost confidence in the Indonesian authorities? Yet another reason to implement the system as it would take the conduct of monetary policy out of Indonesian hands. "If you don't trust these people, if you have weak institutions, weak government, with doubts on their integrity, it is precisely why you should put them out of the decision-making process," Hanke said.

If he was right, the timing wasn't yet ripe. But one thing was clear—either the Suharto clan members didn't understand how the mechanism worked or they had no intention of accepting the discipline such a system imposed.

## THE JAVANESE KING

On March 10, Suharto was reelected to a seventh term by the People's Consultative Assembly under his control. The patriarch was behaving more and more like a Javanese king.

Suharto picked B. J. Habibie as his new vice president. Habibie, a sixty-one-year-old engineer by training, had long been in the presidential circle. He was educated in Germany and worked at aviation giant Messerschmitt-Bölkow-Blohm in the 1970s and now had the record as the longest-serving member of cabinet in his role as Research and Technology Minister. He had long been regarded as a sort of mad professor who was not miserly when it came to using public funds. Among other things, he spearheaded Indonesia's attempts to develop an aeronautical industry. Habibie's publicly listed company IPTN devoured billions of dollars in a project to develop an aircraft for regional transport. According to the tireless Australian sleuth Michael Backman, "Habibie Inc." was a modest replica of "Suharto Inc." —about eighty companies run by the brothers, children, and cousins of the Research and Technology Minister. His treasure island was Batam off Singapore. For two decades, the future vice president worked on transforming Batam into an industrial base and harbor rivaling Singapore. The island was a tropical paradise for subsidies and privileges. For the markets, it was red alert. When rumors surfaced on January 21 that Habibie was the hot favorite to be vice president, the rupiah fell like a rock.

After he was reelected in March, Suharto decided to tell the IMF and the international community where to go. The new cabinet looked like the executive board of Suharto Inc. Uncle Bob was brought in as the new industry and trade minister. And yes, Mr. Monopoly himself was put in charge of dismantling cartels. Mar'ie Muhammad, the public face of the technocrats, lost the post of finance minister to Fuad Bawazier, a trusted ally and financial adviser to the Suharto family. But the icing on the cake of the new cabinet was Tutut, the president's eldest daughter who became minister for social affairs. Tutut was the figurehead for Suharto's nepotism, the vice president of Golkar, and seriously presented by loyal followers of the regime as a potential candidate for succession if the Suharto dynasty was going to remain in power. As minister of social affairs, she had all the grace of Queen Marie-Antoinette, although she wasn't about to tell starving Indonesians to eat cake if they didn't have enough bread. For Indonesians, the problem was chicken, the main source of protein that was now out of the reach of most Indonesian households. "Eat rabbit," she declared while touring some food stalls in Jakarta in March. "The taste of rabbit is just as good as chicken."

## THE MAY REVOLUTION

Political regimes that lost the capacity to adapt were victims of both their failures and successes. The emergence of a middle class and improvements in education were to the credit of the New Order. But the greed represented by Suharto Inc. negated such social developments. Why bother studying for a degree when success was first and foremost a matter of influence peddling and nepotism? How could the intellectual and moral awakening of a generation accommodate a political monarchy where the wishes of a single man dictated the law of the land to more than two hundred million people? What was the possibility for the social consolidation of economic growth in a country where the distribution of wealth was so unequal between the Chinese minority and other ethnic groups? The economic collapse would raise these questions with an acuteness never before seen in Indonesia. And the students provided the necessary, albeit insufficient, response: "Suharto must go."

The rapid disintegration of political regimes that appeared unshakable only months before was a mundane phenomenon that nevertheless surprised people when it happened. In Jakarta too, and it happened quickly.

The hikes in prices of staple goods triggered by the long-deferred removal of subsidies unleashed a new wave of rioting across the country. Students were getting bolder and took their protests outside their campuses. With Suharto out of town for a summit of the Group of Fifteen developing countries in Cairo, soldiers opened fire on a student protest. The four students killed by the troops were from the elite Triskati University. Suharto had suddenly lost the middle class.

Rioting devastated Jakarta. More than a thousand people died, including looters trapped in blazing department stores owned by ethnic Chinese. The Chinese who had the means fled the country, accompanied by expatriates.

In the bloody chaos of the streets, the message was not difficult to read. The house of Liem Sioe Liong was ransacked and set on fire. Rioters systematically destroyed the branches and automatic teller machines of Bank Central Asia, the bank own by Suharto's most prominent Chinese friend.

The pressure from the streets started to crack the edifice patiently built by Suharto over the past thirty-two years. There were defections from what had once been the most loyal pillars of the regime. Students took their protests to the parliament building that soon became the focal point of the crisis. The army had a choice—either assume the cost of human life and forever compromise its special role in Indonesian society or prepare to pull back. It would depend on allegiances. Suharto himself was holed up in the palace with the rest of the clan, resembling a drowning man clutching at anything to stay afloat. But as the patriarch recognized himself in his resignation speech, broadcast live throughout the world, all his dreams had slipped away. "Taking this into account, my feeling is that it would be difficult for me to rule," Suharto said. "In conformance with the 1945 constitution and after seriously considering the point of view of the house of representatives, I have decided to abandon the presidency of the Republic of Indonesia. In conformance with the constitution, Vice President B. J. Habibie will serve the rest of my presidential term. I would like to thank the citizens for their assistance and their support. And I would like to seek their pardon if I have committed any errors or displayed any weaknesses."

## A "NEW DEAL" FOR JAKARTA?

Replacing Suharto was one thing. Dismantling Suharto Inc. was another. The Asian financial crisis had done some of the work by sharply eroding the value of the assets of the clan that, according to estimates, was in debt to the tune of several billion dollars. Those close to Suharto were removed from the government by Habibie and General Wiranto, the head of the armed forces whose actions helped to seal Suharto's fate. Wiranto removed the ambitious General Prabowo Subianto, one of Suharto's son-in-laws, from his position as head of the army's strategic reserve. Suharto's offspring lost lucrative contracts and other monopolistic privileges. The foreign companies that used to jostle for positions in the back rooms of the First Family suddenly found that what was once a trump card was now a handicap. Within a few days, Thames Water of Britain and Lyonnaise des Eaux of France had bought out their once inescapable local partners, Suharto's eldest son Sigit Harjojudanto and the Salim group of Liem Sioe Liong.

But beyond such developments, which included changing the head of an inquiry into the Suharto family wealth, the Habibie administration wasn't expected to dig very deep in uncovering the clan's assets. "Mr. Habibie's administration is guaranteed to do little when it comes to chasing down the Suharto assets. Almost certainly, it was part of a bargain struck by Suharto when he agreed to step aside. But to do so also would be tacit acknowledgment that much of the wealth of the old faces in the new cabinet also is possibly illegitimate and worthy of investigation," Michael Backman wrote. Such potential targets ranged from Habibie himself, whose family had prominent assets under its Timsco group, to newly reappointed Coordinating Minister of the Economy, Finance, and Industry Ginandjar Kartasasmita, the main negotiator for Indonesia's debt rescheduling who had also "thrived" during his years in office.

"In the longer term, the biggest threat to the Suharto empire will not come from the new regime—hamstrung by collective guilt as it is—or from any investigative parliamentary commission," Backman said. "The real threat was low-minded scavenging by other members of the Indonesian elite still eager for their turn at the trough…With some juicy pickings now left without the political cover they once enjoyed, the Suharto corporate carcass is still quite a kill and it is sure to attract a lot of vultures. It takes more than a few days of shuffling the deck chairs at the top to turn around a cultural legacy built up over thirty years."

Suharto wasn't a Marcos and he wasn't a Mobuto either. He was more like a Dr. Jekyll and Mr. Hyde in a large family of dictators. If the accounts of the "smiling general" were closed in the early 1990s, they would have been largely positive. But when Suharto stepped down in 1998, a large part of the accumulated gains over the years had been wiped out. The rupiah's collapse had slashed GDP per capita from twelve hundred dollars to about three hundred dollars, at the lower end of the World Bank's rankings. In 1998, the Indonesian economy would decline by some fifteen percent. Some forty million people would fall below the poverty line. Tens of millions of individuals would be either unemployed or underemployed. A serious drought would exacerbate the financial crisis, damaging crops in a country that had become self-sufficient in rice. And ethnic and separatist tensions would flare across the archipelago, from East Timor to Kalimantan to Aceh. Ethnic Chinese who fled would take with them billions of dollars, transferred to bank accounts in Singapore or Hong Kong. Others would send their children to school abroad to foreign cities like Kuching, capital of the eastern Malaysian state of Sarawak where Chinese could live in peace and study in a language almost identical to Indonesian. But the Chinese would always face the cruel dilemma of whether to go back to a country where they were traditionally made the convenient scapegoats in times of trouble.

The new leaders couldn't simply cut a new deal between the Javanese military hierarchy and its economic agents, the Chinese minority. Despite controlling two-thirds of the country's wealth, the Chinese were subject to political and social discrimination. Indonesians of Chinese origin were second-class citizens, no matter how many generations they had lived there. Their religious identity, often Christian, was respected during periods not marked by violence, but not their cultural identity. Chinese were denied public office and had little political representation. Any "New Deal" in Indonesia would involve redistributing economic power and achieving a finer balance in political and social representation. But the chances for such developments were thin. Indonesia and it neighbors were living dangerously—and not just for a year.

## CORRUPTION VERSUS THE MARKET

In an interview published in *Euromoney* the month before Suharto resigned, André Lee described the attitude of foreign investors to the presidential clan. Lee's adventures in Indonesia had led to the collapse of Hong Kong investment bank Peregrine Investment Holdings earlier in the year.

"We were always aware of it as I think anyone who travels to Indonesia is," Lee said. "I don't know if there has been a single infrastructure project awarded to a non-first-family member. They are involved in many of the major companies and infrastructure projects in Indonesia. It's kind of hard not to, at some point, be involved or have some sort of indirect contact with them."

In reality, foreign companies accepted corruption all too readily in emerging economies. Frank Vogl, the vice president of Transparency International, a nongovernment organization campaigning against corruption, said critics focussed too much on demand rather than supply. "Those who pay bribes are sometimes depicted as innocent parties, forced by ruthless officials to provide kickbacks and do special favors in return for business," Vogl said. "The reality is that both parties to corrupt practices conspire to defraud the public, to undermine fair trade, to waste resources, to frustrate development, and often to increase human suffering."

The story of Suharto Inc. proved, if there was any need, that corruption was not one of those little incidental expenses incurred by developing economies. Western leaders and experts who denounced "crony capitalism" as one of the causes of the Asian crisis only had to look at what their own companies were doing to see that corruption was a two-way street. Rich countries took too long before they acknowledged the problem. And by the end of the twentieth century, it remained to be seen what would become of the OECD convention concluded at the end of 1997, which aimed at combating corruption among officials of foreign governments in international commercial transactions.

The subject was important for Western democracies. Not just because corruption and money laundering went hand in hand, as Frank Vogl pointed out. It was also because some of the money that went under the table in emerging economies had an unfortunate habit of coming back, in large amounts, into the pockets of individuals or political parties in certain Western capitals—intolerable from the point of view of both social equality or public morality.

Treating corruption as a serious distortion to the efficient functioning of markets was inseparable from the advanced state of the market economy itself in industrialized countries. But certain industrialized countries had a problem with that—and still did at the end of the century.

# CHAPTER ELEVEN

# An Afternoon on the Bund

"Can China cope? And can the world cope with China? Because so much is at stake, the answer to both questions must be 'yes'".
—*World Bank*, China in 2020

It was time to go home. By taking the student route for the long holidays that accompanied the end of a posting, we could avoid the pressure of people rushing. Instead of the twelve-hour flight, we opted for the Siberian route separating Tokyo from Paris. we set sail from Yokohama for Shanghai one evening in September 1989. From Shanghai, a night train would take me to Beijing before the long rail journey to Moscow. Six days and six nights contemplating the Great Wall, going back several centuries in time as we crossed Mongolia, washing my tired eyes in Lake Baikal and counting the endless Siberian villages where nothing, especially the misery, seemed to have changed since Gogol. Six days and six nights drinking tea and eating cheap caviar, bought for a song with rubles acquired on the black market. In Novosibirsk it was dark by 4 p.m. But we celebrated my arrival in the Siberian city with grilled chicken wings bought at the station.

Rusting away like the train carriages turned into forgotten homes parked in railway sheds, the Soviet Union was on its deathbed. In Leningrad, the victory of the West could already be felt. From taxis to cafés, the dollarization of the economy was underway. As for China, it was still traumatized from that night in June when kids in uniforms, hostages of their own fear, obeyed an order from aging members of the Communist Party to open fire on a crowd of students. In early October, Beijing was still in a state of siege. Soldiers guarded the entrances to Tiananmen Square, which was open to visitors at fixed times in the morning and afternoon—on presentation of one's passport.

Emptied of tourists, the Forbidden City was like a film set. We were no more than one of a few dozen roaming around the biggest museum in the world. Back in May as the first of many demonstrations were converging on Tiananmen Square, the ancient sanctuary of Manchu emperors was full of Chinese tourists. They came from all over a country overwhelmed by internal migration involving tens of millions of people leaving the countryside for jobs in the cities.

A sharp hike in train fares was one of the first steps the authorities took after the bloodbath on June 4. On the overnight train from Shanghai to Beijing, there was only one other passenger in the first-class carriage—an official from the state-owned railway company.

Shanghai had been serious but serene, eager to open itself up to the rare foreign visitors who hadn't been put off by recent events. The regime in Beijing, that austere city on the windswept steppes of the distant north, could close itself off from the outside world and international contempt. But Shanghai was a port. And when you approached it by sea, even when you couldn't see land, the water suddenly changed color as the mighty Yangtze River flowed into the ocean. The city itself sprawled out across the river. And on Sundays, families would descend upon the Bund for an afternoon walk.

That's where we were, looking across the river to Pudong where the biggest construction site of the century would soon appear, when a group of students approached. Where are you coming from? Where are you going? Japan? France? One spoke Japanese. His dream was to go to Japan, he said, raising his arm to the east. Another spoke French and recited the names of famous writers. The others spoke English. The crowd got bigger. The discussion in three languages attracted other young people and curious onlookers.

The reflex came from an eventful stay, many years earlier, in another communist country. We started glancing left and right to be on the lookout for the arrival of the police, who would surely not ignore this spontaneous meeting. We didn't speak about politics. Well, not openly, at least. But they spoke of their desire to leave, to live, and study somewhere else.

Nothing happened. Night slowly fell and we concluded our afternoon on the Bund, happy but a little disconcerted.

When the blood was flowing in Beijing in June, Shanghai showed it was different. The authorities of the industrial and commercial metropolis that was China's biggest city managed to cool things down in a few days. There was no force, no violence, and no tragedy. The mayor was a man called Zhu Rongji.

## BEIJING AND SHANGHAI

The massacre started on June 3, a little before midnight. The order came from Zhongnanhai, the new forbidden city that was a stone's throw from the square.

The order to put an end to the "chaos" must have come from paramount leader Deng Xiaoping, who was head of the central military commission. But the title of "Butcher of Beijing" went to Li Peng, the prime minister. Throughout the rest of his ten-year term that ended in 1998, Li was subjected to abuse from protestors every time he undertook one of his rare ventures abroad. Yang Shangkun, the Chinese president and deputy chairman of the central military commission, was another suspect.

Back in May, Yang had welcomed thousands of international bankers in the Great Hall of the People opposite Tiananmen Square. The financiers had come to Beijing for the annual meeting of the ADB, the first big international event of this type that China had ever hosted. The scene was disturbing. Inside the hall, the Chinese head of state was trying to charm, with not much talent, a few thousand bankers from across the world. Outside the hall, tens of thousands of students were marching down the Avenue of Heavenly Peace and descending upon the square, calling for democracy and an end to corruption. Deserting the bankers to chat with the students was not a difficult decision. The weather was beautiful, a bit warmer than Paris in May 1968 when student riots rocked the French capital. But dictatorships didn't have the same scruples as democratic regimes and the peasants in People's Liberation Army uniforms knew only one way to restore order—firing on the crowd. There was no official death toll. According to reporters there at the time, it was somewhere between four hundred and eight hundred.

When news of the bloodbath reached Shanghai, the industrial heartland of China exploded with anger. On June 5, a Monday, thousands of protestors blocked the streets. Zhu, the mayor, appealed for calm in a television address. "As mayor, I want to apologize to you for our inability in recent days to enforce the law and ensure the normal livelihood of the people," he said, before lapsing into supreme ambiguity. "What has happened recently in Beijing is now a fact of history and facts of history cannot be concealed by anyone. The whole truth will eventually come to light."

In a land of mechanical puppets droning on with the language of bureaucrats, the speech was unusual. And so too was the man.

## COMMUNIST WITH A HUMAN FACE

Zhu Rongji became the human face of Chinese communism. Within a few months of the massacre, authorities anxious to repair the considerable damage used the mayor of Shanghai as a roving ambassador shuttling between world capitals.

He spoke English with great ease. This was not due to postings at Chinese missions in London or at the United Nations in New York. Zhu learned his English by listening to foreign radio broadcasts while he was raising pigs or making bricks during the lost years of the Cultural Revolution.

Zhu was purged twice. The first time was as a "rightist"—he dared to question the outrageous objectives of the disastrous Great Leap Forward in the late 1950s. The second time was during the Cultural Revolution when Mao Zedong let the Red Guards run wild, and competent technicians such as himself came under suspicion. From 1957 until his rehabilitation in 1979, Zhu remained loyal to the communist cause and survived, like so many others, as his life oscillated between labor camps and obscure party tasks.

In 1987, he became mayor of Shanghai. According to Deng Xiaoping, Zhu was "the only real economic expert in our party." Running the biggest city in China, where he worked with local party chief and future president Jiang Zemin, allowed Zhu to forge a reputation as a great administrator. He was perceptive, honest, brutally decisive, and ruthless when it came to dealing with the inefficient and corrupt bureaucracy. He took an axe to the jungle of red tape to help foreign investors who had come to invest in Shanghai. Zhu was so successful that Deng brought him to Beijing in 1991 to take up the post of vice premier. Jiang was already there, having left Shanghai for Beijing in 1989 when he replaced the "liberal" Zhao Ziyang who was dismissed as secretary general of the Chinese Communist Party after being too accommodating to students.

The events of 1989 derailed the Chinese economic train. The economic slowdown came as the opponents of Deng's economic reforms regained strength. At the same time, China was subjected to economic sanctions by most industrialized countries. In 1991, however, Deng followed in the footsteps of the Chinese emperors before him, embarking on a tour of southern provinces where he galvanized support for further economic reforms. At the time, Deng no longer had any official titles except for being head of the Chinese Bridge Players Association. But words of the patriarch were heeded—a bit too well, as it turned out. By 1993, the economy was overheating and threatening to lead to hyperinflation, notably in the big cities and special economic zones of the coastal areas.

## CHINA IN 2020

The man who put both his feet on the brakes was Zhu Rongji. As Prime Minister Li Peng was recovering from a heart attack, the vice premier took over the reigns of economic policy. He temporarily stepped into the central bank governor's chair and piloted the Chinese economic machine to a soft landing. Inflation, which had reached an annual rate of twenty percent in urban areas, was brought under control and money supply growth slowed to more reasonable levels. Investment in fixed assets also slowed to an annual increase of 18.2 percent in 1996, down from 61.8 percent in 1993. Economic growth also slowed but remained in the vicinity of ten percent. Production prices were also brought under control, leading to an increase in China's international competitiveness and an export boom. Foreign exchange reserves ballooned from eighteen billion dollars in 1993 to more than 140 billion dollars in 1998. Foreign companies rushed to invest in China. Between 1994 and 1996, foreign direct investment in China exceeded one hundred billion dollars—almost half of all direct investment to emerging economies. In 1997 alone, foreign direct investment came to forty billion dollars out of the 107 billion dollars flowing to emerging economies.

All this meant that 1997 was going to be China's big year. Hong Kong, the Pearl of the Orient and the jewel in Britain's colonial crown, was to be returned to Chinese sovereignty at midnight on June 30, ending more than one-and-a-half centuries of colonial humiliation. And the IMF and the World Bank would mark the event by holding their annual meetings in China's new "special administrative region" a couple of months later, the biggest gathering of international financiers ever held in China. In the lead-up to the meeting, the World Bank marked the occasion by publishing some long-range forecasts in a study called *China in 2020*. The study was printed on glossy paper and destined to last, a bit like *The East Asian Miracle* published by the World Bank four years earlier.

The central theme was that the emergence of China as a major economic power had to be considered by its Asian neighbors and the rest of the world as an opportunity and not a threat. If all went well, China would be the world's second-biggest exporter as well as its second-largest importer in 2020. China would also be a major player on international markets ranging from energy to cereals and would also have a respectable presence in world capital markets. The country's 1.2 billion people wouldn't be rich but they wouldn't be poor either.

Of course, "the transformation of an economy as large as China's from low to middle-income status, from rural to urban, from agricultural to industrial (and services), will inevitably cause ripples in the world economy," the study said. But "China's rapid growth and liberalization will be an opportunity for the world economy, not a threat." After all, the emergence of the United States in the nineteenth century and Japan in the twentieth century was "good for the world" and not just the Americans and the Japanese.

The study painted two scenarios, one rosy and one dark, a Chinese blossoming and a "Sinosclerosis" where the promises faded.

In the first, China was "competitive, caring, and confident" as well as being "cleaner and richer" while enjoying "rapid and sustainable growth based on markets and private enterprise."

But if things turned for the worse, prospects for eliminating poverty in poor provinces would recede. "Cities would become tinderboxes of tensions, with growing numbers of poor living in proximity to an increasingly rich elite that manipulated the laws and systems to its benefit," the study recounted. "Foreign investment would be deterred by the opacity of China's trade, legal and investment systems, and growing instability.

Frictions would arise with trading partners and increase the possibility of retaliatory action."

Whatever the outcome, China had "embarked on an extraordinary voyage of change" affecting a fifth of the planet's population. "Much will depend on the ability and resolve of the authorities to maintain the momentum of reforms," the World Bank study reiterated. "Two questions present themselves. Can China cope? And can the world cope with China? Because so much is at stake, the answer to both questions must be 'yes.'"

## A MAN IN A HURRY

"I don't know if this speech is worth 1,150 dollars to get in. I'll do my best but I don't know whether I can satisfy you," Zhu Rongji said. Actually, the financiers gathered for a seminar hosted by the World Bank on September 22, 1997, should have been paying a lot more—the "Chinese economic czar" had emerged in a strengthened position from the fifteenth congress of the Chinese Communist Party that had just renewed the mandate for reform. Zhu's elevation to the post of prime minister was only a few months away, with the next sitting of National People's Congress scheduled for March. Disoriented by the storm that had spread across Southeast Asia since July, those who had paid to hear Zhu speak wanted to be comforted and reassured. But the contents of the speech, which was fairly conventional, undoubtedly counted less than the physical ease, the relaxed manner, and the humor displayed by Zhu. The man lived up to the legend—he was direct, sure of himself, and knew what he was talking about. It was reassuring because so much depended on his abilities.

In September and the months that followed, the position of Chinese leaders was the focus of much anxiety. For foreign investors battered by the storm across the rest of the region, China was an ocean of calm. The renminbi, not fully convertible, was a bastion of stability as other currencies plunged. As the crisis spread to Hong Kong in October followed by South Korea and Japan in November and December, all eyes started increasingly focussing on China—to which point, it became unreasonable.

Zhu's personality played an important role in a world where stardom left no profession untouched. Bakers and cooks had become international stars. And so too, had Zhu Rongji. "You're my idol," a ravishing Hong Kong reporter gushed during a Beijing news conference given by China's newly appointed prime minister the following March. Surrounded by his new government team Zhu spoke for ninety minutes to the hundreds of local and foreign reporters present. The show was broadcast live on national television and cable networks. And that wasn't the only change in protocol.

"I'm not at all good looking," the new prime minister quipped, referring to two American weeklies that had recently run portraits of him. Asked about his falling victim to the antirightist campaign of the late 1950s: "I learned a lot from that experience. But that experience was also unpleasant so I would prefer not to mention it again." On his role in China's new government: "I do not have much to say. Whatever the foreign media call me, China's Gorbachev, economic czar or anything else, I'm not delighted to hear it."

The comparison with the former Soviet leader was particularly unwelcome. Apart from the fact that perestroika hardly benefited its founder, who ended up being eaten by the very forces he unleashed, the official visit by Gorbachev to Beijing in May 1989 only served to encourage protesting students and complicated the resolution of the crisis. But the collapse of the Soviet Union also showed that totalitarian regimes could not reform and survive. President Jiang and his comrades were betting they could and that China would succeed where all other socialist countries had failed. The aim was to assimilate a market economy and a certain amount of democracy in a political and social architecture that preserved the leading role of the Communist Party.

Under the long march of Deng's economic reforms, the Communist Party had lost much of its ideological baggage. The party congress in Beijing in September 1997 took a decisive turn by legitimizing "several forms of public ownership" for state-owned enterprises, paving the way for privatization. "This new theoretical breakthrough will definitely lead to advances in several major aspects in the reform of these enterprises," Zhu told the seminar in Hong Kong.

Chinese leaders had an acute awareness of how crucial the reforms were. The only chance of retaining the "mandate from heaven" to govern the vast empire was to maintain a high level of economic growth that could absorb the cost of social change. And growth couldn't be maintained with a public sector that accounted for a third of industrial output while devouring two-thirds of the country's total lending. Nor could growth be maintained if the cleaning up of the banking system was blocked by the need to keep public enterprises afloat in an ocean of bad debts.

Survival required reforms and Zhu held the cards. "I'm very much concerned that I may fall short of what is expected of me," he told the news conference in Beijing. "However, no matter what is waiting ahead—land mines, an abyss—I have no hesitations or misgivings but shall do whatever I can and devote myself entirely to my people and my country to the last day of my life."

Zhu was a man in a hurry. At sixty-nine years old, he had a five-year mandate to leave his mark when he was appointed prime minister in 1998. And by giving himself three years to clean up industrial and financial state-owned enterprises, he had set his goals high.

## TO DEVALUE OR NOT TO DEVALUE

The challenge for anyone trying to bring a fifth of mankind out of poverty and underdevelopment was already complex and dangerous. A hostile external environment only made matters worse. The crisis in the rest of Asia was bad news for China. A third of the country's exports went to neighboring countries and Chinese exports had been booming since 1993. If exports grew at a slower pace or even started decreasing, how would economic growth be maintained at high enough levels to absorb the millions of new workers coming onto the labor market each year? What was the right response? Should a competitive devaluation of the currency take place?

In addition to these immediate questions, there were also strategic considerations that were almost philosophical in nature. China's neighbors had just gone through the painful experience of letting their banking systems drift. Sudden outflows of short-term capital would not occur in China, however, as the currency was nonconvertible for capital account transactions that were strictly monitored. But the internal risks for China's banking system were huge—at least a quarter of all loans to state-owned enterprises were nonperforming. And after all, a run on local banks couldn't be ruled out. What would happen if depositors emptied their accounts and stuffed piles of renminbi under their beds?

When the rest of the world learned of the unbelievable pyramid of debts built up by South Korea *chaebol* in late 1997, Beijing was embarrassed. During the party congress several months earlier, the Korean model was upheld as an example of how to transform state-owned enterprises into powerful conglomerates that could one day feature in the *Fortune* 500 list of the world's top companies.

The major difference between China and other Asian countries was that the response to all these questions would have to come from the government. For better or worse, China was still an administered economy where authorities had more influence on markets than in liberalized economies.

China's first response to the Asia crisis was to not touch the exchange rate of the renminbi, which was implicitly pegged to the dollar. A devaluation wasn't necessary. And even if it was necessary, it wouldn't be beneficial. It might even be dangerous.

A competitive devaluation wasn't needed because China was already well ahead of its Asian neighbors—it devalued in 1994. And some economists saw the resulting difficulties of other Asian exporters as one of the contributing causes of the regional crisis.

"China's additional competitiveness was at the heart of the process that unleashed the crisis in Southeast Asia," said Kenneth Courtis, chief economist for Deutsche Bank in Tokyo. The Chinese currency's depreciation was amplified by the appreciation of Southeast Asian currencies pegged to the dollar when the yen started plunging in 1995. For Courtis, the Big Three economies of China, Japan, and the United States were the internal trio that brought Southeast Asia crashing to the ground.

"Devaluation?" asked indignant Chinese officials and a good number of economists. "What devaluation?"

From January 1, 1994, China abandoned the official exchange rate of 5.8 yuan to the dollar in preference to the central swap rate of 8.7 yuan to the dollar. On paper the devaluation was more than thirty percent. But in reality, the central swap rate was already being used for most commercial transactions and the average rate was 8.1 yuan to the dollar. So the devaluation was much more modest at around seven percent. But even at the nominal rate, argued Pu Yonghao, economist at Bank of China International in London, the devaluation would have been reduced to only six percent taking into account the differences between inflation in the United States and China (forty percent between 1994 and 1996) and the fact that the Chinese currency had appreciated to 8.3 yuan to the dollar by early 1998.

China could not deny, however, that it had developed a huge manufacturing capacity financed by direct investments from Hong Kong, Taiwan, the United States, and other countries, allowing Chinese exporters to push other Asian exporters aside. But here, the statistical evidence was not conclusive. Chinese exports generally didn't compete directly with exports from the four main ASEAN economies—Indonesia, Malaysia, the Philippines, and Thailand—or South Korea. The exception was textiles, but that was an industry where world trade was distorted by quotas for importing countries. China's advantage in terms of low labor costs and rising productivity in the textile sector mean that it could have eliminated its competitors—if the world market was liberalized.

Fred Hu, head of Asian research at Goldman Sachs, nevertheless estimated that China's share of exports to OECD countries almost doubled between 1990 and 1995, rising from 8.5 percent to more than sixteen percent. The share of the four ASEAN countries climbed more slowly, from twenty-one percent to twenty-three percent in the same period. Those losing share were the newly industrialized economies of South Korea, Taiwan, Hong Kong, and Singapore. In the case of Taiwan and Hong Kong, the decline reflected moves to shift production to Mainland China. "The increase in China's market share thus to an important degree reflects the role of Asia's intraregional direct investment, and China's entry into world trade has not crowded out Southeast Asia's exports in third markets," he said.

"It is impossible to explain the recent financial troubles in Southeast Asia by pointing to China's role in undercutting those countries' competitiveness. The cause of Southeast Asia's economic trouble lies at home."

## GOOD NEIGHBORLINESS

For the same reasons, China had no pressing economic reasons to devalue in 1997. And it also had political reasons not to.

China was repeatedly praised for its responsible attitude during the summit of leaders from the Group of Eight (the seven leading industrialized countries plus Russia) in Birmingham in mid-1998. With Asia in disarray,

China—and its currency—were a pillar of stability. A few weeks earlier Zhu Rongji had been the star of another summit of Asian and European leaders. The new Chinese prime minister met European leaders behind closed doors before being immortalized in handshakes by photographers. Even in Asia, ingratitude knew no bounds. Those who used to denounce the "decadent" West and heap praise on Japan for being the economic motor of the region were now keeping their distance in public. Japan was even discreetly criticized for failing to be the locomotive during a visit to Tokyo in 1998 by Anwar Ibrahim, the Malaysian deputy prime minister and finance minister at the time.

China's assurances were a sharp contrast to Japan's cowardliness. Japan may have contributed billions of dollars to IMF packages for countries needing assistance, but Japanese officials were being constantly reproached. The weak state of Japan's economy meant it could not play the role of regional savior as the United States did with Mexico in 1995. Japan's banking disaster was aggravating the credit crunch in the rest of the region and the weak yen had become a major threat to Asian financial stability.

"Policymaking, vision, and leadership in Japan seem stuck in the darkness of despair. Beijing seems to have it all together," wrote David Roche of *Independent Strategy*. "A small example—avoiding the devaluation of the yuan is an act of Asian statesmanship and leadership—not selflessness, of course— but nevertheless virtues sadly lacking in anything that Japan has done since the Asia crisis began," Roche said. To help the region recover, Japan should be to Asia what the United States was to Mexico in 1995 by pouring in capital and sucking exports back out. "But as an economic locomotive, Japan could not pull the skin off a bowl of congee," he said.

The same conclusion was made by Stephen Roach, chief economist and director of global economics at Morgan Stanley Dean Witter, who observed that China's behavior in leaving its currency unchanged was remarkable. "For a nation steeped in five thousand years of inward-looking tradition, China does not take the outward-looking decision on its currency lightly," he said.

Roach admitted it was in China's interest to prevent the spiral of competitive devaluations spinning out of the country. But in addition, "China gets a lot more—namely, an explicit admission by the G7 that China is the key to any lasting resolution of the Asian crisis."

Both Japan and China were confronted with changes to their economic models. But "Japan is frozen at the switch. China is not. This contrast between China and Japan suggests a new Asian leadership is emerging in the wake of the crisis," Roach said. "I am left with a sense of postcrisis Asia that could well be dominated by the ascendancy of China and the decline of Japan."

For Harry Harding, dean of the Elliot School of International Affairs at George Washington University, neither country was doing much, but the perception was positive for China and negative for Japan. Harding, an expert in Sino-U.S. relations, said Japan's stagnation and China's expansion would have to be prolonged over a long period for a regional shift of economic power to take place. China was acting as a "good neighbor" by not devaluing its currency but would take a long time to become a substitute for Japan, given its relative economic weight.

And in any case, Asia's need for a locomotive was immediate and "not in ten years," observed Maurice "Hank" Greenberg, head of American insurance giant AIG, established in Shanghai before World War II. Asian exports would be going to Japan, not China.

## DEVASTATED BANKS

The Chinese themselves weren't planning to play that role. At least not for the time being. "In China, we have never thought of being a regional leader in the foreseeable future because we have to put our own house in order first," said Long Yongtu, the Chinese vice minister for international trade and economic cooperation. "It's going to be a very difficult transition because there's a long way to go and it's not easy to build a market economy."

Like its Asian neighbors, China was suffering from a cancer in its banking system. And the cancer was in proportion to the size of the patient.

The most conservative estimates showed that nonperforming loans accounted for a quarter of all lending that came to 778 billion dollars at the end of 1997. At this level, the World Bank said the net value of the banking system was already negative—China's banking system was technically insolvent. For some economists, the situation was even worse—estimates of nonperforming loans went as high as fifty percent of all lending.

China's banking assets were concentrated in four main banks after the People's Bank of China was restructured in 1984, losing its commercial banking functions to focus on its main role as central bank instead. The banks—the Industrial and Commercial Bank of China, the People's Construction Bank, the Agricultural Bank of China, and the Bank of China—accounted for between eighty percent and ninety percent of all lending. But their profitability was weak—the average return on assets dropped from 0.31 percent in 1993 to 0.16 in 1996. By comparison, the figure for Hongkong and Shanghai Banking Corp. was 1.5 percent.

The deterioration of their balance sheets reflected the fact that banks were being forced either to lend to unprofitable state-owned enterprises that had no intention of paying the loans back or to make investments according to political criteria with no regard for profitability. The inability to distinguish between commercial banking and what should have been government budget spending was typical for planned economies.

But in China, two decades of frantic investment had not been accompanied by fiscal reforms allowing the government to raise funds through budgetary means. Of total investments of 315 billion dollars in 1997, for example, some 225 billion dollars was ordered by the government and linked to state-owned enterprises. Less than ten percent of this figure—only twenty billion dollars—was covered by government budget spending. "The rest was financed though extra budgetary fiscal levies and through direct bank lending," said Rajiv Lall, executive director at E. M. Warburg Pincus.

In 1994, the government decided to established three "development banks" in a bid to separate public financing from commercial banking activities. But in 1997, Chinese banks other than these three banks had still advanced eighty billion dollars in loans to the public sector out of total lending of 150 billion dollars.

Much of this lending was used to keep afloat state-owned enterprises that would have gone bankrupt years earlier. The state-owned enterprises were caught in a vicious circle. Under the impact of market reforms, their share of industrial output tumbled from eighty-five percent in the late 1980s to about one-third in the late 1990s. But the structure of state-owned enterprises didn't adapt to the new environment at the same pace—too many workers in too many factories were producing too many products that "liberated" consumers didn't want to buy. But putting an end to the vicious circle was a major social risk.

China's state-owned enterprises "constitute much of the fabric of China's society and the sector's health influences more than just the lives of the one hundred million workers who work for them," said Jing Ulrich of Credit Lyonnais Securities Asia.

Destroying the balance sheets of Chinese banks was therefore the price paid for political reluctance to take action. By 1996, the losses of state-owned enterprises swelled to a new record of sixty-eight billion yuan (8.3 billion dollars) and forty-five percent were in the red.

The money came from the savings of Chinese households. Given the lack of development in Chinese financial markets, bank deposits were the main forms of savings. After a decade of rapid growth and underconsumption, these savings were estimated at five thousand billion yuan. But Credit Lyonnais estimated that almost two-thirds, about thirty-two hundred billion yuan, would be swallowed up recapitalizing state-owned enterprises.

"When households in large numbers attempt to withdraw their savings, the insolvency problem of several of China's largest banks will become a liquidity problem," wrote Nicholas Lardy, an economist at the Brookings Institution. "At that point, the central bank will face two alternatives. It could supply funds to banks to meet the demand for withdrawals. This was not unheard of over the past two decades when the central bank extended loans to individual provincial branches of state banks to solve liquidity problems." But done on a large scale, the burgeoning increase in money supply would be inflationary. "A second, more likely, alternative is that the banks will sharply limit customer withdrawals," Lardy said.

The World Bank ruled out a collapse of the Chinese banking system, arguing that the government would put all its weight behind the state-owned banks. But there was no doubt that the Asian crisis increased the "stress" on the system as a whole. The best indicator was the reappearance of a black market for dollars in early 1998, despite the repeated promises from Zhu Rongji that the Chinese currency would not be devalued.

Long Yongtu summarized the Chinese leadership's response to the crisis as a "three S" approach—self-congratulation, serious actions, and strengthening the financial system.

The first stage was Chinese leaders congratulating themselves for not having opened financial markets. "This feeling of self-congratulation didn't last very long when it became apparent that the speculative crisis unleashed a profound economic crisis," Long said.

The serious actions in the second stage were "pursuing economic reforms and the open-door policy to the outside world," the Chinese vice minister said, describing this as the "only solution" to the Asian crisis. "We reached the conclusion very quickly."

Strengthening the financial system, the third stage, was twofold—giving the People's Bank of China real monitoring and regulatory powers, and transforming the banks into real commercial banks.

In China, as in the rest of Asia, this was easier said than done. It involved letting bankers be bankers and that involved an institutional change—cutting the umbilical cord between politicians and banks.

## AUGEAN STABLES

To achieve such a change, Zhu Rongji was relying on Dai Xianglong, governor of the People's Bank of China. Trained as an accountant, Dai used to work at one of the big commercial banks in Shanghai. When Zhu took over as central bank governor in 1993, he brought Dai to Beijing where he did the day-to-day navigation of bringing the Chinese economy down to a soft landing. In his fifties, Dai was part of the new breed of Communist Party officials who didn't mince his words. "If we don't deal with the problems of our financial system, we will not only fail to achieve our main objectives for the next century but we will also jeopardize our national economic security and social stability," he told the standing committee of the National People's Congress in early 1998.

In his speech, Dai outlined the reforms discussed by Chinese leadership behind closed doors the previous November.

The reforms would start with the central bank itself, with the thirty-one provincial branches being merged into twelve regional ones—similar to the Federal Reserve system in the United States. The idea was to remove the pressures from provincial governments which paid salaries and provided housing to "their" central bankers. China wasn't about to embrace the idea of an independent central bank, but it was a start. The central bank headquarters in Beijing would meanwhile set the example in restructuring by at least halving the number of two thousand employees. The People's Bank of China would also get rid of all the residual business from its days as a commercial bank such as broking, insurance, investment, and trust banking activities.

At the same time, the state-owned banks would be required to focus on commercial banking. Lending quotas would be abolished from the beginning of 1999 and banks would have to learn how to evaluate risks and assess profitability. All loans would be classified into one of five categories—normal, special mention, underperforming, doubtful, and write-off.

To recapitalize the banks, the Chinese government would by making a huge bond issue raising 270 billion yuan (32.6 billion dollars) with the idea of achieving the minimum ratio prescribed by the BIS. The BIS ratio required banks with international operations to have risk-weighted capital equivalent to eight percent of their total assets. The ratio for Chinese banks had dropped from 3.9 percent in 1993 to 3.1 percent in 1996.

The four leading banks would also be subjected to competition to make sure they didn't fall back into their old ways. New banks would be established including some from existing rural financial cooperatives.

At the same time, the central bank would try to clean up other parts of the financial sector where abuses and scandals were widespread. Trust and investment companies would be merged and licenses revoked if necessary.

In the Herculean task of Chinese economic development, reforming the financial system was like cleaning the Augean stables. The obstacles to overcome were obviously huge. China's state-owned banks had the highest cost structure in the world and each had hundreds of thousands of employees. Those who kept their jobs would have to graduate from being simple bank tellers to risk evaluators. Banking reforms would shake up old habits and vested interests that would no doubt resist. For Zhu and his technocrats, the battle was being fought on two fronts. Reforming the banking sector and reforming the state-owned enterprises was like the chicken and the egg. Nobody knew which came first but they couldn't exist without each other.

## PRIVATIZATION

"I think the foreign press has overestimated or played up the magnitude of difficulties facing China's state-owned enterprises," Zhu said during his Beijing news conference in March 1998. "When we say that the loss-making percentage of Chinese state-owned enterprises is more than forty percent, we are referring to the number of loss-making companies. At present, China has a total of seventy-nine thousand industrial enterprises that are state-owned, some of which are of very small size, employing only a few dozen workers or even several people...Of that total figure, five hundred extremely large or mega-sized state-owned enterprises account for eighty-five percent of the total profits and taxes submitted to the state. And among those five hundred mega-sized enterprises, only ten percent or fifty companies are loss making. So we believe three years is enough for the majority of loss-making state-owned enterprises to step out of their present difficult situation."

The accent on big enterprises reflected the "catch the big fish and release the small fry" approach endorsed during the fifteenth party congress. In other words, efforts would be made to make big enterprises strong. As for the rest, President Jiang Zemin said the government would "encourage mergers, bankruptcies, and restructuring to create a competitive environment where the survival of the fittest is the rule."

"We must restructure state-owned enterprises strategically, using capital as a tool to bring to the market big companies that operate in different regions and sectors with diversified shareholding structures and multinational operations," Jiang said. And "to accelerate the opening up and renewal of small enterprises, different methods should be adopted such as restructuring, mergers and acquisitions, leasing, shareholding systems, and joint ventures."

The Chinese president defined "shareholding systems" as being "a type of modern capitalist enterprise structure that separates ownership from management and the improvement of operational and financial efficiency." As Jing Ulrich said, this was "de facto privatization."

For the vast majority of public enterprises that survived the upheaval, the state would merely be a minority shareholder like any other, be they managers, workers, private people, or foreign investors. In the longer term, the state would retain control over about three thousand enterprises in strategic sectors such as telecommunications, transport, natural resources, petrochemicals, banking and finance, and of course, defense.

The social and political risks associated with the reform of state-owned enterprises could not be underestimated. If social tensions exploded in a country like China, the dramas associated with the crisis elsewhere in Asia would seem like a simple hors d'oeuvre.

How many enterprises would be involved? It was question that nobody, not even Chinese government officials, could answer with precision. China had five levels of administration from the central government to the commune level, and all of them operated and ran their own enterprises. Credit Lyonnais Securities Asia estimated there were 150,000 of significant size, of which 118,000 were involved in industrial activities.

Recapitalization needs, it estimated, would be fairly limited for the 1,000 biggest enterprises—about 300 billion yuan. For the next 9,000—about 600 billion. But for the other 140,000 enterprises, total financing needs could be as high as 3,200 billion yuan. The reality was that Chinese enterprises didn't have shareholder funds. At the end of 1995, short-term loans from banks represented eighty percent of their total balance sheets and ninety-five percent of their operating funds.

Some of the funds needed for all this would come from banks writing off bad debts that they would never recover, somewhere between thirty percent and fifty percent of all loans. If the central government decided to make up the difference, China's public debt would soar past the European level at about sixty percent of GNP, estimated Carsten Holz, a professor at the University of Science and Technology in Hong Kong.

But China, unlike European countries, had a relatively modest government with public spending representing about ten percent of GNP. Like so many other emerging economies, China was more in need of tax reforms.

Underdeveloped financial markets would pose another problem. Despite rapid growth, the stock markets of Shanghai and Shenzhen were relatively small and incapable of absorbing thousands of new listings.

China didn't have a real corporate bond market either. One way or another, the government and financial intermediaries would have to find a way to securitize the debts of state-owned enterprises, especially the viable ones that were weighed down by debts inherited from the past.

Cleaning up their balance sheets was the main precondition for big Chinese enterprises to regain access to the international capital markets—once the situation in Asia normalized and Hong Kong resumed playing its "go-between" role to the fullest extent.

Finally, foreign direct investment would play not only a quantitative but also a qualitative role that would be different from the past. The days of Chinese "plucking the feathers" of their foreign joint-venture partners in terms of money and technology were over.

### CHAEBOLIZATION

"The South Korean crisis is very, very important for us," said Yi Gang, deputy chief of the Chinese central bank's currency policy division. "There are many similarities with our system such as the relationship between companies and the government and between companies and banks...The lessons from South Korea are very direct."

Keen to develop their own industrial giants, the Chinese thought they had found the answer with *chaebol*, the huge family-controlled conglomerates in South Korea that made everything from oil tankers to nappies. The idea that big was beautiful was alluring even if conglomerates were no longer fashionable in the advanced economies.

"These *chaebols* contributed a lot in transforming Korea from an agricultural country to an emerging industrial one with GNP increasing from 2.1 billion dollars in 1961 to 480 billion dollars in 1996," said an official in Shanghai. "If not for the conglomerates, it would have been absolutely impossible for Korea to achieve such figures." His remarks were shared by numerous Chinese officials. The 120 enterprises chosen to become Chinese conglomerates would get favorable treatment such as easier access to capital, tax benefits, and research funds.

The idea was a Chinese version of the government favoritism that allowed Hyundai, Samsung, Daewoo, and others to reach an outrageous level of dominance over the South Korean economy. Such favoritism included privileged if not exclusive access to bank loans, oligopolistic practices in "strategic" sectors, and the complicity of the government and a powerful bureaucracy seeking to uphold the "national interests" of South Korea.

At the end of 1997, South Korea was nevertheless close to defaulting on its external debt. The IMF arranged an unprecedented support package worth fifty-seven billion dollars to prevent an implosion of the South Korean economy that would have destabilized Japan and the international payments system. And it was the *chaebol* themselves that took most of the blame. Their frantic race to gain market share had been financed by a mountain of debt, largely short-term and mainly denominated in foreign currencies. The ratio of debt to shareholder funds was in the order of five hundred percent. Profitability was pathetic, and obscure accounting practices buried subsidies flowing into a myriad of unprofitable subsidiaries in sectors where they had no expertise.

Given China's tradition of state control and its considerable and dramatic lag in assimilating capitalist culture, it wouldn't be surprising to see *"chaebolization"* have a similar impact in China. That was the view of Wu Jianglin, who was nevertheless the man behind the Chinese government's approach to restructuring large state-owned enterprises. "Many of the conglomerates now being formed are monopolistic, or else they are entering areas where they are not competitive," said the economist from the Development Research Center, the state council's top think-tank. "The relevant government departments claim that this is meant to realize economies of scale. But the real reason is to expand their political power." Wu noted that many large Chinese enterprises were actually former ministries that had changed their status but not their behavior. Grouping business activities with no real synergy was like "welding together several sampans in an attempt to build an aircraft carrier," he said. And the chances of staying afloat were slim. "There is so much experience both in China and abroad that shows it does not work," Wu said.

Another complicating factor would be China's accession to the WTO as privileges extended to state-owned enterprises would become illegal. "These firms will be in a very difficult situation. They will simply not be able to compete."

Jing Ulrich said South Korea's experience illustrated to Chinese officials that putting together diversified companies with no common thread or merging weak companies with strong companies was not a viable solution. China had to rationalize not *"chaebolize"* its enterprises.

Returning from a research trip to China, Clive McDonnel, head of Northeast Asia research at SG Securities in Hong Kong, said the Chinese still wanted to develop big enterprises, but they wanted them to be focussed on one area.

## AVOIDING SOCIAL CHAOS

For China, choosing a model for development was not just an academic argument. Chinese leaders could not fail because society would have to make heavy sacrifices. The "iron rice bowl" was being turned into scrap. Tens of millions of workers whose livelihoods depended on state-owned enterprises would be affected—not just salaries but also housing, health, and pensions.

Chinese unemployment was difficult to measure, especially in rural areas where tens of millions were either underemployed or jobless. The official unemployment rate in the cities—which is what counted considering the social impact of restructuring the public sector—was barely credible at 5.5 percent or ten million people at the end of 1997. The figure excluded workers retrenched by the state.

The fact was that the axe had already fallen on millions of guaranteed jobs, and that layoffs would accelerate in the years to come. One Chinese economist, Feng Lanrui, predicted that the national unemployment rate including rural areas would reach 183 million people by the turn of the century, or twenty-eight percent of the active population of 658 million people.

The sole restructuring in the state-owned textile sector resulted in 1.2 million workers losing their jobs. During the first quarter of 1998, 240,000 people were retrenched. Official figures showed that forty percent either ended up in the service sector, created their own jobs, or emigrated. The government redeployed a quarter and the rest were either retired or unemployed.

In April 1998, the Shanghai municipal government announced that 250,000 jobs in the public sector would be cut over the following year. Some 180,000 would undergo training to prepare for new jobs.

But transforming textile workers, who tended to be young with little education, into employees of big hotels with foreign visitors was a delicate operation and the chances of succeeding were slim. In one case cited by the Chinese press, a contingent of workers abandoned their new jobs in a Beijing hotel on the first day. "The hotel wanted us to bow and fawn the whole day in front of the foreigners. We simply could not do it," one of the rebels was quoted as saying.

The first victims of the increase in unemployment would be the millions of migrant workers in the big cities who did the more difficult and low-paid jobs. In April 1998, the municipality of Beijing ordered that 120,000 immigrant workers among the 1.8 million registered in the capital would have to leave. But replacing them with locals was not always easy. In 1997, the former capital of Nanjing was required to rehire the immigrant workers it had fired because local people refused to work in such jobs.

Chinese authorities were perfectly aware of the problems they faced in phasing out the iron rice bowl culture. China was badly prepared to absorb such change. Like its Asian neighbors, it had no "social safety net" for displaced workers who had been accustomed to receiving generous social benefits throughout their lives as a complement to their modest salaries.

For a while, state-owned enterprises would remain partly responsible for the workers they had retrenched, offering training or social benefits. But they would share the burden with the central government and local authorities. "This is the required link in creating a good social security system," the prime minister said.

The "social philosophy" embraced by Chinese reformists had more in common with American liberalism than Europe's mixed economies. Workers themselves would finance their unemployment insurance themselves according to a formula directly inspired by the United States—benefits would be limited and the size and duration of payments would be in proportion to contributions made.

In changing its social model, China was not doing things by halves. Chinese leaders studied the model of the European welfare state and rejected it—such a system would exert severe strain on state finances and require massive bond issues to fund the additional budget spending. "We have seen the failure of Marxist-style systems of protection in Europe. We know that we can't use the same method," said an official from one Chinese municipality that had pioneered social reforms.

"They went looking for their model in Chile," said Jean-Michel Piveteau, the representative of French bank Paribas in China. He said at least three Chinese missions were sent to study the system operating in the South American country. That meant workers had to finance their future retirement with their own savings. For the world's life insurance companies, the China of Jiang Zemin and Zhu Rongji was emerging as the promised land. After setting up their headquarters in Beijing, the companies started expanding to Shanghai and Guangzhou, the other two cities that had been opened up to foreign insurance companies. And in May 1998, history was made in Shanghai when Hank Greenberg took possession of the very same building on the Bund that had originally been AIG's headquarters. Half a century after Mao Zedong's troops stormed the city, the group founded by Cornelius V. Starr in Shanghai in 1919 was renewing its Chinese roots.

## REFORMING THE STATE

At the dawn of the third millennium, two economic and social adventures without precedent were promising to shape the face of the world—Europe creating a single currency and China choosing a model for development. The success or failure of either would largely determine what happened in the rest of the world.

What Zhu Rongji's reforms signaled was that the period of carrying out experiments in China was coming to an end. The open-door policies and conversion to a market economy launched by Deng in the late 1970s, especially in the special economic zones of the coastal regions, had not only become irreversible, but economic reforms were progressively coming to embrace all levels of Chinese society, including the administrative apparatus of the communist regime.

Among the most striking upheavals endorsed by the National People's Council in March 1998 was the decision to halve the number of bureaucrats employed by the central government from eight million to four million over three years. People wouldn't be fired, of course. The reduction would be achieved through retirements and transfers. Eleven out of forty ministries would disappear, and some would be transformed as state-owned companies such as the energy ministry that had become the National Energy Company. The small army of ministers, vice ministers, and directors deprived of their portfolios and armchairs would be put in charge of monitoring the reforms of state-owned enterprises, advised by American experts. The skepticism among Chinese experts was justified. China's administrative tradition stretched back two millennia and it flourished under the communist regime despite repeated attempts to slim down the bureaucracy.

But leaders in Beijing had at least acknowledged the direct link between economic reforms and pruning back the apparatus of the central government.

"Government organizations that duplicate and overstaff produce regulatory shackles, red tape, corruption, and unhealthy practices. They are also a heavy drain on the state budget," the government's secretary-general Luo Gan said while unveiling the reforms. "There will be obstructions and risks but we don't have a choice. We are going to follow this through to the end." The basic idea was that a country fervently embracing the market economy no longer needed a bureaucracy with such long tentacles. The central government set the example and started giving the means to officials from local collectives to carry out reforms at different levels.

The resistance of bureaucrats to their own demise was only one of the dangers threatening the reforms. Numbed by the Tiananmen massacre, social tensions were rising again. A working group from the central committee of the Communist Party found that the number of strikes and formal protests against working conditions had doubled between 1994 and 1997. Such localized and spontaneous movements involved hundreds of thousands of workers, as seen in Hunan, Jiangxi, and Fujian provinces in mid-1997. In early 1998, riots erupted across China when the central government decided to ban pyramid selling, a practice used by American companies to distribute their products directly to consumers.

The regime took precautions. The reduction of one million men from the ranks of the People's Liberation Army announced during the party congress in 1997 was offset by military police increasing their numbers by five hundred thousand. By mid-1998, there were some 1.2 million military police who were backed by the central committee and ready to face any troubles should they arise.

"A shift in resources and political clout of this magnitude has ominous implications for any would-be labor organizers or spot protesters," wrote Gregory Fossedal, chairman of the Alexis de Tocqueville Institution.

Since the launch of reforms in the late 1970s, Chinese leaders had worked hard to balance the resistance of the supporters and beneficiaries of the old regime by strengthening the positions of those in society who were interested in change. They succeeded after 1994, when the rapid growth in coastal urban areas started to highlight the huge gap with the poor inland rural areas where half a billion Chinese still lived. A series of ad hoc measures was taken to "maximize the enthusiasm of the peasants," Zhu explained in September 1997. The subsequent record grain harvests not only enriched the countryside but also helped reduce inflation that had dropped below one percent by the beginning of 1998.

## A NATION OF HOMEOWNERS

The epic that Chinese economic reforms had become was entering a crucial stage. With the public sector being restructured and the banking system cleaned up, China also had to "maximize the enthusiasm" of the urban masses while making sure the economic machine was running fast enough to absorb the millions of new workers coming onto the labor market each year. So China decided to use housing as a new motor of economic activity. The aim was to transform a nation of subsidized tenants into a nation of homeowners.

"Promoting housing has some strategic advantages in addressing China's problems," Credit Suisse First Boston said. "First, it creates demand without pushing up supply, a vital characteristic given China's chronic oversupply situation. Second, by nature, the housing industry is labor intensive, generating fresh jobs for an economy battling to stem rising unemployment. Third, it has a great multiplier effect with the potential to boost all sectors including banking, construction materials, appliances, and restaurants."

By the late 1990s, barely five percent of the people living in Chinese cities owned their own homes. Most people got their housing from their enterprises or the government, often paying symbolic rents after spending years on the waiting list. But from July 1998, housing reforms went into effect. The main features of the reforms were eliminating subsidized housing and gradually increasing rents in government and enterprise housing from five percent of household income to fifteen percent by 2000. The higher rents would be offset by a monthly allowance payable in cash that would encourage tenants to buy their own homes at favorable prices, supported by loans from the government or enterprise.

The people targeted were medium-income households who were not rich enough to buy property on the open market but still had enough money to finance the purchase of a home provided they had some additional financial assistance.

Money was not a problem as private savings amounted to five thousand billion yuan (more than six hundred billion dollars)—thirteen times the annual amount of foreign direct investment and almost three times the market capitalization of the Shanghai and Shenzhen stock markets combined. The new housing policy would be the most effective way to mobilize these savings. And at the same time, the policy would achieve other objectives by improving the accounts of state-owned enterprises, offering a stable and profitable business to banks, reducing the burden of the state, and supporting domestic demand.

Obstacles existed but they would be gradually removed with the development of primary and secondary markets in mortgages, new banking expertise, and measures to prevent speculation.

"In China, you now have hundreds of millions of people wondering how to get rich enough to buy their own home," enthused one Chinese leader.

## LIKE NINETEENTH-CENTURY AMERICA

In the same way as Chinese officials were inspired to renounce the Japanese-Korean model for their enterprises, they had no reason the follow the national development policies pursued by Japan and South Korea. These mercantilist if not xenophobic policies had became so absurd that they led both countries into an impasse.

Despite the waves caused by the entry of Chinese industries into the international marketplace, export-led growth was not an option for China. An extrapolation by Russel Napier of Credit Lyonnais Securities Asia illustrated why.

"Should exports growth continue to power ahead at the twenty-two percent per annum level (in 1997) to the year 2020, the total exports would be more than double current U.S. GDP. Even assuming that U.S. real growth was 3.8 percent for the next twenty-two years, then China's exports would be the same size as U.S. GDP by 2020," Napier said. The scenario was absurd. But "it is through this prism of export-oriented growth that foreign fund managers see China every day. This is a perspective that has been imported from Southeast Asia and transplanted onto China."

Andrew Freris at BankAmerica Asia noted that the external sector was relatively not that important for China. All of China's economic cycles had been led by capital investment and domestic demand. The net contribution of exports to economic growth was half the contribution from investment. And exports accounted for only 22 percent of China's GNP compared with 42 percent in Thailand, 44 percent in the Philippines, and 90 percent in Malaysia.

"Given China's size, it seems much more likely that it will pursue a growth policy akin to that of the U.S. in the nineteenth century," Napier said.

Such policies focussed on boosting domestic demand and massive spending on infrastructure ranging from railways to canals that opened the whole continent to modern industry.

To finance its investment needs, China knew it had to welcome foreign capital with open arms. The open-door policy had already made China the biggest recipient of foreign capital after the United States with accumulated investment of 220 billion dollars. Between 1994 and 1996, foreign direct investment accelerated sharply to reach one hundred billion dollars—twice the amount of the previous ten years.

Indications were that barriers still protecting some Chinese industries were being lifted and foreign companies were already being allowed to open more subsidiaries in which they had a majority stake rather than being forced into fully-fledged joint ventures with local partners. The reform of state-owned enterprises was meanwhile offering investment opportunities and a clarification of the rules of the game. "We will protect the rights and interests of foreign-funded enterprises according to law and grant them national treatment so that all enterprises, Chinese or foreign-funded, may compete on an equal footing," Zhu said in his Hong Kong speech.

Several examples, notably in the consumer goods and food sectors, proved that this would amount to real competition and that foreign companies would not necessarily beat their Chinese competitors in every case.

## DIFFERENT FACES

"China will not be able to achieve economic growth in isolation of the world," Zhu said.

The major difficulty was that China presented many different faces to the world.

The "good neighbor" that didn't devalue its currency in the interests of regional monetary stability was also an empire with land and sea borders complicated by numerous territorial disputes. And the nuclear power that cooperated with the United States, Russia, France, and Britain to control the proliferation of nuclear weapons in India and Pakistan was also the country that fired missiles into Taiwan waters during the island's election campaign in 1996.

China had formally kept its promise of autonomy for Hong Kong after 1997. But the constitutional system put in place in the new special administrative region guaranteed that the same colonial elite would keep running the territory and that only the allegiances had changed. Still, the first anniversary of the Tiananmen massacre under Chinese rule saw forty thousand people turn out despite torrential rains, and a similar commemoration was held in 1999.

Notwithstanding Zhu's somewhat sober visit to the United States in 1999, marred by allegations of Chinese espionage, his popularity with the foreign press masked the absence of a solid power base. Most of the prime minister's support was among the economic and financial technocrats with whom he had worked most of his life. If the reforms skidded on the slippery road of China's social difficulties, Zhu would be sacrificed to keep the political balance guaranteed by President Jiang Zemin. When Chinese leaders attended the centenary celebrations of Beijing University in May 1998, it was Zhu who got the biggest round of applause from the students, not Jiang. Chinese censors ensured the incident wasn't seen by television audiences.

"If China is to take its rightful place in the modern world, it must choose constructive engagement with that world," the American Assistant Secretary of State Stanley Roth said in Hong Kong in October 1997.

"As Deng Xiaoping rightly pointed out, the most brilliant of China's golden ages—the Sung and the T'ang—occurred when the Middle Kingdom was most open to the outside world," Roth said. "As in Deng's time and as in ancient eras, there is tension today between the vision of an open China and that of a closed China. Some voices seem to suggest that China should 'protect' its people by restricting their access to information, the lifeblood of today's economy, and operate by its own rules when interacting with other nations. Neither is possible for long and would do great harm to China's modernization."

# CHAPTER TWELVE

# Democracy Is Our Destiny

"The Koreans' great dream was to become like the Japanese,
and the bad news is they succeeded."

—*Rudiger Dornbush, economics professor at*
*Massachusetts Institute of Technology*

In Singapore, the post of information and arts minister was long held by a military man. Brigadier-General George Yeo was no ordinary soldier. Educated at the best American universities, he was more at home handling arguments in polemics than weapons. All the same, you had to be Lee Kuan Yew, the founding father of Singapore, to hand the cultural portfolio over to a man coming out of the barracks. The Lion City didn't start asserting itself as the cultural capital of Southeast Asia until the 1990s when it saw the competitive advantages of intellectual and artistic creation. It wasn't that Lee Kuan Yew, who by that time had retired from the premiership to become a "senior minister" in the cabinet, didn't care about cultural things. On the contrary. Asserting himself as the top Confucian in Asia, the man who ruled Singapore with an iron hand for thirty years observed and commented on world affairs through a prism that was essentially cultural. Starting with the display of authority founded on respect for the family hierarchy, Lee's vision of "Asian values" was opposed to the concept of Western democratic and civil liberties that had been enshrined in the Universal Declaration of Human Rights. Throughout Asia, he soon became the inspiration for authoritarian leaders and intellectuals troubled by four centuries of Western predominance. The main challenge for Asia's political leaders and opinion makers was to make sure such thinking and behavior was maintained as economic development dragged societies from the nineteenth century into the twenty-first century in a single generation. By the end of the twentieth century, GNP per capita was higher in Singapore than Britain, the former colonial power. Singapore's middle class had one of the best education systems in the world and nearly everyone was at least bilingual with English having the same status as the three other official languages of Mandarin, Malay, and Tamil. Lee, who led Singapore to independence in 1958, was brought up speaking English. He was known as Harry and didn't learn to write Chinese properly until World War II when he found himself working for the Japanese. Some even said he was more comfortable in the language of Shakespeare than the language of Confucius. But contradictions were essential to understanding economic and social history, especially between advanced economic development and democratic backwardness. Such hiatuses were not confined to developing economies or economies in transition. Even in the oldest and most solidly established democracies, adapting institutions to economic and social advances was a permanent challenge. In any case, it was a good topic to bring up in an interview with George Yeo when the opportunity arose during a French ministerial visit to the island state in 1993.

Singapore was prosperous, advanced, and stable. It had obviously succeeded in getting people of various races and religions to live together in peace. Wasn't it time to lighten up a bit? Why all these laws that made people laugh—the prohibition against walking around naked in a hotel room, against forgetting to flush the toilet, and against importing chewing gum? Not to mention the laws that made people cry—literally in the case of those sentenced to corporal punishment by caning, which apart from being particularly painful could leave permanent scars. Why the refusal to let a legal and civilized opposition breathe freely, why the rejection of any criticism by the foreign media, and why such Orwellian controls? Why not trust the maturity and spirit of responsibility among Singapore's three million people? The time given to journalists to ask questions, all questions, was often the right of the person being interviewed not to reply. And that's what George Yeo indicated—foreigners, including the ones asking such incongruous questions on that particular day, were not "part of the family." Singapore was a family. It was more delicate than it seemed and would be threatened if its private affairs were displayed in public. It was a bit like a policeman telling a crowd of curious onlookers to move on.

## SMOKESCREEN

In 1994, the American publication *Foreign Affairs* published a long conversation between its director Fareed Zakaria and Lee Kuan Yew under the title "Culture is Destiny." "The fundamental difference between Western concepts of society and East Asian concepts...is that Eastern societies believe that the individual exists in the context of the family. He is not pristine and separate. The family is part of the extended family, and then friends and the wider society. The ruler or the government does not try to provide for a person what the family best provides," Lee said. On the other hand, "in the West, especially after World War II, the government came to be seen as so successful that it could fulfill all the obligations that in less modern societies are fulfilled by the family." The senior minister quoted a Chinese aphorism that captured the idea—*Xiushen qijia zhiguo pingtianxia. Xiushen* meant to look after yourself, cultivate yourself, do everything to make yourself useful. *Qijia* meant looking after the family, *zhiguo* meant looking after your country, and *pingtianxia* signified that all was peaceful under heaven. "It is the basic concept of our civilization," Lee said. "Governments will come, governments will go, but this endures. We start with self-reliance. In the West today it is the opposite. The government says give me a popular mandate and I will solve all society's problems."

Lee asserted that this attitude had led to problems in Western societies ranging from drugs and single mothers to violence in schools. But Singapore had a "cultural backdrop—the belief in thrift, hard work, filial piety, and loyalty in the extended family, and most of all, the respect for scholarship and learning" had led to Singapore's success. Lee also asserted that the World Bank study on Asia's economic success had underestimated the importance of cultural factors. "Getting the fundamentals right would help but these societies will not succeed in the same way as East Asia did because certain driving forces will be absent," he said. Lee said Asian countries had to make sure they didn't lose their identities as they modernized. "We have left the past behind and there is an underlying unease that there will be nothing left of us that is part of the old. The Japanese have solved this problem to some extent. Japan has become an industrial society while remaining essentially Japanese in its human relations." The Taiwanese and Koreans were doing the same but it was something Asian countries had to do themselves, not something the Americans could solve for them. "Therefore you will find people unreceptive to the idea that they be Westernized. Modernized, yes, in the sense that they have accepted the inevitability of science and technology and the change in the lifestyles they bring."

Systems of governments in Asia would change. "But it will not end up like the American or British or French or German systems," Lee said. He added that he was "not intellectually convinced that one-man, one-vote is the best," and suggested giving two votes to all men over the age of forty with families—they would likely be more careful if they were voting for their children as well.

"Let me be frank," the former prime minister said. "If we did not have the good points of the West to guide us, we wouldn't have got out of our backwardness. We would have been a backward economy with a backward society. But we do not want all of the West."

How did "culture" explain the Asian economic miracle? How were "Asian values" different from Western values? And especially how did they justify a way of governing that was different from Western democracy and that was supposed to have played a key role in the spectacular economic progress of the region? Until the financial fury broke in 1997, Lee Kuan Yew found numerous willing ears in the West. At an international monetary conference in London in 1994, Sir Charles Powell, head of Jardine Matheson Holdings, the parent of the legendary Hong Kong trading company, admitted that many Asian governments were authoritarian. But they were stable and let markets operate while increasing liberalization.

Philip Tose, whose investment Bank Peregrine Investment Holdings was bankrupted by its adventures with Suharto Inc., was a keen apologist for authoritarian regimes from Indonesia to Burma. And Tose would blame the economic backwardness of the Philippines and India on the democratic traditions of both countries. Interestingly, the Philippines missed the turnoff to the Asian miracle under the Marcos dictatorship and only started to catch up under the democratic administrations of Corazon Aquino, and especially Fidel Ramos. And India, like so many other developing countries, paid the price of a socialist economic model combined with protectionism and a stifling bureaucracy before undergoing an economic renovation under the liberal policies of finance minister Manmohan Singh. Commenting on his Lee Kuan Yew interview, Fareed Zakaria asked his readers: "If culture is destiny, what explains a culture's failure in one area and success in another? If Confucianism explains the economic boom in East Asia today, does it not also explain that region's stagnation for four centuries?"

Handling the culture argument was delicate. Should "Asian values" be held responsible for the financial assault of 1997? Was "crony capitalism"—denounced by the same Western financiers who openly tolerated it for years—a specific Asian "cultural" trait? The idea was absurd—corruption and nepotism knew no borders and had been around for centuries. They clashed with laws and institutions according to formulas that were universal.

There was also the idea that cultural differences were an obstacle to reciprocal understanding. Take George Yeo—you're different, you're not part of the family, you can't understand.

"There is an Asian culture, a powerful and distinctive culture in this part of the world," Richard Holbrooke told a conference organized by Credit Suisse First Boston in Hong Kong in March 1998. "However, the values—the so-called Asian values, strong family values, good education, hard work, cohesiveness of the society—those are all things that Americans and Europeans share." In other words, they were universal values. "People who are talking about sovereignty and Asian values are really setting up a smokescreen in order to prevent scrutiny of their balance sheet," the future American ambassador to the United Nations said. "The Asian economies that have entered the mainstream of the global economy, and those closed countries that have entered it—Korea, Taiwan, China, the four tigers, Japan—cannot have it both ways. They can't go to the capital markets to borrow money and then say we won't show you our books; we play by different rules. If they want to remain isolated like North Korea and remain backward and totalitarian and despotic, then that's another route. But if you want to be part of the international community, you have to play by international rules."

## KIM DAE JUNG REPLIES

Depicting the debate as an East-West clash would be misleading. There were big fans of "Asian values" in the West and powerful voices in Asia itself rejected the notion. None was stronger than Kim Dae Jung who at the age of seventy-three became the democratically elected President of the Republic of Korea in December 1997.

At the end of 1994, Kim Dae Jung had his future behind him. He had stood for the presidency three times and had lost on each occasion, not always at the ballot box. He was known as D. J. to distinguish him from Kim Jong Pil, who would eventually become his prime minister, and Kim Young Sam, who was president at the time.

Kim Dae Jung had been in politics for decades and was now in semiretirement. A former dissident, his only title in 1994 was as chairman of the Kim Dae Jung Foundation for Peace in the Asia-Pacific. It was in this capacity that he picked up his pen to reply to Lee Kuan Yew. The letter was published in the November-December issue of *Foreign Affairs* and is worth quoting at length.

Kim Dae Jung described Lee Kuan Yew as the "most articulate" among Asia's authoritarian leaders but said his remarks were "self serving" and contrary to the facts, going against Asian history itself.

"It is not true, as Lee alleges, that Asian governments shy away from intervening in private matters and taking on all of society's problems. Asian governments intrude much more than Western governments into the daily affairs of individuals and families," Kim said. South Korean households had to attend monthly neighborhood meetings to receive government directives and discuss local affairs while the Japanese government constantly intruded into the business world to protect perceived national interests. Kim also denounced the "Orwellian extreme of social engineering" in Singapore. "The fact that Lee's Singapore, a small city-state, needs a near-totalitarian police state to assert control over its citizens contradicts his assertion that everything would be all right if governments would refrain from interfering in the private affairs of the family." Singapore was the sort of place where the government decided to hold a national day of fun because it decided the people weren't amusing themselves enough. And Singapore would soon announce plans for new legislation forcing children to take care of their aging parents. For the moment, however, Kim focussed on some of the stringent regulations in such areas as chewing gum, spitting, smoking, and littering. "Such facts fly in the face of his assertion that East Asia's governments are minimalist. Lee makes these false claims to justify his rejection of Western-style democracy," the future South Korean president said.

"No one can argue with Lee's objection to 'foisting' an alien system 'indiscriminately on societies in which it will not work.' The question is whether democracy is a system so alien to Asian culture that it will not work," Kim said. "A thorough analysis makes it clear that Asia has a rich heritage of democracy-oriented philosophies and traditions." He noted that English political philosopher John Locke shared the same "democratic ideals" as the Chinese philosopher Meng-tzu some two thousand years before. Meng-tzu preached that people had the right to overthrow governments in the name of heaven if they were not being righteously ruled. Asia also had a long history of "democratic institutions"—when Europe was being run by a procession of feudal lords, China and Korea had already established prefecture systems for about two thousand years. The civil service in both countries followed meritocracy whereby even the sons of high-ranking officials had to pass civil service examinations if they wanted to be appointed to official positions—unlike Europe where appointments were largely considered on the basis of class. Kim Dae Jung, whose country was the most Confucian in Asia, obviously had a different reading of Chinese literature from Lee Kuan Yew. In both China and Korea, Kim noted that "freedom of speech was highly valued, based on the understanding that the nation's fate depended on it. Confucian scholars were taught that remonstration against an erring monarch was a paramount duty." While Asians developed the fundamental ideas for democracy well before Europe, comprehensive and effective electoral democracy was formalized first by the Europeans, the invention of the electoral system being the "greatest accomplishment" of Europe.

"Asia has no practical alternative to democracy," Kim Dae Jung said, noting that democracy had been consistently practiced in Japan and India since the end of World War II while "people power" had proven to be a resilient force in other Asian countries. Asia should therefore help build a "global democracy" by learning from Western countries that suffered many problems in building their systems.

"Asia should lose no time in firmly establishing democracy and strengthening human rights," Kim said. "The biggest obstacle is not its cultural heritage but the resistance of authoritarian rulers and their apologists. Asia has much to offer the rest of the world. Its rich heritage of democracy-oriented philosophies and traditions can make a significant contribution to the evolution of global democracy. Culture is not necessarily our destiny. Democracy is."

## DEMOCRACY MADE IN KOREA

The letter was even more important in the sense that it was Kim Dae Jung and it applied to South Korea. When it was caught up in the turmoil of the Asian storm toward the end of 1997, the financial crisis took on a new dimension. Not only because South Korea was the world's eleventh largest economy, an industrial and commercial heavyweight that was heavily integrated into the global division of labor and not just capsizing the flimsy rafts of Southeast Asia. And not unique because Western and particularly Japanese banks were exposed to such an extent that it was dangerous for the international banking system. And not necessarily because South Korea was still technically at war with North Korea and was located on a sensitive tectonic plate where the interests of the United States, China, Russia, and Japan converged. It was also because South Korea represented the fastest ever transition from an underdeveloped rural nation ruled by dictators to an industrialized urban country ruled by democracy. And the Koreans succeeded in a very difficult environment.

South Korea had benefited from international economic growth marked by a sharp increase in global trade. But following in Japan's footsteps, it did not enjoy the same advantages—especially in the financial area. And given its cycle of development, it got involved way too early in the sorts of distrustful and hostile reactions that were typical of old industrial nations. If you could accuse Japan of receiving a lot and giving little by hitching a free ride on the train of global trade, it was a lot more complicated in the case of South Korea. While dreaming of being another Japan, it refused to accept that others could reject the unfortunate Japanese precedent and limit its ambitions to accede to the ranks of industrial powers. When Japan's economy boomed during the Korean War in the 1950s, Koreans were dying of bombs and hunger in what was a particularly atrocious conflict. And despite the protectionism that warranted criticism, South Korea never posted the sorts of structural trade surpluses manufactured by the Japanese economic machine.

In terms of social and democratic development, the most obvious comparisons for South Korea were Spain and Portugal. During the 1970s, both countries went through transitions to democracy. In Spain, biological evolution did away with General Francisco Franco. And in Portugal, colonial warfare slowly sapped the life out of the fifty-year dictatorship of Antonio Salazar and Marcelo Caetano, triggering a revolt among young military officers who no longer wanted to die in the African savannah under a hot sun. In both cases, internal movements played a major role. Society decided it could no longer put up with police terror, religious obscurantism, economic backwardness, and international isolation. Spain and Portugal wanted to bring their colonial splendor of centuries past to a continent that was living in the late twentieth century. The presence of neighboring democracies, adherence to the enlightenment of European civilization, clandestine exchanges of ideas, and the refuge given to dissidents paved the way for the reversal. Protests across Europe against the execution of the "Burgos Six" by Franco was a founding moment for a new European identity. If European governments and sun-seeking tourists had been closing their eyes to the embarrassing realities of the dictatorships on the Iberian peninsula, they made honorable amends. Integration into the European Community became a powerful means of consolidating democracy. Spain and Portugal benefited considerably from membership and used it to catch up economically. Europe gained enormously with the refocussing toward the southern "Club Med" countries paving the way for European economic and monetary union (EMU). If only a simple extension of the German mark zone, monetary union—like the Australian bird with the same name—wouldn't have been able to fly.

Who were South Korea's democratic neighbors—Stalinist North Korea, communist China? What was the example to follow and where would the moral and material support come from—nearby Japan or distant America? Japanese society was democratic but its political structures and morals were not really a proper model with a big fan club across Asia.

The role of the United States was complex. Washington wanted South Korea to be solid and stable—it had tens of thousands of troops stationed in the last major outpost of the Cold War where the two adversaries had not even signed a cease-fire. At the same time, the hundreds of thousands of Koreans who went to study in the United States didn't come back with MBA's and Ph.D's alone. The ability to think and be oneself was an active virus. Koreans would nevertheless achieve democracy themselves, with the same fierceness and passion they showed in extracting themselves from poverty, enduring shortages, working double shifts for meager salaries, and putting up with the quasi-militarization of economic life for two decades. With all its qualities and faults, it would be democracy made in Korea.

The Americans intervened on two known occasions to halt the excesses of military dictatorship—once in 1961 and again in 1987. On both occasions, Kim Dae Jung was involved.

## IN THE FACE OF DEATH

On August 8, 1973, Kim had just had lunch with another Korean opposition figure in central Tokyo when he was grabbed by a group of men, beaten up, chloroformed, blindfolded, thrown into a car, and eventually put on a cargo plane for South Korea. The operation, which could have been right out of a spy movie, was the work of the Korean Central Intelligence Agency (KCIA), South Korea's version of the CIA. The role of KCIA agents was to hunt down those opposed to Park Chung Hee, the South Korean dictator. Kim Dae Jung was the first. In 1970, Kim had lost in presidential elections called to "legalize" Park's seizure of power in a military coup in 1961. It was the first, but not the last, time that Kim would stand in an election he would have no doubt won if voting had been fair. After coming so close to defeat, Park decided not to take any more chances with elections and he ripped up the last democratic scraps of the constitution and officially established a dictatorship in 1972. Kim had been receiving medical treatment in Japan and decided to stay, continuing from abroad his one-man battle against Park that went back to 1961 when he was first elected to parliament. When American CIA agents in Seoul learned that Kim had been kidnapped, U.S. Ambassador Philip Habib tried to bluff the South Koreans. He personally warned Park that the elimination of Kim would have serious repercussions on ties between Washington and Seoul. While details of what transpired were still not clear twenty-five years later, the whole affair lasted about forty-eight hours. Kim was still alive but put under house arrest in Seoul where he would spend the next nine years when he wasn't in prison.

In 1979, a mysterious settling of scores took place, although this was more like a gangster movie. Park was assassinated by the KCIA chief in the Blue House, the presidential residence. But it wasn't the end of military dictatorship. In the chaos that followed Park's assassination, a brutal figure emerged—General Chun Doo Hwan. Chun unleashed a bloodbath in the southern city of Kwangju, a traditional hotbed where Kim was from. Chun declared war on the insurgents who had taken control of the city and dispatched special troops. At least two hundred people were killed. Kim was thrown in prison and in a summary trial a few months later sentenced to death for treason.

Pressure from the teams working under outgoing President Jimmy Carter and newly elected President Ronald Reagan saved Kim's life.

He was expelled to the United States just before Christmas in 1982. In America, Kim put to work the English he had started learning in jail, widening his political and philosophical horizons through his contact with the Western world. With popular resistance against the Chun regime growing, Kim decided to go home in 1985. American officials accompanied him on the plane to avoid the same tragedy as Benigno Aquino, the Philippine opposition leader who was Kim's friend and companion in exile in the United States. As Aquino was getting out of the plane that brought him back to Manila, he was shot to death by agents of Philippine dictator Ferdinand Marcos. Kim returned to his home in Seoul that was under monitoring. Electoral fraud deprived him of a victory in the 1987 presidential poll that was won by Roh Tae Woo, who had been Chun's companion in arms at the South Korean military academy.

## UNFINISHED BUSINESS

Roh took over a country that was completely different from the miserable and largely rural South Korea that Park inherited in the early 1960s. The country had been transformed and had a strong industrial base in heavy industries. A quarter of the forty million inhabitants were concentrated in the area around Seoul, which had undergone an unprecedented demographic explosion. South Korea was young, urban, well educated, and ready to enjoy the fruits of the economic miracle. Roh's term was marked by protests—students in the streets calling for democratic freedoms and workers in factories demanding wage increases and trade union rights. The police state started falling apart and freedom of the press gradually increased. In sector after sector, year after year, salaries rose sharply. On the economic front, the developments were welcomed—domestic demand grew and helped to rebalance an economy that had been relying too much on external demand through booming exports.

But in matching growth with political development, South Korean leaders missed a crucial opportunity that would have alleviated the dramatic effects of the economic crisis that unfolded in 1997. The outcome of the election of 1992, which Kim contested for a third time, was sealed two years earlier in a questionable compromise between Roh's party and an opposition party headed by Kim Young Sam, a former comrade of Kim Dae Jung. Voters chose Kim Young Sam as their first civilian president in thirty years. But Kim Young Sam had an ambiguous mandate. His financial backers—the powerful conglomerates that dominated all aspects of the economy—expected him to rule as the head of a conservative coalition that would perpetuate the Japanese-style alliance between politicians, bureaucrats, and businessmen. But the public wanted to settle scores with the former military dictators. People were demanding radical reforms, and first and foremost an end to corruption. Kim Young Sam had given a pledge. The subsequent trial of Chun and Roh was broadcast live on television, becoming an emotional drama that was almost unbearable for many Koreans. Apart from Chun's role in the Kwangju massacre, there were allegations of corruption. Chun was hated so much that he didn't attend the opening ceremony of the Seoul Olympic Games in 1988 out of fear of being booed. The trial uncovered the extent of the corruption of those around Chun including his own wife. Roh fed his former military companion to a wild and hungry public. After making a televised apology, Chun and the former first lady fled to a Buddhist sanctuary where they remained in exile doing penance for two years.

The trial in 1993 shed a brutal light on the scale of corruption and the trough from which leaders fed. Chun and Roh managed to collectively siphon off one billion dollars. Chun was given a suspended death sentence and sentenced to life in prison, and Roh got seventeen years, although both were later pardoned after Kim Dae Jung became president. In addition, three thousand officials lost their jobs and dozens of business executives were sentenced including Kim Woo Choong, the founding chairman of Daewoo. But Kim Young Sam's reform drive would soon come up against an old contradiction—how could you clean up economic and political life without questioning the very structures behind South Korea's success? How could you touch the edifice without causing everything to collapse?

## JAPANESE MILITARY SCHOOL

The father of South Korea's economic miracle wasn't an economist, a financier, or even a politician. Park Chung Hee was a general and a dictator who ruled the country for eighteen years. He found his economic strategy in Japan.

"In Japan, Park had a familiar model for Korea to follow," wrote Mark Clifford in his book *Troubled Tiger*. "It was the Japan of the 1930s and 1940s that Park was familiar with, however, and this militarized model left a stain on the path of Korean development that remains even today."

Korea lived the first half of the twentieth century under Japanese colonial rule. Park was a military cadet in the Japanese Imperial Army and was sent to Manchukuo, the Japanese puppet-state in northeast China that bordered Korea. There he witnessed firsthand an economy that was entirely run by the government, with the cooperation of a regimented private sector. The same model and men who implemented it strongly influenced Japan's reconstruction after World War II. The model was then transplanted to South Korea when Park came to power after the Korean War.

"Under Park, the state controlled virtually all economic activities in South Korea," wrote Clifford, a former correspondent of *The Far Eastern Economic Review* in Seoul. "The government approved all bank loans, granted licenses for virtually all businesses, and controlled many prices. In this, the Korean economy copied much of the Japanese model, but with a heavier emphasis on political and military influences in the running of the economy."

Park adopted Japanese-style economic planning. The instruments he put in place—economic planning councils in the finance ministry and the international trade and industry ministry—were clones from Japan. Seoul National University, established during the Japanese occupation, served the same role in training top bureaucrats in South Korea as Tokyo University did in Japan. Using the Japanese military model, Park forced all companies into a myriad of industrial associations, appointing retired soldiers to head the most important ones. The associations were used to monitor the activities of the private sector. And when companies failed, the government stepped in. Park meanwhile awarded the task of developing a national steel industry to Park Tae Joon, a young colonel who studied engineering at Waseda, one of the top universities in Tokyo. The young colonel would become the "high priest of steel," founding Pohang Iron and Steel (POSCO) in 1968 and running it until his fall from grace in 1992. POSCO became a leader in technology, productivity, and—rare for a public company—profitability. By the 1990s, it rivaled Japan's Nippon Steel Corp. as the world's biggest steel maker.

In most cases, however, it was the private groups who helped Park Chung Hee realize his industrial ambitions. He chose men personally, less for their expertise and more for their entrepreneurial spirit and taste for risk—people like Hyundai's founder Chung Ju Yung and Daewoo's founder Kim Woo Chong. The government set goals in various sectors ranging from oil refining and shipbuilding to cement, chemicals, and mechanical equipment. The government awarded licenses and provided logistics by ordering banks to lend funds to certain clients. All macroeconomic policies from trade to credit were subordinated to the creation of Korea Inc. The result was a group of conglomerates called *chaebol*, family-owned groups resembling the *zaibatsu* that dominated the Japanese economy before World War II. Their influence on the South Korean economy was impressive. Clifford reported that the combined sales of the ten top conglomerates accounted for fifteen percent of GNP in 1974, rising to almost two-thirds in 1984.

The cardinal rule for the *chaebol* was that capital had no cost. Each group could easily borrow funds from banks that were as familiar with risk as the Sahara was with snow. Proceeds of loans were used for investment, repaying old loans, or paying interest on those occasions when it was being charged. The inflation that came with rapid economic growth eroded the debt burden and the *chaebol* subsidized their subsidiaries to expand into an endless stream of new activities. Profitability didn't count but market share did. Ownership was concentrated in the hands of the founder and his family. Management too. When it existed, accounting procedures were opaque. The management style was authoritarian and patriarchal—decisions were instantaneous and risks could be taken even if some of the crazier ideas weren't successful.

The model was perfect for the rebirth of a rural country that was underdeveloped. Labor was abundant and, for a long time, cheap. Workers endured nineteenth-century-style conditions—twelve-hour shifts, sometimes seven days a week. The police state was there to guarantee peace if need be. The threat from North Korea was real. But it was also a pretext to persecute those who dared to raise their voice in huge conglomerates that were run with military discipline.

## CHAEBOL ADRIFT

The flaws of the system would become more and more distinct as the 1980s progressed. The business structure was completely unbalanced—beneath the thirty or so conglomerates that made up Korea Inc. was a semideserted landscape filled with subcontractors.

Small independent companies with innovative ideas had little chance of surviving when most of the credit was being siphoned off by the giants. One sign of the primitive nature of the Korean model was the "curb market" where borrowers who didn't have access to bank loans could raise funds provided by households at usurious rates of interest.

The lack of absence of diversification became a heavy handicap to the building of a sophisticated and flexible economy. South Korean officials were aware of this and an initial attempt was made under Roh Tae Woo to curb the *chaebol's* stranglehold over the economy. The conglomerates were told to focus on three core activities and to raise more funds by listing their shares on the stock market, allowing the banks to lend more funds to small and medium-sized independent companies. The policy failed miserably, showing that the government had lost control of the very creatures it had developed. The *chaebol* owners were intent on perpetuating their autocratic control over groups that now comprised dozens of different companies and hundreds of thousands of employees.

Corruption was the inevitable result of a system based on collusion among politicians, bureaucrats, bankers, and industrialists. It ensured the rules of the game were followed. And it reached outrageous levels under Chun and Roh.

And after all, why worry? The economic machine was still working. The *chaebol* had completely dominated the domestic market and were now trying to conquer the world. They started with building sites in the Middle East, where their foremen and workers imported from home could mix concrete at unbeatable prices. Following in Japan's footsteps, the South Korean conglomerates then started exporting cars to America. The strategy was simple— replace Japanese carmakers in the middle to bottom end of the market that had been more or less abandoned by Western rivals.

To cut down on wage costs at home, the South Koreans also adopted the Japanese strategy of shifting production to cheaper locations in Asia. From Bangladesh to Vietnam, many of the companies manufacturing clothes and sports shoes with well-known brand names were South Korean (and given American sensibilities to "sweatshops" in Asia, this generated some concern for companies like Nike).

Success made the South Koreans bolder. In sectors where the ability to invest huge amounts of money was what counted, they took on the Japanese at their own game. Samsung Electronics soon became the world's biggest producer of dynamic random access memory (DRAM) chips, a huge but largely volatile market that depended on the ability to develop new generations of memory chips as others became obsolete. The conglomerates also benefited from the establishment of diplomatic relations between South Korea and China in the early 1990s as well as the gradual integration of the former Soviet empire into the world market. South Korea's less sophisticated and cheaper products were well adapted to the resources of hundreds of millions of new consumers.

The discipline imposed by Park Chung Hee had long disappeared. The favorite game soon became trampling on each other's flower beds as all of the conglomerates sought to enter the same market. The egos of the founders decided each conglomerate's strategy. In a management environment dominated by family bloodlines and Confucian obedience, there was no opposition. In the rare cases where they existed, minority shareholders from outside had barely any impact.

Korea Inc. was manufacturing excess capacity. The red ink flowed. And the banks continued lending—they didn't know how to do anything else—as if they were shoveling coal into a steam engine running at full speed. The problem was that the train conductor was still on the platform. And the train wasn't going anywhere.

The car industry illustrated the problem well. While the Asian storm was already starting to hit South Korean shores, the Samsung group was opening champagne to celebrate the birth of its latest child, Samsung Motors. The country's biggest conglomerate after Hyundai had just invested 2.5 billion dollars to enter an industry whose excess capacity worldwide had been aggravated by the activities of South Korea carmakers led by Hyundai and Daewoo. And the third-largest carmaker, Kia Motors, had just gone bankrupt.

The huge debt financing Samsung's foray into cars was guaranteed by Samsung Electronics, the jewel in the conglomerate's crown. Only 123 million dollars came from Samsung's own funds.

The first half of the 1990s offered South Korea the last chance to stop before the approaching abyss. But the machine kept accelerating, the major cause being internal—the reformist ambitions of Kim Young Sam were stuck. In a country with a vast pool of economic talent, the problem was not with failing to diagnose the deficiencies of the model. The problem was trying to prescribe remedies to a patient who refused to believe he was ill.

It got worse with two serious errors in assessing the international situation.

## CAUGHT OFF GUARD AND GOING AGAINST THE GRAIN

The first was specifically Korean. When the yen started to ascend to new heights in 1993, the conglomerates thought their time had come. They gambled that the appreciation of the yen, which reached 79 to the dollar in early 1995, was a lasting phenomenon that wouldn't be reversed. The conclusion was typical of Korean management—full steam ahead. With its steel, ships, home appliances, electronics, and cars, South Korea soon became a replica of the Japanese export machine. With the soaring yen and a weak won, the time had come for South Koreans to pull the rug from under the feet of their Japanese rivals in world markets. The passion for investment and market share turned into a raging obsession. Typical was the attitude displayed by Kim Woo Chong, the founder of Daewoo and the last of his generation still acting as chairman. Founded in 1968 with five employees, Daewoo expanded from textiles into heavy industry and then cars and electronics. The group, whose name meant Big Universe, had worldwide sales of more than fifty billion dollars in 1996, although the figure was inflated by transactions between subsidiaries. South Korea's fourth-largest conglomerate was also a pioneer in expanding abroad, with one hundred thousand employees in foreign countries. In the earlier 1990s, "President Kim" unveiled a global strategy involving fifteen billion dollars in investment in the period up to 2005. By this date, he wanted Daewoo to be among the world's top ten carmakers, boosting annual capacity from 1.7 million units to 2.5 million units with most of the growth coming from abroad, especially in emerging markets. Major targets were Eastern Europe, where Kim was betting on an enlargement of the European Union, along with China and the rest of Asia, notably Vietnam, where Daewoo had become the biggest single foreign investor. The group was also aiming for ten percent of the world electronics market. Kim shocked the world industrial establishment when he offered to buy Thomson Multimedia, a subsidiary of the French state-owned company Thomson SA, a financial disaster but a gold mine of technology. Blocked for political and social reasons, Kim denounced French industrial xenophobia. He wasn't entirely wrong. But given South Korean behavior toward foreign investment and products in their own country, it was a case of the pot calling the kettle black. But the failure in France didn't dent the ambitions of the group—Daewoo still aimed to have one thousand subsidiaries by 2005 with two hundred fifty thousand employees on five continents. Other Korean groups had similar ambitions to those of Kim Woo Chong. The plans were well underway with the money and the investments raised when American policy changed in April 1995. Suddenly, the strong yen was out and the strong dollar was in. The Koreans were caught off guard.

The other error was the failed negotiations for South Korea's entry into the OECD. Statistically speaking, South Korea's case for joining the OECD was undeniable. It was the world's eleventh largest economy with GNP per capital exceeding eleven thousand dollars that was more than Mexico. The United States had pushed for Mexico's entry on the basis of its membership in the North American Free Trade Association (NAFTA) that comprised the United States, Canada, and Mexico. But to admit Mexico and South Korea into their ranks, the OECD had to close its eyes to certain shortcomings. That was no shock. It happened in clubs all the time—new members were expected to improve themselves through contact with older members, learning how to act and live according to the same rules. Negotiations with South Korea were nevertheless long and difficult. In the area of trade, the country was fiercely protectionist. But the most delicate issues were liberalizing and opening South Korea's financial markets. Westerners learned only too late the secret of the country's success—they had to raise their own capital while their South Korean rivals did not. The bill was around somewhere but it was never brought to the table, and certainly not by the banks. Opaque accounting procedures allowed losses to be masked, transferred from one subsidiary to another. Wide-ranging financial reforms were the only way to improve the rules of the game. Pierre Duquesne, deputy director of multilateral affairs at the French treasury who later became economic adviser to Prime Minister Lionel Jospin, said France was alone in pushing the issue. "The Japanese were pushing in favor of the Koreans. The Americans and the other Europeans said nothing. We were the only ones blocking," Duquesne said. "The Koreans were constantly coming to see us and it turned into a foreign policy issue. We obtained a certain number of concessions. But France was always seen as the ugly duckling." At the same time, France was bidding for a high-speed railway project linking Seoul with Pusan. Nothing was simple.

The outcome was partial liberalization that was timid and stretched out over time, insufficient to clean up the financial system or introduce the discipline of the market. But for South Korean banks, it was like throwing the reins to the horse. With new freedoms in external operations, the banks increased their own debts and those of their clients.

In the 1980s, reducing South Korea's external debt—mainly public-sector borrowings and relatively modest—was considered a national priority. The same scruples were lacking in the 1990s when South Korean banks and conglomerates rushed to the international capital markets to finance an orgy of investment. The figures were disturbing—total external debt swelled from 54.4 billion dollars in 1994 to 78.4 billion dollars in 1995 to 160.7 billion dollars in 1996. In terms of servicing the debt, the amount was reasonable. But not the maturities—short-term debt ballooned from fourteen billion dollars in 1994 to seventy-three billion dollars in 1996. By 1997, forty-seven percent of the country's debt carried maturities of between three and twelve months. At the same time, domestic debt was surging too. Investment banks, including many recently established by the conglomerates, issued one trillion won worth of commercial paper in 1995, rising to six trillion won in 1996 and twelve trillion won by the middle of 1997. Half of the thirty investment banks had been operating for less than two years. Some lent as much as 120 percent of their shareholder funds to single borrowers such as Kia Motors.

## HANBO'S FAILURE

"Korea's foreign debt is conglomerate debt," wrote David Roche of *Independent Strategy*. "There is virtually no public sector debt. Sure, a lot of foreign debt is in the banks but the banks lend it to the conglomerates. And the conglomerates doubled the foreign money they got from their own banks by borrowing the same sum again in foreign markets and forgetting to report it. Then the conglomerates doubled their money again by borrowing from the supine banks to inflate domestic debt (that admittedly double counts the banks' lending on their foreign borrowings) to 155 percent of gross domestic product. That figure rises to near two hundred percent of GDP if corporate bonds bought and guaranteed by banks are included. All that would be fine if the conglomerates ever earned a return on assets equal to the cost of their debts, and if their debts did not average three hundred percent of shareholders' funds. But quoted Korean corporations have earned a return on assets equal to the cost of borrowing only once in the past seven years and are now deep into the red even before interest payments."

How was this possible? Just ask Chung Tae Soo, the founding chairman of Hanbo Iron and Steel, the country's second-largest steelmaker and the core company in the Hanbo group. But arranging interviews with Chung was difficult.

He was rotting in jail. When Hanbo Iron and Steel collapsed in January 1997, it left a mountain of debt of six trillion won (almost seven billion dollars at the time). It also left gaping holes in the accounts of South Korean banks and a huge political scandal that directly involved President Kim Young Sam. If there was a single event marking the end for Korea Inc., the collapse of Hanbo was it.

With shareholder funds of three hundred billion won, Chung was able to borrow five thousand billion won to build a giant new steel mill. Where did the money come from? From the "old boys," the six big banks led by Korea First Bank that were nominally private but actually run by the government, controlling seventy percent of all lending. An inquiry found that Korea First Bank had lent more than one trillion won to Hanbo while Chohung Bank lent six hundred forty billion won, Korea Exchange Bank 421 billion won, and Seoul Bank 205 billion won. Those who approved the loans apparently didn't look at the steelmaker's balance sheet—investments in 1996 exceeded one thousand billion won while the company's cash flow was barely sixty billion won.

What was the key to the mystery? It was partly South Korea's traditional banking practices, whereby banks acted as development institutions lending funds according to government economic policy rather than commercial banks that evaluated risks and the potential for profit. But in Hanbo's case, the main key was corruption.

Chung Tae Soo was a recidivist. He had already been involved in political scandals. Korea First Bank was no virgin either—its former chairman Chul Soo Ree was arrested in May 1996 for making illegal loans in exchange for kickbacks. But the key figure in the Hanbo affair appeared to be Kim Hyun Chul, the son of President Kim Young Sam and also a friend of Chung Bo Keun, the son of the Hanbo chairman. The Korean public was convinced that the Hanbo chairman financed the president's election campaign in 1992, ensuring himself the complacency of the banks. The president's son was soon thrown into prison for his involvement in another scandal and Kim Young Sam's ratings plunged, forcing him to spend his final months in office as a lame-duck president.

Hanbo's collapse was symptomatic of the gangrene infecting Korea Inc. It was followed by the failure of another steelmaker, Sammi, and several other companies such as Jinro, Dainong, and Kia, with each bankruptcy digging a bigger hole for the grave of the South Korean banking system. During the course of 1997 alone, bad debts would balloon to twenty-six thousand billion won.

## CAUGHT IN A NUTCRACKER

Hanbo Iron and Steel was supposed to have been another POSCO. But the sad reality was that the madness of Korea Inc.'s big ideas coincided with the loss of its international competitiveness

In a study released in October 1997, international management consultants Booze-Allen and Hamilton described South Korea as being caught in a nutcracker. "The wide-ranging systemic impediments, in particular high cost and rigid financing options, inflexible labor conditions, and widespread bureaucratic intervention have prevented the economy from responding to emerging challenges," said Kevin Jones, the vice president who carried out the study commissioned by Korean institutions themselves. "As a consequence, Korea finds itself in a competitive nutcracker between advanced knowledge-based nations like Japan and rapidly growing low-cost economies like China."

The pressure on South Korea came from four directions including China, with its advantages of cost and economies of scale in the same industries, and Japan, that was increasingly locating production abroad, had its own technology, and was maybe going to liberalize its domestic economy. Additional pressure came from the international economy, which was more complex, more oriented toward global services, and divided into big free-trade zones, and the new global companies founded on knowledge-based industries that had extensive networks with multicultural abilities.

The nutcracker led South Korea in the wrong direction, as its external trade figures showed. Between 1987 and 1996, exports to developed economies dropped from seventy percent to forty percent of all exports while the ratio of exports to developing countries doubled from thirty percent to sixty percent. While it enjoyed trade surpluses at the end of the 1980s, South Korea had a trade deficit of 35 billion dollars with developed countries in 1996, only partly offset by a surplus of fifteen billion dollars with developing nations. In other words, South Korea was selling less and less to sophisticated and creditworthy consumers in rich countries and more and more to consumers who had less money and were therefore less picky. South Korean exporters were weak against the strong and strong against the weak—hardly a recipe for success.

Another study, by McKinsey and Co., identified severe shortcomings in productivity in eight key industries and found that the rate for South Korean companies was barely half that of its American rivals. South Korea may have been the world's fifth-largest carmaker, but top manufacturer Hyundai produced only 27.9 cars for each employee in 1996 compared with 44.7 for Toyota in 1974 when Japanese industry was at a similar stage of development.

"In manufacturing, Korea has massively invested in the best available technology. But because of protectionism and poor corporate governance in banks and companies, it was not forced to adopt best managerial policies," the McKinsey report said.

What was the remedy? Allowing market forces to work, according to the separate report by Booze-Allen and Hamilton. "The government should take a drastically reduced role in the economy and abstain from the micromanagement of the economy," it reported. "To do so, the government should devolve its economic management functions to the market and create an independent agency, the Liberalization Policy Board, to ensure an open fair and fully competitive environment for all major sectors of the economy...Increased foreign investment will also foster greater competition in all sectors of the economy."

For McKinsey, reforms had to include radical liberalization in the service sector. The reason was major—the service sector would have to absorb workers retrenched by manufacturers in an effort to reverse their considerable lag in productivity.

Booze-Allen said the painful changes implied the establishment of a new triangular social contract among the government, companies, and workers. The old relations between the government and the business world, previously based on orientation and protection on one side and investment on the other, would have to give way to a market economy guaranteed by rules. The rules would be between the government and workers, with security accompanying discipline and with the new relationship based on freedom and development along with personal responsibility. The new rules would also be between labor and capital with employment and dedication replaced by career opportunities and greater flexibility.

The diagnosis was hardly new and the remedies weren't original either. What were the chances of them being implemented? Before December 1997, the chances were almost zero. The last attempted reform of President Kim Young Sam had focussed on the labor market. It failed one year earlier with massive strikes.

## BLESSING IN DISGUISE

"I think Asia's economic crisis stems mainly from a lack of democracy," Kim Dae Jung told *Time* magazine in March 1998 just after he was sworn in as president. "In democratic countries, there is not the same kind of collusion between businessmen and the government. If we develop both democracy and a market economy, we can expect successful results in the near future." The new South Korean president was true to his words. In his response to Lee Kuan Yew in *Foreign Affairs* in 1994, he noted that "some people concluded that the Soviet demise was the result of the victory of capitalism over socialism. But I believe it represented the triumph of democracy over dictatorship."

In his interview with *Time* in 1998, Kim said he had recently met with the *chaebol*. "I told them I would welcome them if they adhere to market principles and are competitive. I asked them to reform their financial structure and establish transparency so that everybody inside and outside Korea will believe their financial statements. I told them that I don't favor or disfavor any particular company. I would like everyone who produces the cheapest and best goods to be winners in international competition. If not, I am sorry to say, they must disappear.

"Such reforms would not even be thinkable without the IMF's provisions. It would have been very difficult to achieve them because the *chaebol* would have resisted. So I am determined to utilize the IMF's reform provisions to transform our economic system so we can prepare to rebound in the twenty-first century. This is a blessing in disguise for us."

The other hope for South Korea was Kim's election itself. "I have faced death five times, spent six years in prison and ten years in exile, but I never lost my faith, physically or mentally," he said. The election victory only days before Christmas in 1997 wasn't only due to the extraordinary endurance of this devout Catholic. It was also the fruit of chance and necessity.

The storm hit South Korea right in the middle of the election campaign, weakening the chances of the government candidate. In a pragmatic move, Kim Dae Jung entered into an alliance—considered unholy by many—with the liberal conservatives of Kim Jong Pil, who had been close to the former dictator Park Chung Hee many years earlier. Kim Jong Pil was also behind the establishment of the KCIA, whose agents came close to assassinating Kim Dae Jung in 1973. According to public opinion, the election was the cleanest in modern Korean history.

Chance and necessity worked well. At a time when South Korea had to carry out nothing less than an economic renaissance, the man put in control was what Clifford called a "supreme outsider"—for somebody in politics for almost half a century, Kim had the most limited links possible with the economic and financial establishment. He was not only the persecuted dissident, the "Nelson Mandela of Asia," Kim was also the first president from South Cholla, the poor province in the south that was distrusted by its more prosperous neighbors. With Kim rejecting the idea of exacting revenge, his election raised the possibility of less provincial factionalism in South Korean politics. And in a country where xenophobia was legendary, Kim was committed to opening South Korea to the outside world following his years of exile abroad.

## THE *CHAEBOL* RESIST

Where Kim wanted to lead the country he had just taken over was clear. "Whether Korea survives and develops in the future will depend on how much we can go out in the world and how much we can receive the world at home," he told *The Far Eastern Economic Review* in early 1998.

But it wouldn't be all clear sailing.

The external environment was unfavorable. The meltdown in other parts of Asia was depriving South Korean industry of export markets at the same time as domestic demand was declining sharply. And far more than any other country in Asia, the crisis in Japan was a threat rather than a positive development. The international community had contributed to a massive package of financial assistance to prevent a default with unpredictable consequences. But despite all the nice words, the punishment was severe. As Michel Camdessus said, nothing would be like before.

"Capitalism without bankruptcy is like Christianity without hell. There is no systemic means of controlling sinful excesses," David Roche said. And for South Korea, it looked like hell was just around the corner. "At the core of the Korean meltdown is a mountain of unserviceable corporate debt owed by self-liquidating corporations that make up 30-40 percent of output," Roche said. "The only cure is for the banks that own the bad debts to go bust and the assets that the bad debt financed to be liquidated or scrapped. That way, about 40-50 percent of Korean industrial capacity would disappear. The conglomerates would start operating profitably but on a much smaller scale."

There was little likelihood of the *chaebol* accepting the idea of trimming so much fat. And according to You Jong Keun, the governor of North Cholla province, the conglomerates were resisting. You was educated at Rutgers University in the United States and was among the academics adhering to free-market principles that Kim Dae Jung was consulting to rebuild the country. During a closed-door meeting with foreign investors organized by Credit Suisse First Boston in early 1998, You warned of *chaebol* resistance at least 10 times, according to a diplomat present. "Over-leveraged firms will have to retrench and restructure quickly in order to survive," he told *Asiaweek*. "And the government will not help the banks the next time they get in trouble. Our Fair Trade Commission, before an apologist for the *chaebol*, will be reincarnated as an enforcer of fair competition."

In his war against the conglomerates, Kim Dae Jung found some unexpected allies such as Park Tae Joon, the legendary founder of POSCO, who could teach a few lessons about discipline to some of the other industrial giants founded under Park Chung Hee. A highly profitable group with a relatively low debt burden like POSCO had everything to gain if its local rivals were submitted to market discipline. The state-owned steelmaker was forced to come to the rescue of Hanbo and Sammi when they collapsed. And if South Korea's excess capacity in steel was finally eliminated, POSCO would be the first to benefit. The company was already listed on the New York Stock Exchange and also targeted for privatization.

At the same time, many foreign banks were petrified of seeing these dinosaurs perish. The banks had recklessly financed the frenzy of investment by Korea Inc. Their shareholders were stuck with the bill and repayments of more or less doubtful debts with *chaebol* subsidiaries had been guaranteed at the group level.

Workers were meanwhile torn apart. Since national union leaders met with Michel Camdessus in December 1997 when the IMF signed its agreement with the government in Seoul, trade unions had acted responsibly. For having brought the "IMF era" upon them, workers wanted the leaders of the industrial empires punished. But at the same time, workers would pay a heavy price for the restructuring of Korea Inc. In a country where unemployment was virtually nonexistent, about ten thousand workers started losing their jobs every week in 1997. South Korea would soon have something in common with its European partners in the OECD—an unemployment rate of more than 10 percent. South Korean companies were like their Japanese counterparts in providing social benefits to their employees. Those who lost their jobs lost everything—health insurance and retirement benefits as well as their own identities and social standing. The creation of a "social safety net" was on the priorities of the adjustment program drawn up by the IMF. But the transition from one system to another would not prevent tragedies. The divorce rate rose, crime increased, and more babies were abandoned.

Kim Dae Jung was not just a prophet of democracy. He was also the prophet of globalization.

"We're no longer in the era of national competition but of world competition," Kim told *The Far Eastern Economic Review*. "Under the WTO system, capital doesn't have nationality. What is important is *where* that capital is invested and used by businesses. Our own companies have made investments in dozens of other countries. Does this mean we are colonizing them?"

Foreign investment would bring new jobs to replace those destroyed by the conglomerates, and methods of management and know-how previously ignored by South Korean groups at their own risk and peril. Foreign investment would also bring discipline.

"The reason we have been suspicious about foreign investment is because of our history as a Japanese colony. But this is rapidly changing because of our people's higher education levels," Kim said.

Foreign investors needed to be reassured that South Korea would renounce the open displays of xenophobia that regularly filled the pages of the international press. These ranged from the regular boycotts of foreign products, which resumed as the crisis got worse, to outright attacks on owners of foreign cars. Foreign bankers hadn't forgotten the troubles with unions at their branches in Seoul during the 1980s. And as both General Motors and Michelin found out, Western companies knew that joint ventures with Korean partners could be a bitter experience. If they came back, they would want to be able to control their activities themselves.

Xenophobia was a luxury Korea Inc. couldn't afford. The country was no longer a cheap export base. If it wanted to avoid a dramatic and sustained decrease in the size of its economy and its peoples' standard of living, South Korea had only one card left to play. This was to integrate itself into the world economy, which signaled an opening up to foreign products and investment, without backtracking and without second thoughts. Kim Dae Jung was no reincarnation of Don Quixote. His analysis and views were clear-headed. But he wasn't just tilting at windmills.

# The Most Powerful
# Man in Asia

"For now, if Camdessus wants to restructure an entire continent,
no one can stop him."

Asiaweek, *May 1998*

Kuala Lumpur had its colonial-era train station and its twin towers, the tallest in the world. And it also had its traffic jams. Like most cities in East Asia that grew too quickly, the Malaysian capital was choking in automobiles. During rush hours, it was impossible to find a taxi. And to be able to drive faster than you could walk, you had to be a minister or Michel Camdessus. On December 2, 1997, the managing director of the IMF was speeding to the airport in a white Mercedes preceded by two police motorcycles and a security vehicle. Brigitte, his wife, politely offered to sit next to the driver in the "death seat" up front. The IMF chief was allowed to take his wife on these trips. It was covered by expenses and perfectly legal. To attract the best candidates for the top job, the IMF considered it was important to let the managing director's wife regularly escape from the closed atmosphere of Washington on a regular basis. When he arrived in the Malaysian capital for a meeting of finance ministers from ASEAN and six other countries, the IMF chief had promised me an exclusive interview. But with his program squeezed by the upheaval surrounding the deepening crisis in South Korea, the drive to the airport became the only chance before Camdessus left for Bangkok, where he was scheduled to address a trade union gathering. The next stopover would be Seoul, where intense negotiations between IMF officials and the South Korean government would be at their height. Michel Camdessus gladly agreed to hold the tape recorder as we spoke.

Speaking on the record, Camdessus was not necessarily going to stop over in Seoul. But on an off-the-record basis, the IMF chief admitted he had decided to go but that results were not guaranteed.

"I'm not going to stay in Seoul forever," he said. "I've got a lot of things to do and I hope these negotiations are concluded quickly." The stakes weren't small—it involved whether the world's eleventh biggest economy was about to default. The South Korean won had become the latest victim of the financial turmoil sweeping Asia. When the markets opened each day, the won would plunge by its daily limit within the space of a few minutes and the markets would close. Worth about nine hundred won to the dollar at the beginning of the year, the South Korean currency was now flirting with the barrier of two thousand won. The central bank's coffers were almost empty—foreign exchange reserves were down to five billion dollars, enough to meet the country's import bill for only ten days. As it had elsewhere in Asia, the currency's collapse had suddenly inflated the mountain of debt owed by local companies that was denominated in foreign currencies. For several weeks, Michel Camdessus had made it known that the IMF was ready to intervene if asked by Seoul. Thailand and Indonesia had already sought the IMF's assistance but South Korea posed a very different problem. It was more fully integrated into the world economy, as shown by its recent admission to the OECD, the Paris-based club of rich countries. Lending to South Korean industrial groups by international banks, especially Japanese and European institutions, amounted to tens of billions of dollars. South Korean companies had expanded beyond their borders to North America and Southeast Asia, and more recently to China and Eastern Europe. And encouraged by financial liberalization measures adopted as part of joining the OECD, South Korean banks had been venturing abroad, subscribing to Indonesian corporate bond issues and playing the stock markets in Moscow and Kiev.

Several weeks earlier on his way to Manila during stopovers in Frankfurt and Tokyo, Larry Summers, the number-two man in the U.S. Treasury, had proposed a rescue plan for South Korea. The proposed cost caused a shudder—between forty billion dollars and sixty billion dollars, as much if not more than the record amount put together for Mexico in 1995. Discussions between the IMF and South Korea started in late November but had been, as one might have expected, particularly rough over the previous few days.

"They've got a nerve," the IMF chief said, using a particularly colloquial French term to describe the Korean "negotiating tactics" as he arrived in the lobby of the Renaissance Hotel in Kuala Lumpur on November 30. For the third time in several days, South Korea's finance ministry had asserted in leaks to the local press that an agreement had been reached with the IMF. Camdessus issued a formal denial, this time in English, before disappearing into an elevator. Over the next forty-eight hours, the phones would be buzzing between Kuala Lumpur and Seoul. Camdessus directed operations from his suite on the twenty-fourth floor of the Renaissance. In Seoul, the IMF negotiators had established their base camp at the Hilton with Asia-Pacific director Hubert Neiss leading the team. The agreement was virtually completed on December 2 but Camdessus imposed a condition—the text of the accord had to be endorsed by all three candidates in upcoming presidential elections before Christmas. Whoever was elected would have to honor the signature of the outgoing head of state, Kim Young Sam.

During the stopover in Bangkok, Michel Camdessus was confident that an agreement had been reached. "South Korea was on the brink of a financial disaster," he said. What would the collapse of the world's eleventh biggest economy have been like? Kenneth Courtis, chief economist for the Asia-Pacific region at Deutsche Bank, later said that it would have been "the most serious threat to the international financial system since the Bretton Woods system collapsed in the early 1970s." A South Korea default would have led to a rupture in the global payments system. International lending and investment in South Korea exceeded two hundred billion dollars and contagion would have left a powder trail. All this next to Japan whose own financial system was about to implode.

## DISMANTLING KOREA INC.

South Korean officials would try to make use of the explosive situation by using a classic procedure. As the old joke went, if you owe ten pounds to the Bank of England, you get thrown in jail, but if you owe a million pounds, they invite you to sit on the board. How many times had the notion of "too big too fail" been used to justify public rescues of institutions whose failure would threaten the entire banking system? With globalization, the same could be said of sovereign risk. The default of a country was almost a mundane occurrence during the Latin American debt crisis in the 1980s but it was now something that had to be avoided at all cost. And the IMF determined the price to be paid.

When the turbulence started getting this rough, the pilot had to have nerves of steel. And in the car driving to Kuala Lumpur airport, Michel Camdessus was calm.

The South Koreans were using blackmail but the markets were under pressure too, imploring an agreement.

"I don't care," Camdessus said, adding that Seoul could either accept the IMF's conditions or not get the money. The conditions? "In all of the key issues we're discussing, the Koreans have to show me that they themselves are making maximum efforts that we can reasonably demand. As we speak now, I'm not sure whether I'll give the green light for the IMF to take part in the Korean program."

More important than the amount of financial support was the program itself lasting at least three years "that gives good assurances that things won't be the same afterwards and that the vulnerabilities and handicaps we discovered in Korea will be treated," Camdessus said. It involved "liberalizing external exchanges, opening up to capital flows that are normal for an industrial power of this size, cleaning up financial structures excessively controlled for too long, and abandoning certain exceptions and favors, which perhaps were useful to allow this economy to grow rapidly for a certain period but which obviously don't correspond any more to the needs of an advanced economy in a globalized world."

Korea Inc.—the economic and social architecture that transformed a country from the ruins of war into one of the world's biggest industrial heavyweights in less than two generations was in the hot seat. As the IMF chief pointed out, it wasn't just the financial system that was implicated.

"A model of economic and social development represents a cease-fire between social and political forces, and it's a lot harder to question when it's been successful for such a long time," he said.

The events were clearly not a run of the mill balance of payments crisis, the sorts of economic ills the IMF had been curing for decades. For South Korea, major surgery was involved.

What justified this meddling in the internal affairs of a sovereign country was financial assistance. And Camdessus didn't hide the fact that he was negotiating on behalf of his shareholders—the leading industrialized countries that dominated the IMF board—and that they were watching developments closely and showing no signs of budging in the face of Seoul's intransigence. "They're absolutely right. We're committing a sizeable amount," he said. "We have a crisis with a major partner in the international community in terms of finance and trade. Just like we do for small developing countries, it's quite normal that efforts made by the international community are subject, with all due allowances, to equally significant efforts by the recipient country."

At fifty-seven billion dollars, the amount was indeed sizeable. Under the same format used for Thailand and Indonesia that was formalized in the Manila Framework, South Korea would get a first line of defense from multilateral institutions, the IMF alone contributing a record twenty-one billion dollars. A second line of defense comprising twenty billion dollars in commitments from various countries would be on standby. The accord was announced in Seoul in December 3.

## NEW JOB

During the interview in late 1997, Camdessus was quite aware that nothing would ever be the same for the IMF. Established in 1944, the multilateral institution had entered the twenty-first century a few years before everyone else with the Mexican crisis in 1994-95. "During the twentieth century, the problems we had to resolve usually stemmed from muddled government policies, whether they were loose monetary policies or fanciful budget policies," the IMF chief said. "Maybe because we were working too hard monitoring and putting public affairs back into order, policies facilitating complacency in the private sector appeared in the shadows as the public sector was being straightened out. They either went unnoticed or were tolerated in the booming environment that ruled over this region for such a long time. As soon as the house of cards was shaken, we witnessed the collapse of economies based on too much credit and not enough shareholder funds and direct investment."

For the IMF, treating problems in the private sector wasn't only new it was "certainly a lot more complex and I'm not going to tell you that we have all the right answers...Until now, we haven't had any experience dealing with banks or the private sector...In terms of manpower and technology, the IMF doesn't have all the means of dealing with this in the same way as the problems of public finance or currencies. We're in the process of learning a new job."

The nature of the Asian crisis—sick private companies rather than problems with public finances and indigestion caused by unproductive investments rather than overconsumption—would not only prompt the IMF to venture into new territory, the IMF would also be scrutinized, for the legitimacy of its actions and its very existence would be questioned. Never before had the IMF appeared so powerful across an entire region—and never before had the attacks been so virulent either.

In the 1970s and 1980s, it was common to see "anti-IMF" protests when extravagant Latin American governments, for example, were forced to slash subsidies in areas such as public transport or staple goods. The IMF was denounced as an instrument of "yankee imperialism" in protests where ideology mixed with the Cold War.

In East Asia in the late 1990s, it was a different story. In Bangkok, for example, the government was shouted down for its inability to implement the restructuring program agreed to with the IMF.

And in Jakarta, the remark by President Suharto's close friend Bob Hasan that "this is the Republic of Indonesia not the Republic of the IMF" did not have its intended effect. Stanley Fischer, the number-two man in the IMF, said in Tokyo several months later that it was remarkable that Indonesians weren't blaming the IMF despite recent unrest. Indonesians knew there were deeper reasons for social instability, he said, adding that it was also remarkable that the IMF program itself had the support of many Indonesian groups.

In South Korea, December 3 was declared a "day of national humiliation" and the IMF letters were used to promote massive sales in stores and depict social dramas such as workers committing suicide or parents abandoning their children. Overall, however, Asian public opinion was remarkably clear-headed when it came to the causes of the suffering. And the IMF's diagnosis of the problem helped. "Publishing a letter of intent effectively throws the spotlight on the whole system of corruption," one IMF official said, referring to Indonesia. Even Malaysian Prime Minister Mahathir Mohamad, who discreetly sought IMF advice on several occasions, described Camdessus as "quite independent" despite his virulent attacks on the recolonization of Asia.

Such independence sometimes caused serious problems for Camdessus in dealing with the main IMF shareholders. At the same time, however, it also earned him respect from developing nations.

After a particularly stormy meeting of the IMF's interim committee in Madrid in 1994, certain members of the G7—and not just the United States—vowed to punish Camdessus, accused of fomenting a front of developing countries to support his proposal for an major increase in IMF capital resources. The IMF chief was popular with the Latin Americans—he spoke fluent Spanish, picked up when his father was working as a journalist in San Sebastian. Camdessus was also popular with the Africans, whom he would tirelessly defend, but was accused of neglecting his European constituents a bit too much.

A few weeks after the Madrid meeting, the peso crisis in Mexico allowed Camdessus to stage a spectacular comeback by reviving the White House rescue plan that got stuck in Congress. Without even waiting for the green light from the IMF board, he decided in forty-eight hours to give the go ahead for eighteen billion dollars in assistance to Mexico on February 1, 1995. Camdessus was criticized by some shareholders, notably the Germans who said he was being "geographically selective"—a charge that wouldn't be repeated later when a package to Russia was arranged. But in May 1996, the IMF board conferred Camdessus with an unprecedented third term for another five years.

For their handling of the Asian crisis, IMF officials were under the most pressure in Washington, where they were subjected to virulent attacks from the American political and financial establishment. And it was in Washington—not Seoul or Jakarta—where the IMF's actions became a domestic political issue, taken hostage by the American contribution to the increase in its capital resources.

## DIPLOMAT AND ADMINISTRATOR

"He leads no country, he commands no military. He serves in no government, he answers to no electorate. He does not run a billion-dollar business or head a million-member organization. He is not even Asian. Which is exactly the point. The most powerful man in Asia this year does not need to control a political party or army. It does not matter if he is (or is not) respected or popular, even here, most of the time. Michel Camdessus is the interloper—twelve months ago, no one would have expected him to be where he is today. Which is presiding over the one hundred billion dollar rescue, and reform of Asia."

When it named him as Asia's most powerful person in 1998, the weekly magazine *Asiaweek* assumed that Michel Camdessus had been absorbed by the institution. If he wanted, the managing director could have remained in his office at 19th Street in Washington, allowing the IMF teams to do the groundwork, giving his stamp of approval and defending his position before the IMF board. After all, that's what his predecessor Jacques de Larosière did brilliantly during the Latin American debt crisis of the 1980s, barely leaving his chair.

Why bother going all the way to Jakarta and risk having your photo taken in a situation deemed humiliating by much of Asian public opinion? "I do it often but I'm happy to do things at close range," Camdessus said before leaving for Seoul. "It's good for the morale of the troops who are up all night negotiating. It's also good for the people we're negotiating with who want to be able to look you straight in the eye when they're signing an agreement. So I'm going to exchange some heavy looks with the Koreans."

Such a personal commitment recognized that diplomacy involved contact between human beings. In this respect, financial diplomacy was the same as diplomacy between states, even if force was expressed in terms of billions of dollars rather than the number of armored divisions and nuclear warheads. Diplomacy had a common language—not just the spoken language, which was usually English, but also the language of ideas, the theoretical baggage common to technocrats from all corners of the world. The basic principles were the market economy, monetary stability, financial orthodoxy, privatization, dismantling trade barriers, and liberalizing capital flows. The theory was largely taught at American universities, where for half a century the best brains from developing countries received their education. The economic policies of Indonesian President Suharto were defined by the "Berkeley Mafia" and similar teams had long been in place in Latin America, more recently taking over in Eastern Europe. For China, it would only be a matter of time. The most stubborn countries, like Japan and France, relied on strong cultural traditions to maintain educational systems that were suspicious of different ideas.

The IMF was able to use these skills in bringing together financial officials from 180 countries on temporary transfers to Washington and diversifying the hiring of its permanent staff as much as possible. Those who had worked at the IMF or World Bank could be found in finance ministries and central banks across the globe and often found themselves on the other side of the negotiating table when IMF officials made their annual visits to member countries.

How did one go about becoming the managing director of the International Monetary Fund?

You had to be European, and it helped to be French. Tradition for more than half a century dictated that the head of the IMF was always a non-American, which had been taken to mean a European. Such historical privilege was not so shocking given the combined European share of the IMF's capital. The fifteen members of the European Union held thirty percent, almost twice as much as the Americans, and consolidating European participation was justified with the birth of the Euro in 1999.

Because it was established at an international monetary conference in the New Hampshire retreat of Bretton Woods in 1944, the IMF had employed only seven managing directors by the end of the twentieth century. Three Frenchmen held the position for more than half the period—Pierre Paul Schweizer (1963-73), Jacques de Larosière (1978-87) and Michel Camdessus (1987- ). The success of French candidates wasn't by chance. France had a political desire to see its own people running international institutions to help maintain the influence of a power that had otherwise become "average" in all respects. But that wasn't the only factor. The head of the IMF wasn't supposed to be an economist but an administrator and a diplomat, two areas where France tended to excel due to tradition and training. France may have been able to provide top rate education in mathematics, for example, but it could never rival America in economics. And in any case, those in charge of hiring staff at the IMF would have considered the economics background of Michel Camdessus as insufficient—he did have a standard political science degree at the Institute of Political Studies in Paris before attending the National Administration School, known as Ena, the elite training ground for senior bureaucrats in France.

When he graduated from Ena in 1960, Camdessus joined the French treasury. In the 1960s and 1970s—well before privatization, financial liberalization, and European integration came along—people joining the Treasury were generalists. They dealt with everything from macroeconomic policy and state-owned enterprises to international finance and exchange rates as well overseeing as the Bank of France, which was not independent. About the only thing the Treasury didn't deal with was the government budget that came under a different section of the finance ministry.

Camdessus would normally have ended his career as the number two man in the Treasury before getting a cushy job in a public-sector financial institution or joining the private sector. He hadn't graduated from Ena in the top ranks of the elite—they went off to become public auditors, the fast-track for promotion in France's financial elite. So the chances for a simple civil administrator like Camdessus getting the top job in the Treasury were remote. Before the Socialist victory of François Mitterrand put an end to twenty-three years of conservative rule in 1981, the position of Treasury Director had been promised to Michel Pébereau, an up and coming public auditor (who would later become chairman of Banque Nationale de Paris). But politics decided otherwise. The incumbent Treasury Director Jean-Yves Haberer was no socialist but apparently switched sides at the last minute when it became clear that the liberal president Valéry Giscard d'Estaing was going to lose. Haberer went off to become chairman of the newly nationalized Compagnie Financière de Paribas. But Camdessus wasn't won over. He may have regarded the left as his political family but he was one of the minority in the French bureaucratic elite whose sympathies were more "social" than socialist.

More important were the positions held by Camdessus within the Treasury. From 1978 to 1984, he chaired the Paris Club of creditor countries involved in rescheduling the debts of developing nations. And from 1982 to 1984, he headed the powerful but little-known committee in charge of running the European Monetary System. In August of 1984, he was appointed deputy governor of the Bank of France and then governor of the central bank from November, succeeding Renaud de La Genière who left to take up the reins at Compagnie de Suez, the other French investment bank that had been nationalized at the same time as Paribas. Camdessus had been serving as France's alternate governor to the IMF since 1983 and became governor in 1984. Under the first government of cohabitation under Mitterrand, the governor of the Bank of France was pushed as the candidate to replace Jacques de Larosière in Washington. And after a surprising amount of to-ing and froing involving the Dutch candidate Onno Ruding, Michel Camdessus become managing director of the IMF at the beginning of 1987.

## AMERICA: ABSENTMINDED OR HOSTILE

"I'd like to get rid of the head of the IMF. He's a socialist from France," said Trent Lott, leader of the Republican majority in the United States Senate. "Am I being too rude?"

By 1998, Camdessus was caught up in politics. He became the target of the American right. The activities of the IMF in Asia triggered a lively debate between academics in the United States and Asia. The attacks were unkind but they were also based on serious and legitimate concerns. But there was nothing serious or legitimate in the way the IMF was dragged into domestic politics in the United States. And in Asia itself, the situation became embarrassing for Americans. "I wouldn't recommend the American Congress as a model to anyone," said Richard Holbrooke, the former number-two man in the State Department. It was also a good ammunition for Eisuke Sakakibara, the number-two man in the Japanese finance ministry who was always on the defensive over allegations that Tokyo had aggravated the Asian crisis. He could now describe America as an inward-looking superpower.

As for the IMF being run by a French socialist, the remarks by Trent Lott prompted quite a few laughs in Paris, not to mention some sections of the

Socialist Party. In their official dealings with the French government, the IMF and Camdessus himself had severely criticized France's structural impediments and cultural inflexibilities. Like many others around the world, Camdessus was irritated "to see sixty million people convinced that they are right and the rest of the world is wrong," one Frenchman working at the IMF said.

Of more concern was the fact that Asian crisis was treated by American public opinion and the mass media as mere distraction of the "real story" at the end of the twentieth century—the sexual escapades of the president of the United States with a White House intern. The world's sole superpower was suddenly obsessed with the sordid details of Bill Clinton's relationship with Monica Lewinsky as the futures of hundreds of millions of people in Asia were at stake.

Frustrated in its attempts to damage Clinton with financial and sexual scandals, the American right turned its revenge on the IMF. The political environment was such that congressional approval for Washington's contribution to boosting the IMF's capital reserves could be held hostage by the anti-abortion lobby. In late 1998, Congress was still blocking America's fourteen billion dollar contribution to the ninety billion dollar increase approved by shareholders at the annual meeting in Hong Kong a year earlier. When the IMF had to help out Russia in July, it was forced to use an emergency funding mechanism as the increase still had not been approved.

The anti-IMF tirades were soon taken up by the editorial page of The Wall Street Journal, which tended to be a law unto itself, run by small group of journalists distinct from the rest of the editorial team.

"Michel Camdessus, who's asking the U.S. taxpayer for a fresh eighteen billion dollars for the International Monetary Fund, personally takes home 224,650 dollars a year as head of that august body," an editorial said. That was more than the president of the United States, and a lot more than a congressman voting on the IMF package. And what's more, it snorted, salaries of IMF officials were tax free.

"What all this means is that IMF staffers, in prescribing policies for the world at large, do not have to live with their own medicine," the editorial reported. "Indeed, if only IMF policy shapers had some of their own pocket change at risk, they just might prove a tad more cautious about pushing for things like higher taxes and bigger bailouts."

The debate was not new. Under pressure from members of Congress who were less concerned about taxpayers when it came to benefiting their own constituents, the United States had pushed for a freeze or a reduction in IMF salaries. The Americans lost. The reality of the marketplace was that tax-free salaries offered by the IMF were lower than what was available on Wall Street or in London and even some universities in the United States. With twenty-two hundred employees, the IMF bureaucracy was in fact relatively light considering the number of members had grown to 182 by the end of the 1990s, increasing the number of trips that had to be taken.

Bankers had a reputation for having short memories and repeatedly making the same mistakes. A case in point was Walter Wriston, the former head of Citibank. Wriston joined forces with former Secretary of State George Schultz and former Treasury Secretary William Simon in calling for the IMF to be eliminated. "The IMF is ineffective, unnecessary, and obsolete," they wrote in a piece published by *The Wall Street Journal*. "Once the Asian crisis is over, we should abolish the one we have."

The argument put forth by these three musketeers was that IMF efforts were "effective in distorting markets. Every investment has an associated risk, and investors seeking higher returns must accept higher risks. The IMF interferes with this fundamental market mechanism by encouraging investors to seek out risky markets on the assumption that if their investments turn sour, they still stand a good chance of getting their money back through IMF bailouts. This kind of interference will only encourage more crises." IMF officials were dumbfounded that Walter Wriston had even dared to put his name to such a piece of writing. "This is the same man who told his officers in Latin America in the 1970s to keep lending and lending because sovereign countries never defaulted," one said. "When the Latin American debt crisis erupted at the beginning of the 1980s, Citibank had lent the equivalent of two times its capital to Brazil alone, without even talking about other countries. If the IMF hadn't been there, Wriston would have lost his bank and his pension."

## MORAL HAZARD

Walter Wriston illustrated how hypocritical the criticisms of the IMF could be. It seemed that the most effective way of combating moral hazard was firstly to make those guilty pay dearly for their mistakes, and secondly to do everything possible to prevent the mistakes from being repeated.

"Nobody is more concerned about moral hazard than me," Camdessus said during the interview in late 1997. "But I would like to point out that the term 'bail out' is a particularly unsuitable way of describing IMF intervention. It's a nautical term. If you refloat the *Titanic*, it doesn't mean it can sail again. The IMF doesn't bail out countries. It returns the boat to the water only after ensuring that it's been repaired and that it can sail peacefully after mechanisms, procedures, and rules have been put into place. Rather than bailing out, I would say we're bringing the vessel back onto an even keel by ensuring that it's seaworthy."

Moral hazard was not an acute problem affecting sovereign countries and governments. In this respect, "I don't talk about moral hazard because I don't know of any country that would lead its economy into a disaster because it knows it's going to get bailed out one day by the IMF,"

Camdessus said. "Certainly no country wants to go through the experience of Mexico with having an additional 1.3 million unemployed people because they did stupid things with *tesobonos*. And I think no country today would want to spend several weeks or several months making the huge effort that Korea is going to have to achieve to bring its economy into the twenty-first century." Events would show that the punishment was more severe than expected.

Did moral hazard involve the investors who gambled recklessly on the financial markets of Asian countries? In this area, the sanction of the market—a concept cherished by Wriston and his cohorts—was swift and ruthless. The hundreds of billions of dollars that disappeared in the collapse of stock prices and currencies had to have been lost by somebody.

What about the local financial institutions that helped to accelerate the Asian financial crisis? In each of the countries where it intervened, namely Thailand, Indonesia, and South Korea, the IMF insisted that the owners and creditors of the banks paid for their mistakes while protecting depositors, especially small ones. But purging financial systems was more difficult to negotiate and carry out when the banks were caught up in powerful interests in ruling circles, especially in Thailand and Indonesia. The IMF had to overcome "the myth that banks are unsinkable," Camdessus said, adding that it was "psychologically, technically, and politically very difficult to recognize that this could no longer be applied to a world where financial institutions had to be placed under equal competitive, financing, and operating conditions."

Making owners pay for the failures of their banks wasn't always easy because of practices tolerated in the past.

"In some countries, certain shareholders of banks break the rules by borrowing amounts from these banks that are much bigger than their actual shareholdings. Such arrangements allow them to risk almost nothing if the bank fails," said Philippe Delhaise, the head of Thomson BankWatch Asia.

The moral hazard argument was strongest for the international banks that had lent so much to the countries now in trouble. In an annex to its *World Economic Outlook* released in early 1998, the IMF said, "it may be difficult to avoid moral hazard altogether" with foreign creditors. "There may well be scope for arrangements in which foreign banks agree to roll over short-term loans at reasonable risk premiums at times when they would not normally choose to do so."

The negotiations on South Korea's short-term debt in December 1997 provided a reality check. American investment banks J. P. Morgan and Goldman Sachs came up with two rival refinancing plans that were similar and based on market conditions at the time.

South Korea was to issue bonds at penal rates of interest to raise funds to repay more than twenty billion dollars in debt coming due within three months. The commission being sought was two hundred million dollars in the case of J. P. Morgan whose man in charge of negotiations was Ernest Stern—a former vice president of the World Bank involved in rescheduling Latin American debt in the 1980s. The South Koreans as well as the Japanese and European commercial banks were up in arms—whether they were debtors or creditors, it was their money. And the American banks were much less exposed to South Korea than their competitors. The plan finally adopted was close to the proposal of Société Générale, which represented the French banks in negotiations at the Citibank headquarters in New York. With a South Korean government guarantee, the debt was rescheduled to one, two, or three years at rates that averaged 250 basis points—two and a half percentage points—above the London Interbank Offer Rate (LIBOR), the rate banks in London charged each other for funds. In the case of Indonesia, the terms were more generous and included a long grace period as Indonesian debtors were completely unable to meet their obligations.

Should there have been an institutional mechanism automatically bringing banks into the process of resolving financial crises? "This question has received focus since the Mexico crisis and renewed attention in view of recent developments in Asia," said David Nellor, the number-two man in the IMF's regional office in Tokyo. "There are no easy answers. Some have suggested the equivalent of an international bankruptcy court or code, and that the international system needs to find a way to authorize a temporary stay on payments in external financial crises."

In 1996, the Group of Ten (actually eleven—the G7 plus Belgium. the Netherlands, Sweden, and Switzerland) considered the idea of allowing orderly suspensions of payment obligations to allow countries in trouble to negotiate identical terms with all their creditors. The terms were supposed to be generous enough to allow a country to emerge from a crisis but not too generous to avoid scaring off future creditors. The issue was complicated because the foreign debt of a country was not just bank loans from dozens or even hundreds of banks. Foreign debt increasingly included bonds held by thousands or tens of thousands of investors.

"This led the working group to suggest that the terms of sovereign bonds might in future allow for the possibility of standstills and recognize explicitly the agreement of creditors to allow others to negotiate on their behalf," said Jon Shields, the British representative to the IMF.

As David Nellor noted, "In considering options in this area, enormous care must be taken to ensure that the debts are serviced in all but extreme circumstances and to avoid the dangers of contagion. An effort to involve the private sector in solving the debt problems in one country could lead to capital outflows from other countries if care is not taken."

## SELF-CRITICISM

Blamed for failing to punish the culprits, the IMF was also blamed for not issuing any warnings.

In Thailand, the IMF was specifically accused of not predicting the crisis. But it was in good company. Most private-sector economists—notably those who had the harshest words of criticism for the IMF—didn't see it coming either.

The IMF carried out an internal review in a confidential report that was partly published by *The Financial Times* in March 1998 and confirmed by IMF officials. The report indicated that the overheating of the Thai economy started to worry IMF economists as early as 1993. During its annual consultations with Thailand in 1994, IMF officials recommended that the practice of fixing the baht's exchange rate to the dollar be abandoned to slow down the rapid inflow of foreign capital. Greater exchange rate flexibility signaled an appreciation of the baht. But the IMF board didn't endorse the recommendation, during the consultations in 1995, the Thai authorities resisted IMF suggestions to tighten monetary policy and allow the baht to rise. In March 1996, by which time Thailand's current account deficit was ballooning dangerously, the IMF again suggested allowing the currency to appreciate while tightening fiscal policy. And in a warning that came too late, the IMF highlighted the risks involved with massive inflows of short-term capital encouraged by the creation of the Bangkok International Banking Facility. After the IMF board considered the report of the team's visit to Bangkok, Michel Camdessus wrote personally to the finance minister in July 1996 to request greater monetary flexibility.

The conclusions of the board's discussions were published in the IMF's annual report in 1997. The report showed similar warnings were issued to Malaysia and Indonesia. According to the IMF, the huge current account deficit of around eight percent of GNP had increased Thailand's vulnerability to economic shocks and adverse changes in market sentiment. It diplomatically pointed out that inflows of short-term capital were relatively high and suggested that Thailand be cautious in relying on foreign savings while taking swift action to curb the current account deficit. But monetary measures and caution adopted to control massive inflows of volatile short-term capital were no substitute for fundamental policies in the longer term. And while the baht's stability had served Thailand well in the past, greater flexibility was urged to increase monetary independence and reduce the encouragement given to inflows of short-term capital. Increased monitoring of the bank sector was also recommended.

And so this was the scenario for Thailand—a crisis of confidence triggered by the sudden realization of how big the trade and financial imbalances were after ten years of rapid growth. And this was followed by a liquidity crisis and a huge outflow of capital, leaving a banking sector drowning in speculative property lending in its wake.

The IMF warnings wouldn't be heard. They were inconveniently written in the diplomatic and financial jargon of a multilateral institution and buried among the eulogies for the overall performance of the countries under its review. What's more, they were confidential and the seriousness of the situation in the banking sector was underestimated, as the IMF would later admit. And in any case, the authorities in Bangkok didn't want to know. From late 1996, when the initial speculative selling of the baht began, the IMF became more concerned. Camdessus wrote letters and visited Thailand discreetly on several occasions. In January 1997, proposals to clean up the financial sector were part of a three-point IMF plan recommended to the Thai government. The IMF offered technical assistance. In March, before issuing a general warning in Hong Kong on the financial risks associated with the Asian miracle, Camdessus took advantage of an APEC meeting in the Thai resort of Phuket to appeal for the exchange rate issue to be tackled once and for all. The IMF recommended devaluing the baht and replacing the fixed rate against the dollar with a wide range allowing it to fluctuate against a basket of currencies. At that stage, the IMF officials were not aware of the scale of intervention by the Bank of Thailand to offset speculative selling of the currency at that stage. And neither Michel Camdessus nor Stanley Fischer would be able to get a clear answer from the Thais during the next round of meetings in April-May. The horrible truth—that the central bank coffers were empty with the reserves tied up in the forward market—would not emerge until August when Thailand finally decided to appeal for IMF help.

## WORLD BANK VERSUS IMF

The IMF was a fireman. It could have been more strict when its fire inspectors made their annual visits. And it could have been firm in asking the owner of the house of Thailand to get rid of the inflammable materials stored in the attic. But as long as there was no fire, it could only intervene with the owner's approval. Axes, ladders, and hoses could be deployed only when the house was on fire and threatening neighboring houses. And fighting the fire resulted in lot of water damage. But what else could a fireman do?

Blamed for not seeing the fire coming, the IMF found itself criticized again when its firemen used the traditional means to put it out—a sharp rise in interest rates to stabilize the exchange rate and budget austerity to get room to maneuver to put the house back in order. The old fiscal remedies, prescribed during the Latin American crises triggered by extravagant public spending, only made this worse in countries used to balanced budgets or even surpluses. And interest rate hikes were a bad prescription as they only worsened the condition of the only real patients—the banks and companies that were choking on their own debts.

In the crowd of critics rushing to burn effigies of Michel Camdessus and Stan Fischer, there were two who stood out—the imposing figure of Joseph

Stiglitz and the slender Jeffrey Sachs, the Laurel and Hardy of the IMF-bashing circus.

In their own way, both were part of organizations that rivaled or competed with the IMF.

Stiglitz was vice president and senior economist of the World Bank. Despite all the nice words about cooperation between the two "sisters" born in Bretton Woods in 1944, the Asian crisis highlighted the ancient rivalries between the World Bank and the IMF.

Sachs was one of the growing number of American academics who "earned a little on the side" by advising governments in emerging countries or private banks. As director of the Harvard Institute for International Development, he became known as economic adviser to the Russian government between 1991 and 1994, when he ceded his position to the IMF. If Stiglitz came from the second big supermarket in town, Sachs was the small storekeeper battling the methods used by large-scale distributors.

"The IMF has become the Typhoid Mary of emerging markets, spreading recessions in country after country," Jeffrey Sachs wrote in *The New York Times* in June 1998. "It lends its client governments money to repay foreign investors, with the condition that the government jack up interest rates, cut the flow of credits to the banking system, and close weak banks. The measures kill the economies and further undermine investors' confidence. It would be more sensible to keep interest rates moderate and let the economies continue to grow."

In an address to the Chicago Council on Foreign Relations several months earlier, Joseph Stiglitz gave an equally harsh assessment of the IMF. His speech on "the role of international financial institutions in the current global economy" was, however, more cryptic and more systematic than the attack by Sachs.

The World Bank vice president said "specific policies in East Asia shaped the incentives that led to the build up of vulnerability"—namely, currencies pegged to the dollar and the "sterilization of capital flows" to prevent the currencies from appreciating. "The sterilization entailed high domestic interest rates, thus driving a large wedge between domestic and international interest rates, creating an additional incentive for companies to borrow from abroad." The third policy was liberalizing capital accounts, facilitating the huge inflows of foreign funds. Although Stiglitz didn't mention it, the policies were endorsed if not encouraged by the IMF. "The ideological position is that financial market liberalization is important because it also leads to faster economic growth, by reducing distortions in the market economy," Stiglitz said. "But both empirical evidence and recent economic theory cast doubt on that proposition."

So what were the lessons of all this?

"One lesson is that we have to become more sensitive to the relationship between what economists divide into the 'macroeconomy' (output, the trade balances, interest rates, exchange rates) and the 'microeconomy' (especially the financial system). At first blush, the obvious answer is to increase the rate of return, to increase the interest rates," Stiglitz said. The problem was that people were already pulling their money out of the country anyway. "Higher interest rates increase the promised return, but in many circumstances they will also create financial strains, leading to bankruptcies, and thus increasing the expectations of default," he said, adding that this could make it less attractive to keep money in the country—the exact opposite of what the policy aimed to achieve.

Moreover, "policies that increase the likelihood of a major economic downturn inevitably increase the risk premium," Stiglitz said. And furthermore, economists "cannot ignore the political consequences" of their policies. "We know that there are systematic relationships between economic downturns and political disturbances, and we know that an enhanced likelihood of political disturbances will weaken confidence in the economy. This is not rocket science, even if is not taught in standard economics courses."

Stiglitz also noted that the Asian crisis was "another reminder of the complexity of the relationship between exchange rates and exports." The boost to exports could be much less than expected if there were corporate failures "that cascade into the bankruptcies of financial institutions and a generalized credit crunch...Addressing the problems in the financial sector and trying to remedy the shortfalls in credit may be as important a determinant of exports as the exchange rate."

But "another set of lessons concerns financial restructuring, particularly the need to maintain the payments system and credit in the process of financial reforms," Stiglitz said, referring to the precedent set by the Resolution Trust Corp. in the United States. Its role in cleaning up the savings and loans mess of the late 1980s was being promoted by the IMF as a model for Asia. But despite all the planning and huge staff of the U.S. agency, "it is generally acknowledged that the U.S. economy suffered a credit crunch that was partly responsible for the depth and persistence of the 1990-91 recession."

In an obvious reference to Indonesia, Stiglitz also noted that governments announcing they will not guarantee private banks "can easily generate a run on the private banks, especially if the government shuts down some banks but leaves doubts about the health of some of the remaining banks. Restructuring done the wrong way can create havoc. It can lead to credit crunches, contributing to the insolvency of firms that otherwise would have survived."

And the World Bank economist implicitly criticized the IMF for being overly ambitious in its new crusade against crony capitalism. "The policy regimes we adopt must be robust against at least a modicum of human fallibility," he said. "Airplanes are not designed just to be flown by ace pilots, and nuclear power plants have built into them a huge margin of safety for human error."

His conclusion?

"In approaching the challenges of globalization, we must eschew ideology and oversimplified models," Stiglitz said. "We must not let the perfect be the enemy of the good. As one of my friends puts it, it is better to have a leaky umbrella than no umbrella at all."

## STAN FISCHER'S DEFENSE

In June 1998, Toyoo Gyohten invited Stanley Fischer to address a seminar in Tokyo organized by the International Institute of Monetary Affairs. And Fischer gave a systematic defense of the IMF's actions in East Asia. If Camdessus was the administrator and diplomat of the IMF, Fischer was the chief technician. The first assistant director was the mentor for an army of a thousand IMF economists—including several graduates of Harvard.

In Thailand, Indonesia, and South Korea "the first order of business was to restore confidence in the currency," Fischer said. "To achieve this, countries had to make it more attractive to hold domestic currency that, in turn, required increasing interest rates temporarily—even if higher interest rate costs complicate the situation of weak banks and corporations." It was an old remedy but it worked to contain the fallout of the "tequila crisis" in Latin America in 1994-95, and more recently in Brazil, the Czech Republic, Hong Kong, and Russia. "Once confidence is restored, interest rates can return to more normal levels—and they are in both Korea and Thailand."

Why not adopt a "kinder, gentler Asian way" by allowing lower interest rates and a sharper currency depreciation? Firstly, because the currency declines were already excessive. Individual countries and the companies with big foreign debts "stand to suffer far more from a steep slide in the value of their domestic currency than from a temporary rise in domestic interest rates," Fischer said. And action had to be taken fast as confidence would continue to erode if raising interest rates was delayed. Furthermore, competitive devaluations were a "way of spreading the crisis" and were "precisely the type of devaluation the IMF has an obligation to prevent."

On budgetary tightening, "the balance is a particularly fine one," Fischer said. But at the outset, fiscal tightening was needed to "make room in the budgets for the future costs of financial restructuring" and reduce current account deficits—particularly crucial in Thailand's case. Because of this, the size of the adjustment was three percent of GNP in Thailand, three times the level in Indonesia and twice the level in South Korea. When the economy weakened more than expected in all three countries, the IMF generally agreed to let budget deficits widen to let automatic stabilizers operate. But "in two cases, IMF staff suggested a higher fiscal deficit than country authorities were willing to accept," Fischer said. "Asian countries are not generally in favor of large deficits."

But "macroeconomic adjustment is not the main element in the programs of Thailand, Indonesia, and Korea," he added. "Rather, financial sector restructuring and other structural reforms are central to each program because the problems they deal with—weak financial institutions, inadequate bank regulation and supervision, and the complicated and nontransparent relations among governments, banks, and corporations—lie at the heart of the economic crisis in each country."

It was primarily a question of efficiency. Confidence wouldn't return if problems were either not treated or treated badly—as the events in Russia in mid-1998 showed. And as Fischer told his mainly Japanese audience, Japan showed that the refusal to carry out structural reforms would only prolong the difficulties. He also urged Japan to adopt a "comprehensive and transparent" approach to fix the country's bad debt problems once and for all.

In developing countries, the IMF was often accused of double standards—of tolerating practices in industrialized countries while fighting the same practices in adjustment programs for countries less fortunate and less powerful. The accusation was largely unfair. The difference was that rich countries were in a position to ignore equally harsh recommendations from the IMF because they didn't have to go begging. And putting aside the financial aspect as it was already the world's largest creditor nation, IMF intervention in Japan could have been justified too. The country was in difficulty, its decade-long stagnation was adversely affecting the regional and global economies, and its political and bureaucratic elite could not cure the illness. The Japanese wouldn't necessarily have been worse off, and the rest of the world—East Asia especially—would have undoubtedly been much better off.

Such a scenario went right to the heart of the issue of IMF intervention. When and according to what criteria did a multilateral institution have the right to dictate its laws to a sovereign state?

## ABUSE OF POWER?

The question of whether the IMF was abusing its power was taken up by Martin Feldstein, economics professor at Harvard University and chairman of the National Bureau of Economic Research.

"The fundamental issue is the appropriate role for an international agency and its technical staff in dealing with sovereign countries that come to it for assistance," he wrote in the March-April 1998 edition of *Foreign Affairs*. "It is important to remember that the IMF cannot initiate programs but develops a program for a member country only when that country seeks help. The country is then the IMF's client or patient, but not its ward. The legitimate political institutions of the country should determine a nation's economic structure and the nature of its institutions. A nation's desperate need for short-term financial help does not give the IMF the moral right to substitute its technical judgments for the outcomes of a nation's political process."

Feldstein argued that the detailed IMF reforms for South Korea, ranging from corporate restructuring to liberalizing markets and removing trade barriers, would probably improve things in the long term but were not needed for the country to regain access to capital markets. "What Korea needed was coordinated action by creditor banks to restructure its short-term debt, lengthening their maturity and providing additional temporary credits to help meet the interest obligations," he said.

South Korea faced "temporary illiquidity rather than fundamental insolvency" and the primary need was to persuade foreign creditors to keep lending by rolling over loans as they came due. "By emphasizing the structural and institutional problems of the Korean economy, the fund's program and rhetoric gave the opposite impression," Feldstein said. And several features of the IMF plan were what foreign countries had long been trying to get South Korea to adopt, such as lowering trade barriers to certain Japanese products and opening the financial sector to foreign competition. "Koreans and others saw this aspect of the plan as an abuse of IMF power to force Korea at a time of weakness to accept trade and investment policies it had previously rejected," Feldstein said. The risk was that emerging economies would follow Malaysia's example and do everything they could to avoid asking the IMF for help. And the other danger was that they might be tempted to follow the example of Hong Kong, Singapore, Taiwan, and China to use their trade surpluses to accumulate foreign exchange reserves, building up war chests of financial assets rather than using scarce reserves in more productive areas such as importing new plants and equipment.

"The IMF should eschew the temptation to use currency crises as an opportunity to force fundamental structural and institutional reforms on countries, however useful they may be in the long term, unless they are absolutely necessary to revive access to international funds," Feldstein said.

Stan Fischer addressed the questions raised by his former Harvard colleague during his speech in Tokyo. On the question of whether it was really necessary to restore access to international capital markets, "the answer in the case of the Asian programs is yes," Fischer said. But on distinguishing between "technical" matters and improper interference, "the answer here is complicated," he said, noting that there were no accepted definitions. "Banking sector reform is a highly technical issue, far more than the size of the budget deficit—a policy consideration Feldstein is apparently willing to accept as fit for inclusion in a fund program. Nor is it clear why trade liberalization—that has long been part of IMF and World Bank programs—is any less an intrusion on a sovereign government than banking sector reform. Nor does Feldstein explain why the programs supported by the fund in the transition economies including Russia—that are far more detailed, far more structural, and in many countries as controversial as Asia—are acceptable but those in Asia are not." And would the IMF ask for similar changes in Europe if industrialized countries practiced similar policies to Asian countries and had a fund program? "The answer here is a straightforward yes," Fischer said.

If there were two observations to be made, one was that the notion of economic sovereignty was relative, involving countries entering into trade and financial exchanges with their neighbors and the rest of the word. Absolute sovereignty is called autarchy—like in communist Albania or North Korea. When a country had reached the level of integration into the world economy as South Korea had, it no longer deserved to be called the "hermit kingdom"—even if there were still some heavy traces of traditional xenophobia in some of its behavior.

The second observation was that some structural reforms "dictated" by the IMF had been on the drawing board of the national authorities themselves and were in the interest of the general public. Unfortunately—and it really was very, very unfortunate—they were either difficult or impossible to implement because of vested interests. This was particularly true in the case of South Korea, whether it was excessive *chaebol* dominance over the economy or excessively rigid labor markets.

## LENDER OF LAST RESORT

In fact, Stanley Fischer replied, Feldstein's criticisms ignored the most important question. "Does this program address the underlying causes of the crisis? There is neither point nor excuse for the international community to provide financial assistance to a country unless that country takes measures to prevent future such crises," Fischer said.

Implicitly, this involved the very role of the IMF itself. And some of its critics argued that it should play the role of lender of last resort. The Wall Street Journal argued in an editorial that there was such a role for the IMF when fundamentally sound currencies were being subjected to temporary attacks. The editorial in May 1998 accused the IMF of being responsible for riots in Indonesia and the fall of Suharto. In short, the IMF should play a scaled-down role on the global scene similar to a central bank operating within its national boundaries—provide liquidity when the currency comes under attack or if all or part of the financial system is threatened with insolvency.

The approach raised several problems. First, there was the Sachs argument that the economies and currencies of East Asian economies were fundamentally sound and that the crisis was the result of a financial panic and nothing else. One could then assume that the lender of last resort was supposed to intervene unconditionally. This had been the ulterior motive of those promoting the Asian Monetary Fund who wanted to remove or heavily dilute the conditions that would have otherwise been imposed by the IMF.

But on the national scale, intervention by a central bank acting as lender of last resort was neither unconditional nor free. Supporting a currency involved using the interest rate weapon, sometimes violently. And rushing to the aid of a troubled financial institution often meant taking over its management and getting rid of its executives before transferring it to a healthy rival or calling in the receivers. When Barings fell into problems with its "rogue trader" Nick Leeson in Singapore, Bank of England Governor Eddie George spent a weekend putting together a plan that ended two centuries of independence and transferred the business to Dutch bank ING. And in France, the central bank governor could fleece other banks if an insolvent financial institution needed to be bailed out. How could the choice between life and death be carried out on a global scale? By putting a country under the direct control of the IMF and replacing the prevailing arrangements whereby adjustment programs were negotiated with its representatives?

In any case, the IMF wasn't a lender of last resort. As David Nellor pointed out, it was like a credit union or a cooperative in which members had a common interest in promoting international economic cooperation. This was carried out by monitoring activities, on behalf of all members, to predict any difficulties. If there was a crisis, it was in the "common interest" of the 182 members to remedy the situation with market interest rates and terms that guaranteed the ability to repay. Some countries were in arrears with the IMF. But no member had ever defaulted, the most desperate being able to benefit from schemes to reduce the principal amount owed or interest payments. "The IMF is not a charitable institution," Nellor said. "It is not an aid agency. And its operations are not carried out at taxpayer expense. Rather, it is a revolving fund—the resources made available by member governments are lent out, they are repaid with interest, they are lent out again."

The advantages of multilateralism were varied. As a club, the IMF could speak with members without threatening their national susceptibilities in the same way as bilateral talks could. "It also brings about needed policy changes in situations where a bilateral approach would almost surely be rebuffed," Nellor said. Secondly, the IMF had shown its ability to treat international crises, often on very short notice. These ranged from balances of payments crises triggered by the two oil price shocks of the 1970s to the peso crisis in Mexico in 1994-95. Other crises included the economic consequences of the Gulf War and the delicate transition to market economies by countries in the former Soviet bloc. "The IMF provides a highly effective mechanism for sharing the responsibility of supporting the international monetary system," Nellor said. How could the United States deal with such crises alone and at what price? It was the biggest shareholder in the IMF but only accounted for eighteen percent of its capital. The Mexican crisis proved that despite a major strategic interest, the Americans could not act alone either politically or financially. And neither could Germany, whose banks were up to their neck in Russian debt, act alone in pulling the government in Moscow out of its frequent messes.

What would the world be like without the IMF? In a piece of financial fiction, Thomas Friedman of *The New York Times* painted a scenario for "the first anniversary of the closing of the IMF." It was June 15, 1999, and the ruble had dropped to fifty thousand to the dollar. Russia's new president, former general Alexander Lebed who had deposed Boris Yeltsin in a coup d'etat, had decided to turn the country into a major export machine by selling military technology and material including enriched uranium on the international market. At the same time, Thailand and South Korea were appealing for emergency financial assistance from the United States Congress. In its bid to get ten billion dollars from Washington, Seoul had hired George Schultz, William Simon, and Walter Wriston—the trio who had earlier campaigned to close the IMF. But South Korea was rejecting American demands to end birth control and allow U.S. companies to acquire one hundred percent of South Korean companies. The American embassy in Seoul had been ransacked. Martial law had been declared in Thailand, Malaysia, and Indonesia where anti-Chinese riots were raging. The trade deficit of the United States had ballooned to four hundred billion dollars. The dollar had jumped to three hundred yen but the Dow Jones Industrial Average had plunged to 6,660 points. Pat Buchanan and Ross Perot, the right-wing fundamentalist and the right-wing eccentric, were neck and neck in the presidential election polls. The United States called for an emergency meeting to discuss the creation of some sort of international monetary fund, offering to host the meeting in Bretton Woods, a small town in New Hampshire.

"But the other world powers, showing contempt for weak U.S. leadership, insisted on Shanghai."

## YELLOW CARD

When the system of exchange rates established in Bretton Woods in 1944 collapsed in the early 1970s, it appeared that the writing was on the wall for the IMF, which had been established to guarantee the smooth running of the system that no longer existed. But the IMF showed a remarkable ability to reinvent itself. This was partly due to the self-preservation instinct of any bureaucracy and the skills of successive managing directors. But that wasn't enough. Each new international crisis highlighted the usefulness of the IMF and also the need to adapt itself to new ways, procedures, and operations. The Asian crisis was no exception to this rule.

Among the deficiencies highlighted by the Mexican crisis was the lack of information that would have allowed markets to get a clearer picture of what was going on and limit the impact of the "tequila effect" on other emerging economies. During the summit of leading industrialized countries in Halifax in 1995, the IMF requested and received a mandate to improve the collection and dissemination of statistical data. The Asian crisis showed that the goal was far from being achieved. Even if they were willing, emerging economies didn't always have the means to furnish lists of figures that were too ambitious. The excuse offered by recalcitrant governments was that less criteria would allow statistics to be targeted properly.

But how could the IMF call for greater transparency when the organization itself was excessively worried about confidentiality? The question was raised well before the Asian crisis during the fiftieth anniversary of the IMF and the World Bank in 1994. Under the leadership of former U.S. Federal Reserve Chairman Paul Volcker, the Bretton Woods Commission called for voluntary publication of a country's annual consultations with the IMF. The idea was adopted by a few countries—the problem being that they tended to be the best students whose report cards were glowing with praise. The weaker but hard-working students as well as the dunces had to show greater enthusiasm.

What was the IMF supposed to do when governments refused to listen to calls to change economic policies, as Bangkok did in 1996?

In 1998, the interim committee of the IMF made suggestions. Michel Camdessus said they involved a "progressive strengthening of our language" with the IMF adopting the "yellow card" approach used as a warning in soccer games. Raising the yellow card more often would involve the managing director writing to governments that would then have to respond to the IMF's executive council within a certain period. "It is the strong hope of the committee that the IMF will never be in the situation to have to resort to the 'red card' of going public with its negative opinion on a given country," Camdessus said. But the dilemma between triggering a crisis and being ignored could be overcome if the IMF made more of its assessments available to the public.

Such changes were important as long as they didn't lead to a transfer of responsibility—the IMF couldn't be a substitute for the international rating agencies or investors that were responsible for assessing the risks of sovereign and corporate borrowers themselves. Nor could the IMF substitute for central banks in the role of policing commercial banks in their respective jurisdictions. Greater statistical transparency was meanwhile in the interests of borrowers as much as assessing risk was the job of investors. The call by George Soros—for an international institution funded by taxpayers to be established alongside the IMF to guarantee some of the risks undertaken by private investors—was heresy. National credit guarantee companies like Coface in France and Hermes in Germany had already cost small fortunes to taxpayers in those two countries. Public funds were used to cover political risks taken by elected governments themselves—Iraq and Algeria in the case of France. The Soros idea of accepting moral hazard was like accepting that drug consumption was inevitable and not a problem to be fought.

The IMF was necessary because improving preventative measures would not stop new crises from emerging. When the IMF undertook emergency measures and stepped in yet again to rescue Russia from the abyss in mid-1998, those who had been criticizing the massive bailouts in Asia so loudly suddenly couldn't be heard—except for Jeffrey Sachs, of course. The silence was particularly deafening in Germany, for reasons not difficult to understand. But as French Treasury chief Jean Lemierre asked: "After the Russian decision, hasn't the moral hazard debate become theoretical?"

## HE WHO PAYS...RULES!

The Asian crisis initiated a global debate on a "new international financial architecture" and what role the IMF should play. The technical aspects weren't that interesting but the political dimensions were. Given its positive impact but also the negative fallout from contagion, the very nature of globalization led to a widening of the IMF's mandate during the meeting of the interim committee in April 1998. The IMF's expertise in microeconomic reforms was widespread, especially in the area of strengthening the financial systems of member countries. It was asked to inquire more actively about the real economic situations in member countries and to be a tougher referee, to use the football imagery of Camdessus. The same meeting of the interim committee approved a code of conduct for budget transparency. And in a follow-up to the annual meeting in Hong Kong, it confirmed preparations to modify the IMF's articles to give it a mandate to promote the gradual and orderly liberalization of capital flows. The Asian crisis had not questioned the validity of capital liberalization itself, only the violent and disorderly manner of the flows.

In other words, membership obligations for the IMF club were becoming more urgent, rules were getting stricter and intrusions into daily lives more inquisitive. What ever happened to the rights of the members? Every member of any club knew that the type of democracy followed was special. Membership was voluntary and consensus was preferred to open confrontation or an actual vote (voting was rare in the IMF executive council). And some members—notably the older and more influential ones—were obviously more equal than others.

On the eve of the summit of leading industrialized countries in Birmingham in May 1998, Camdessus asked: "Is there anything that could be done to strengthen what one might call the political accountability or legitimacy of our institutions? At this stage, this would require at least a few organizational changes, which would make more explicit the ties that bind us to the governments we depend on."

Camdessus suggested two paths—through the IMF itself or through the Group of Seven industrialized countries, the oldest and richest members of the club.

On the first idea, he took up the idea of French Economy and Finance Minister Dominique Strauss-Kahn of "revitalizing" the IMF interim committee by transforming the consultative body into a "council" with real decision-making powers.

"It could become an essential structure because no other can match the scope of its responsibility and the legitimacy of its members, who are collectively responsible for key developments in the world economy," Camdessus said.

Grouping twenty-four member countries, the interim committee met twice a year in spring and autumn—just before the annual meeting of the council of governors when all members were present. The interim committee didn't just include the big industrialized countries but also large developing countries such as Brazil, China, and India. It also included European countries such as the Netherlands, Belgium, and Switzerland whose commercial and financial importance outweighed their relatively small size. The idea of transforming the committee into a decision-making body wasn't new. It was considered in the Jamaica Accords of 1974 but postponed due to what was then the experimental nature of the committee that was only created in 1970. Moreover, many of the twenty-four members of the interim committee were among the twenty-four members of the IMF board of directors. During a meeting in Germany in mid 1999, G7 finance ministers took initial steps toward expanding the role of the interim committee.

As for the second proposal, Camdessus said the G7 "feels the need to embrace emerging market countries but is unclear about how to go about it and finds it difficult to come up with acceptable ways of choosing its partners."

The composition of the G7 was a problem that went back to the Plaza Accord between Group of Five countries in 1985. Until then, the G5 was a largely discreet group involved in technical decisions. With the Plaza Accord, it was suddenly thrust up onto the world stage with global responsibilities. Adding Italy and Canada to the G5 and making it the G7 was questionable—why not the Netherlands that had a bigger presence in international banking? And the gradual addition of Russia to the annual summits of the seven leading industrialized countries didn't clarify things either, especially when journalists started calling the summits "G8" meetings. Russia was neither an advanced industrial power nor a stable democracy, and it certainly didn't take part in meetings between finance ministers and central bank governors from the G7 countries. The creation of the European Central Bank in 1999 complicated things even further for the G7, although at least the initial chairmanship of Wim Duisenberg of the Netherlands could make the Dutch feel better for a while.

Faced with such problems, Camdessus suggested that the G7/G8 might want to enlarge its annual summits every two years to invite the sixteen countries on the executive council of the IMF and the World Bank, along with the heads of the IMF, the World Bank, WTO, and the United Nations "that could become a fourth humanitarian and social pillar of the world system."

The Lyons summit in 1996 set a partial precedent toward the establishment of a G24 with French host President Jacques Chirac organizing a special session with Michel Camdessus, World Bank president James Wolfensohn, and WTO director general Renato Ruggiero.

And even if his ideas were greeted with skepticism and objections over logistics, Camdessus said "they need to be discussed" by IMF members. "They could provide a concrete way of recognizing that each medium-sized or developing country must have a more equitable share of responsibility for the future of the world economy, a share they believe is unjustly denied them in the present institutional arrangements of the international financial system."

Naive optimism had to be avoided. Global financial integration required a "democratic" widening of the structures in the system. But it couldn't be effective and durable if it didn't follow precedents and the hierarchy of responsibilities.

Jean Lemierre, the head of the French Treasury, said the debate involved two basic questions—which forums and what powers?

"On the first point, it seems obvious to me that we need a forum where a number of countries can express themselves," he said. "It's legitimate for somebody like Pedro Malan (the Brazilian finance minister) and the representatives of India or China to be able to express themselves. It's in the G7's interest to talk with other countries and share technical and political experiences given that the Asian crisis, following the Mexican crisis, has highlighted the fallout that affects all of us. For the G7 and the IMF, it's a question of geographical legitimacy."

But the political dimension was more complicated, as Lemierre himself admitted when referring to the French proposal to transform the interim committee into a decision-making body.

"Let's be clear," he said. "It's a question of legitimacy for the IMF. But in America, there's a refusal to give the IMF political legitimacy."

Was this the reason why the White House invited twenty-two finance ministers to an evening at the Willard Hotel in Washington in early 1998? The event, hosted by Treasury Secretary Robert Rubin, was held on the sidelines of the spring meeting of the interim committee and the arbitrary makeup of the group—immediately baptized as the "G22"—wounded a few prides. "We agree with Larry Summers on the need for a forum of between twenty and twenty-five members. The problems are with the choice and the prerogatives," Lemierre said.

"The legitimacy of the G7 would be comforted and enriched by a larger group. But that should not reduce the weight and role of the G7 for the simple reason that it's the G7 who pays," he said. The leading industrialized countries were not only the main shareholders in the IMF and the World Bank. The G7 countries—plus maybe the Netherlands and Switzerland—were the ones who had the global banking risk. "The G7 has proven its effectiveness," Lemierre said. And it was particularly effective during the South Korean crisis. "The G7 became a war room. We worked day and night to convince the banks to reschedule the debts and it turned out to be effective. If the G7's usefulness is disputed after all that, then I've lost the plot."

# CHAPTER FOURTEEN

# Breaking the Bank

"Banking itself is a disaster-prone nineteenth-century technology."
—*Merton Miller, winner of the Nobel Prize for economics*

Banking crises are not exceptional events. They have always existed, at least since the emergence of bankers whose sole purpose in life was to take risks, in this case the risk of not being repaid.

Between 1975 and 1997, IMF figures showed that fifty-four banking crises erupted across the world. Banking crises were often preceded, accompanied, or followed by currency crises—and there were 158 of them during the same period. East Asia was in good company.

Banking crises affected all countries—rich and poor, big and small, and from both the North and the South. The United States went through a difficult period with its savings and loans crisis, prompting the liquidation or merger of twenty-five hundred financial institutions between 1980 and 1992. Latin America spent most of the 1980s in shock from the banking crisis that broke out at the beginning of what would later be called the "lost decade." Sri Lanka suffered terribly between 1989 and 1993, the same period that large-scale intervention by authorities saved banks from imploding in Finland, Norway, and Sweden. And let's not forget Japan, which spent most of the 1990s vainly trying to conceal the terminal state of its financial system. Or France, where the Credit Lyonnais disaster would have provoked "systemic risk" if the bank that wanted to be Europe's biggest had not been state owned.

The figures compiled by the IMF showed that it was better to be rich and healthy than poor and sick—banking crises were more common in emerging economies than industrialized ones (forty-two versus twelve), and crises in developing nations were more costly to resolve.

Banking crises also became more frequent beginning in the mid-1980s, raising questions about financial liberalization policies adopted by several countries around the same time. But it often turned out that liberalization was just exposing the excesses of the preceding period, when lending was strictly controlled by governments. You had to study the past before insulting the future. At the same time, Sri Lanka and China showed that governments could keep tight reins on banks but still ruin their financial systems.

## ANATOMY OF THE CRISIS

What is a banking crisis? Edward Kane, a specialist in the field who taught at Boston College, said it was best understood as "an open (and typically prolonged) struggle between economic sectors" over "how to allocate across society an unpaid bill for losses that have accumulated or are still accumulating at banks."

Kane also confirmed what everyone had known for ages, verified once again by the Asian crisis, that banks were a special breed that required special treatment when they were sick or dying. Bank failures weren't just any old bankruptcy.

How did banking crises develop? In a presentation to a seminar in Hong Kong in late 1997, Kane distinguished five separate stages.

In the "embryonic phase," losses suffered during the cyclical expansion of the economy started to accumulate. The origins of the losses varied from one cycle to the next and from one country to the next. It might be aggressive lending by banks, especially newcomers, or political pressure to lend to certain borrowers such as private individuals or sectors of the economy. But it might also be an excessive concentration of risks, a worsening internal climate, an external shock, or lapses on the part of the authorities supervising banks (notably state-owned ones). The accumulation of hidden losses was helped by deficiencies in accounting or supervision.

The second phase was the "accelerating risk-shifting stage" in which managers intensified risk-taking and loss-causing activities, marked by the beginning of silent runs and increasing collateralization of deposits owned by "informed customers" of the banks. Supervisors gambled they could finesse the pain of allocating losses to taxpayers by combining cheerful public statements with time-buying disciplinary action.

Next came the "emergency hospitalization stage" as more depositors learned about insolvencies and the silent run generated more noise. Two characteristic symptoms of this stage were media reports about sky-high deposit rates and even runs, as well as open talk among authorities about plans for assigning losses through bailouts, mergers, or closures. "This phase may drag on for years (as it has in Japan) or its may last only a few weeks," Kane said.

The fourth phase was the "recapitalization stage" with losses absorbed or softened by a combination of cures. The easiest cure was when the nation's economy was in good shape and the health of the survivors enhanced by the exit of ruined banks during the hospitalization stage, reducing competitive pressures. Here, the injection of taxpayer money usually played an important role.

Finally was the "incentive reform and blame distribution stage" where heads rolled and scapegoats were designated to keep the public happy while whitewashing the well-connected parties who deserved to be held accountable. During this stage, incentives to renew the cycle of loss-shifting were often wished away. "Even when genuine reforms are adopted, risk-shifting opportunities are eventually renewed," Kane said. Taxpayers forget quickly, and memories of the crisis fade, along with financial discipline. As David Roche used to say, bankers could be distinguished by two features—short memories and IQ's that were below average.

## AN OCEAN OF LOSSES

The banking crises in East Asia in the late 1990s more or less followed Kane's script. The main uncertainties were the duration and the final cost.

But there were numerous ways to evaluate the gravity of a banking crisis. Two widely used ratios were the cost of restructuring banks as a percentage of a country's GDP and the total amount of nonperforming loans as a proportion of all lending. In the late 1990s, recapitalizing a bank involved making sure it had enough capital to cover eight percent of all loans—the basic standard set a decade earlier by the BIS in Basel.

In the last two decades of the twentieth century, Argentina's crisis between 1980 and 1982 won hands down with a restructuring cost amounting to fifty-five percent of GDP. Resolving Chile's crisis between 1981 and 1985 came to forty-one percent of GDP. The ratios were lower for industrialized countries—seven percent of GDP for the United States and five percent for Sweden.

Sri Lanka won the bad debt prize with nonperforming loans amounting to thirty-five percent of all lending, followed closely by Malaysia where a third of bank loans were rotten between 1985 and 1988.

American investment bank J. P. Morgan said the banking crisis in East Asia was one of the worst in modern history back in April 1998—well before the loss of financial assets had run its full course. The cost of recapitalizing banks was twenty percent of GDP in the case of Indonesia, Malaysia, and Japan, the world's second-largest economy. In South Korea and Thailand, the cost was estimated at thirty percent.

Nonperforming loans (NPL's) were estimated at between 15 percent and 20 percent of all lending in Japan, between 15 and 25 percent in Malaysia, between 25 percent and 30 percent in South Korea and Thailand, and between 30 percent and 35 percent in Indonesia.

Around the same time, the credit rating agency Fitch-IBCA estimated the ratio of nonperforming loans in Indonesia as high as fifty percent of all lending. And in the climate created by the failure of Yamaichi Securities and Hokkaido Takushoku Bank, Japan decided to delay its rapid corrective action plan by a year.

J. P. Morgan calculated that if Asian banks made provisions for bad debts, the solvency ratios would be negative to the tune of minus 17 percent for Indonesian banks, minus 11 percent for Thai banks, minus 10 percent for South Korean banks and minus 4 percent for Malaysian and Japanese banks.

Roy Ramos, who headed the banking analysis team at Goldman Sachs (Asia) in Hong Kong, described the scenario in Thailand, "With a credit to GDP ratio exceeding 150 percent and an NPL (nonperforming loan) ratio likely to reach 25 percent, bad loans should peak at close to 40 percent of GDP," he said. "Assuming a fairly generous 50 percent NPL recovery ratio, this suggests ultimate losses equal to 20 percent of GDP. That would be a full three years of good economic growth, assuming Thailand can still grow at 7 percent each year post-financial crisis."

In South Korea, it was believed that cleaning up the banking mess could require an injection of as much as one hundred billion dollars—almost two times the size of the IMF-led multilateral assistance package to the country that was already the biggest in IMF history.

Given the implications of such figures, it wasn't surprising that governments and shareholders were tempted to follow the example of Japan—conceal the size of the problem and pretend it didn't exist in the hope that it would eventually go away.

Following the Japanese model, the central banks of Thailand, Indonesia, Malaysia, and South Korea used their central banks to inject enormous amounts of liquidity into their banking systems. At the end of 1996, the Bank of Thailand owed six hundred million baht to the financial system. A year later, the financial system owed the central bank 583 billion baht. Similar developments took place in South Korea, where the central bank went from being a 3.1 trillion won debtor to a 35.5 trillion won creditor in the same period. In Indonesia, the central bank's deficit with the financial system of 5.5 trillion rupiah in December 1996 swung to a surplus of 47.3 trillion rupiah in February 1998.

## MORATORIUM

Japan was rich and powerful. It was the biggest creditor nation on earth with more than one thousand billion dollars in net assets abroad. So it stuck its head in the sand like an ostrich. And paid the price with seven years of stagnation, coming within a whisker of financial implosion at the end of 1997 before plunging into recession once again when it was caught up in the Asian crisis. By mid-1998, Japan's defiance toward the state of its financial system's health was such that credit-rating agency Moody's announced a review of Japan's triple-A rating for sovereign debt, the top ranking available in the international markets and a status enjoyed by few countries. Few people were really surprised—it was a bit like a five-star hotel being told it might lose its rating after refusing to clean up the mess in the kitchen for seven years.

But waiting was a luxury the fragile economies elsewhere in Asia couldn't enjoy—for different but equally pressing reasons.

Banking sectors in other Asian countries were heavily indebted to foreign lenders, and the funds involved were often short-term borrowings. According to BIS figures, the external debt of Asian countries outside of Japan was 367 billion dollars at the end of 1996 of which 226 billion was short-term debt maturing in less than a year. The combined debt of the banking sector was 160 billion dollars with the breakdown varying between countries. In Indonesia, the debt of the private sector excluding financial institutions was almost three-quarters of the total amount. In South Korea, the situation was almost reversed with the banking sector accounting for two-thirds.

In Thailand, Indonesia, and South Korea, the financial and banking crisis rapidly became a debt crisis, precipitating IMF intervention and the mobilization of more than one hundred billion dollars by the international community to prevent a repayment default or a moratorium on external debt.

"Debt moratoriums are in no one's interest—governments, private sectors, banks, or bond investors," Roy Ramos said. "As the mid-1980s reschedulings in Mexico, Brazil, Argentina, and the Philippines show, debt moratoriums help cause painful recessions, prolonged periods of net capital outflows, and years of lost economic momentum."

In the case of East Asia, reviving economic growth would come from a sharp increase in exports. But this was a goal that was impossible to achieve if the credit system wasn't working any more. A year after the financial squall hit, the exports of the countries most affected hadn't really taken off in a big way. The spectacular improvement in current account balances had largely been a result of collapsing imports. Was anyone really surprised if international banks didn't honor a letter of credit from an Indonesian bank?

The truth was that the 1997 crisis made major surgery inevitable—the disease had been diagnosed long before but the patient had chosen to ignore it. The crisis also interrupted experts at the World Bank who were busy editing a study on banking reform in Asia.

"In a world that is increasingly integrated financially, East Asia can no longer postpone difficult choices—the penalty of maintaining a fragile, underdeveloped banking system is too severe," the World Bank wrote in the mid-1997 report. The report was entitled *Are Financial Sector Weaknesses Undermining the East Asian Miracle?* The response to that particular question would soon become clear.

## UNFINISHED LIBERALIZATION

The World Bank—and this didn't surprise anybody—asserted that it wasn't financial liberalization itself that was the problem. "First, initial conditions matter. Countries rarely start to reform when the financial system is performing well," the report noted. "Many countries pursue change only after a financial crisis intensifies, making it difficult to assign causality." But timing is decisive. "Countries that move faster with reforms during good times and slower during bad times can cope more easily with the inevitable adjustment costs."

As an example, the study cited Malaysia, where the banking system was restructured in the mid-1980s. Another two examples were the Philippines and Taiwan, which restructured their banking systems after earlier crises. Both countries were less affected by the financial turmoil in 1997.

The point was that liberalization was nearly always unfinished business.

"Countries that have liberalized interest rates, credit controls, and international capital flows often failed to upgrade accounting and reporting standards, strengthen the legal system, create better incentives for bankers, and address other institutional issues," the World Bank said. The improvement in "human capital" in the financial sector was also neglected, the entry of new banks was insufficiently controlled (as in South Korea and Indonesia), and privatizations were carried out poorly (as in Mexico).

It was hardly surprising. "Liberalization is inexpensive: fast and easy to implement; building institutional capacity is expensive: slow and complex. Thus many countries have done the quick and easy reforms first," the study said.

The 1997 crisis imposed a new order. In the adjustment programs dictated by the IMF in Thailand, Indonesia, and South Korea, cleaning up the banking systems was a priority. It rested on two pillars—opening to foreign competition and creating an institutional and regulatory framework conforming to international standards. In the second area, the World Bank was supposed to play a major role with technical and financial assistance.

## PUNISH THE REAL CULPRITS

"The convalescence period for the banking systems affected by the crisis would be long and painful. And it didn't have any chance of succeeding," warned Thomson BankWatch Asia chief Philippe Delhaise, "unless at least two conditions were fulfilled—the real culprits had to be punished and the same mistakes couldn't be repeated when the medication was being administered."

Drawing up a new banking landscape was not just a technical job. From Mexico to Scandinavia to the United States, various therapies had been tested. The therapies would be used in Asia, with some adjustments. Equally important were the moral and political aspects.

The immediate moral question was punishing the guilty parties. But in banking, it was never that easy. There were depositors, shareholders, creditors, supervisory authorities, and taxpayers—who would pay for the mess and in what proportion? "In Asia, these groups end up sharing the cost of a bankruptcy using proportions that defy common sense," Delhaise said. "The shareholders are nearly always the culprits. They own the bank, they choose the management, and they received dividends…It is morally indispensable that they are be the first to pay for their mistakes."

Authorities supposedly supervising the banks that failed should also be punished and replaced, and every effort possible should be taken to make sure banks are supervised properly in the future. "The greed of the owners of the banks and the complacency of the authorities largely made the current turmoil in Asia a lot more painful than it would have been," Delhaise said. Edward Kane argued that individual authorities should be punished for underestimating losses and the resulting exposure to taxpayers who had to foot the bill. "Taxpayers must subject top regulators to personal penalties and tie those penalties carefully to reproducible estimates of the monetary damages that taxpayers suffer when they are asked to rely on disinformation," he said. Kane suggested a series of measures to improve the quality of information on banking risks and their prevention, notably the publication of the assessment of individual banks by authorities.

The next moral issue was to ensure that decisions to use taxpayer funds were clear and democratic. This was almost never the case. In early 1998, the administration of Mexican President Ernesto Zedillo presented to parliament the bill for bailing out the banking system after the crisis three years earlier—550 billion pesos or 65 billion dollars. The tardy revelation represented funds injected into the financial system by the deposit-guarantee agency FOBAPROA to recapitalize sick banks and acquire bad debts. The scheme would more or less prove to be the inspiration for the bailing out of Asian banking systems. And in Mexico's case, it took the government three years to get members of parliament to approve the bill that would eventually be charged to taxpayers. "Where else in the world can a president freely dispose of 14.5 percent of gross domestic product and then ask Congress to sign a blank check?" an independent Mexican lawmaker asked. "The banking crisis underscores the lack of accountability of the executive. It is unacceptable and it must change." He was Mexican but he might as well have been French—how much of the Credit Lyonnais bailout bill would French taxpayers have to foot?

In resolving banking crises, it was also important to make sure the prescription was right. Remedies applied to banking systems in industrialized countries might not necessarily be transferable to the systems in developing economies.

On this point, Kane and Delhaise agreed. "G10 countries have made measures of a bank's risk-based capital position the centerpiece of modern banking supervision," Kane said, referring to the BIS ratio requiring that banks have risk-weighted capital equivalent to eight percent of their total assets. But for Kane, the system was inefficient because it was based on figures and not economic values. The BIS ratio mechanically sought to limit the size of balance sheets. Kane argued that it would be better to improve information and monitoring with incentives to make sure the authorities were doing their jobs properly. On the other hand, limiting the size of balance sheets imposed a costly burden on prudent banks, but didn't prevent banks and taxpayers from being exploited by those who were overly aggressive. "Overworking these restrictions imposes costly burdens on safe-driver banks, burdens that do not protect strong banks and taxpayers from being exploited by aggressive banks," Kane said.

Delhaise agreed that too much emphasis had been put on the BIS ratio. "The structure of interest rates, operating costs, market profit potential, and other factors determine what solvency ratios can be reasonably achieved by financial institutions," he said.

Imposing a uniform ratio of eight percent—originally conceived as a voluntary ratio for banks in OECD countries—caused banks in some countries to drift. "It forced all banks in these countries to start fiddling with their accounts and find sources of profit to increase their capital," Delhaise said. Such activities took place in banks from Indonesia to Ukraine to South Korea. Delhaise argued that people should be more realistic. In some countries, "banks cannot achieve a ratio of more than three percent," he said. That might bar them from the interbank market but wouldn't prevent them from servicing the local economy.

Instead of getting obsessed over a ratio that was too ambitious, it was much more important for authorities to act before the real situation of a bank became negative. The Bank of Thailand could have been told in the late 1980s that six or seven of the country's fifteen banks should have been shut down. In Indonesia, twenty-five of the top forty banks should not have been operating before the crisis struck in 1997. "If they used the normal criteria used by normal people, South Koreans should have shut down ten of the twenty leading banks ten years ago—the solvency ratio before the crisis was minus ten percent and it's now minus twenty percent," Delhaise said.

"Darwin's process of elimination didn't work in Asia. How many banks really collapsed? How many owners of banks lost their shirts? Before the crisis, hardly any."

## CREDIT RISK

The crisis in 1997 was a call to order. For Merton Miller, it illustrated his "credit risk" concept of the crisis.

"Credit risk is ever present in financial markets and is realized whenever borrowers cannot or will not repay their loans on the original terms," Miller said. "In a properly regulated banking system, the rules would require banks to write those bad loans down to market value, taking the losses into income. Recognizing bad loan losses that way, however, erodes the bank's capital ratios, and banks whose capital ratios are impaired—or close to it—cannot make new loans. They can thus no longer play their traditional role of greasing the wheels of commerce."

What made the situation worse in Asia, compared with the American crisis in the late 1980s, for example, was the extremely high dependence on bank financing. Bank lending accounted for between fifty percent and eighty percent of all financial assets in Asian countries compared with barely twenty percent in the United States.

Asian companies were like households—there were hardly any other means of financing apart from bank loans. That made managing a banking crisis all the more delicate. For this reason, "many of the countries of the area have long been reluctant to force their banks to recognize and write off their bad loans. The governments and bank regulators in Southeast Asia feared that recognizing bad loans would impair the capital of their banks and lead to a liquidity freeze-up that would damage the economy severely," Miller said.

Governments behaved like gamblers betting double or nothing in the hope of making up any losses in the next game. They lost the bet. And then the casino closed down. "For those countries with weak banking systems, which includes most of Southeast Asia except for Hong Kong and possibly Singapore and Taiwan, a more rational system of bad loan recognition must be developed that, in turn, means huge amounts of new capital must be pumped in to make banks capable of playing their role in the savings-investment process," Miller said "The countries must recognize, however, that the needed capital can come from only one source—foreigners. And that those foreigners will be unwilling to put their capital in without substantially more control over the management of that capital than many locals are willing to give up to outsiders."

Rebuilding a solid banking system while inviting foreigners to come and work on the construction site was an urgent and necessary task. But it wasn't enough. In the longer term, Asia had to move away from a financial model that had just proven to be dangerous and outdated. "Banking is at the root of the problem," Miller said. "Banking itself is a disaster-prone nineteenth-century technology."

It was true—the crisis had done little for the reputation of the entire international banking community, not just the Asian banks.

The common feeling was that after so many disasters, both at home and exotic places abroad, bankers hadn't learned a thing. The fact was that immediately after the Mexican crisis of 1994-95, there was a surge in net lending to the five Asian countries most affected by the crisis. According to the Institute for International Finance, net lending to South Korea, Indonesia, Malaysia, Thailand, and the Philippines jumped from 23.4 billion dollars in 1994 to 55.7 billion dollars in 1996. Just as serious was the propensity to lend without restraint when things were fine and the tendency of bankers to brutally turn off the tap when things got bad. The guilt of the bankers was highlighted by Martin Wolf, a former World Bank economist who fired volleys of bullets at bankers from his editorial chair at The Financial Times.

Wolf noted that bank lending was so volatile in the capital flows of the five Asian countries that the balance swung from net private inflows of ninety-three billion dollars in 1996 to net outflows of twelve billion dollars in 1997.

The swing was the equivalent of ten percent of the combined GDP of the five countries before the crisis. "The real villains are our old friends, the commercial banks, whose net lending jumped from twenty-four billion dollars in 1994 to fifty-six billion dollars in 1996 before turning into net repayment of twenty-one billion dollars (in 1997)," he said. At the end of 1997, Japanese banks had lent almost one hundred billion dollars to these five countries, amounting to twenty-six percent of their stock market capitalization and two percent of the entire GDP of Japan. The ratios were similar for European banks, with German and French banks at the top of the list.

The figures nevertheless showed that international banks had learned at least some lessons from the past. During the Latin American debt crisis in the 1980s, it was discovered that certain big American banks such as Citibank and Chase Manhattan had lent amounts exceeding their entire shareholder funds to certain countries. Under the BIS, supervision of banks had since improved. Banks might keep doing the same stupid things but at least they were a lot more solid. And so it was in Basel, the Swiss city where the BIS is headquartered, that the heads of the big commercial banks came to perform their act of contrition amid much secrecy in January 1998. Invited by the council of central bank governors from the Group of Ten, they had to explain why they had closed their eyes to excessive lending and also why they had ignored the alarm bells.

For Merton Miller, the final solution to the repeated mistakes of banks was simply to manage without them, in every way possible. "We must look ahead ultimately to reducing our dependence on banks as suppliers of capital to industry, partly by shrinking the banking industry itself but even more by steadily expanding the number and variety of market alternatives to bank loans—everything from leasing to junk bonds that, after all, are really just liquid, negotiable commercial loans," he said. "Here, as so often in economic life, we must rely on decentralization and diversification—in this case, diversification of financing alternatives—and not on the presumed superior judgments of large banks and their regulators for directing capital to its most productive uses."

While the Asian crisis prompted a torrent of polemics, there was one point where a large consensus had emerged—it was imperative for East Asia to change its way of financing economic development.

"It's obvious," Philippe Delhaise said. "Why did banking systems explode in Asia? The reply is that they grew too quickly because the weight of financial support for regional development was carried by the banks and not capital markets. Banking systems leapt ahead at a furious pace that was much faster than the economic growth of these countries that was already phenomenal. It ended with growth being fuelled by bank loans instead of other forms of credit."

## BOND MARKET VIGILANTES

"We built highways to move people safely and efficiently, but we do not pay as much attention to the building of financial highways to move money safely and efficiently," said Joseph Yam, head of the Hong Kong Monetary Authority. "We built airports and planes to fly people, again safely and efficiently, around and across international boundaries to enhance their mobility to that they can interact with each other for their mutual benefit. Why do we not do as much for money or capital, the mobility of which from one marketplace to another arguably is of equal importance?"

It was July 14, 1997, and Yam had decided to use the podium of an Asian debt conference organized by *Asia Finance* magazine to climb up on his favorite horse—the need to develop debt markets in Asia.

For Yam, the absence of a regional debt market was yet another example of how Asia had a quasi-colonial dependence on the big financial centers in the United States and Europe. It was a bit of a paradox—the region with the highest saving rates in the world went to New York or London for its financial intermediation.

The risks of such dependence were highlighted only two weeks earlier when the Bank of Thailand resigned itself to floating the baht. "Stability of the Thai economy and its currency has been adversely affected by an overreliance on short-term foreign borrowing for investment activities and the overextension of property-related lending by banks and nonbank financial institutions," Yam said. "Had there been a mature debt market to mobilize efficiently long-term domestic or foreign savings to meet long-term investment needs, the reliance on short-term foreign capital, which is inherently volatile, would have been reduced."

It was perfectly true that a debt market was the indispensable foundation for a solid financial infrastructure. Without bond markets, savings had no choice but to end up in banks, where the money was safe but the returns were low, or the stock market where the returns were higher but with bigger risks. In developed countries, bond markets grew with the needs of governments to finance deficit spending and the amounts of capital involved were often two or three times bigger than the capital tied up in equity markets. In Asia, it was the reverse. Adrian Churn, who invested in Asian bond markets as manager of the Tiger Fund for Merrill Lynch, did some calculations. He found that the total stock market capitalization in Asia was about three thousand billion dollars before the crisis really got underway. If the ratio for Asia was to be more similar to the advanced economies, regional bond markets should have been at least ten times the miserable size they were that was about six hundred billion dollars.

If Asia was backward when it came to bond markets, there were good and not so good reasons. The best of the good reasons was obvious—Asian governments ran balanced budgets and sometimes even surpluses, so there was no need to issue bonds to cover deficit spending. But the absence or paucity of government bonds meant there was no benchmark for the rest of the market. And without a benchmark yield curve for sovereign risk, which should command the lowest interest rates, it was difficult to work out the interest rate spread for nonsovereign borrowers that should pay more to borrow given the higher risk to investors. Moreover, international rating agencies used to assess the level of risk associated with certain borrowers had only recently started expanding in Asia.

The worst reason for Asia being a bond market backwater was less obvious—owners of Asian companies, often families, didn't want to subject themselves to the vigilance of the bond market. Asian companies preferred to borrow from friends who were bankers or, better still, banks owned by family members—nobody looked too deeply into the accounts of the company or the risk involved. And in other cases, the policy of borrowing from banks could be dictated by governments for "strategic" reasons—as was the case in South Korea where some conglomerates were burdened with bank loans representing as much as six times their shareholder funds.

The absence of bond markets allowed these same governments, who practiced the virtues of balanced budgets, to tolerate the monetary debauchery that was going on in the private sector. "The absence of proper domestic currency bond markets in Asia has created an unnatural bias for the Asian investors toward boom-bust cycles with their associated easy money," said Russel Napier of Credit Lyonnais Securities Asia. "Asian investors have never had the bond market vigilantes looking over their shoulders, prepared to dump domestic currency bonds and increase the risk-free rate should the monetary juices start flowing too freely...In that environment, with no bond market providing salutary inflation warnings, the Asian investor was searching for monetary excess and even rewarding it. This is not the normal approach to investment, and the wreckage of overinvestment strewn across the region is testament to the imprudence of such abnormal cravings. Surely investors cannot still be seeking to reward such impudence?"

Almost two years after the storm broke, APEC finance ministers pledged to put priority on developing regional bond markets at their annual meeting on the Malaysian island of Langkawi in May 1999.

Japanese Finance Minister Kiichi Miyazawa noted, a bit late, as it turned out, that the existence of bond markets might have eased the severity of the crisis two years earlier. Instead of pulling their money out of Asia, foreign investors withdrawing from collapsing stock markets could have reinvested the funds in bonds, which would have been more attractive given the rising interest rates at the time. The APEC ministers acknowledged the urgent need to develop benchmark yield curves by getting governments to raise funds by issuing in domestic markets. But in Malaysia's case, the urgency of the issue seemed to have fallen on deaf ears. A few days later it went ahead with a one billion dollar bond issue—in New York. If the purpose of borrowing abroad was to reduce the cost of funds, it was apparently news to the Malaysian government. The bonds were a full 330 basis points—3.3 percentage points—over the corresponding rate for U.S. Treasury bonds, the main benchmark for emerging economies. The bonds were priced so cheaply to attract investors that Malaysian debt was suddenly cheaper than debt issued by Thailand. Even Malaysia's strongest critics would never have argued that the government in Kuala Lumpur was a bigger credit risk than the government in Bangkok. But more important for the politicians basking in the glory of the "successful" bond issue back home, it showed that even foreigners were now confident in the policies of Prime Minister Mahathir Mohamad—who was fighting a rearguard battle against domestic critics after jailing Anwar Ibrahim, the ousted deputy premier and former finance minister. The increasingly unpopular Mahathir also faced elections within a year.

## ANDRÉ LEE RETURNS

After the storm passed, the landscape was turned upside down. Governments with little or no debt suddenly needed huge sums of cash. As the economic slowdown turned into a recession, government budgets fell into the red—even in Hong Kong. Saving banking systems and recapitalizing them inexorably led to the colossal losses of the private sector becoming a public concern. In Thailand as in Indonesia, in South Korea as in China, and eventually Japan, a big part of the debt would be transferred to governments. And governments had to refinance the newly acquired private debt with public debt by raising funds on domestic or international markets.

"When the current crisis is over, the governments of Asia will have had to have issued significant domestic currency debt to finance the bailout program and repay the IMF," Russel Napier said. If Asia wanted a bond market, it would certainly get what it was asking for.

The scenario meant that fixed-income specialists had their future mapped out ahead of them in Asia. Including André Lee, no doubt. Yes, the same André Lee who made his fortune by "inventing" the Asian junk bond market, leading Peregrine International Holdings to ruin along the way. Since the collapse of the Hong Kong investment bank Peregrine in early 1998, André Lee had been laying low and wasn't talking (except for one interview granted to *Euromoney* magazine). So the curiosity was intense when it turned out that André Lee himself was going to speak on May 21 at the annual investors forum organized by Credit Lyonnais Securities Asia in Hong Kong.

Even if it shocked certain right-thinking people, inviting André Lee to address the forum was logical. Like his competitors, Credit Lyonnais Securities Asia boss Gary Coull was betting on the regional bond market taking off. Notwithstanding his mistakes, André Lee offered precious professional experience.

It was impossible to defend free-market philosophy without admitting the right to make mistakes, even big ones. That's what Philippine central bank governor Gabriel Singson was explaining when he recounted a joke about the brilliant company manager who was explaining the secrets of his success to a journalist. "Good decisions," the manager said. The journalist asked the manager how he reached good decisions. "Experience," he replied. And how did the manager acquire all this experience? "Bad decisions," he said. In the market economy, mistakes had a price. You paid the price, but only once. André Lee lost his job and it would be up to Hong Kong's judiciary to decide if Peregrine managers committed anything illegal against their shareholders or clients. For everything else, financiers weren't particularly indulgent. They were realistic.

It was Russel Napier who introduced André Lee to the auditorium. The press had been removed (well, there might have been an exception), and Russel Napier spoke. "Even from the back of the room, you can see that he doesn't wear horns," he said as he introduced the next speaker.

What did André Lee say? He said Asia needed money, and lots of it. "Asia needs to be recapitalized...if this crisis is to come to an end," he said. It wasn't particularly original, but the figures he gave were. "The banking system can be wiped out one hundred times in Korea," Lee continued. But "Koreans still have money. It is in won. There are Koreans that have far more money than the chaebol ever had. It is more a question of who has it and where it will go. The winners of tomorrow are not the players of today." The problem was that "the Asians with the money have not yet started to spend it," he said.

Lee said there was a "key perception gap between the expectations of how markets should operate and about how they operate in reality, a growing gap in perception between people that operate in the Asian markets and the ones who say how the markets should operate. The wider the perception gap, the bigger the volatility and the longer the recovery will take." In other words, the assets devalued by the crisis should be evaluated realistically and sold off—exactly the opposite of what had been going on in Japan. "Beware of the false prophets. Nothing will come closer to the truth unless Asian countries start to address the bad loans—and to write down loans takes capital and courage." Lee noted that debt-for-equity swaps were a "practical alternative that banks and companies can understand and implement." And "Asian debt markets are not dead in any sense. They will resume growth as soon as banks resume lending as they should."

Asian companies that survived would be those making radical adaptations to the new environment. "Companies relying on old political connections have not yet proven their ability to survive," Lee said, adding that the regulatory and fiscal climate had to change with the rules of the game being defined and applied. "The Asian crisis got worse because some countries not having the proper regulatory climate made things get worse. If the function of the regulatory framework is to make sure that each bureaucrat gets his share, then it will take time to change." But "the message is clear—if you are going to open a market, then open it. It's better to keep it shut than to keep it half-open. What I am talking about is sea changes about the business ways in Asia and that will take much more time than people think. It will take the Asian economies at least ten years to get through."

## EUROPEAN EXAMPLE

Time was not the only barrier Asia had to overcome to create a solid financial infrastructure. There was also the absence of a monetary framework corresponding to regional needs. The dependence on the dollar, accompanied by Japan's incapacity or refusal to let the yen become the main reserve currency for the region, had heavily penalized the region. The integral floating of currencies imposed by the victory of "speculation" was not a long-term solution for fragile economies. And so the crisis prompted considerable debate about what sort of exchange-rate arrangements would be put in place in the more or less distant future.

There was no shortage of proposals. One was to use local currencies for trade between members of ASEAN that comprised ten countries by 1999. But the effect would have been largely cosmetic. The idea to use the Singapore dollar as a regional currency for ASEAN countries was also proposed. Brunei effectively did already. But the idea was rejected by the rulers of the city-state. Whatever the intrinsic merits, they were perfectly aware that an economy of three million people didn't have a solid enough basis to support a monetary instrument used by hundreds of millions of individuals from Indonesia to the Philippines. As for the yen, the Japanese currency might have missed its chance. If an Asian currency came into being in two or three decades, some now thought that the anchor currency could well be the Chinese renminbi.

Malaysia simply gave up after a year and reverted to the old system of pegging the exchange rate to the dollar, imposing capital controls, ending convertibility of the currency, and withdrawing high-denomination bank notes from circulation. The drastic measures bought the government time—and prevented undue pressure on the exchange rate when a political crisis followed the sacking and arrest of Anwar Ibrahim, the finance minister. While working well as a short-term panacea, economists agreed that it was not sustainable and that economic distortions would only get worse over the longer term. Indeed, within months of the rate being fixed at 3.8 ringgit to the dollar, other Asian currencies had appreciated, and it was not long before the Malaysian currency was widely considered to be at least ten percent undervalued.

The failed attempt to establish a currency board system in Indonesia didn't extinguish the debate. Hong Kong's experience with its currency board system during and after the storm revealed the advantages and constraints of such a mechanism. But there was no doubt a country could keep its hat in the storm if—and it was a very big if—the authorities and the population were willing to put on a straitjacket and accept the implications such as losing independence over monetary policy. But whatever happened with exchange-rate arrangements, solutions would be on a case-by-case basis and there would be no unified response to the challenges brought by the crisis.

Could Asia learn anything from Europe? While the question would have once seemed incongruous, it took on a new legitimacy as the Asian crisis unfolded at the same time the Europe Union embarked on the final phase of economic and monetary union. While the European exchange rate mechanism shuddered under the impact of the Mexican peso crisis in 1995, it didn't flinch at all when the tsunami swept across East Asia two years later. But before dreaming of Frankfurt, where the European Central Bank was located, Asia would have been better off looking at London where the euromarkets were born back in the early 1950s.

Why should a similar "asiadollar" market not develop in Asia? All that was needed to create a vast Asian bond market was a financial center with a pool of dollars and enough borrowers and investors.

For Kenneth Courtis, Asia faced a paradox. "Over the next decade, hundreds of billions of dollars worth of assets from Tokyo to Jakarta are going to be restructured," he said. "Given the current state of affairs, most of these deals will be structured in Asia and will frequently be financed with Asian money. After all, the countries of the region will be generating huge current account surpluses as they rebuild their economies, just like Japan will keep doing. These surpluses will have to be recycled in the international markets and a lot of this paper will end up back in Asia. But in terms of financial benefits, the real added value will be in the euromarket."

Asia after the crisis would therefore resemble Asia before the crisis—its weak financial infrastructure meant that a large part of local savings would be deployed in New York or London. These savings would be managed outside the region and would act in the same way as foreign capital, heading for the exits when the weather got rough.

The euromarket was born during the early 1950s when the Soviet Union decided it would be safer to keep its dollar-denominated assets in Europe. The first bank to lend dollars in London was a Paris-based Soviet bank known as Banque Commerciale pour l'Europe du Nord, also know as "EUROBANQUE" for telex transactions. For tax reasons, American companies operating in Europe weren't too keen on repatriating their hard-earned dollars and followed in the Soviet bank's footsteps by lending their dollars in London. Soon there were borrowers of all nationalities, starting with Americans, seeking to borrow dollars in the new market in London that was totally unregulated by British authorities. The eurodollar market expanded and other currencies were borrowed and lent in the same way, leading to the birth of euromark, eurofranc, eurosterling, and other eurocurrencies. The offshore market boosted the standing of London as an international financial center without affecting British monetary policy as the funds were being borrowed and lent by nonresidents.

Courtis proposed that Hong Kong "dollarize" its financial center in a similar fashion. Why Hong Kong? Because monetary stability—a condition for being an international financial center—was being threatened by the growing stock market capitalization that was getting increasingly bigger as a proportion of GDP. This expansion was inevitable given the role Hong Kong played for Chinese companies wanting to access the international capital market. But it also led to huge quantities of Hong Kong dollars being held by speculators; that is exactly what happened in September 1997.

"As market capitalization soars with the acceleration of reforms in China, speculators will gets their hands on huge quantities of Hong Kong dollars simply by playing the stock market. They'll be in a position where they cannot lose," Courtis said. By short selling shares and the selling of the Hong Kong dollar forward at the same time, speculators would encourage monetary authorities to raise interest rates to support the currency, fuelling the stock market's decline even more. If the peg held, they could make money out of the plunge in share prices—as seen in September 1997 and again in August 1998. And if the peg broke and the Hong Kong dollar fell, they'd win on two fronts at the same time.

"Authorities could contain the process in the past, including the recent turmoil, because market capitalization was sufficiently small. But in the future, it will become increasingly difficult as reforms progress in China and the capitalization of the Hong Kong market takes off."

To start dollarizing Hong Kong's financial market, Chinese companies could list their shares on the local market in dollars rather than Hong Kong currency. The earlier "red chip fever" of Chinese companies listing in Hong Kong dollars had already caused the territory's money supply to blow out in the past. Listing in U.S. dollars would reduce the risks for the peg, and companies raising funds would be able to enjoy lower interest rates. At the same time, volatility in Hong Kong's money supply would be reduced. And other Asian companies could follow in the footsteps of Chinese companies.

"Major company listings in U.S. dollars would immediately open the door to Hong Kong joining New York and London as one of the three pillars of what would rapidly emerge as a twenty-four-hour market," Courtis said. "It was on a similar basis that the euromarket developed, with real long-term demand for dollars in Europe. And that was how London became Europe's financial center."

## A CURRENCY FOR ASIA

The emergence of the euromarket was one of the factors contributing to the birth of the single European currency, the euro, in 1990. The existence of a big offshore financial center in London allowed European borrowers, including governments themselves, to overcome constraints in their own markets. At the same time, the euromarket worked as an incentive to bring these scattered financial activities under a larger roof. With the single market for goods and services along with monetary cooperation, financial integration became one of the engines of European growth, offering crucial material support to the indispensable political will.

Whenever the idea of Asian monetary union was raised, Asian officials usually responded by saying that the region was too diverse (which was true) or that the level of intraregional trade was much less developed than in Europe or that the historical mutual distrust between countries in the region was still too strong.

But they tended to forget what Europe was like before the Treaty of Rome. The historical wounds between France and Germany were great, and building a unified Europe was always accompanied by doubts, sarcasm, and even outright hostility.

Like Europe before it, the East Asian region had just measured the cost of being disunited. And it was a very high price to pay for the "conventional wisdom" that everything from corruption and lack of democracy to crony capitalism should stay the same. But East Asia would never return to the previous status quo. It would be forced it reinvent itself.

"Asia needs a regional currency and the creation of an 'asian' would result in a boom in investment, trade, and tourism," said Mark Mobius. "The time has never been better to consider such an idea."

Mobius was no dreamer. He managed twenty billion dollars for Templeton Asset Management and was considered the guru of emerging markets, carrying his premature baldness to the four corners of the earth. Mobius proposed a currency board system for the whole region, an "Asian Money Board" responsible for defending a single currency, the asian, a unit of account for Asia

"What should the 'asian' be based on? Gold, of course. Gold has always been a store of value in Asia and is respected as the last resort in times of crisis," Mobius said. Why not the dollar? "No, because to do so would be short-sighted. We are interested in long-term stability. With the introduction of the euro, the U.S. dollar may lose its status as the world's international currency." And recalling the skepticism that accompanied European efforts to create a single currency, Mobius said: "Don't listen to the timid."

# The Giant Panda Disappears

---

"If mankind eradicates the habitat of the giant panda, then the panda ceases to exist in the wild….The IMF package…is a mandate to eradicate the existing habitat of Asia's corporates."
—*Russel Napier, strategist at Credit Lyonnais Securities Asia*

Morris Chang was the father of Taiwan's semiconductor industry. As a young graduate of the Massachusetts Institute of Technology, he was hired by Texas Instruments in 1958. He stayed for twenty-five years, rising to the position of vice president in charge of the group's semiconductor activities worldwide. By 1985, he was running a company called General Instrument Corp. when he was called home by the Taiwan government and given the chairmanship of the Institute for Industrial Technology Research. It was one of those think-tanks established by the Chinese Nationalist government with the aim of making the island a center of industrial excellence. He ran the Institute until 1994. But Dr. Morris Chang, who did his doctorate at Stanford University in 1964, was no armchair researcher. "I am a professional manager myself," he used to say. In 1987, he became one of the founders of Taiwan Semiconductor Manufacturing Co. Ltd. (TSMC), where he was managing director until becoming chairman in 1997. But before being a business—nothing less than the world's top manufacturer, in its own way, of semiconductors—TSMC was a concept, and a rather clever one too. The semiconductor industry was outrageously expensive, devouring huge amounts of capital investment. Launching a new production line could require more than a billion dollars in fresh money. The really expensive process was the fabrication of silicon wafers, on which the semiconductors were stamped. At the same time, progress in the industry depended on those who designed the semiconductors that were found in all electronic equipment and modern electrical appliances by the end of the twentieth century. "We liberated the industry from the burden of raising capital and allowed small companies to enter," Chang explained. TSMC was a foundry. Its wafer fabrication activities were based on the designs and specifications of its clients, some two hundred companies across the world. "Ten years ago, launching a semiconductor company required one hundred million dollars. Today—five million, twenty times less. We changed the rules of the game," Chang said.

Globally focussed on a single activity and extremely profitable with a return on shareholder funds estimated at 40 percent, TSMC symbolized the New Age of Asian industry. It was also representative of a model of development—Taiwan Inc.—that showed an exceptionally strong ability to resist the virus of the Asian crisis.

## ASIAN MANAGEMENT GOES ON TRIAL

In June 1998, the Japanese business daily *Nihon Keizai Shimbun* had the bright idea of inviting Morris Chang to Tokyo to speak at a conference on the "Advantages and Disadvantages of Asian-style Management." The newspaper also decided to invite some representatives from the dinosaurs of Asian industry, those creatures from the golden age when conglomerates ruled the region. On stage with Chang were Kim Woo Choong, the chairman of South Korea's Daewoo, and the high priest of Japanese-style management himself, NEC Corp. Chairman Tadahiro Sekimoto.

From his long stay in the United States, Morris Chang hadn't just brought impressive technical and management expertise back to Asia. He also had a refreshingly frank way of speaking.

"So-called Asian-style corporate management has to change fundamentally. It may be difficult to change for old established companies with entrenched Asian styles but new companies are emerging," the Taiwanese businessman told the audience, including his Japanese and Korean colleagues.

"TSMC does not follow so-called Asian style-corporate management. Competition is global in nature and to survive requires a company with global standards," he said.

The Taiwan company's management style was "also applied in most world-class companies even if some of those are not traditionally emphasized in traditional Asian companies."

At TSMC, the working language most widely used was English and the board worked efficiently. It wasn't a room for recording the decisions of the chairman, like in a South Korean conglomerate, or the Japanese-style "parliament" with forty members of the board trying to achieve a group consensus. The TSMC board set the general direction but left the day-to-day running of the business to the managers.

"Our profit is very much a function of our management, in which we emphasize innovation and individualism," Chang said. "We encourage an open environment in which everybody is free to speak his mind."

TSMC's cost structure was the lowest in the industry worldwide. Salaries represented only eight percent of costs and were supplemented with stock options, for which TSMC was one of the pioneers in Taiwan. "A middle-level manager can make a million dollars over a few years," Chang said. In 1998, TSMC had the third-largest market capitalization of all companies in emerging markets with the exception of Hong Kong and Singapore.

The exceptional profitability of TSMC was linked to its high production yields—the proportion of finished products without defects, the Achilles heel of the semiconductor industry. "We are getting higher prices because we are providing better services and enjoy higher confidence from our customers," Chang said. The formula was so effective that TSMC was even getting orders from big chipmakers with their own wafer fabrication facilities. This was a "marriage made in heaven," Chang said. "They need us and we need them. When they work in partnership with TSMC, they are very competitive in competing with companies that have their own foundries."

But TSMC had not grown complacent with success. "We are very paranoid. We are always afraid that we may lose our competitiveness," Chang said. "We certainly have no plans to move into any other business than foundry. We think there is a great future for at least thirteen years. In any case, that is the business that we know best and are very good at. We want to become the premier foundry in the world and the supplier to a lot of big companies. We can become a ten billion dollar company within six to seven years while keeping the same kind of return on earnings.

"It is time to take stock of the whole thing of Asia management," Chang said. "The world cannot wait for us to change very slowly. There are very good Asian values, such as closeness of families and emphasis on education. But those values are certainly eliminating cronyism and promoting openness. A lot of people are talking about culture as something that is very slow to change. Look at Mainland China, today they are as capitalistic as anybody. Culture can change very rapidly," he said. "Companies used to grow on the ground of their connections with the government. That model has crashed."

## KIM WOO CHOONG PERSISTS

If you followed Dr. Chang's lesson and did exactly the opposite, the result might be something like Daewoo—diversification in every direction, weak or negative profitability, a mediocre level of technology, intense concentration of personal power, management based on obedience, and obscure accounting practices.

Among the big corporate bosses in South Korea, Kim Woo Choong distinguished himself as someone who learned nothing from his mistakes. At sixty-one, he was one of the last *chaebol* founders who still exercised absolute power. He was also the flag carrier of resistance of the conglomerates to the restructuring prescribed by the IMF and endorsed by the new administration of President Kim Dae Jung. As fate would have it, the Daewoo chairman was also head of the Federation of Korean Industries at the height of the crisis. And Kim Woo Choong was happy to drag his feet even more than his main rivals—Hyundai, Samsung, LG, and Sunkyong—when it came to cleaning up Daewoo whose debts amounted to almost five times shareholder funds. Using the principle that the best line of defense was to attack, he decided to accelerate. So Daewoo Motors, the group's automobile division, took over failed carmaker Ssangyong Motors at a time when the economic crisis had halved its sales (and those of its competitors). "Daewoo will overcome the crisis by expanding," he told his employees.

Such obstinate voluntarism was typical of South Korean economic development. But the founder of Daewoo didn't know how to speak any other language. "What is important for the region today is self confidence," Kim said in his response to Morris Chang at the conference in Tokyo. "We have to grow out of this pessimism, regain courage for the future. But rather than confidence, we see confusion around us."

"Many changes are now being imposed on the basis of U.S. economic rights and wrongs," he said. But South Korean productivity was only a third of American productivity. "It is an excessive comparison to say that Korea is a complete failure. We have been trying very hard to improve our competitiveness. This kind of comparison will only discourage us."

For Kim, "borrowing from overseas is today seen as a sin but it has had positive effects in the past." And the high levels of debt as a percentage of shareholder funds in South Korea should be seen in the context of the country's high level of savings and not be judged by American or European criteria. "Debt was used to build factories and facilities worth one trillion dollars. It has not been wasted like in South America," he said. Invoking the "Asian values" of Singapore's Lee Kuan Yew, the Daewoo chairman asserted that "global culture should take into account cultural characteristics." South Korea, for example, was traditionally homogenous and rural—it didn't have the same diversity as the United States. "Discharging people because of a mergers or acquisitions will be very difficult," he said.

In South Korea, "the concept of competition, which is the basis of the market economy, has not been established and that stands in the way of corporate transparency," Kim said.

And then came a confession that shed some light on the South Korea disaster. "Somehow, we did not expect the financial industry to become an element of competition. It is basically based in advanced countries," Kim said. "The cost of money will be the big element in the twenty-first century. We did not have enough time for capital formation compared to advanced countries—we were depending on leading world banks for financing."

Kim said governments in South Korea had prevented big companies from going into finance. "That's why we are very behind. Korean companies had to pay for their capital three times as much as Western countries," he said.

It was formally correct to say that South Korean companies paid dearly for their financial resources. But the truth was that they also "borrowed" without having an obligation to repay. Otherwise, how was it possible to explain how this rarity of capital was not reflected in the prudent use of such a precious resource, which was in fact wasted in building massive industrial excess capacity? Kim Woo Choong also seemed to have forgotten that pressure to diversify *chaebol* funding by opening their share registers to outside shareholders triggered fierce resistance from the founders and their families who tried to reverse the reforms. "Family first," Kim said. "Oriental philosophy puts blood members first." When they were finally forced to accept outsiders, both Koreans and foreigners, the *chaebol* cheerfully trampled on their rights. Given the performance of South Korea's "investment banks," one could only tremble at the thought of how a *chaebol* bank would have been managed.

"There is not yet a consensus within all the ministries and among the people on whether Korea needs big companies or not, and whether they contribute to the country's prosperity," Kim said.

His response wasn't really surprising. "In my view, they are really necessary because of international competition," he said. "Our only resources are human resources. We made big investments in facilities. We need to operate our facilities to increase our added value. That is the only way for South Korea to survive. In order to operate in world markets, we need to be big to survive."

A year later, South Korean creditors put Daewoo under an emergency rescue program to avert bankruptcy, with the company agreeing to sell off twelve of its twenty-five subsidiaries to raise cash. But foreign creditors claimed they were not being treated equally and by September 1999 fears were growing of a second crisis. The bill for Kim Woo Choong's reckless expansion came to 50 billion dollars.

## DARWINIAN SELECTION

The Korean *chaebol*, the Japanese *keiretsu*, the Indonesian monopolies, and even the family-run empires of the Chinese diaspora in Southeast Asia were born and grew up in a well-defined environment. One of the main factors was the importance of "relations"—what some people called "crony capitalism" and what Chinese called *guangxi* or connections. Other factors were determined protectionism even with the appearance of open economies and cheap capital provided by a captive banking system helped by asset price inflation, especially in the property sector. And then there was the existence of government-approved monopolies and oligopolies that distorted business activities and the more or less general absence of bankruptcy laws or the inability to apply them. And then there was the final ingredient, currency stability.

"Anybody who has read the IMF package for the distressed jurisdictions must be struck by the massive structural changes that it demands or implies," said Russel Napier, the Credit Lyonnais Securities Asia strategist. "It is a mandate to eradicate the existing habitat of Asia's corporates."

The new environment was based on free and open competition along with transparency. The environment was deflationary with asset prices falling. The cost of capital was higher and exchange rates were flexible. Bankers would be independent and bankruptcy would be an effective sanction, depriving Asian companies of their traditional defenses. "If mankind eradicates the habitat of the giant panda, then the panda ceases to exist in the wild," Napier said. "Deprived of the ability to graze in the bamboo groves of Sichuan, the giant panda does not have the option to retrain as an orthodontist and move to Milton Keynes."

Asian companies were going to have to learn to live in a new environment, exposed to their most formidable predators, the big multinational companies. And they didn't have much time whereas their Western predecessors had one or two decades.

Who should they follow—Morris Chang or Kim Woo Choong?

"We believe Taiwan Inc. will accelerate market share gains against Korea Inc. and Japan Inc. due to more focused, competitive management, closer ties with U.S. companies and greater financial strength at both a macro and corporate level," wrote Goldman Sachs, the American investment bank. "Ultimately, we believe the Taiwanese model (low leverage, self-financing, niche focus) will aid continued accelerating gains over the Korean and Japanese model (vertically integrated, diversified, size focus) and the Korean and Japanese companies will have to operate more like Taiwanese companies to survive."

Victor Fung, head of the Hong Kong Trade Development Council, made similar remarks. Speaking at the Asia Society in Hong Kong in mid-1998, he said the writing was on the wall for the age of the conglomerates where families operated in protected markets comfortable in the knowledge that they enjoyed special relationships. What Asia needed, Fung said, were well-targeted companies capable of meeting the challenge of global competition.

The message primarily targeted the family empires of the Overseas Chinese that represented, along with Japanese keiretsu and Korean chaebol, the third type of Asian enterprise confronted with the challenge of globalization. This type of enterprise had a special name too.

## THE CHINESE BAMBOO NETWORK

The Overseas Chinese diaspora in Southeast Asia had unrivalled economic power. If it was a single country, it would have had about as many inhabitants as France—between fifty million and sixty million people (including Hong Kong and Taiwan). And if it was a single economy, it would have almost been as big as China with GDP of around 450 billion dollars and a population one-twentieth the size.

In Southeast Asia, the local Chinese communities represented less than ten percent of the total population. But ethnic Chinese accounted for almost ninety percent of the billionaires (in dollars). Whether they had kept their original names, like the Kuok family of Malaysia or the Liem family in Indonesia, or whether they had "localized" them, like the Cojuangco family in the Philippines or the Sophonpanitch family in Thailand, the large merchant families of the diaspora had an economic weight that went well beyond the demographics of population. It was still the case in Malaysia, where the Chinese accounted for almost a third of the population but had less economic dominance than before as a result of an affirmative action program favoring the indigenous majority which had given birth to a new class of ethnic Malay entrepreneurs.

Chinese emigration to Southeast Asia went back to the thirteenth century although the big waves of immigrants occurred several centuries later, triggered by unrest and famine in Imperial China and then civil war ending with the communist victory in 1949. The immigrants were a fairly homogenous group in the sense that they nearly all came from the two southern coastal provinces of Guangdong and Fujian as well as the southern island of Hainan (that is now a province). Links were not primarily between Chinese as such but between people from the same area in China and the distinctive dialect groups that tended to be mutually unintelligible despite sharing the same writing system. The main dialects spoken in Southeast Asia were Cantonese (most people originating from Guangdong province), Hokkien (southern Fujian province), Teochiu (Shantou in northern Guangdong), Hakka (mainly northern Guangdong and southern Fujian), Fuzhou (Fuzhou in northern Fujian), and Hainanese (Hainan Island).

Immigration over the generations was controlled by clans. And the Chinese clans established their own mutual support groups that came to play an important economic role.

"Mutual help societies assisted new arrivals to settle and lent money to members for specific purposes," according to *Overseas Chinese Business Networks In Asia*, a study prepared by Michael Backman for the Australian Department for Foreign Affairs and Trade.

"In this manner, the ethnic Chinese created a cohesive web of interlocking organizations and relationships that provided a firm and stable framework within which traditional society could be recreated, maintained, and developed and whose individual members could prosper far from home. This characteristic of Chinese settlement in East Asia significantly underpinned the ethnic Chinese business community's later commercial ascendancy," the study reported.

Such networks went back generations but were remarkably resilient— much of the food trading in Southeast Asia, for example, was still being undertaken by Teochiu families at the end of the twentieth century. And Hakka families tended to be strong in optical wear businesses, traditional pharmacies, and pawnshops. "A growing trend is to form clan associations based on dialect," the study noted.

China's open-door policy favored this process, with Chinese living in different countries in Southeast Asia coming together to invest in their area of origin in China.

Traditional Chinese entrepreneurship was characteristic and marked by a long history.

It was primarily a small or medium-sized family-run business, with any conglomerates tending to be groups of certain businesses.

Management was highly centralized and the strategy for expanding was thin margins offset by high volumes, strict controls, and rapid rotation of stock to reduce capital requirements. The Chinese networks minimized transaction costs and financing was internal, as were legal and other services such as research and development.

Modern management techniques were gradually introduced as the abacus gave way to the computer.

"Nevertheless, today many of these business—even the largest regional conglomerates—continue to reflect a family-oriented structure, including an essentially patriarchal style of top-level management in which individual members of the controlling family still play a key role," the Australian study said.

Sons and daughters were sent abroad to study and acquire the necessary qualifications to come back and take charge of the different parts of the business. Conglomerates were extremely diversified, with activities ranging from manufacturing and trading to transport, hotels, and newspapers—not to forget the almost universal infatuation with property development. "Almost all either own or are closely associated with one or more private banks, from which they can tap expansion funds," the study said. But that didn't exclude ties with foreign banks or joint ventures with international companies.

Opening the share register to outsiders was strictly controlled through corporate structures that ensured the holding company and the jewels of the empire to remain in family hands and sheltered from prying eyes. Cross shareholdings, exchanges of management, and even marriages helped to consolidate the ties between groups.

Such a recipe for success ensured that the Chinese business communities had a competitive advantage, frequently decisive, over their rare indigenous rivals. But their success wasn't entirely their own doing. "Governments have also played an important role in creating a suitable environment for the commercial flair of ethnic Chinese entrepreneurs," the Australian study said. "In some cases, their advantage is enhanced through developing symbiotic relations with local indigenous elites." And some of the tie-ups were devastating— such as Indonesia's President Suharto with Liem Sioe Liong, and Philippine President Ferdinand Marcos with Eduardo Cojuangco.

## NEW ORDER?

The financial fury that devastated East Asia tore up entire patches of the Chinese bamboo network. It was most obvious in Indonesia where the breakup of Suharto Inc. and anti-Chinese riots carried a heavy cost, not just for prominent figures like Liem Sioe Liong but to tens of thousands of Chinese entrepreneurs and merchants. In Thailand, some of the leading Chinese families were ruined or greatly impoverished by the crisis. Their domination of the banking and the industrial landscape would never be the same.

Compared with the South Korean conglomerates, the big family-owned Chinese groups of Southeast Asia had the advantage of spreading their risks across the entire region while using the Chinese citadels of Hong Kong and Singapore as havens of security. The Indonesian group Salim controlled by Liem Sioe Liong had powerful links with the First Pacific group in Hong Kong. The Riady family, the big Chinese family of Jakarta that was questioned over its contributions to the Democratic Party coffers and Bill Clinton's presidential campaign, also had a powerful presence in Hong Kong, notably through the Lippo group. And following in the footsteps of Thai food giant Charoen Pokphand, controlled by the Chearavanont family, most of the overseas Chinese groups had been investing massively in China. But overall, it was the activities in Southeast Asia that were worst affected by the crisis.

If the IMF managed to impose new rules—ranging from ending monopolies to introducing transparent accounting, normal financial systems, and effective corporate laws—the survival of the giant panda would be seriously compromised.

More transparent, more universal, and more global, the new rules of the game could also challenge the role of overseas Chinese as the inescapable and onerous intermediaries and partners used by multinational companies wanting to do business in Southeast Asia. Lyonnaise des Eaux had already gone through the experience of suddenly finding its Indonesian partner too cumbersome. So why did such a big French company have to hold the hand of New World boss Chen Yu Tong every time it wanted to set foot in China?

Multinational companies would benefit from the new order but others would too—such as parts of the Chinese network in Thailand, for example, with their "cousins" in Taiwan or Singapore. The government in Singapore openly declared that it hoped the Asian crisis would be an opportunity for its banks to become regional players (provided they didn't lose their shirts in Indonesia). Others would benefit from the new order too. In South Korea, both within and outside the *chaebol*, there were world-class companies like POSCO and Samsung Electronics, which were ready for the new era. And there were Japanese industrial champions, especially those born outside of the *keiretsu* families. Japanese companies like Toyota, Sony, and Honda had long been in the top league.

The Asian jungle would never become a French garden. In any case, the manicured geometry of the French garden was hardly representative of the market economy that required greater imagination and freedom, like an English garden. To let good specimens flourish, gardeners had to trim the surroundings and sacrifice the less worthy specimens. Sometimes a storm did the job.

# EPILOGUE

The natural question after any disaster was if the drama could have been avoided or at least the destructive effects minimized. But there was also another question—how to avert a new crisis and make preparations to limit the negative fallout.

It wasn't human nature to accept disasters. The Dutch built dikes to keep the North Sea at bay. The Japanese spent billions dollars on seismic research in an attempt to limit the damage caused by frequent earthquakes. The Chinese were building the Three Gorges Dam, the world's largest, in an effort to tame the wild waters of the Yangtze River that flooded again in 1998. Some natural disasters were caused by humans—deforestation along the banks of the Yangtze, for example, or forest fires in Indonesia that turned the El Niño phenomenon into a disaster for many Southeast Asian cities left choking in a thick blanket of haze in 1997.

Humans felt much better when they had control over events. That's why modern economic policies, whether Keynesian or monetarist, tried to go against cycles, with some "theories" even asserting that cycles were dead. And just like the thirty-year boom in Europe after World War II, people thought Asia was "different," enjoying immunity from economic cycles.

Jim Walker, chief economist at Credit Lyonnais Securities Asia, was one of the first to start ringing the alarm bells over the disturbing developments in Thailand. Why did so many economists and strategists, including the World Bank, write about Asia as if it had banished the business cycle to the dustbins of economic history?

"The answer lies partly in our deep-rooted misunderstanding and unknowledge of what makes the macro economy tick," he said. "It also partly lies in our unwillingness to accept economic forces that are beyond the control of governments and central banks."

In this fin-de-siécle account of capitalism at the end of the twentieth century, the cycle was being driven more than ever by the creation and circulation of money, the commodity of universal exchange.

From miracle to debacle, developments in East Asia during the 1990s were almost a perfect illustration of the cycle. During the boom, the expansion of credit accelerated and interest rates were artificially low. Investment in production capacities was followed by excessive investment and finally bad investment in nonproductive areas. Economies grew rapidly and asset price inflation ballooned. With the collapse came severe credit crunches, punitive interest rates, and the destruction of financial assets. And real assets too.

Cycles were now "global," like the new borderless world.

## THE PLAZA CYCLE

The Plaza Accord of September 1985 ignited the world credit cycle, the second since the collapse of the Bretton Woods system in the early 1970s.

The previous cycle had its roots in the first oil price shock of 1974, with the hike in crude oil prices by OPEC triggering a transfer of wealth from oil consumers to oil producers. Western banks ended up with vast deposits of "petrodollars" and much of the world fell into a period of stagflation with little or no economic growth accompanied by high inflation. The bankers found their new El Dorado in Latin America. But the first credit cycle after the collapse of the Bretton Woods system ended in disaster a few years later. Oil prices plunged after the second oil shock of 1979 and interest rates soared in the United States, triggering the debt crisis in Mexico in 1982.

The Plaza Cycle started in Japan a few years later when it became a vast pool of liquidity for the rest of the world, recycling its current account surpluses. Japan started exporting huge amounts of capital in the form of foreign direct investment by manufacturers and portfolio investment by investors, mainly in the U.S. Treasury bond market. To relieve the adverse effects of the strong yen on Japanese exporters, the Bank of Japan eased monetary policy. Interest rates fell and the bubble was created.

From Japan, much of the excess liquidity flowed to Asia. And the "Asian miracle" soon became the magnet for capital from all over the world—not just the old international banks, which had already forgotten their disastrous forays into Latin America, but also the many newcomers who owed their existence to financial deregulation.

## NEW MARKETS, NEW PLAYERS

In a timely address, American economist Henry Kaufman delivered a speech on "the elusiveness of reasonable financial behavior" to a conference in Philadelphia in November 1997.

"The nature of financial assets has changed," he said. "Modern financial markets are increasingly based on a bewildering assortment of securitized assets." The new tradable instruments, based on anything from credit card receivables to car loans, "have fundamentally changed the character of the credit markets. When the familiar kinds of assets are on the books of a traditional financial institution, they are usually held to maturity and carried at par. But from the time these same assets are packaged and sold as securities, their values are determined in the marketplace."

The marketplace had also changed with new players—governments, companies, financial aristocrats, and industrial commoners—who came to sell their debt products. Traditional bankers and insurance company executives now had to deal with a whole range of new competitors including hedge funds. "These institutions are distinguished by their emphasis on short-term performance, their heavy use of leverage, and their ability to move in and out of markets—whether equities, bonds, currencies, or commodities—wherever they believe the returns will be the highest," Kaufman said. And while they included the "oft-reviled hedge funds," similar activities were being carried out by major banks and securities companies, some insurance companies, and even nonfinancial companies.

And finally savers themselves joined the fray through increasingly popular mutual funds, which overtook bank deposits in the United States in the early 1990s and continued to expand for the rest of the decade. By 1998, the combined value of mutual funds was worth five thousand billion dollars compared with only forty-seven hundred billion dollars for total banking assets. The amount invested by mutual funds in the stock market alone jumped from thirty-five billion dollars in 1981 to three hundred forty billion dollars in 1991 and twenty-four hundred billion dollars in 1998, just before the correction on Wall Street imposed by the Asian and Russian crises.

Fund managers didn't invest in reality, they invested in concepts. And in the last decade of the twentieth century, the world financial mania was for emerging markets.

Just like any other mania in history, it went from a rational stage to a complete frenzy.

Marc Faber, the Doctor Doom of Hong Kong, spent twenty years studying cycles, dissecting manias and investment bubbles.

"New eras," he wrote, were periods during which a "displacement" promised great profit opportunities. Mania was a psychiatric term used to describe any "abnormal state of excitement, usually associated with a loss of touch with reality or rationality." And an investment mania was the "terminal phase of a market upswing characterized by a euphoric mood during which more and more people, usually without any special knowledge, want to make money by switching out of cash into real or financial assets."

Faber drew up a nonexhaustive list of manias throughout history. It started with the property mania in Athens in 333 B.C. before jumping to the tulip mania in the Netherlands from 1634 to 1637. Then there was the Mississippi share mania in France in 1719 and 1720, and the Californian real-estate boom from 1886 to 1887. Of course, there was also the American stock market boom, starting in 1924 that led to "the mother of all crashes" in 1929. More recent stock market manias occurred in Hong Kong from 1970 to 1973 and in Mexico from 1978 to 1981. And in the United States, there were successive manias for silver, gold, and oil between 1979 and 1989 (not to mention the real-estate mania from 1986 to 1989). And then there was the Japanese "bubble" between 1985 and 1990 and the "red chip fever" in Hong Kong in 1997 just before the Asian storm hit.

In other words, human failings were an unknown quantity that tended to exaggerate cyclical fluctuations.

## THE AMERICAN BUBBLE

Was Marc Faber getting ready to enlarge his inventory by adding the United States in the last few years of the twentieth century?

One man who thought so was Karl Richebacher, former economist with German bank Dresdner who authored an investment publication called *The Richebacher Letter*.

"Anyone knowledgeable in economic and monetary history is well aware that booming 'bubble economies' have regularly been mistaken for economic miracles," Richebacher wrote in March 1998. "This glowing misconception tends to be evoked by the coincidence of three bubble features—first, soaring asset prices generating tremendous wealth effects; second, low goods price inflation; third, strong economic growth. Thus the U.S. economy in the late 1920s, the Japanese economy in the late 1980s, and more recently, the Southeast Asian economies. In fact, it lies in the very nature of 'bubble economies' to look like the best of all possible worlds, until the bubble bursts."

The reality was that the United States grew faster than Japan and Europe during the 1990s but that growth was low by historical standards. Inflation remained an American problem given excessive growth in domestic demand, reflected in a permanent trade deficit, and the lowest savings and investment rates in the industrialized world. And supposed technology-linked productivity gains had less to do with increased use of computers and more to do with the soaring output of computer manufacturers. "In short, the technology-led productivity miracle has been taking place in just that single narrow sector—nowhere else. It has eluded the economy as a whole," Richebacher said.

And the bubble was being inflated by frenzied buying by American consumers, whose savings rate was close to zero in late 1998. "In other words, the key driver of the U.S. economy's recent strong growth was a virtual collapse of private savings," he said. "To speak under the condition of extremely healthy economic growth is really the height of economic ignorance. It has created a belief in a 'free lunch,' where consumers think they can raise their spending levels, while soaring stock prices take care of their retirement."

In other words, government debt precipitated the Mexican crisis in 1994, private-sector debt triggered the Asian crisis in 1997, and now household debt generated by consumers was hanging like a sword of Damocles over the American economy.

And like Japan and East Asia before, it was asset price inflation in the United States that was providing the "collateral guarantee" through soaring stock and property prices—American households were refinancing their mortgages and using their credit cards to buy more shares in an ever-rising market.

"This is a credit bubble *par excellence*. The financial leverage applied here is even for America of unprecedented scope," Richebacher wrote, noting that it was basically a massive "carry trade" of short-term borrowings put back into long-term investments, the same practice that had such a devastating impact in Asia.

In 1995, Federal Reserve Board Chairman Alan Greenspan warned of the "irrational exuberance" being displayed in American financial markets. But the words were not followed up by deeds, raising the suspicion that the U.S. central bank had become a prisoner of the bubble just like the Bank of Japan and the Bank of Thailand before—petrified of triggering an explosion while trying to cool things down. Richebacher was described as caught in the "Granddaddy of Bubbles" running out of control. What would happen when it finally burst, like all the bubbles before it?

In a bid to reverse the threat of a deflationary spiral leading to depression in Asia, the Federal Reserve led the world's central banks in launching an unprecedented policy of reflation. Across the world, there were 130 cuts in interest rates in several months. The result was a torrent of liquidity, similar to that which followed the global stock market crash of 1987. In September 1998, the world came close to the abyss once again—this time with the threat of a failure at hedge fund Long Term Capital Management and a new Russian debt crisis. For Kenneth Courtis, the world economy had entered a new state of "thrombosis"—Alan Greenspan and the other doctors at the world's central banks had injected the patient with massive amounts of fluids to get rid of a blood clot. The problem, the Deutsche Bank economist said, was that prolonged use of this sort of treatment would cause the veins to burst, resulting in the death of the patient. Much of Japan's excess liquidity, which played a key role in contributing to the Asian crisis, had meanwhile wound up in Wall Street by the middle of 1999. "The next crisis will be a lot more serious as it will be a dollar crisis," said Patrick Arthus, head of economic research at France's Caisse des Depots et Consignations, the country's biggest state-owned financial institution. "It will probably start with the bubble economy and the debt exploding in the United States."

## BACK TO THE AUSTRIAN SCHOOL

What could be done? Jim Walker of Credit Lyonnais Securities suggested we all go back to school, the Austrian school. People in the China of President Jiang Zemin were avid readers of Friedrich von Hayek, the last and best-known economist of the Austrian school that dominated economic thinking between 1870 and 1930. China read von Hayek and so did Margaret Thatcher. But the successor to Carl Menger and Joseph Schumpeter, the founder and star pupil of the Austrian school, also ran a research institute on business cycles in the 1920s. But the problem with the Austrians, Walker said, was their conclusions that cycles were inevitable. "As surely as night follows day, bust follows boom and there is nothing that technocrats and politicians can do about it," he said. "This admission of impotence is a bitter pill for human beings to swallow. It is even more difficult for politicians."

The Great Depression of the 1930s put the final nail in the coffin of the Austrian school when John Maynard Keynes came along and suggested the "virility-filled panacea" of government-led growth through budget deficits to overcome cyclical downturns. And when Keynesians, as faithful to their hero as Stalinists were to Marx, started leading countries into stagflation and bankruptcy in the 1970s, monetarism came along as the new creed for the 1980s. And derivations were still around in the 1990s, across OECD countries and within the IMF. "The assumption is that active economic management of a number of economic variables—one or other specific measures of money supply, the budget deficit—will result in a smoothly running economy, devoid of business cycles," Walker said. "Monetarism, like Keynesianism, is a virile interventionist macroeconomic approach. It also ignores fundamental human traits about confidence and expectations and fails to appreciate the malinvestment forces unleashed when bank credit growth forces the market rates of interest below the natural rate that would otherwise prevail in the economy. For Austrians, impotence begins when the distortionary boom gets underway in the first place—from then on, the bust is always an inevitability. The trick is, via supervision and regulation of the banks, to keep it contained in the first place."

The IMF's focus on developing sound banking systems subject to proper monitoring and regulations was a belated recognition of the Austrian approach, as was its focus on transparency, good governance, or for that matter all the adjustment programs putting priority on structural reforms.

Financial deregulation, and the power of markets achieved through dis-intermediation, increased the ability for heavy punishment to be dished out immediately as soon as mistakes were made. So the temptation to shoot the messenger was strong. And much was made of Chile's controls on short-term capital flows, seen as a means of protecting the country from evil "specula-tors." People forgot that the controls were implemented after Chile went through one of the worst banking crises in history in the early 1980s. And controls on short-term capital could be cushioned by countries capable of attracting inflows of long-term capital.

The real alternative to portfolio investment—that was by nature volatile—was not exchange controls nor reintermediation through banks that endlessly repeatedly the same mistakes. It was foreign direct investment. In other words, the doors could be either open or shut. Thailand refused to sell foreigners a single plot of land. But it left its banking system at the mercy of fund managers straight out of university who were living on the other side of the world. As far as national concepts of sovereignty went, it was quite remarkable.

## DEMOCRACY

For politicians in emerging economies, the lesson was clear, even if it was obviously difficult to carry out. Instead of resorting to inward-looking measures such as intervention and protectionism—cures that were worse than the illness itself—the best way out of the crisis would be to create institutional and legal frameworks enabling developing economies to hold on to their hats when the going got rough. The single ingredient was democracy. Politicians weren't supposed to run economies by taking the place of market participants. Their job was to develop good institutions and make sure they worked. The end of government intervention did not mean the death of politics. It was too easy to forget that the "first crisis of the twenty-first century" in Mexico in 1994-95 erupted amid signs that the ruling Institutional Revolutionary Party was starting to decompose after seventy years in power. The East Asian crisis showed that democratic societies, or at least those on the way to democracy, had greater capacity to withstand the shock than countries ruled by authoritarian regimes.

East Asia could build a new destiny for itself by fully drawing on the lessons of the unprecedented crisis. The choice was up to the authorities. Whether they survived the storm or came to power because of it, the end of the twentieth century witnessed a remarkable rise in the awareness of the political and institutional foundations of economic growth from South Korea to Indonesia. The alternatives were consistency or complacency. Consistency in the democratic, social, and political upgrading of the Asian development model would remain an unprecedented adventure even after discounting the effects of the crisis. The alternative was complacency toward the old recipes for "success," the compromises and dirty tricks of the past. The ability of East Asia to resume growth was never seriously questioned. What was at stake was the capacity to cope with external shocks that would inevitably happen again. As Confucius said: "Whoever makes a mistake and doesn't correct it is making another mistake."